Women Preachers and Prophets through Two Millennia of Christianity

Women Preachers and Prophets through Two Millennia of Christianity

EDITED BY

Beverly Mayne Kienzle and Pamela J. Walker

UNIVERSITY OF CALIFORNIA PRESS

Berkeley   Los Angeles   London

University of California Press
Berkeley and Los Angeles, California

University of California Press, Ltd.
London, England

© 1998 by
The Regents of the University of California

Library of Congress Cataloging-in-Publication Data

Women preachers and prophets through two millennia of Christianity/edited by Beverly
  Mayne Kienzle and Pamela J. Walker.
      p.   cm.
    Includes bibliographical references and index.
    ISBN 0–520–20921–4 (hardcover : alk. paper).—ISBN 0–520–20922–2 (pbk. : alk.
paper)
      1. Women clergy—History. 2. Women evangelists—History. 3. Sex role—Religious
aspects—Christianity—History. 4. Women in Christianity—History. I. Kienzle, Beverly
Mayne. II. Walker, Pamela J., 1960–   .
  BV676.W556   1998
  270'.082—dc21   97–30743
                                                                                CIP

Printed in the United States of America
9 8 7 6 5 4 3 2 1

The paper used in this publication meets the minimum requirements of American National
Standards for Information Sciences—Permanence of Paper for Printed Library Materials,
ANSI Z39.48–1984.

For Kathleen Cary Kienzle,
my daughter, my sister, my friend,
in celebration of her twenty-first birthday

And for M., who is eloquent in word and in silence.

CONTENTS

LIST OF ILLUSTRATIONS

PREFACE: AUTHORITY AND DEFINITION

The letters of Virginia Cary Hudson Cleveland (1894–1954),[1] Beverly Kien-zle's grandmother, illustrate the issues of authority and definition that have surrounded the act of preaching for women during the nearly twenty centuries of Christianity. Virginia *taught* at Calvary Episcopal Church in Louisville, Kentucky; she regularly instructed the Women's Auxiliary and adult Sunday school classes designed to prepare her audience for better appreciating the rector's sermon. Her letters contain occasional references to complaints about her teaching's encroaching either in time or in authority on the rector's message. Virginia also *taught* Sunday school classes at the Methodist church in Cloverport, Kentucky, where her family had a country house. Her audience included Methodists, Baptists, and two Jews, whose insights on the Hebrew Scriptures she treasured. Most were simple country folk who came to town on Sundays, attracted by the dynamic lessons of their ecumenical teacher. Virginia also gave religious instruction in another setting, the Goodwill Chapel in downtown Louisville; she called that instruction *preaching*. There she was the authorized voice; she even had her rector's permission. To her daughter she wrote: "At a church council meeting some weeks ago I was asked to be the Episcopal representative to the Goodwill Chapel for Lent. I soon learned that my responsibilities meant the whole shebang, including preaching on Ash Wednesday and Good Friday. . . . These people at the chapel are a forlorn folk who must at times feel that God has forgotten them. Our work is simple: to bring spiritual encouragement and assurance to them." Virginia's preaching was so well received that she was asked to deliver additional sermons. The chapel superintendent said to her, "The la-di-da words of some of the robed preachers do not go over down here. These are simple and plain people who want a simple truth."

Some of the women whose stories are told in this book spoke a simple truth and others a message embedded in figurative language; both groups found their modes of expression in the Scriptures. Some based their authority solely on divine inspiration; others were authorized by their communities and a few by the hierarchy of the dominant church. Their voices call for the examination of what constitutes preaching and for the recognition that preaching can be defined with and without restrictive categories. Broadly viewed, preaching is the delivering of a religious discourse—a sermon—by a preacher to an audience. More narrowly construed, the term *preaching* designates that the sermon is delivered by an authorized cleric within the context of a worship service or liturgy.[2] That definition incorporates restrictive categories: the control over designation of the preacher and over time and space within the liturgy or worship service.

Throughout the twenty centuries of the Christian era, a narrow definition of preaching has served as an instrument for delegitimizing acts of religious discourse that fall within the bounds of the broader definition. The voices of women, saddled with accusations of theological and biological inferiority, have been especially constrained and delegitimized. Although prophesying has been recognized as an activity accessible to women, preaching generally has not. Restrictions have obstructed recognition of the spirit's voice when enunciated by a woman; the name *preaching* has been withheld to deny legitimacy or pronounced to issue condemnation.

Yet the women discussed in this volume participated in preaching, some within the narrow definition and some within the broader one. The label applied to their discourse and to the expression of their voices varies according to the perception of their right to authority. Their contemporaries may have wished either to sanction or to condemn these women; they bent the language to reflect their approval or condemnation of the women's actions. Instances of prophesying, teaching, or the like have sometimes been labeled preaching when they fell under suspicion. Women themselves have sometimes used language that reflected the boundaries of authority. Repeatedly women have been described, or have chosen to describe themselves, as prophesying, teaching, or performing some other authorized act when preaching was prohibited to them.

Despite the centuries of prohibitions grounded on Paul's injunctions against women teaching in the public assembly, many women throughout the history of Christianity have preached, claiming authority for themselves through the inspiration of the Holy Spirit and also finding alternate routes for expression such as writing, teaching, and singing. Some independent-minded communities of men and women have recognized female voices as authoritative and have even adopted structures that grant authority to women's voices. The recurring presence of women's preaching attests to both the continuing struggle within Christianity over problems of authority and the indomitable spirit of women's voices.

This book explores the diverse voices of Christian women who claimed the authority to preach and prophesy and analyzes their relationships to broader Christian communities from the second century to the twentieth. The essays vary somewhat in length for deliberate reasons: a lesser-known community such as the Moravians or one widely misunderstood such as the Cathars requires a lengthier explanation of its organizational background than do more familiar institutions or communities. Similarly, the essay on the figure of Mary Magdalene provides a transition from early to late antique and medieval Christianity and thus merits an extensive development of its subject.

The contributors to this volume are scholars in folklore, church history, social and political history, history of art, religion, literary criticism, and biblical studies. All take an interdisciplinary approach to their topics, transcending narrowly construed limits of academic disciplines in order to explore and elucidate the broad cultural context of their subjects. Similarly, their sources are extensive and varied, including Scripture, sermons, art, polemical literature, letters, diaries, chronicles, inquisitors' manuals, devotional works, and fiction.

The essays in this volume all break new ground. For the premodern period, they represent some of the first studies in the expanding research on women preachers and women's preaching. Even the exemplary Hildegard of Bingen has received little attention for her sermons, although she preached publicly with approbation. A new edition of her gospel homilies is being prepared and translated into English, and essays examining Hildegard's preaching are scheduled to appear.[3] The connection medieval society made between a woman's preaching and demonic possession has also been brought to light in the case of Sigewize, a woman inspired by Hildegard and judged as possessed by a demon because of her desire to preach publicly.[4] Other studies on medieval women's preaching were either published or being undertaken as this volume was being completed: an article on the preaching of Lollard women; an edition of Umiltà of Faenza's sermons and their translation into English; a major study on Birgitta of Sweden and an essay on her role as preacher and prophet; and a dissertation on gender and authority in late medieval preaching.[5] Still other research on the sermons of medieval women has already been stimulated by the discussion around this volume.

For the modern period, existing research is more extensive, especially on the nineteenth century, but a focus on preaching in the field of women's history is still a neglected area. The eighteenth and nineteenth centuries witnessed a profusion of new denominations and sectarian movements among Protestants. Women preachers contributed to the birth and growth of these movements. Certainly they had predecessors in Anne Hutchinson (1591–1643), who was expelled from Massachusetts, and in the seventeenth-century Quakers in England and America, but in the later period, women from both new and established denominations preached in greater numbers and sometimes with institutional sanction. Scholars have explored why these phenomena emerged in their respective periods, the significance of women's religious leadership for their theology and practice, and their relationship to modern women's rights campaigns that also took root during those centuries.[6] Names of eighteenth- and nineteenth-century women who preached have become familiar in recent years. Among them are Sarah Osborn (b. 1714), religious instructor to whites and free blacks in eighteenth-century Rhode Island; Barbara Ruckle Heck (1734–1804), called the "Mother of American Methodism"; Jarena Lee (1783–1836), a preacher who challenged the African Methodist Episcopal Church to sanction her work; Mary Barritt Taft (1772–1851), a British Methodist whose preaching divided the Wesleyan Methodist Connexion; Sojourner Truth (ca. 1797–1883), emancipated slave, abolitionist, and independent preacher; Phoebe Palmer (1807–1874), holiness preacher and author; Mary Baker Eddy (1821–1910), founder of Christian Science; and Antoinette Brown, ordained a Congregationalist minister in 1853.

Yet, although exemplary women have received increased scholarly attention in the last ten to fifteen years, their preaching and sermons generally have not been the focus of research. Many women have been studied more for their political campaigns than for their preaching and religious vision. Scholars, moreover, have often presented them as unique individuals. This volume is concerned with individual women but equally with the movements that fostered women's preaching and with placing women preachers within the history of Christianity. During the 1980s and 1990s, increasing numbers of women have entered the Christian ministry, and they are producing literature directed toward contemporary women preachers and their preaching. These contemporary works on women's sermons, like the recent scholarship on modern women, generally have not examined the scope of women's preaching over the centuries and have not uncovered the extensive reach of historical precedent that is demonstrated in this book, with its panorama of women's preaching over the two millennia of Christianity. Although this volume is not a comprehensive history of women's preaching, it does take the first step toward creating a fuller view by illustrating both the persistence of women's voices and the consistency of the strategies used against them. It challenges the narrow definition of preaching that has constricted the study of women's voices and explores how alternative routes for expression such as prophecy and teaching fall within a larger view of what constitutes preaching. It also demonstrates how distinctions between preaching and related avenues of expression have been either blurred or sharpened in attempts to legitimize or delegitimize women's religious speech. Thus this volume establishes a broad and creative basis for recounting the history of women preachers and their sermons.

The essays begin with a contemporary perspective that reflects on the analysis of women's preaching in the present and its relationship to the past. Elaine Lawless's introduction, "The Issue of Blood: Reinstating Women into the Tradition," draws on years of research focused on contemporary women's preaching, first in Pentecostal communities and more recently in mainline Protestant denominations. She asks how contemporary women's preaching can illuminate the past and, at the same time, how studying the past can reinforce women's claims to the right to preach in the present. Lawless's work listening to, recording, and analyzing actual sermons delivered by women differs from the research of other contributors to the volume, who reconstruct limited historical evidence to write a history of women's preaching. Nonetheless, Lawless draws significant parallels between women's sermons today and the writing of a history of preaching that includes women. Both are about reinstating women and their experiences into the tradition. Just as a woman's story (the story of the woman with an issue of blood) is omitted from the present-day lectionary but brought into one of the sermons Lawless cites, so too women's preaching has been excluded from the historical record but is being reinserted by the essays in this volume.

Elaine Lawless's look at contemporary women's preaching is balanced by Karen King's afterword, "Voices of the Spirit: Exercising Power, Embracing Responsibility," in which King reviews the questions posed by the essays in this volume and raises issues for contemporary scholars. King notes how key scriptural passages and biased notions of women's nature and rightful place have been used to attempt to silence women for centuries. Women, however, have developed means to claim their right to preach, employing other passages of scripture that justify their speaking, renaming their speech acts, challenging institutional restrictions, and creating alternative institutions. King demonstrates that comparison of the women preachers featured in this volume reveals a range of common strategies and convictions. She ends with questions that merit further scholarly research and highlights the new perspectives on Christianity, past and present, that the volume opens up.

Ten of the essays in this volume deal with Christianity before the Reformation. The essays of Karen King and Karen Jo Torjesen focus on early Christian communities. King introduces the conflicts over women's leadership in early Christian communities, and through her analysis of the *Gospel of Mary* (Magdalene) explores the nature of prophetic speech and its relationship to gender. Torjesen examines artistic representations of the female *orans*, a woman depicted in a posture of prayer and previously interpreted as a symbol of the church or of the soul. Torjesen argues that viewers in antiquity would have associated the *orans* with women's praying, prophesying, and preaching, and she places examples of those activities within the broader interpretive framework of women's participation in early Christian worship.

Katherine Ludwig Jansen's essay on Mary Magdalene builds a bridge from early and late antique to medieval Christianity. Jansen traces the confusion in Magdalene's identity, concretized by Gregory the Great, and demonstrates how interpretations of Magdalene's preaching and vocation as *apostolorum apostola* encapsulate conflicting and ambiguous views toward the phenomenon of a preaching woman. Magdalene was hailed as the proclaimer of Jesus' resurrection and the evangelizer of Gaul: some described her as the recipient of a special dispensation from the Pauline ban on women's preaching; others simply and enthusiastically praised her. Although the church prohibited women's preaching, Magdalene appeared as a preaching figure in sermons, art, liturgy, and popular and sacred literature.

Dissident groups in medieval Christianity allowed women greater participation in religious life, as described in the essays by Beverly Mayne Kienzle and Anne Brenon. Kienzle analyzes the evidence for the preaching of Waldensian women and the patterns of rhetoric and thought discernible in the polemical literature directed against the Waldensians in the late twelfth and early thirteenth centuries. Brenon traces the historical evidence for women's participation in Catharism and defines the pastoral and sacerdotal functions of women in the Cathar churches of Languedoc. Inquisition records attest to the presence of women among preachers and believers alike.

Within orthodox circles women found ways to express their voices by exploiting alternatives to preaching: primarily teaching and prophecy. Nicole Bériou explores legislation prohibiting women from preaching and demonstrates how they nevertheless developed and received praise for their role as teachers of the faith. Carolyn Muessig analyzes the lines demarcating preaching and prophecy and tells the story of a famous male preacher who advocated singing as an acceptable channel of expression for cloistered women, one that he described in terms like those used for the activity of preaching. Darleen Pryds and Roberto Rusconi focus on medieval Italy, where exemplary women, biblical figures and later saints, expanded the boundaries of practice and imagination. Pryds brings to life Rose of Viterbo, a teenage Italian laywoman of the thirteenth century who preached publicly in her native city with the knowledge and approbation of church officials. The two *vitae* circulated as part of her canonization process portray her speaking publicly, and the second—a fifteenth-century text—describes her speech specifically as preaching. Rusconi analyzes the Italian iconography of women known generally through hagiographical literature: early saints such as Mary Magdalene, Cecilia, and Catherine of Alexandria, and medieval figures such as Rose of Viterbo, Umiltà of Faenza, and Catherine of Siena. The artistic representation of these exemplary women documents the public recognition of their preaching as a mark of holiness.

Of the eight essays examining the period from the Reformation to the twentieth century, two focus on the Reformation, when Christians struggled with questions of individual and institutional authority, the distinctions between clergy and laity, and the claims of established and emergent denominations. Women's preaching was one aspect of these broader issues. Edith Dolnikowski investigates how John Foxe's influential *Acts and Monuments* used stories of women who publicly proclaimed their faith to demonstrate the vital importance of reading and preaching the Gospel in the vernacular. The emphasis on women's voices underscored the tenet that any Christian, male or female, lay or clergy, could and should offer public witness. The seventeenth-century Catholic Reformation provides the context for Linda Lierheimer's treatment of the apostolate of the French Ursulines. The Ursulines were among the European women who began to teach, nurse, and missionize, thereby creating new models of public, female, religious activity. Although they never officially claimed the role of preacher, the Ursulines assumed public religious authority when they taught and attracted followers to their chapels. Their activities, alternately termed preaching and teaching, illustrate how closely religious teaching approximates preaching and how the boundaries between the two could be purposefully blurred to create a space for female voices.

Two essays bring to light religious communities of the eighteenth century that valued women's participation and voice. Peter Vogt examines the German Moravians, a Pietist group in which, under the leadership of Count Zinzendorf (1700–1760), women assumed leadership, preached, and held ministerial office. Vogt describes how this community's theology and practice, with its emphasis on a biblical version of community and spiritual experience, opened up opportunities for women. Phyllis Mack analyzes the world of eighteenth-century British Quaker women, who were noted social reformers and activists as well as quietists seeking self-transcendence and mystical insight. These women had a strong legacy in the radicalism of the seventeenth-century sectarians, and Mack raises questions about their gains and losses during the Enlightenment, the relationship between religion and women's political consciousness, and how a new understanding of "soul" shaped women's religious life.

Nineteenth-century women are the subject of two essays. Judylyn Ryan compares the ministry of two African American women, Maria Stewart and the fictional Baby Suggs, holy—a character created by Toni Morrison. Ryan emphasizes the vitality and significance of Christianity and African cosmology, which meet in the lives of these two women and account for their conviction that they were entitled to and capable of spiritual leadership. Ryan also uses fiction to recover the lives of enslaved African American women who left no written record of their ministry. Pamela Walker studies Catherine Booth and the women of the British Salvation Army, analyzing how the Army created a unique female ministry by drawing upon Methodist, revivalist, and holiness theologies as well as the particular culture of urban, working-class communities in Victorian England. Walker suggests comparisons between Booth's reading of Scripture and that of other sectarians, including Quakers and Moravians. She also explores the relationships among theology, religious practice, and culture.

The final two essays examine the early twentieth century. Yvonne Chireau explores the career of Mother Leaf Anderson, the leader of a New Orleans Spiritual church. The Spiritual churches offered diverse beliefs and practices blending Christianity with neo-African religions. Mother Leaf Anderson and her contemporaries used their authority to create spiritual practices that subverted the conventions of gender, and they established agencies to promote social justice and the well-being of their congregations. Finally, Jacqueline deVries focuses on the British women suffragists who after 1918 became preachers and campaigners for women's right to preach. DeVries continues the investigation of questions about the sources of women's spiritual authority as she traces the connections between women's preaching and political activism and the suffragists' vision of the vote as a means of achieving a more godly nation.

The idea of a history of women's preaching began to interest Beverly Kienzle and Pamela Walker when they met at Harvard Divinity School and began discussing similarities between the twelfth-century Waldensians and the nineteenth-century Salvation Army. Divided by seven hundred years and significant theological differences, the two movements nonetheless dealt with similar questions about women's authority and voice. The discussions between Kienzle and Walker led to a panel at the 1994 American Academy of Religion meetings entitled "Women's Voices in the Church" and then to Beverly Kienzle's proposal to compile a book about women preachers and prophets in the history of Christianity. The contributors to this volume also participated in a conference conceived and organized by Phyllis Mack at the Rutgers Center for Historical Analysis in November 1995: "Women Preaching in the Christian Tradition."

We owe our gratitude to many who helped shape and produce this book. Phyllis Mack and the staff at Rutgers were responsible for a successful conference; Lynn Strawbridge deserves special mention in this regard. Constance Buchanan, now at the Ford Foundation, and the faculty and staff associated with the Women's Studies in Religion Program at Harvard Divinity School brought together the editors and other contributors to the volume; the Harvard program has provided a stimulating and productive intellectual environment for scholarship on gender and religion. Stanley Holwitz, assistant director of the University of California Press, provided persuasive enthusiasm and sound advice from our first conversation with him. Others at the Press deserving our thanks are Harry Asforis, editorial assistant; Janet Mowery, copy editor; and Sue Heinemann, project editor, who guided the book smoothly through the phases of production. Our reviewers provided insightful comments that helped to shape and improve the book. Our thanks to Tammy Zambo for her outstanding work preparing the index and to Paul Dervis for helping us complete it. We are also grateful to the dean of arts at Carleton University and to Harvard Divinity School for their support. Kathleen Shanahan, staff assistant at Harvard Divinity School, was the person behind the scenes without whose intellect and organizational talents the book could never have been completed so quickly. Finally, we each express our gratitude to the people closest to us for their moral and intellectual support: for Beverly, Judith Rhodes, priest and preacher par excellence, Lewis Mayne, Ann Cleveland, and Edward and Kathleen Kienzle; for Pamela, Susan Whitney and their extended families, especially Elizabeth Walker.

NOTES

1. Author of four volumes of essays and letters published by her daughter, Virginia Cleveland Mayne: the best-selling *O Ye Jigs and Juleps* (New York: Macmillan, 1962, 1989); *Credos and Quips* (New York: Macmillan, 1964); *Flapdoodle, Trust and Obey* (New York: Harper and Row, 1966); *Close Your Eyes When Praying* (New York: Harper and Row, 1968). The passages cited below appear in *Flapdoodle*, pp. 72, 76.

2. An extensive definition of the sermon in the Middle Ages is offered in Beverly Mayne Kienzle, "The Typology of the Medieval Sermon and Its Development in the Middle Ages: Report on Work in Progress," in *De l'homélie au sermon: Histoire de la prédication médiévale*, ed. Jacqueline Hamesse (Louvain-la-Neuve: Université Catholique de Louvain, 1993), pp. 83–88. See also *The Sermon*, ed. Beverly Mayne Kienzle, forthcoming in the series *Typologie des sources du moyen âge* (Turnhout, Belgium: Brepols, 1998).

3. *Expositiones evangeliorum*, ed. Beverly Mayne Kienzle and Carolyn Muessig, with the assistance of Monika Costard and Angelika Lozar, in preparation for the *Corpus Christianorum Continuatio Mediaevalis;* translation by Fay Martineau and B. M. Kienzle for Cistercian Publications. Articles include B. M. Kienzle, "'Operatrix in Vinea Domini': Hildegard of Bingen's Preaching and Polemics against the Cathars," *Heresis* 26 (1997); Barbara Newman, "Three-Part Invention: The 'Vita S. Hildegardis' and Mystical Hagiography," in Charles Burnett and Peter Dronke, eds. *Hildegard of Bingen: The Context of Her Thought and Art* (London: Warburg Institute, 1998).

4. Newman, "Three-Part Invention."

5. Alcuin Blamires, "Women and Preaching in Medieval Orthodoxy, Heresy and Saints' Lives," *Viator* 26 (1995): 135–52; Maria Adele Simonetti, ed., *I sermoni di Umiltà da faenza: Studio ed edizione* (Spoleto: Centro italiano di studi sull'alto medioevo, 1995), English translation in preparation by Catherine Mooney; Claire Sahlin, "Birgitta of Sweden and the Voice of Prophecy: A Study of Gender and Religious Authority in the Later Middle Ages" (Ph.D. diss., Harvard University, 1996); C. Sahlin, "The Prophetess as Preacher: Birgitta of Sweden and the Voice of Prophecy," *Medieval Sermon Studies* 40 (Fall 1997):29–44; Claire Waters, "Doctrine Embodied: Gender, Performance, and Authority in Late-Medieval Preaching" (Ph.D. diss., Northwestern University, 1998).

6. Some influential titles from this extensive scholarship include: William Andrews,

Sisters of the Spirit (Bloomington: Indiana University Press, 1986); Wendy Chmielewski et al., eds., *Women in Spiritual and Communitarian Societies in the United States* (Syracuse, N.Y.: Syracuse University Press, 1994); Nancy Hardesty, *Women Called to Witness: Evangelical Feminism in the Nineteenth Century* (Nashville, Tenn.: Abingdon Press, 1984); Brian Heeney, *The Women's Movement in the Church of England, 1850–1930* (Oxford: Clarendon Press, 1988); Susan Juster, *Disorderly Women: Sexual Politics and Evangelicalism in Revolutionary New England* (Ithaca, N.Y.: Cornell University Press, 1995); Susan Juster and Lisa McFarlene, eds., *A Mighty Baptism: Race, Gender, and the Creation of American Protestantism* (Ithaca, N.Y.: Cornell University Press, 1996); Christine Krueger, *The Reader's Repentance: Women Preachers, Women Writers and Nineteenth-Century Social Discourse* (Chicago: University of Chicago Press, 1992); Nell Painter, *Sojourner Truth: A Life, a Symbol* (New York: W. W. Norton, 1996); Alex Owen, *The Darkened Room: Women, Power and Spiritualism in Late Victorian England* (London: Virago, 1989); Marjorie Proctor Smith, *Women in Shaker Community and Worship* (Lewiston, N.Y.: Edwin Mellen Press, 1985); Rosemary Radford Ruether and Rosemary Skinner Keller, eds., *Women and American Religion*, 3 vols. (San Francisco: Harper and Row, 1981); Deborah Valenze, *Prophetic Sons and Daughters: Female Preaching and Popular Religion in Industrial England* (Princeton, N.J.: Princeton University Press, 1985); and Judith Weisenfeld and Richard Newman, eds., *This Far by Faith* (New York: Routledge, 1996).

The Issue of Blood

Reinstating Women into the Tradition

Elaine J. Lawless

On a warm and sunny June morning nearly ten years ago, I sat in the cool, dark sanctuary of Calvary Episcopal Church in Columbia, Missouri, aware of the high holy church atmosphere, taking in the vivid colors of the small but dramatic stained-glass windows, the dark wood of the altar rail, the Eucharist table, the ornate elevated pulpit worthy of a seventeenth-century cathedral. This was a new field research position for me: to sit in a "high church" seeking to continue my studies of women in the pulpit. In the preceding years I had entered many warehouse-like Pentecostal assemblies and one-room "tabernacles" lucky to have a wood-burning stove, an American flag, and sometimes a donated piano. In contrast to the noisy ambiance of those "spirit-filled" congregations, the tone of this self-conscious Episcopal space was set by the hushed voices of arriving congregants, the quiet shuffling of feet, the swish of the priest's garb, the smell of the candles, and the deep tones of the huge organ. And when the priest turned to face her audience, I caught my breath as I watched my friend Tamsen Whistler raise her arms in the voluminous butterfly sleeves of the priest's robe and invite her congregation to worship with her. We stood at her invitation and joined in the standard, deeply ritualized, ancient liturgy associated with the Episcopal tradition.

This anthology is about the role of women in Christian preaching, broadly defined. It traces a tradition that helped to place Tamsen Whistler in the pulpit. Instead of conducting fieldwork with contemporary women preachers, as I do, most of the contributors to this book generally work within an intellectual space of historical reconstruction, re-membering, hypothesis, conjecture, and quilting together of fragments.[1] Because of a dearth of information, the loss of official records, and the bias against recognizing women's contributions, their research is often based on the sketchiest of evidence; these scholars work steadfastly to recreate some sense of the heritage of women preaching. And their persistence pays off; they reveal that women have been preaching in the Christian tradition from the earliest of historical moments, perhaps only days after Jesus Christ was crucified and his resurrection announced. Beginning with Mary Magdalene's instruction from the risen Christ to "Go and tell," a tradition of women preaching can be documented. It is a story, however spotty, about how women have followed Christ's directive, about how they have "told" even as they have needed to negotiate the contexts for that telling. Restoring the contribution of women to the history of preaching allows for the construction of a new story about the preaching tradition. Rewriting women into the record, re-membering women whose names have been deleted, restoring women's place and voices in the record of Christian preaching is a vital first step toward reclaiming women's right to that space, both then and today.

Unlike the work of other researchers in this collective endeavor, my ethnographic research can take me, on any given Sunday, only a few blocks or miles to record a woman preacher preaching from any number of pulpits in the midwestern university town where I live and in the areas nearby. This is actually not unusual. Women are filling pulpits all over the country in record numbers, albeit often in the smaller and less prestigious churches, where the salaries are low and never match the grueling workload. Sometimes a single minister serves several small churches. Indeed, some ministers who are also new mothers serve churches that are miles apart, forcing them to juggle work and family, negotiating bottles and car seats while traveling rugged Missouri roads to reach small towns and far-flung rural areas.

In conducting my field research, I tape-record the actual, verbatim texts of women's sermons—a luxury enjoyed by few, if any, of my colleagues in this anthology. I can interview the preachers and the members of their congregations, as well as transcribe the texts of their tape-recorded sermons. The texts of their life stories, the interviews I have conducted with them, and the tape-recorded dialogues we have shared over the years of my research about their lives and their ministries provide a rich tapestry of information upon which I depend for my writing, thinking, and teaching. I do not need to hypothesize or reconstruct what women might be preaching in this moment which ushers in the momentous move into a new millennium. At least for the women in my field studies, I know what they are preaching, and I can share that with my readers. What I do have to reconstruct and hypothesize, however, is how their work illuminates the historical record of women preaching and how it may reflect back upon the prejudices and discrimination, the denial and the persecution, of other women who dared to claim the pulpit before them. What is the heritage of the women I have come to know so well? Can their lives and words help to uncover the depths of the biases against their voices in the pulpit? Do their messages provide a path toward their own inclusion in this largely male circle? Can the pulpit language, imagery, and rhetorical style of contemporary women preachers help us to fill in the gaps where their foresisters' words have survived only in fragments? Are there clues in evidence that guide us toward an understanding of the substance of feminine voices, female spirituality, and women's way of knowing God?

My own work began in the mid-1970s with Pentecostal laywomen, preachers, and pastors in middle America and continues with mainline denominational pastors and chaplains. This work suggests a kind of religious breadth that may serve us well as we think about women who seek the pulpit. In the early 1980s, my training as a folklorist took me to very small, autonomous Pentecostal congregations in southern Indiana that were largely, if not exclusively, female. Generally, the pastors ministering to these small groups of female believers were male. In these small religious contexts, I was drawn to document the wide variety of religious expressive behaviors and verbal arts that were performed and displayed in a typical Pentecostal service. As I. M. Lewis and others have noted, the women predominated in their participation, standing in the pews to testify at great length, weeping, praying for God's mercy and intercession in their lives, singing, dancing, swaying and shouting in the spirit, seeking the spirit's manifestation through tongue speaking, "falling out" on the floor, being slain by the spirit, or jerking spasmodically as the spirit entered their willing bodies.[2] Women who had grown up in this charged religious atmosphere had cultivated the ritualized behaviors and the formulaic discourse through observation and participation.

At the time I did not recognize that I was observing "women preaching," for men stood in the pulpit, serving as pastors and guides for the female congregations. Yet in my earliest published work I addressed the possibility that the women's testimonies were acts of preaching.[3] Although these testifying women stood in their places in the pews (rather than behind the pulpit), they delivered long, elaborate testimonies that went far beyond what I had learned to anticipate as a testimony text.

In general, testimonies are short but often emotional declarations of the evidence of God's intervention and consolation in the testifier's life. Testimonies are viewed as obligatory; believers need to acknowledge God's goodwill in their lives.[4] Most often testimonies in the Pentecostal service begin with the standardized statement, "I just want to stand and give my testimony." Then, in a highly formulaic and (at times) nearly chanting delivery, the testifier recounts the miraculous deeds of God during the past days. These testimonies are perceived as important testaments to God's intervention in every believer's most mundane daily experiences and to more spectacular "miracles" that God has performed—a typical example might be the unexpected arrival of a check in the mail when the refrigerator was empty and the children had begun to get hungry, or a story about losing an important document only to have God reveal its whereabouts.

I found Pentecostal women's testimonies to be highly formulaic, typical of the oral tradition. These poetic texts exhibit the creative use of repetition, imagery, and structural format; they are rarely didactic, often emotionally charged, rhetorically persuasive, rhythmic, and artistically rendered. These oral, formulaic testimonies are contemporary examples of similar epic and poetic genres in folklore.[5] While the actual words, or the order of words, may change from testimony to testimony, the formulaic patterns inherent in this female verbal art are certainly discernible, as are the rhythmic patterns of the "lines" and the oral, poetic style of delivery. With study, I came to recognize both the dynamic and the conservative elements in these "spontaneously" delivered verbal affidavits, noting how the style, the language, the patterning, and the content are all part of their shared religious verbal art (folklore).[6] As is typical in the context of oral tradition, the group determined the form, content, and structure of the texts, while individual performers put their nuances upon a traditional form that had been passed down from generation to generation and from believer to believer. Inherent in the performances was the recognition of a critical audience ready to pass judgment upon the competence of the performance.[7] Good testimonies are warmly received by other group members. Often an "Amen" or "Tell it Sister" accompanies the delivery of a testimony or punctuates its end. Length is not regulated. It does not appear that shorter or longer testimonies are received differently or preferred.

But the analysis that took me beyond the oral formulaic aspects of the testimonies broke new ground in terms of genre identification. In one congregation, for example, I noticed that the testifying women, usually three or four in a single service, occasionally "took over" the entire service. And their testimonies often sounded more like sermons than like testimonies. Because they delivered their testimonies (sermons) from the pews (never from the pulpit), the testifying women did not pose a threat to the male who claimed the pulpit as his own. In many ways, though, the testifiers were preaching, and they frequently testified or preached long into the night, so long that the pastor was not able to deliver his own sermon. My suggestion that the women were actually "preaching" (when they were supposed to be testifying) raises two issues that have a direct bearing on this volume: one, what women say and do may be classified as preaching even though the content and format, presentation and performance, of the verbal act are not immediately discernible as preaching. Two, these performances of women in the religious context may be seen as political acts—as manipulative, strategic, thoughtful, and intentional acts of rhetorical empowerment. Women can and do preach when and where they are able. It behooves us then to pay close attention to all aspects of these "testimonies." Not only are form, content, structure, imagery, patterning, and formulas important in our study of women's religious verbal art, but also the very acts of when and where, how and by whom, these acts are delivered, critiqued, and acknowledged. Would anyone in the congregation exclaim, "Gee, Sister Helen certainly can preach!" if she had only stood in the "testifying" space? Or, is part of the safety of "preaching" from the pew inherent in the fact that both the women delivering these "testimonies" and their audience/group members would never refer to their text as a sermon or to their delivery as preaching. Rather, the critique for competence would rest solidly on the collective agreement that what had been delivered was, indeed, a testimony.

The following testimony, recorded on tape in 1980, illustrates some of what I have been discussing.[8] It may be significant to note that the performer of this testimony was a licensed, not an ordained, preacher (licensing is generally accomplished through a short correspondence course). Hence, she probably knew the characteristics of a sermon and the difference between a sermon and a testimony, as did her listeners. Yet, this highly charged, rhetorically marked "sermon" was delivered in the mode and space of a testimony:

Blessed Jesus. Thank you Jesus.
Tonight I love the Lord.
I thank him tonight
And I praise him
Because I know he's real in my heart
This night.
As we sang that song "Jesus on the main line"
It just made me think, you know,
When you dig around sometimes
You get down there
And you get these little streams.
You know, these little streams
They're just not enough,
There's just not enough water there.
But when we hit that main line,
Hallelujah,
You've got plenty of water,
You've got plenty,
When you get Jesus on the main line.
Hallelujah.
You've got just what you need.
You know, those little trinkles
They don't do much for me,
Thank you Jesus,
For I've been under the Holy Spout.
Hallelujah.
It does a whole lot more for me,
Thank you Jesus.
Hallelujah.
You know I might make you stay up for a while

Because, praise the Lord,
Hallelujah,
I know he is real!
Whooooooooo!
Glory!
I know he is real tonight.
You know when I sing
And when I testify,
Everyone looks at me
And they think I'm kind of
Peculiar.
But you know tonight
We are a peculiar people.
But you know something?
I'm not ashamed of Jesus.
Hallelujah.
Because this is the Lord
That I sing
That I testify for
That I stomp my feet for
That I clap my hands for
It's Jesus Christ
And I love him tonight,
Lord,
And he is worthy
Of all praises,
Everything,
Everything
That we can possibly do for him
He is worthy of it
This night.
Hallelujah!
Whooooooooooooooooo

Blessed Jesus. Thank you Jesus.
Tonight I love the Lord.
I thank him tonight
And I praise him
Because I know he's real in my heart
This night.[9]

The first lines of this testimony offer two different aspects of the verbal repertoire of the speaker. "Blessed Jesus" and "Thank you Jesus" are formulaic phrases that one might find in several religious genres—prayer, testimony, sermon, even tongue speaking. Bruce Rosenberg might identify such phrases as clichéd "fillers" or "stalls" that give the performer time to think about the next line, or they may be inherent components of the testimony mode itself.[10]

The next lines identify the text more clearly as testimony, with the obligatory testifying language: "Tonight I love the Lord. I thank him tonight and I praise him because I know he's real in my heart." Yet, the next section of this testimony ought to focus on *how* this woman *knows* God is real in her heart; what made her say this? What did God do that week for her, specifically, that can attest to God's constant care and ability to deliver? But instead of offering these basic components of the Pentecostal testimony, this performer leaps directly into what I would argue is a "preaching mode." Her sisters in faith in that small congregation may also have recognized her rhetoric as preaching; they appeared to endorse and respond enthusiastically to her testimony, as well as that of others, supporting a collective effort that prevented the pastor from delivering the actual sermon.

My study of sermons actually delivered by women from the pulpit has taken me to Pentecostal churches in southern Indiana and southern Missouri, where women serve both as traveling preachers and as official pastors of churches. Many Pentecostal associations officially deny women access to the pulpit, so how, I wondered, did these women secure their rights to the pulpit? I have concluded from my research that their access is a product of their claims to a personal "call from God." Because Pentecostals place such a high value on and believe so deeply in personal interactions with an immanent God (as opposed to a less accessible transcendent God), any "call to preach" is taken seriously and thus provides the validation for a woman's claim to the pulpit. God can and does, the believers all agree, work in mysterious ways and could be using a woman's voice for the work of the kingdom. And they would not dare to question the voice of God. Still, the woman making such claims must convince them that her call is genuine, her motives above reproach, and her aspirations not personal but spiritual and religiously based.[11]

But what about the women who now have access to the pulpits of some of the mainline denominations in this country—what and how do they preach? I find that their sermons address many of the same concerns that the contributors to this volume do. Often they remember the women who have been ignored in the biblical canon and left out of the official liturgy. Their sermons often collapse strictly defined genre markers in an attempt to expand the possibilities for spiritual and religious exploration—allowing testimonies, for example, to move in style and delivery toward sermonizing; allowing song and dance into liturgical performances; fusing modes of teaching and preaching, prophecy, and prayer. Their sermons reinforce female imagery of God as evidenced in relationships and connections; women preachers rely, in their sermons, on women's narratives, women's experiences, women's ways of knowing who God is as a way to tell "the other half of the story"; they preach inclusion, family, and community. They are bold, even revolutionary in their insistence that the biblical canon must be reviewed and redefined; that denominational and official religious stances must be decentered and reexamined; that church hymns, prayers, Bibles, sermons, and all other genres of religious discourse must be stripped of their male bias and replaced with inclusionary language that embraces all religious seekers; that all persons deserve to be treated humanely, fairly, and with love; that age, race, and sexual discrimination must end before other global problems can be resolved; that the earth is God's body and that all persons living must learn to treat it as the very essence of God's being; and that their female voices are part of a new dialogic paradigm that is taking root in the religious arena, both here and abroad, and these voices ring clear and true, bringing God's people back to a truer reality of what it means to be Christian.

I want to examine how some of these themes are presented in a sermon delivered by the Reverend Tamsen Whistler at the Episcopal service I described earlier; the lectionary readings were Deuteronomy 15:7–11; 2 Corinthians 8:1–9; Mark 5:22–24, 35b–43 (June 26, 1988). She called the sermon "A Woman's Faith" and began with the following Gospel passage:

"And one of the leaders of the synagogue named Jairus came
and when he saw him, fell at his feet and begged him repeatedly,
'My little daughter is at the point of death.
Come and lay your hands on her,
so that she may be made well, and live.'
So he went with him.

. . . .

—Some people came from the leader's house to say,
'Your daughter is dead. Why trouble the teacher any further?'
But overhearing what they said,
Jesus said to the leader of the synagogue,
'Do not fear, only believe.'
He allowed no one to follow him except Peter, James, and John,
        the brother of James.
When they came to the house of the leader of the synagogue,
he saw a commotion, people weeping and wailing loudly.
When he had entered, he said to them,
'Why do you make a commotion and weep?
The child is not dead but sleeping.'
And they laughed at him.
Then he put them all outside,
and took the child's father and mother and those who were with him,
and went in where the child was.
He took her by the hand and said to her,
'Talitha cum,'
which means, 'Little girl, get up!'
And immediately the girl got up and began to walk about
(she was twelve years of age).
At this they were overcome with amazement.

He strictly ordered them that no one should know this,
and told them to give her something to eat."

The Gospel passage this morning
is a fairly straightforward miracle story,
particularly dramatic
because beyond healing,
Jesus raises someone from the dead.
A twelve-year-old is restored to life
because of her parents' faith.
There's a pattern to miracle stories in the Bible,
and what we have heard this morning
follows the pattern pretty well:
Human resources are exhausted.
Jairus in desperation approaches Jesus.
Jesus encounters opposition in the pressing crowd
and the jeering mourners.
The miracle itself is private—
only parents and three disciples
witness Jesus' raising the girl.
Jesus both touches and speaks to the child.
Everyone is astonished
when she gets up and walks.
After requesting silence about the miracle
and making sure that the child eats,
Jesus leaves.

At issue here for us
in the twentieth century
is often the question,
"Is this really a miracle?
Did it really happen?"
But we can trap ourselves
so effectively
in the "Is it real" question
that we may not move beyond it
to the real issue:
the issue of faith.
Do we believe that God
can intervene in our lives?
Can we reorganize God's action?

And there's another issue also,
which lies in the fact
that what the lectionary provides for us
this morning
in the healing of Jairus's daughter
is only part of the story.
You may have noticed in your bulletins

that what we heard a short while ago
were verses 22–24 and 35–43
of the fifth chapter of Mark.
Verses 25–34, which we did not read,
contain another story,
another healing miracle,
which interrupts the story of Jairus's daughter,
while providing an explanation
of Jesus' delay in reaching Jairus's house.
Let me read this passage.

[Reads Mark 5:25–34]
"And a large crowd followed him and pressed in on him.
Now there was a woman who had been suffering from hemorrhages
for twelve years.
She had endured much under many physicians,
and had spent all that she had; and she was no better,
but rather grew worse.
She had heard about Jesus, and came up behind him in the crowd
and touched his cloak,
for she said, 'If I but touch his clothes, I will be made well.'

Immediately her hemorrhage stopped;
and she felt in her body that she was healed of her disease.

Immediately aware that power had gone forth from him,
Jesus turned about in the crowd and said,
'Who touched my clothes?'
And his disciples said to him,
'You see the crowd pressing in on you;
how can you say, "Who touched me?"'
He looked all around to see who had done it.
But the woman, knowing what had happened to her,
came in fear and trembling, fell down before him,
and told him her whole story.
He said to her, 'Daughter, your faith has made you well;
go in peace, and be healed of your disease.'"

An obvious question here,
of course,
is why did the designers of our lectionary
leave the woman with the twelve-year issue of blood
out of the story of Jairus's daughter?
We could get caught for a long time
in speculation about this,
and probably the explanation
is something simple like,
"The story of Jairus's daughter
stands on its own" or

"one healing makes the point as well as two"
or "the hemorrhaging woman is less tasteful
than the little girl."
It's apparently fairly clear
in the oldest Greek manuscripts of Mark
that the healing of the hemorrhaging woman
is written in better Greek
than the healing of Jairus's daughter.
So the writer of Mark
probably inserted the story to begin with.
Perhaps our lectionary designers left it out
because it began as an insertion.
Whatever the reason,
it's been left out.
But I think it's important that we consider it;
first, because the use of the "story within a story"
is fairly typical to the Gospel of Mark,
but primarily because
the two stories together
offer us more about the nature of Jesus
and faith
than either story does on its own.

Without the story
of the hemorrhaging woman,
the healing of Jairus's daughter
invites us to concentrate
on the beautiful vision of a child lost,
now restored to her parents.
It is possible for us to talk about
the great spiritual meaning
of the child's return to life
without giving much thought
to the physical—
beyond the touch of Jesus' hand
and his command
that she be given something to eat.
We can be thrilled
that Jesus has acted
in such a dramatic way,
and we can recognize that children,
as well as adults,
are recipients of God's grace.

But we can stand outside the story
and watch.
And we can speculate
about the reality of miracles.

We can sidetrack ourselves,
while we admire the great spiritual revelation
of the child's return to life.

If we consider the healing
of the hemorrhaging woman
in the context of the healing of Jairus's daughter,
we find powerful contrasts.
The hemorrhaging woman
is not somebody we'd want to be around.
She's drained and desperate.
She's spent all her savings
seeking a cure,
and she's only grown worse.
For twelve years—
as long as Jairus's daughter has been alive—
the hemorrhaging woman
has been denied access
to the practice of her religion,
because she's unclean.
Close contact
with another human by her
renders that other person unclean, also.
The woman is an outcast,
one to be avoided,
one for whom life
within the structure of a supportive community
is impossible.
She is unclean;
and no decent person
should have anything to do with her.

In her desperation,
the woman forces herself through the crowd
toward Jesus,
seeking only to touch his clothing
to heal herself.
But the healing comes from Jesus.
She touches his garment
and feels within her body
that she is cured.
And he feels within his body
that someone has touched him.
His disciples think he is silly
to seek a particular person
in a pressing crowd,
but he recognizes
that a particular individual

has encountered him,
and he looks for her.
Overwhelmed by the fact of her new wholeness,
the woman is frightened.
Nevertheless,
she goes to Jesus as he seeks her,
and she tells him her whole story.
His response to her?
"Daughter, go in peace.
Your faith has healed you."
Another miracle, to be sure,
but the two stories together
help bring home to us
that an encounter with Jesus Christ
on any level
involves both the physical,
concrete world
and dialogue with Jesus Christ.
The reality of experience
is imperative
in our relationship with God.
We don't simply encounter Jesus Christ
on some esoteric plane
separate from our daily lives.
Instead, we encounter God in Christ
in our physical being,
our life in the world,
and our death.
The encounter involves both touch
and conversation.
Without the dialogue
between Jesus and the woman,
Jesus and the child,
and the child's parents,
the miracles have little meaning.
Without the dialogue,
what happens simply happens
and there's nothing to allay
the resulting fear.
When the woman is healed,
she is frightened.
Jesus gives peace
by acknowledging her faith,
and that's a miracle
beyond the physical healing.
We are like the hemorrhaging woman
and the little girl

because we are embodied beings.
We will undergo physical and emotional pain;
and we will die.
We are like them also
in that we know the world
through our physical presence,
through our senses as well as our thoughts,
and we need both
for wholeness in our daily lives.
The physical aspect of our lives
is not somehow separate
from our spiritual development.
We have to live that development out
in our bodies,
in the world,
in the here and now,
in the decisions we make,
in our connections with those around us.
How do we participate
in God's healing action?
We touch each other;
we talk to each other.
We love.

These stories are given to us
that we might learn something about faith,
not that we get sidetracked
on the issue of whether they really happened,
whether they're really miracles,
but that we might focus on the issue
of how it is that we encounter God.

Do we believe in the resurrection?
How do we live that belief,
act it out in our physical lives?
Can we recognize that concrete action—
touch and dialogue—
are the way we know each other
and the Christ within us?
Body and blood,
word and action—
the miracle of faith
lies in the concrete,
the particular,
the physical,
our daily lives.

We eat and drink together
that we might more fully know

our connection with each other,
with the hemorrhaging woman,
the dead and living child,
the crucified and risen Christ.
Amen.[12]

What is immediately evident in this sermon is that the priest has dared to question the authority of the lectionary writers. Not only has she read the portions of the Scripture that were left out of the lectionary, she proceeds to preach the sermon on that "left-out" portion and, in the process, to chastise the lectionary writers for their discrimination and their unwillingness to deal with the disturbing story of the hemorrhaging woman. She has elected to restore this unlikely story into the lectionary scripture reading and re-member the hemorrhaging woman into the religious canon. Furthermore, in focusing on this woman's story she has provided a framework for reinstating women into the biblical story on the one hand, and into the contemporary religious scene on the other.

Why did the lectionary writers omit the story of the hemorrhaging woman? Tamsen Whistler offers several possible reasons: the story of the healed child stands alone; perhaps they felt one healing story would suffice; or perhaps the story of the hemorrhaging woman was too distasteful. But, she argues, none of these reasons will suffice. Both stories are needed to provide a complete picture, just as we might argue that the experiences of women are essential to getting the full picture. The innocent twelve-year-old girl, mourned by her parents, is a child healed, brought back to life by Jesus. But by itself, this healing story focuses too much on the miraculous as awe-inspiring. The story of the risen child cannot stand alone. The faith exhibited is not her faith; it is not even, in some ways, her story. The story is about the father's faith and Jesus' own assurance that he could bring the child back to life. But the story of the hemorrhaging woman is a story of one woman's experience with a blood flow that would not stop—a raging flow of blood that has lasted as long as the young child visited by Jesus has been alive. Because of the Jewish culture in which she lived, which labeled her perpetually unclean, not fit to engage in any religious or sexual activities, and because of the physical debilitation rendered on her by the excessive blood flow and the failure of the physicians to heal her, she is a broken woman, an outcast. Tamsen described her in strong details.

What separates this woman from the rest of her community is her femaleness, of course—the blood flow that will not cease. The society had created elaborate ways to deal with women's "unclean" nature as it occurred naturally once a month: via the mikvah (cleansing bath at the conclusion of the menstrual flow) a woman could be reincorporated into the collective whole and become active again in the religious community.[13] But this woman has been isolated and denounced because she is in a constant unclean state. Jesus' followers did not want him to touch her, talk to her, and certainly not heal her. But Jesus does, and with his act, he reinstates her into the community. She is unclean no more; she is now a woman with a regulated blood flow, therefore a woman who can be re-incorporated. We might extend this metaphor to understand that both the biblical story and Tamsen Whistler's sermon serve to reincorporate women into the collective, community story. Women were written out because, as women, they were perceived to be unclean and unworthy. Jesus' healing of the woman served to reinsert her into the community and into the story. Certainly, Tamsen's act of reinserting the woman's story into the lectionary reading and into her sermon serves to reinstate and reinsert women's experiences into the biblical canon and into the collective, supportive story of Christians. *Both* stories are necessary, she tells her congregation, in order to understand the complete story of Christ as it pertains to people's daily lives.

Tamsen Whistler's sermon is also a subtle critique of the typical sermons delivered on these passages. We can, she says, get caught up in arguing about whether these are actual miracles. But such arguments divert us from the real purpose of these stories, which is to tell us how faith works. These healings are possible, she claims, only through the *physical interactions and dialogue* of the faithful with the healer, Jesus Christ. The hemorrhaging woman reaches out to touch Jesus. He stops to demand who has touched him for healing. Tamsen claims that the healing is not complete until the woman *actually converses with Jesus*. He asks her a question and "she tells him her whole story." Only then does he say to her: "Daughter, go in peace. Your faith has healed you." Tamsen asks:

> Can we recognize that concrete actions—
> touch and dialogue—
> are the way we know each other
> and the Christ within us?

Like many of the women in my studies, she builds her message on a theology of connection, human and divine. The last lines of her sermon invite her congregation to the Eucharist table, with Christ, the woman, and the risen child. In a brilliant metaphorical twist, the risen child in the healing story becomes the risen Christ (child), and the body and blood of Christ at the Eucharist table are remembered via the blood of the hemorrhaging woman.

> We eat and drink together
> that we might more fully know
> our connection with each other,
> with the hemorrhaging woman,
> the dead and living child,
> the crucified and risen Christ.

With these words, she has not offered an unpolluted symbolic Eucharist table to her congregants; she has, rather, invited them to the table replete with living images both human and divine, connected, re-membered, re-inserted, re-vived, after being interrupted, separated, dead. Here there is life and blood:

Take this and eat; this is my body.
Drink, this is my blood.

The sermons of women serve to reinsert women into a religious history that has sought to deny their stories as contributing to the larger, collective story of Christians sharing traditions. Women's sermons are about connection and dialogue, about inclusion and broadening perspectives; they draw upon and build around women's experiences, women's language, and women's ways of being in the world.[14] Their messages are of restoration and healing, like Tamsen's sermon on the hemorrhaging woman—the story that was omitted from the lectionary but told nonetheless.

NOTES

1. Elisabeth Schüssler Fiorenza, *In Memory of Her: A Feminist Theological Reconstruction of Christian Origins* (New York: Crossroad, 1993); and Schüssler Fiorenza, "The 'Quilting' of Women's History: Phoebe of Cenchreae," in Paula M. Cooey, Sharon A. Farmer, and Mary Ellen Ross, eds., *Embodied Love: Sensuality and Relationship as Feminist Values* (San Francisco: Harper and Row, 1987).

2. I. M. Lewis, *Ecstatic Religion* (Middlesex, England: Penguin, 1971).

3. See Elaine J. Lawless, "Shouting for the Lord: The Power of Women's Speech in the Pentecostal Service," *Journal of American Folklore* 96 (1983): 433–57; and Lawless, *God's Peculiar People: Women's Voices and Folk Tradition in a Pentecostal Church* (Lexington: University Press of Kentucky, 1988).

4. See Elaine J. Lawless, "'I Know If I Don't Bear My Testimony I'll Lose It': Mormon Women's Testimonies," *Kentucky Folklore Quarterly* 30 (1984): 32–49.

5. See Bruce Rosenberg, "The Formulaic Quality of Spontaneous Sermons," *Journal of American Folklore* 83 (1970): 3–20; and Rosenberg, *The Art of the American Folk Preacher* (New York: Oxford University Press, 1970). See also John Miles Foley, *Immanent Art: From Structure to Meaning in Traditional Oral Epic* (Bloomington: Indiana University Press, 1991); and Foley, *The Singer of Tales in Performance* (Bloomington: Indiana University Press, 1995).

6. Cf. Barre Toelken, *The Dynamics of Folklore* (Boston: Houghton Mifflin, 1979), pp. 34–39.

7. "Performance-theory folkloristics" recognizes all delivered verbal art as "performance" before a critical audience that critiques it for its "competence." See especially Richard Bauman, *Verbal Art as Performance* (Rowley, Mass.: Newbury House, 1977), p. 11; and Marta Weigel, "Women as Verbal Artists," *Frontiers*, Special Issue, Vol. 3 (Fall 1978): 1–9.

8. See Lawless, *God's Peculiar People*, pp. 102–3 ff.

9. This poetic rendering of her testimony is in keeping with current ethnopoetic renderings of verbally performed art; see Dennis Tedlock, "On the Translation of Style in Oral Narrative," *Journal of American Folklore* 84 (1971): 114–33; and Tedlock, *The Spoken Word and the Work of Interpretation* (Philadelphia: University of Pennsylvania Press, 1983). The line endings correspond to the performer's pauses for breath in performance. Because this text was rendered spontaneously and extemporaneously, it is difficult to match the written rendition with the artistically superior verbal rendering. Even a cursory glance at this text reveals characteristics of the text that might mark it as "testimony."

10. See Rosenberg, "Spontaneous Sermons," and *American Folk Preacher*, pp. 53–56.

11. See Elaine J. Lawless, *Handmaidens of the Lord: Pentecostal Women Preachers and Traditional Religion* (Philadelphia: University of Pennsylvania Press, 1988).

12. The sermon is printed here with the permission of Tamsen Whistler; transcription of the taped sermon was done by the author.

13. See Mary Douglas, *Purity and Danger* (London: Routledge, 1966).

14. See Elaine J. Lawless, *Women Preaching Revolution: Seeking Connection in a Disconnected Time* (Philadelphia: University of Pennsylvania Press, 1996).

PART ONE

Early Christianity

ONE

Prophetic Power and Women's Authority

The Case of the *Gospel of Mary* (Magdalene)

Karen L. King

In every century, including our own, history records women exercising leadership in Christian communities, and in every century that leadership has been contested, beginning in the early church and continuing through contemporary battles over the ordination and ministry of women. Although there are important exceptions,[1] in the first centuries the majority of the clear cases of women's leadership based their legitimacy on claims to prophetic experience.

Arguments against the public exercise of women's leadership over men, such as those in 1 Corinthians 14 and 1 Timothy 2, provide indirect evidence that women were in fact practicing public speech—otherwise why bother to prohibit them?[2] We also have direct evidence concerning the Corinthian women prophets—Philip's daughters, Ammia of Philadelphia, Philumene, the visionary martyr Perpetua, and several leaders of the Montanist movement, including Maximilla, Priscilla (Prisca), and Quintilla. All these women were accepted as prophets and exercised authority within Christian groups. There is, however, one additional work that lets us see a woman actually exercising leadership and hear what arguments were made to support that leadership: the *Gospel of Mary* (Magdalene).

We knew nothing about the existence of the *Gospel of Mary* until extensive fragments of a Coptic translation and two additional Greek fragments came to light in Egypt during the late nineteenth and twentieth centuries.[3] The first part of the work contains a postresurrection dialogue between the Savior and his disciples, among whom Mary Magdalene plays an important role.[4] After the Savior departs, controversy erupts among the disciples over the veracity of a vision Mary had of the Savior. The work confidently confirms Mary's vision and her leadership role among the disciples in the face of challenges from other disciples, especially Andrew and Peter.

In this essay I ask: What is prophecy? How does prophecy occur? Is prophecy a gendered phenomenon? What specific views support women's prophetic leadership? How are debates over prophecy centrally tied to conceptions of the nature of humanity and humanity's relationship to God? My main example is the *Gospel of Mary*. The issues surrounding women's prophetic experience in the *Gospel of Mary* were intertwined with early Christian attitudes toward the body and sexuality, ethical perspectives, and issues of authority and leadership. Moreover, Mary's prophecy directly impinged upon the interpretation of the teachings of Jesus and questioned the value of apostolic tradition.[5] In short, at stake here are the central issues of early Christian theology and church organization that were under debate in the formative centuries of Christianity. The analysis below follows the lead of Elisabeth Schüssler Fiorenza in purposefully treating the work within the context of early Christian debates over authority and leadership.[6] It presumes that prophetic authority and women's leadership were widely practiced, and it places the *Gospel of Mary* rhetorically within the controversies over those practices. Comparison with the works of Tertullian and others uncovers the ways in which prophecy, the body, ethics, and community organization are intertwined. In conclusion, I make some tentative suggestions about a complex of elements that may constitute a pattern of early Christian teaching and practice that was favorable to women's prophetic leadership and indeed to whose formation women may have substantially contributed.

WHAT IS PROPHECY?

In early Christianity, the term *prophecy* referred to a direct communication of the Deity to the prophet or through the prophet as medium. But beyond this simple definition, authentic prophecy encompassed a wide range of experiences that were not always distinguished. Prophecy might have interpreted the past, spoken to the present, or predicted the future. Prophetic inspiration could have been auditory or visionary or both. It could have occurred while someone was awake or through dreams during sleep.[7] It could have been ecstatic, or not.[8] It could have been remembered by the prophet after the trance, or not. It could have occurred while the prophet's soul or spirit was in the body or out of it. Sometimes it involved a spiritual journey while the body itself lay suspended in a stupor. At other times, the Spirit was understood to speak directly through the mouth of the prophet. The personality of the prophet was sometimes present, sometimes obscured by the divine presence.

The prophet played a variety of leadership roles. Usually the prophet had only an informal role, but a few churches seem to have had an official office of prophet.[9] The prophet provided guidance, interpreted Scripture, commanded, and declared. Often the prophet was the recipient of instruction and then passed that divine instruction on to others.[10]

Prophetic citations appear in early Christian literature as pithy oracles, and in narrative accounts of visionary experiences or ecstatic journeys.[11] Because of the variety of prophetic speech in early Christianity, clear distinctions were not always made among the functions of teaching, prophecy, prayer, and speaking in tongues, and their accompanying roles of leadership. One of Paul's projects in Corinthians seems to have been precisely to introduce these distinctions, but he was apparently not very successful.[12] In the *Didache*, for example, the prophet not only provides instruction but also performs the Eucharist and leads prayer. In the second century, Tertullian understood the prophet to play a variety of roles, including revealing prophecy, interpreting Scripture, and directing discipline within the community.[13] Once a prophet's knowledge of God was acknowledged, her status as a teacher was ensured. Even where the role of teacher had become more formalized, it was still connected with prophetic inspiration.[14]

In the *Gospel of Mary*, it is Mary Magdalene who plays the role of the prophet.[15] She receives a vision of the Lord and assumes the roles of comforter and teacher to the other disciples, admonishing them to be resolute. She turns their hearts toward the "Good" so that they begin to discuss the words of the Savior.[16] In the Berlin Codex, the content of her speech is described as a revelation of "what is hidden." She is thus clearly functioning in the role of the prophetic revealer to the other disciples.

Mary clearly remembers her vision, since she is able to recount it later, and there are no indications of a state of trance or possession distinct from sleep. The dream was both auditory and visionary in that she not only saw the Savior but also heard him.[17] Indeed they were able to converse, and the dream account consists primarily of a dialogue between Mary and the Savior.[18]

Prophetic experience in the *Gospel of Mary* has at least two distinct functions: to forge a relationship between the human and the divine,[19] and to claim legitimacy for the work's teaching. The appeal to prophecy implies a claim to the truth and the authority of the teaching of the Savior as it is interpreted by the *Gospel of Mary*, the legitimacy of Mary Magdalene's leadership role, and the text's theory about how visions are seen. Each of these claims was contested in the context of inner-Christian controversy.

HOW DOES PROPHECY OCCUR?

Mary has a vision in which she asks the Savior, "'Lord, how does a person who sees a vision see it—[with] the soul [or] with the spirit?' The Savior answered, 'One does not see with the soul or with the spirit, but with the mind which exists between these two—that is [what] sees the vision and that is w[hat . . .].'"[20] (At this point the text unfortunately breaks off into an extensive lacuna.)

This passage is interesting in that it is the only case in antiquity I am aware of in which the question of how a vision occurs is discussed in the context of the vision itself. Usually the question is raised in philosophical discussions, where the assumed context is the school. The Savior's conversation with Mary also resembles a pedagogical discussion between a teacher and student. Here, however, the authoritativeness of the answer is not dependent upon mere human wisdom, but is based on divine revelation, since the teacher is the Savior. It may be that the author of the *Gospel of Mary* thought to gain more authority for its viewpoint by making the answer come from divine revelation. Putting the answer on the lips of the Savior also attests to how serious the author thought the issue was; he or she did not want to leave the answer to the vagaries of human controversy. What are those issues?

The question of how prophecy occurred was of concern to early Christian theologians because the answer implied a particular view about the nature of God and humanity, and about their relationship—and there were, as will be seen, serious theological and practical implications involved in how that relationship was defined.[21] Those issues are exposed by comparing the *Gospel of Mary* with the views of Tertullian, an African theologian of the late second and early third century.

Both Tertullian and the *Gospel of Mary* highly valued women's prophetic experiences. There the similarity ends. For Tertullian, the self is a dyadic being composed of body and soul in unified relation.[22] For the *Gospel of Mary*, the self is triadic, composed of body, soul, and mind.[23] For both Tertullian and the *Gospel of Mary*, however, the term *spirit* signifies the divine presence.

Tertullian argues strongly against anthropologies of the self that, on the one hand, confuse the mortal soul and the divine spirit, or, on the other hand, divide the soul from its ruling function, the mind. In doing so, Tertullian wants to maintain a strong differentiation between the human and the divine and a relatively unified view of the self.[24] The *Gospel of Mary* is more interested in emphasizing the link between the human and the divine as the basis of hope for salvation, and it sees the soul in the body as a self divided against itself.

Tertullian argues that the soul is corporeal (having form, limitation, length, breadth, and height).[25] It is shaped in the form of the human body and even "has its own eyes and ears owing to which people see and hear the Lord;[26] it also has other limbs through which it experiences thoughts and engages in dreams."[27] To support his point, Tertullian relies not only on arguments from the physician Soranus and Stoic philosophers;[28] his clinching argument comes from a vision of the soul by a woman prophet. During church services she experienced ecstatic visions and after the service reported them to the men leaders, who examined them to determine whether they were true. Once she saw a soul in bodily form that could be grasped by the hand.[29] Tertullian cites this vision as prophetic proof that the soul is corporeal.[30] Because the soul is material, the resurrection of the believer is, for Tertullian, a bodily resurrection—that includes both the material body and the material soul.[31]

These material souls even have gender, which they receive simultaneously with the flesh "such that neither substance controls the cause of sex."[32] Sexual differentiation is thus natural to the soul's very existence, and gender differences and gender hierarchy are inscribed by Tertullian onto the soul itself. It is therefore no surprise to learn that Adam's soul was more complete than Eve's, according to Tertullian.[33]

In contrast, the *Gospel of Mary* argues that the most fundamental self, the soul, is not material but spiritual in nature. According to the Savior, the soul's attachment to the body is the cause of sickness and death.[34] This perspective does not mean, however, that the body is considered to be evil or that the work points toward ascetic practices. Indeed, if the soul is in proper relationship to God, the disturbing passion that wracks the body will be overcome. Ultimately, however, the body will not be saved or resurrected. The story of the soul's rise in Mary's vision emphasizes this point. While the soul ascends to its immortal rest, the material body returns to its root.[35] As with Tertullian, it is a woman's prophetic vision that establishes the truth of this teaching.

The *Gospel of Mary* also does not consider souls to be gendered; sexuality and the gender differences inscribed on the body belong to the material nature that must ultimately be transcended. Gender differentiations are therefore illusory insofar as they are inscribed on bodies that will cease to exist.

Important moral perspectives come into play here. For both Tertullian and the *Gospel of Mary*, sin clouds the divine nature of the soul, dimming its perception of God; only the pure soul may commune with God—and even then only because of the intervention of the Spirit. Their understandings of what constitutes sin, however, are quite different. For Tertullian, sin is the transgression of moral laws; moral reflection, therefore, focuses on determining correct behaviors. For the *Gospel of Mary*, sin is "adultery"—that is, the improper mixing of matter with the divine soul. Such mixing results in sickness and death.[36] Moral reflection focuses on interior spiritual development as a way to overcome physical pain and death. For the *Gospel of Mary*, it is the teaching of the risen Savior that brings salvation; whereas for Tertullian, the resurrected Jesus ensures the physical resurrection of the believer.

These views about the fundamental character of human beings are reflected in their views of how prophecy occurs. Tertullian held that all souls have some measure of original goodness on the basis of which they can prophesy.[37] The experience of prophecy signals the restored purity of the soul from its corruption by sin after it has embraced the Christian faith.[38] Prophetic experience occurs when the soul steps from the body in ecstasy.[39] Ecstasy ("the departure of the senses and the appearance of madness") is common to sleep, and Tertullian associates this state with dreaming. Not all dreams, however, are prophetic. Dreams can come from three sources: demons, God, and the soul itself.[40] In prophecy, the soul is moved by the divine Spirit from without,[41] and it is clear that, for Tertullian, this movement from without is manifest in ecstasy.[42]

The primary difference between Tertullian and the *Gospel of Mary* concerns the participation of materiality in the visual experience. For Tertullian, the material self is able to perceive the Divine if it is purified of sin, although the purified, material soul's senses, including the mind, are dimmed while experiencing the vision. For the *Gospel of Mary*, however, it is not the soul that sees the vision, but the mind acting as a mediator between the sensory perceptions of the soul and the divine spirit. The bodily senses themselves obscure the capacity to perceive divine things. But because the mind is not associated with the senses, it is not dimmed by the presence of the Spirit.[43]

The *Gospel of Mary* clearly agrees with Tertullian that only spiritually advanced souls have visionary experiences. Mary, for example, is praised by the Savior because she has not "wavered" at the sight of him.[44] The Savior ascribes Mary's stability to the fact that her mind is concentrated on spiritual matters. Mary has clearly achieved the purity of mind necessary to see the Savior and converse with him. The vision is a mark of that purity and her closeness to God.[45] Note too that her stability is in marked contrast with the contentious fearfulness of the other disciples.

Tertullian and the *Gospel of Mary* differ in their conceptions of the fundamental nature of the person (whether one is corporeal or incorporeal), the character of sexual differentiation and gender roles (whether natural or illusory), and the role of the mind in human relationship to God (whether dimmed or potent). They do, however, share some beliefs: that only the pure can see God in visions, that attachment to the body dims the spiritual comprehension of the soul, and that visions are authoritative for Christian teaching and practice.[46]

Their differing attitudes toward the body are directly tied to valuations of traditional Mediterranean patriarchal gender roles. For Tertullian, these roles are based in nature; for the *Gospel of Mary*, they are illusory. Their attitudes toward the role of women as prophets fit their respective perspectives. Because gender is irrelevant in the *Gospel of Mary*, it is possible to imagine Mary taking on the role of Savior at his departure, engaging in public instruction of the other disciples. In Tertullian, where the subordination of women is understood to be a fact of nature, the woman prophet had no speech during the public community gathering, but her visions were examined by male elders after the "people" had left. It was up to them to determine the authenticity and truth of her revelations. Her prophetic experience was highly valued, but her role as a public leader was not.[47]

IS PROPHECY A GENDERED PHENOMENON?

We are now in a position to ask if prophecy in Mediterranean antiquity was a gendered phenomenon. The answer is clearly no if we mean that prophecy was restricted to women. It clearly was not. But the answer is yes in consideration of a number of other factors, including social status, sexual status, and the conception of prophecy as penetration of a person by the Spirit.

Social Status

Prophetic experience affects the social status of women and men differently. Women are not more given to ecstatic experience than men, but the social-political contexts of their experience differ.[48] The best study to date for an early Christian context is that of Antoinette Clark Wire on the Corinthian women prophets. The exercise of prophetic gifts affected differently the status of the men and women who joined the Corinthian community. The status of women of all classes, she argues, shows a rise, while the status of elite males may have suffered a decline.[49] We can speculate that the status of lower-class males, especially slaves, would also have been enhanced.

Although there is much less information to work with sociologically in the *Gospel of Mary*, within the narrative it seems clear that Mary's status in terms of wisdom, power, honor, and gender is high. One reason that Peter opposes Mary is that her leadership lowers his gender status, and he is not willing to accept that loss.

A second point concerns the moral aspects of ecstatic prophecy. Wire identifies two different ethical orientations in the Corinthian community: "The ethics fostered [by the women prophets] are release from external authorities and communal expression of divine authority, not the ethics of self-discipline and community order."[50] In 1 Corinthians, Paul, on the other hand, is extremely interested in bringing order and discipline into the Corinthian community. In a similar vein, Tertullian objected to the lack of order in certain Christian communities, which he considered to be heretical.[51] In these churches, roles were not formalized or permanent; rather the movement of the Spirit determined the functions members performed at various times. In practice, this apparently meant that women sometimes performed all the functions of church leadership: "Just so the women heretics, how bold! For they are to teach, to discuss, to perform exorcisms, to give hope of cures—perhaps even to baptize."[52] In both 1 Corinthians and Tertullian, the call for order and discipline in distinguishing among roles coincides with the marginalization of women and their subordination to male control.[53]

In contrast, an ethic similar to that of the Corinthian women prophets appears in the *Gospel of Mary*. Here sin is understood not as right and wrong actions in the material world, but in terms of spiritual development conceived as turning one's self toward the Good. Moreover, in the *Gospel of Mary*, the Savior goes out of his way to warn the disciples against constraining themselves by laying down any rule or law beyond what he appointed for them. Like the Corinthian women prophets, the *Gospel of Mary* fostered an ethics of "release from external authorities and communal expression of divine authority." The different ethical attitudes toward order and discipline by Paul and Tertullian on the one hand, and by the Corinthian women prophets and the *Gospel of Mary* on the other, correlate with positions that would give each the highest social status relative to the other. The freedom of the spirit opened more possibilities for the exercise of women's authority and leadership than did the order and discipline ethics of Paul and Tertullian.

A third way in which prophecy affected the social status of women and men differently concerns social gendered roles. For both the Corinthian women prophets and the *Gospel of Mary*, the practice of women's exercise of authority is tied to attitudes that did not define women's identity in terms of their roles in marriage and motherhood.[54] Since the identity and status of men were defined less in terms of their sexual roles than were women's identity and status, these attitudes would have had less impact on their social status.[55]

Public Roles and Sexual Status

The second way in which prophecy can be considered to be gendered concerns the public roles of the prophet.[56] In speaking, preaching, teaching, and praying aloud in the presence of the whole community, women's sexual status was evaluated differently than men's.

Our ancient sources, whether Christian or other, often explicitly note the sexual status of women in discussing their prophetic experience, while such observation is rare for men prophets. Moreover, this attention consistently plays a rhetorical role and forms a clear pattern: When women's prophetic status is positively valued, their sexual purity is emphasized, often by pointing out that they were virgins, chaste widows, or even occasionally devoted wives.[57] But when a writer opposes a woman, her sexual status becomes an explicit basis for condemnation.[58] One particularly clear example is Tertullian's condemnation of the prophet Philumene. After twice calling her a "virgin" and affirming that she had a "vigorous spirit," he then dismisses her completely with the unsubstantiated charge that later she "became an enormous prostitute," thereby closing the entire discussion on a note of indisputable moral finality.[59] Tertullian can make this charge seem plausible because he associates her "erroneous" teachings with penetration by evil spirits and hence sexual pollution.[60] Such examples of sexual condemnation could easily be multiplied.[61]

This rhetorical move—condemning a woman prophet on the basis of sexual immorality—points to a wider and more problematic issue. Because of the wide acceptance of their authority as messengers of the gods in antiquity, prophets and their prophecies potentially had enormous power to direct people's lives, political events, and public opinion.[62] Prophecy represents a dramatic claim to authority, both for the prophet and for the message. Hence serious issues of power and authority were at stake in distinguishing true from false prophets.

For Christians, the rhetoric was clear: true prophets were inspired by divine agency; false prophets were inspired by the devil and his demons.[63] In practice, however, distinguishing the two was trickier. The problem was that it was not possible to tell the difference on formal grounds. The task was to gaze beyond the seeming of things to discern the true nature and essence of both prophet and prophecy. The ideal way to discern the truth of a prophet lay in seeing whether the prophecy came true or not. When this possibility was not available (either because the prophecy was not a prediction or because it was too soon to tell), criteria[64] centered on the moral character of the prophet[65] and whether the content of the prophetic message was found to be palatable (that is, whether it conformed to one's interpretation of scripture and tradition).[66]

In the case of women's prophecy, the judgment about a woman's moral character was determined by whether she conformed to the established social gender roles of wife and mother and kept silent in church assemblies.[67] In the cases of the Corinthian women prophets, the virgin daughters of Philip, the Montanist women prophets, and Perpetua, there seem to be good warrants for supposing that at least some women prophets withdrew from their roles as wives and mothers. One aim of the opposition to their public leadership involved restoring women to these roles. It is not a coincidence that 1 Timothy links its condemnation of women's public speech with a call for women to bear children in order to ensure their salvation.[68] The judgment of moral character led to a double bind for women: in order for women's prophecy to be considered authentic, women needed to give up its public practice. The ambiguity and tension we witness in many of the sources reflect the contradictions of this dilemma.

We are now in a position to address the question of why every prominent stream of theology and practice within early Christianity that supported women's leadership was sharply opposed, even decried as heretical. Insofar as women based their legitimacy on prophetic experience, the so-called "dampening of the prophetic spirit" in the history of Christianity coincided with the exclusion of women from positions of leadership. Although this phenomenon cannot be reduced to a single cause, such as the formation of canon,[69] one element (among others) that came into play was basing the evaluation of the authenticity of a prophetic utterance on conformity to patriarchal social gender roles. Such evaluation inscribed patriarchal values onto early Christian communal practice so as to exclude women's legitimate exercise of authority.

It is therefore interesting that this issue is not raised by the *Gospel of Mary*. Its view that authority is not gendered may have excluded such considerations, so that the *Gospel of Mary* does not provide an expected patriarchal position, even to contest it.

Ruth Padel has also argued that in early Greek thought, because a woman's body has more openings than a man's, it was considered to be more permeable, making women more susceptible to the entrance of spirits.[70] To my knowledge, this conceptuality is nowhere explicitly present in early Christianity. In the case of the *Gospel of Mary*, the dissociation of prophetic experience from the body may have excluded it by definition. Nonetheless, the continued emphasis in other texts on the sexual purity or impurity of women prophets may carry this conceptuality subliminally.[71]

Indeed, although no one in the *Gospel of Mary* accuses Mary Magdalene of sexual immorality, the early portrait of Mary as a prominent disciple was almost fully eclipsed in Christianity by the later portrait of Mary as the repentant prostitute. This revised edition of Mary's story was secured by identifying her with the sinner in Luke 7:36–50 and the adulteress in John 8:1–11. These identifications laid the foundation for the portrait of the Mary so well known from medieval and Renaissance times as the repentant whore, the "Venus in sackcloth," the counterpoint to the virgin mother of God, the representative of fallen female sexuality redeemed.

Penetration and Feminization

Padel's observation also leads us to the third way in which prophecy can be viewed as a gendered phenomenon.[72] Prophecy is sometimes understood as the penetration of the body by a spirit, and thus was sometimes conceived and expressed in sexual terms. As a consequence of a system of heterosexual gender symbolization in which the penetrator is symbolically masculine and the penetrated is symbolically feminine, the penetrated body of the prophet could be understood to be either feminine or feminized. Literature of the Roman period is replete with imagery of divine marriage, impregnation, erotic entry, and seduction,[73] and Tertullian uses the metaphor of marriage to speak of the Christian reception of the Spirit.[74] Origen also discusses the operation of the Spirit in prayer with sexually penetrating language.[75]

Cross-culturally a common pattern among polytheistic societies is that men are "married" to female divinities, women to male divinities.[76] In a monotheistic tradition where God is envisioned almost solely in male terms, the understanding of possession as marriage or erotic penetration can potentially pose special problems because it implies that women are the natural complements to a male God and that men are implicitly feminized and/or involved in homoerotic relations.[77] Both the polytheistic and the monotheistic patterns presume a heterosexual perspective.

One masked way in which this phenomenon may be appearing in the Christian works considered here is as a competition for the attention of God. Wire has suggested that part of Paul's arguments for the women Corinthian prophets wearing veils included a conception of sin as competition for God's glory. The women prophets apparently did not feel this threat.[78]

In the *Gospel of Mary*, the portrayal of male anxiety about competition among the disciples for the Savior's affection may belong to this perspective. Peter is happy to concede that the Savior loved Mary "more than other women," but he cannot bear the thought that the Savior may have loved her more than he loved the male disciples.[79] In suggesting that this competition is due to males being threatened by a woman for the favor of a male God, some may think that I am reading too much into the work. Indeed, it has been argued that gender is not an issue in the work at all.[80] Yet whether or not the presentation of gender conflict in the text was consciously intentional, it may nonetheless be significant that the portrayal of the conflict fits the patterns of ancient gender conceptuality so fully. We do not need to ascribe conscious intent in order to suggest operative cultural patterns.[81]

Sarah Coakley has astutely pointed out that this kind of gender conceptuality does not work when prophetic experience is understood not as penetration of the Spirit but as the flight of the soul out of the body.[82] Only the former implies the feminization of the prophet and the prophet's loss of self-control. It may be that the avid rejection of ecstatic experience by writers such as the fourth-century bishop Epiphanius is directly tied to the rejection of the implications of sexual penetration and the feminization of the prophet. At any rate, the gendered character of prophecy needs to be qualified according to the particular type of prophetic conceptualization being considered.

The body-denying tendency of the *Gospel of Mary* seems to reject a sexual conceptuality for prophetic experience in its creation of an ungendered space around prophetic inspiration. Mary is not feminized by her vision, because she is not penetrated nor does she lose control. Her experience is one of mind, acting as a mediator between the spirit and the soul. Her authority is buttressed by tying it to a rejection of a penetrating sexual model of prophecy.

VIEWS THAT ARE ENABLING FOR WOMEN'S LEADERSHIP

We are now in a position to hazard an answer to the question: What specific views contributed to enabling women's leadership within early Christian communities in the Mediterranean world?

The most significant factor seems to have been the attitude toward the body. Rejection of the body as the location of the self was accompanied by a rejection of the value of the patriarchal social gender roles inscribed on the bodies of men and women. For women this meant two things: First, a woman's identity and spirituality could be developed apart from her roles as wife and mother (or slave), whether she actually withdrew from those roles or not. Second, she could exercise leadership on the basis of spiritual achievement apart from gender status and without conforming to established social gender roles. Hence attitudes toward the body were central determiners of women's public leadership. The attitudes in the *Gospel of Mary* that rejected or devalued the body in relation to the spirit (or soul) opened up ungendered space, in which leadership functions were exercised on the basis of spiritual achievement and prophetic inspiration.[83]

Contemporary readers may feel ambivalent about this position. Although Tertullian linked sexual differentiation inseparably to a system of hierarchical patriarchal gender roles that contemporary feminism rejects,[84] his theology placed a high value on the body and gave marriage and childbearing positive signification, as some forms of contemporary feminism would like to do. The *Gospel of Mary* supports women's leadership but at the cost of women's bodies, insofar as women's power was achieved through the transcendence of gender and bodily sexual differentiation altogether. If women exercised legitimate leadership only at the price of their identity as women and the valuing of their own bodies, there would seem to be little here of value for contemporary women except yet another narrative of loss.

This conclusion would, however, be incomplete for two reasons. First, it is true that the *Gospel of Mary* attempts to resolve conflict over authority by arguing for the ideal of a common humanity based on the transcendence of bodily distinctions. In so doing, the work erases the political significance of real differences of class, gender, and ethnicity in antiquity. But transcendence is not bought at the expense of ignoring or erasing awareness of injustice and suffering. Instead, the ideal of transcendence is tied to a sharp criticism of social injustice and illegitimate domination. In Mary's vision of the rise of the soul, spiritual power is depicted as the empowerment of the enslaved soul in its (successful) battle against the forces of ignorance, jealousy, lust, wrath, and illegitimate domination.[85] The work's resolution of conflict ties the erasure of difference to the simultaneous elimination of injustice and suffering. Transcendence and justice are linked, so that authority is based on spiritual maturity rather than bodily differentiations.

Second, whether controlled by men or not, women's prophetic speech was highly valued in early Christian movements and contributed to the construction of early Christian teaching and practice. By placing the teaching of the *Gospel of Mary* side by side with the theology of the Corinthian women prophets,[86] the Montanist oracles, and Perpetua's prison diary, it is possible to discern shared views about teaching and practice:

> Theological reflection centered on the experience of the person of the risen Christ more than the crucified Savior.[87] Jesus was understood primarily as a teacher and mediator of wisdom rather than as ruler and judge.
>
> Direct access to God is possible for all through the Spirit. The possession of the Spirit is available to anyone. Those who are more spiritually advanced give what they have freely to all without claim to a fixed hierarchical ordering of power. An ethics of freedom and spiritual development is emphasized over an ethics of order and control.
>
> Identity as a Christian is constructed apart from gender roles, sex, and childbearing (with or without actually abandoning these roles). Gender is itself contested as a "natural" category in the face of the power of God's Spirit at work in the community and the world.
>
> In Christian community, the unity, power, and perfection of the Spirit are present now, not just in some future time.

These elements may not be unique to women's religious thought or always result in women's leadership, but as a constellation they point toward one type of theologizing that was meaningful to some early Christian women, that had a place for women's legitimate exercise of prophetic leadership, and to whose construction women contributed. If we look to these elements, we are able to discern important contributions of women to early Christian theology and praxis. These elements also provide an important location for discussing some aspects of early Christian women's spiritual lives: their exercise of leadership, their ideals, their attraction to Christianity, and what gave meaning to their self-identity as Christians.

NOTES

This paper was written during a fellowship year at the Harvard Divinity School in the Women's Studies in Religion Program. My sincerest appreciation for this support and for the warm cordiality of colleagues there. I would like to thank Constance Buchanan, the program director, and my fellow fellows, Denise Ackerman, Caroline Ford, Sri Padma, and Judylyn Ryan, for their encouragement, criticism, and support. I would also like to express special appreciation to François Bovon, Bernadette Brooten, Alan Callahan, Sarah Coakley, Helmut Koester, and Elisabeth Schüssler Fiorenza for their critical and constructive comments on earlier drafts of this essay.

1. For example, the authority of Priscilla (Acts of the Apostles 18:26; Romans 16:3–5) and Phoebe (Rom. 16:3) is not said to be based on prophetic experience.

See Elisabeth Schüssler Fiorenza, *In Memory of Her: A Feminist Theological Reconstruction of Christian Origins* (New York: Crossroad, 1985), part II. Moreover, William Tabbernee's work on Montanist epigraphic data provides information about at least one woman who was recognized as a presbyter, in addition to three women who held the title of "prophet." The distinction may mean that the presbyter held her position on some basis other than prophetic power (see *The Social Identity of the Montanists: The Epigraphic Data* [Macon, Ga.: Mercer Press, forthcoming]). Other evidence from detractors suggests that Montanist women held offices of bishop and priest in the third and fourth centuries (see Epiphanius, *Panarion* 49.2–3). Non-Montanist women were ordained as priests in fifth-century Italy and Sicily (see Gelasius, *Epistle* 14, 26, and the discussion of Giorgio Otranto in Mary Ann Rossi, "Priesthood, Precedent, and Prejudice: On Recovering the Women Priests of Early Christianity," *Journal of Feminist Studies in Religion* 7 [1991]: 73–93). But see also Cyprian (*Epistula* 74, 10), who tells of an ecstatic woman prophet from Asia Minor who celebrated the Eucharist and performed baptisms.

2. See Schüssler Fiorenza, *In Memory of Her*, pp. 230–33, 288–91; and Linda Maloney, "Pastoral Epistles," and Antoinette Clark Wire, "I Corinthians," both in *Searching the Scriptures*, vol. 2: *A Feminist Commentary*, ed. Elisabeth Schüssler Fiorenza (New York: Crossroad, 1994), pp. 361–80 and 185–89, respectively.

3. See Carl Schmidt, "Ein vorirenäisches gnostisches Originalwerk im koptischer Sprache," in *Sitzungsberichte der preussischen Akademie der Wissenschaften zu Berlin* (Berlin: Verlag der Akademie der Wissenschaften, 1896), p. 839; Walther Till and Hans-Martin Schenke, *Die gnostischen Schriften des koptischen Papyrus Berolinensis 8502*, 2d ed., *Texte und Untersuchungen* 60 (Berlin: Akademie Verlag, 1972), pp. 1–2, 24–25; C. H. Roberts, "463. The Gospel of Mary," in *Catalogue of the Greek Papyri in the John Rylands Library*, vol. 3 (Manchester University Press, 1938), pp. 18–23; P. J. Parsons, "3525: Gospel of Mary," in *The Oxyrhynchus Papyri*, vol. 50, Graeco-Roman Memoirs, no. 70 (London: Egypt Exploration Society, 1983), pp. 12–14; Dieter Lührman, "Die griechische Fragmente des Mariaevangeliums POxy 3525 und PRyl 463," *Novum Testamentum* 30, no. 4 (1988): 321–38; Karen L. King, "The Gospel of Mary Magdalene," Schüssler Fiorenza, ed., *Searching the Scriptures*, vol. 2: *A Feminist Commentary*, p. 625. All references to the *Gospel of Mary* are from Karen L. King, "The Gospel of Mary," in *The Complete Gospels: Annotated Scholars Version*, rev. and exp. ed., ed. Robert J. Miller (Sonoma, Calif: Polebridge Press, 1994), pp. 357–66, and follow its notation system. Citations by manuscript, page, and line numbers are given in the notes as well.

4. For more on the genre of the work as a postresurrection dialogue, see Karen L. King, "The Gospel of Mary," in *Early Christian Apocrypha: Apocalypses*, ed. Adela Collins and Martha Himmelfarb (Santa Rosa, Calif.: Polebridge Press, forthcoming). For more on the portrait of Mary Magdalene, see King, "The Gospel of Mary" in *Searching the Scriptures*, pp. 617–20.

5. For an argument that the Jesus traditions in the *Gospel of Mary* are literarily independent of any known literature, see King, "The Jesus Tradition in the *Gospel of Mary*," paper read at the Society of Biblical Literature Annual Meeting, New Orleans, November 25, 1996. For more on the controversy over apostolic authority, see King, "The Gospel of Mary" in *Searching the Scriptures*, pp. 621–25.

6. In an extremely important section of her path-breaking work, *In Memory of Her* (pp. 294–315), Schüssler Fiorenza provides the paradigmatic treatment of the issues raised in this essay concerning (1) the importance of prophecy and prophetic leadership by men and women in early Christian movements, and (2) the exclusion of women from offices of leadership. Among other topics, she discusses ecstasy, the criteria for judging the truth of prophecy, sexual charges against women prophets, and the controversy literature that pits Mary Magdalene and Peter against each other.

7. The revelations of the "Shepherd" apparently occurred in sleep (*Shepherd of Hermas, Vision* 1.3–4). See also the examples in John Hanson, "Dreams and Visions in the Graeco-Roman World and Early Christianity," in *Aufstieg und Niedergang der römischen Welt* II, Principat, 23.2, ed. Wolfgang Haase (Berlin: Walter de Gruyter, 1980), pp. 1396–1427.

8. An excellent example of a women prophesying without ecstasy is given by Dio Chrysostom, *The First Discourse on Kingship*, 52–56.

9. See Anne Jensen, *Gottes selbstbewusste Töchter: Frauenemanzipation im frühen Christentum* (Freiburg: Herder, 1992), pp. 263–65.

10. See Revelations or *Shepherd of Hermas*.

11. For the types of oracles present in early Christian literature, see David Aune, *Prophecy in Early Christianity and the Ancient Mediterranean World* (Grand Rapids, Mich.: Eerdmans, 1983), pp. 320–25. For the literary character of dream-vision reports, see Hanson, "Dreams and Visions." For visionary experiences, see the *Gospel of Mary* and *The Shepherd of Hermas*. For ecstatic journeys, see Rev. 4:1–2 and following; *Shepherd of Hermas* I, 1; *Apocryphon of James* 15.13–23.

12. See Antoinette Clark Wire, *Corinthian Women Prophets: A Reconstruction through Paul's Rhetoric* (Minneapolis: Fortress Press, 1990), p. 283. Paul's lack of success was no doubt due in part to the fact that such distinctions were not clearly applied by others in the surrounding shared cultures.

13. See *On the Veiling of Virgins*, 1.8; see also Epiphanius, *Panarion* 48.13.1.

14. See 1 Tim. 4:13–14. James L. Ash argues that prophecy was appropriated by the episcopate at the expense of women's prophetic leadership; see "The Decline of Ecstatic Prophecy in the Early Church," *Theological Studies* 37 (1976): 227–52; see also Schüssler Fiorenza, *In Memory of Her*, pp. 294–309. This view is opposed by Cecil M. Robeck, *Prophecy in Carthage: Perpetua, Tertullian and Cyprian* (Cleveland: Pilgrim Press, 1992), 203–5.

15. It is notable that the postresurrection appearance of the Savior to the disciples does not have the same status as Mary's visionary experience. In other situations, such an appearance could well be conceived as prophetic.

16. *Gospel of Mary* 5.9–10; Codex Berolinensis 8502 (hereafter BG) 9.20–24; *Papyrus Oxyrhnchus* 12–14.

17. The Greek term used by the *Gospel of Mary* to describe the vision, ὅραμα, seems to indicate that the vision came to Mary while sleeping. The term appears in both the Coptic (as a transliterated noun) and the Greek (with the prep. ἐν in the dative) versions. Schmidt had already called Mary's vision a *Traumerscheinung*, but without explanation ("Ein vorirenäisches gnostisches Originalwerk," p. 840). The phrase to see "in a dream" (Greek: ἐν ὁράματι) occurs only three times in the Greek literature

of the second century (according to the Thesaurus Linguae Graecae: Clement of Alexandria, *Paedagogus* 2.11; Justin Martyr, *Dialogue with Trypho* 31.3.5; and *Shepherd of Hermas* I.3.10). In all three cases, it appears in Christian literature and refers to a vision perceived in sleep. The first two instances refer to the dream of Daniel in Daniel 7:9–28 (Septuagint); the third to a dream containing a revelation dialogue between Hermas and the "old woman." Daniel was famous in early Christianity as an expert in dream interpretation; an acrostic dream book attributed to him by a Byzantine Christian author survives in a sixteenth-century manuscript; see Naphtali Lewis, *The Interpretation of Dreams and Portents* (Toronto: Samuel Stevens Hakkert, 1976), pp. 87–95. Artemidorus uses the term ὅραμα (nom. sing.) only once in his work on the interpretation of dreams, but there it refers also to the content of meaningful dreams (*Oneirocriticon* I, 2, 13–17).

18. Cf. *The Shepherd of Hermas.*

19. See Patricia Cox Miller, *Dreams in Late Antiquity: Studies in the Imagination of Culture* (Princeton, N.J.: Princeton University Press, 1994), p. 35.

20. *Gospel of Mary* 7.5–6; BG 10.16–23.

21. Elaine Pagels has noted that limiting apostolic authority to those who had witnessed the earthly career of Jesus was part of a strategy to secure exclusive legitimacy for bishops and presbyters against those who based their authority in the continued revelation of the resurrected Lord in dreams and visions. For more on the controversy over the connections between prophetic experience and church leadership, see Elaine Pagels, "Visions, Appearances, and Apostolic Authority: Gnostic and Orthodox Traditions," in *Gnosis: Festschrift für Hans Jonas,* ed. Barbara Aland (Göttingen: Vandenhoeck and Ruprecht, 1978), pp. 415–30.

22. Tertullian's view is close to Stoic views on the corporeality of the soul.

23. This view is shared by many Platonists of this period (see Plutarch, *The Face on the Moon,* 28).

24. See *De anima* 12 and 18–19.

25. *De anima* 9.1.

26. Some manuscripts read "Paul" instead of "people"; see J. H. Waszink, *Tertulliani. De anima* (Amsterdam: J. M. Meulenhoff, 1947), text, p. 12 n. 15. This change may represent an attempt to limit the scope of prophetic inspiration, or to make Tertullian appear less "Montanist" and more orthodox.

27. *De anima* 9.8.

28. For a discussion of Tertullian's reliance on Soranus and the Stoics, see H. Diels, *Doxographi Graeci* (Berlin, 1879), p. 204; H. Karpp, "Sorans vier Bücher *Peri psyches* and Tertullians Schrift *De anima,*" *Zeitschrift für die neutestamentliche Wissenschaft* 33 (1934): 31–47; Waszink, *Tertulliani. De anima,* pp. 21–47. Tertullian probably got much of his material from the doxographical work of Soranus and Arius.

29. *De anima* 9.4.

30. That the content of ecstatic experience accords with or conforms to the needs and beliefs of the broader culture, the specific circumstances, audience perceptions, and even public opinion confirms that such experiences are fully embedded and need to be studied in their specific cultural and social-historical contexts; see Ann Taves, "Knowing through the Body: Dissociative Religious Experience in the African-American and British-American Methodist Traditions," *Journal of Religion* 73

(1993): 200–222; I. M. Lewis, *Ecstatic Religion. A Study of Shamanism and Spirit Possession*, 2d ed. (London: Routledge, 1989), p. 142.

31. Here Tertullian departs from the views of Soranus and the Stoics. He argues strongly against their views on the fate of the soul after death, and that sense perception is fallible. He also argues against the Platonic views on metempsychosis because they endanger his view that the flesh is resurrected.

32. *De anima* 36.2 (text in Waszink, *Tertulliani*, p. 52).

33. *De anima* 36.4.

34. *Gospel of Mary* 3.7–13; BG 7.20–8.10.

35. Whether that root is matter or nothingness cannot be determined with certainty from the text.

36. See further, King, "The Gospel of Mary" in *Searching the Scriptures*, pp. 603–5.

37. See *De anima* 41.3–4.

38. Ibid., 41.4.

39. Ibid., 45.2, 3. Clement of Alexandria, *Paed.* II, 9, largely follows the same dream theory. See also Cicero, *De divinatione* I.30.62–63; I.50.113–51.116.

40. *De anima* 47. Cf. Cicero on the views of Posidonius, *De divinatione* I.30.

41. See *De anima* 6.3.

42. *Against Marcion*, 4.22. Cf. Cicero, *De divinatione* I.31.66; and Plutarch, *Oracles at Delphi* 397A–C.

43. Here the *Gospel of Mary* repeats a view widely accepted in antiquity (see Cicero, *De divinatione* I.30.63; *Asclepius* 18), and one that is found among a number of Christian authors (see Justin Martyr, *Dialogue with Trypho* 3–6; Origen, *Contra Celsum* VI, 69; *Acts of Thomas* 65).

44. *Gospel of Mary* 7.3–4; BG 10.14–16.

45. Cf. Seneca, *Natural Questions* I, pref. 11–13.

46. Both hold that the Savior taught his disciples while alive in the body, after his resurrection, and continues to teach through prophetic experience. It is unclear, however, whether they would differentially value these types of teaching; see Gerard P. Luttikhuizen, "The Evaluation of the Teaching of Jesus in Christian Gnostic Revelation Dialogues," *Novum Testamentum* 30, no. 2 (1988): 158–68.

47. It is possible that Tertullian later modified his views of women's public prophetic leadership as a result of influence from Montanist practice.

48. I. M. Lewis has argued that cross-cultural comparison from anthropology yields three patterns in which gender and status are linked to ecstatic religious experience and ethical perspectives: "Here we may, I think, distinguish three distinct, although not always completely exclusive patterns [in the sexual identity of shamans]. First, in central religions, where possession is a precondition for the full exercise of the religious vocation, those selected by the deities are typically men. Secondly, where an established male priesthood, which does not depend upon ecstatic illumination for its authority, controls the central morality cult, women and men of subordinate social categories may be allowed a limited franchise as inspired auxiliaries. Thirdly, these disadvantaged social categories are also those which supply the membership of peripheral possession cults, irrespective of whether ecstasy also occurs in the central religion. Thus in general, it seems that the moral evaluation of possession tends to reflect social and sexual distinctions.

Amoral powers select their mounts from women or socially restricted categories of men: those divinities which uphold public morality are less narrowly circumscribed in their choice of human hosts" (Lewis, *Ecstatic Religion*, pp. 158–59). By "amoral" Lewis seems to mean powers that have values different from or in conflict with the hegemonic values of the society. It needs to be explored whether and in what respects Christianity in some locations or in certain forms might be classified as a "peripheral religion."

49. See Wire, *Corinthian Women Prophets*, pp. 65, 66–67, 70–71.

50. Ibid., p. 184.

51. *De praescriptione hereticorum* 41.

52. Ibid., 41.5.

53. It should be noted that this reading of 1 Corinthians applies to the current state of the text within the canon, which includes 14:33b–35. Wire argues that this passage belongs to Paul, but it has been widely regarded as an interpolation. The point is significant in determining Paul's attitude toward women's leadership, if not gender: Did he mean (married) women to be silenced entirely within the church, or could he envision them providing leadership in the community within the scope of their gender roles (symbolized by wearing a veil when praying and prophesying)?

54. Wire links the move of women into public roles of prayer and prophecy with their withdrawal from sexual relations (Wire, *Corinthian Women Prophets*, pp. 65, 82–93). The *Gospel of Mary*'s attitude toward the body may have had a similar result, although that is not certain.

55. Similarly, if men withdrew from sexual relationships, that action would have had a different and in some regards a lesser impact on their social status.

56. Here a word of caution is necessary. In noting the important role of ancient Mediterranean *ideologies* that relegated women to the household or "private" sphere and men to the civic or "public" sphere, it is important not to take these ideologies as fully descriptive of actual practices. The presence of women in public places and the presence of men in domestic spheres varied considerably by class, status, occupation, geographic area, urban or rural setting, and occasion (for example, women were present at civic religious celebrations; and patriarchal patterns were replicated in the domestic sphere as well as in civic areas, albeit somewhat differently). It is important to strike a balance between naming the real effects of such domineering ideology in restricting women's lives and affirming the ways in which women exercised agency within the patriarchal contexts of ancient societies. To do less is to reinscribe the silence about women's agency, as well as women's subjection.

57. Wire, *Corinthian Women Prophets*, has collected a list of examples. See Diodorus of Sicily, *The Library of History* XVI, 26.26; Ovid, *Metamorphoses*, XIV, 129–46, 151–53; *The Confession and Prayer of Asenath*; Plutarch, *The Oracles at Delphi* 405CD; Plutarch, *Lives: Numa* 5 and 8; Pausanias, *Description of Greece* II.24.1; Philo, *On the Contemplative Life*.

58. As is common with witchcraft accusations against both men and women, the charges here are raised because their conservative opponents feel they have overstepped acceptable boundaries by advocating changes in established relations and

practices (see, for example, Lewis, *Ecstatic Religion*, pp. 108–9). Ideology that attempts to relegate women to areas separate from politics can be used against them in a kind of circular social logic.

Although women's presence was the normal practice in Christian worship, Karen Torjesen has argued that a woman exercising public leadership could be open to charges of immorality; see Karen Jo Torjesen, *When Women Were Priests: Women's Leadership in the Early Church and the Scandal of Their Subordination in the Rise of Christianity* (San Francisco: Harper San Francisco, 1993), pp. 143–49.

59. Tertullian, *de Praescriptione hereticorum* 6 and 30.

60. We learn, by the way, that her prophecies had been collected and written down by a male disciple. She was apparently a significant enough threat to warrant condemnation.

61. For example, Priscilla's virginity is called into question by Apollonius (Eusebius, *Historia Ecclesiastica* V.18); the Asian woman prophet noted by Cyprian is accused of seducing a deacon (Cyprian, *Epistle* 74.10). Note, too, that the male heretic Marcus was also accused of seducing women (Irenaeus, *Adversus Haereses* I.13.1–4).

62. For a fuller discussion, see David Potter, *Prophets and Emperors: Human and Divine Authority from Augustus to Theodosius* (Cambridge, Mass.: Harvard University Press, 1994).

63. See Tertullian, *De anima* 11.

64. Tertullian believed that true prophecy was ecstatic and implied the prophet's loss of sensibility (see *Against Marcion* V, 8). This view is vigorously opposed in Epiphanius, *Panarion* 48.1–13.

65. See, for example, *Didache* 10.7; 11; 13; 15.1–2.

66. With Tertullian prophecy is the basis for testing the truth (*De anima* 2–4), and the truth can be used to test prophecy (*On Monogamy*, 2.3).

67. See Tertullian, *Against Marcion*, V.8. The issue of conformity to the teachings of the churches was also invoked in these debates, but this point was rather polemical in the first and second centuries since "the rule of the faith" had not yet been clearly established. The issue of conformity thus pointed anxiously to the spectral absence of a normative standard against which prophecy could be measured. So in practice, questions about the truth of prophecy take us right into the middle of debates over the meaning of Jesus' teaching, interpretation of Scripture, community organization, and leadership. The *Gospel of Mary* is fully engaged in these debates. (See "The Gospel of Mary," *Searching the Scriptures*, pp. 621–25.)

68. According to Wire, part of Paul's attempts to silence the women prophets included getting them back into marital relationships (see Wire, *Corinthian Women Prophets*, pp. 25, 32, 34, 64, 75, 76). Her discussion assumes that 1 Corinthians 14:33b–35 is not an interpolation.

69. Suggested by Adolph von Harnack; see Ash, "The Decline," p. 227.

70. See Ruth Padel, "Women: Model for Possession by Greek Daemons," in *Images of Women in Antiquity*, ed. Averil Cameron and Amélie Kuhrt (Detroit: Wayne State University Press, 1983), pp. 3–19.

71. For example, in Paul's insistence that the women prophets in Corinth need to cover their heads because of the angels!

72. Padel, "Women," p. 14.

73. See, for example, among the examples given by Wire, *Corinthian Women Prophets*: Pausanias, *Description of Greece* X, 12; Philo, *On the Cherubim* 41, 47; *Odes of Solomon* 33; Lucan, *Pharasalia* or *The Civil Wars* V. 120–225; Irenaeus, *Adversus Haereses* I.13.1–4.

74. *De anima* 41.4. One might note, too, that the term "adultery" is used in a way that is reminiscent of the Savior's use of the term in the *Gospel of Mary* 3.4; BG 7.13–16, where adultery refers to the soul's improper love of the body.

75. *On Prayer* II, 1 ff.; XI.1. I wish to thank Sarah Coakley for this example.

76. See Lewis, *Ecstatic Religion*, pp. 50–56. It can be noted in passing that this pattern, whereby the male has a female spiritual guide, is operative in the *Shepherd of Hermas* and *Allogenes*, for example.

77. See Howard Eilberg Schwartz, *God's Phallus and Other Problems for Men and Monotheism* (Boston: Beacon Press, 1994), esp. pp. 4, 137–38.

78. Wire, *Corinthian Women Prophets*, p. 133; see also p. 182. Cf. the Montanist oracle in Tertullian, *Concerning Flight* 9.4.

79. Cf. *Gospel of Mary* 6.1; BG 10.1–3 with *Gospel of Mary* 10.4; *PRyl.* 463, recto, lines 15–16.

80. See Pheme Perkins, *The Gnostic Dialogue: The Early Church and the Crisis of Gnosticism*, Studies in Contemporary Biblical and Theological Problems (New York: Paulist Press, 1980), pp. 136–37.

81. See Pierre Bourdieu, *Outline of a Theory of Practice*, Cambridge Studies in Social Anthropology 16 (Cambridge: Cambridge University Press, 1977), p. 16.

82. She made this observation in a private conversation with the author.

83. The tendency toward asceticism involved the rejection or devaluation of marriage and the social gender roles that accompanied it, but in contrast to the *Gospel of Mary*, the ideology of these materials seems to be expressed most often as women "becoming male." See, for example, Rosemary Ruether, "Mothers of the Church: Ascetic Women in the Late Patristic Age," in *Women of Spirit: Female Leaders in the Jewish and Christian Traditions*, ed. Rosemary Ruether and Eleanor McLaughlin (New York: Simon and Schuster, 1979), pp. 71–98; Ross Kraemer, "The Conversion of Women to Ascetic Forms of Christianity" *Signs* 6 (1980/81): 298–307; Elizabeth Castelli, "Virginity and Its Meaning for Women's Sexuality in Early Christianity," *Journal of Feminist Studies in Religion* 2, no. 1 (1986): 61–88; Virgina Burrus, *Chastity as Autonomy: Women in the Stories of the Apocryphal Acts*, Studies in Women and Religion 23 (Lewiston, N.Y.: Edwin Mellen Press, 1987).

84. By this statement I do not mean to imply that the body constitutes a blank slate upon which gender is written. See the critiques of this view by Jean Comaroff, *Bodies of Power, Spirit of Resistance: The Culture and History of a South African People* (Chicago: University of Chicago Press, 1985), pp. 6–9; Judith Butler, *Bodies That Matter: On the Discursive Limits of 'Sex'* (New York: Routledge, 1993), pp. 27–55. Tertullian actually comes closer to these current feminist views when he says that sex and gender, body and soul, come into being simultaneously, and one cannot be thought without the others. The challenge he raises to Christian feminist theology is to say that God has created not only the body and the soul but sex and gender as well. All are natural because they are derived from God. A feminist analysis of this position needs

to consider not only the body as a creature but also the implications of God-given gender—an interesting but not insuperable problem.

85. See, for example, the soul's battle against the powers (*Gospel of Mary* 9; BG 15.1–17.6; see King, "The Gospel of Mary," *Searching the Scriptures*, pp. 612–14).

86. Based on the reconstruction of Wire, *Corinthian Woman Prophets*.

87. Interestingly, this is true even in the case of the martyr Perpetua. One might expect her to identify with the suffering Christ, but it is the risen Christ she encounters in her vision, and it is victory she experiences in her combat in the arena, not passive endurance in the face of suffering.

TWO

The Early Christian *Orans*

An Artistic Representation
of Women's Liturgical Prayer and Prophecy

Karen Jo Torjesen

The topic of women preaching during the period of early Christianity raises questions about women's authority, women's public speaking, women's liturgical roles, and most important, women's access to ecclesiastical offices— questions about the influence of Greco-Roman notions of gender on women's leadership. The historical sources for this early period are limited; contemporary scholars are dependent on the writings of theologians from the third through the sixth centuries, a period characterized by increasing masculinization of church leadership.[1] These theologians generally do not concern themselves with women's activities, and when women make "cameo" appearances in literary texts their portraits are often distorted by the gender bias of the age. Consequently, when positively represented, a woman who prophesied, preached, or taught was pictured as doing so in a private or domestic space; otherwise she would be caricatured as a public woman— wanton, sexualized, and usurping male authority.[2]

For alternatives to the representations of the preaching woman found in literary sources, feminist scholars have turned to other sources, such as epitaphs, statues, paintings, and dedicatory inscriptions. Here scholars have found evidence that Jewish women were elders and rulers of synagogues and that Christian women were deacons and priests or presbyters.[3] Artistic sources such as catacomb paintings, reliefs on sarcophagi, and church mosaics have provided further evidence of women presiding over eucharistic celebrations and holding the office of bishop.[4] This chapter examines the enigmatic figure of a female praying, which proliferated in Christian art from the second through the sixth centuries. Although this figure has traditionally been interpreted simply as a symbol of the church or the soul, a closer examination suggests that the viewers in antiquity would have associated her with women's praying, prophesying, and preaching.

Art historians have named this figure the *orans*, a person praying, because of the typical posture of outstretched arms and upturned face.[5] The *orans* is ubiquitous, painted in catacomb frescoes, carved in relief on sarcophagi, cast in rings, and sealed in gold glass—catacombs alone contain more than two hundred depictions of this praying figure.[6] This familiar figure is even drawn on a liturgical treatise, inscribed on Egyptian funerary stelae, and appears as late as the sixth century on Merovingian bronze plaques.[7] Although male figures are occasionally found in this traditional posture, the overwhelming number of *orantes* are female, which raises the question: Why is this symbol gendered female?

IDENTIFIED *ORANTES*

The earliest artistic appearances of the *orans* are found in catacomb paintings dating from the early second century. Frescoes in the catacombs of Priscilla and Callistus depict several Old Testament figures in this posture of prayer—Daniel attended by lions, the three Hebrew children in the fiery oven, Susanna with the accusing elders, and Isaac about to be sacrificed.[8] Since each of these stories celebrates salvation from death, the portrayal of these figures in the posture of prayer reminds the viewer of the power of prayer and the promise of salvation. For the second-century Christian visiting these burial places, these portrayals connected the powerful prayer of the Old Testament saints with the inspired prayer and prophecy that took place in their own assemblies.

Occasionally the figure of the *orans* is identified with a name, presumably the name of the deceased, and accompanied by a prayer for the departed— for example *Dionysios in pace, Zoe in pace* (Dionysios be at peace, Zoe be at peace). By the third century requests for intercession appear along with prayers for the dead—for example, *in pace et pete pro nobis* (be at peace and pray for us). The *orans* representing the deceased is often set in a background of trees, flowers, lights, lamps, birds, or water, motifs signifying the presence of the *orans* in paradise.

In the fourth century, certain martyrs were portrayed in the posture of the *orans*—Laurentius, Januarius, Tecla, Cecilia, and Agnes—and there was as well a whole icononographic tradition of Mary as an *orans*.[9] J. Sauer notes that because the apostles are never portrayed in this posture of prayer it may have been believed that there was a special connection between women and prayer.[10] In the Cappadocian iconography of the tenth and eleventh centuries, the gesture of the *orans* becomes the attribute of the ascetics and the hermits and especially of the women ascetics and nuns whose holiness, won through asceticism, earned them an honor equivalent to that of the martyrs.[11] The Byzantine presentation of Mary as an *orans* is likely the successor to the martyr *orans*.[12]

There are pagan antecedents for the use of the *orans* in a funerary setting, although the meaning of the gesture of these *orantes* is much debated among scholars, as is the difference between Christian and non-Christian use of the gesture. Egyptian funerary stelae portray a male *orans* flanked by a falcon and jackal, by two jackals, or by the icons of the Egyptian gods Anubis and Horis.[13] There are also literary references to this posture of prayer in Cicero, Virgil, and Apuleius.[14] The fact that in this collection of pagan *orantes* the figure at prayer is always male makes the predominantly female *orans* of Christian art even more interesting.

THE ANONYMOUS *ORANS*

The overwhelming number of portrayals of the *orans* are anonymous. Often she is portrayed alone, sometimes standing between two sheep or two trees, sometimes accompanied by doves. While the posture of the anonymous *orans* remains fixed, there is much variation in her clothing. She appears wearing the Roman toga with two stripes, the Greek pallium, a short tunic with a mantle, barefoot and sandaled, veiled and unveiled. The *orans* can be featured alone framed by a medallion or in groups of two or three. As early as the second century, the *orans* was paired with the good shepherd, a theme that became popular in third- and fourth-century funerary art.

Whether as a solitary figure or in a setting with other figures, the anonymous *orans* is universally female, and that gendered female image endured for six centuries. In other words, when the figure of the *orans* functions symbolically it is a gendered image.

THE SCHOLARLY DEBATE

To my knowledge, no one has done a gender analysis on the *orans* as a symbol. The old question posed by art historians, "What does this symbol mean?" must be asked in relation to a new question, "Why is this symbol gendered female?" The meaning of this posture and the significance of its funerary setting have been debated for more than a hundred years, but no consensus has emerged. Interpreters of early Christian art have been primarily scholars of the patristic period. "Patristic" defines a theological chronology for church history, which focuses on the "orthodox" writers of the first five centuries, the "Fathers," whose work laid the theological foundations for the Christian church. Their approach to the period of the early church has been shaped by their interest in showing continuities in doctrine and liturgical practice from the early church to the contemporary church. Not surprisingly, these scholars have often shared their church's assumption that women were not ordained in the early church and that their ministries did not have a public character.

The femaleness of the *orans* has been something of a stumbling block for these historians of Christian art who have attempted to explain its symbolism by making superficial connections between the *orans* and the church or the soul. De Rossi interprets the *orans* as a symbol of the church based on the third-century pairing of the praying woman and the good shepherd, whom he interprets as a symbol of Christ.[15] Other historians elaborate on this association, explaining the *orans* as the collective of souls to be saved (Wessel) or the church's ministries personified as a woman (Jossi).[16] A second line of interpretation explains the *orans* as a symbol of the soul, portrayed as a young virgin to indicate its state of purity (Leclerq); with the motifs of palm trees, sheep, and doves indicating the state of blessedness in paradise (Liell); with the soul awaiting judgment (Stuiber); or with the soul of the deceased acting as an intercessor (Neuss).[17]

There are serious problems with both theories. If the *orans* is a symbol of the church when she is paired with the good shepherd, what meaning would groups of two and even three *orantes* accompanying the good shepherd have, and why the funerary context? Furthermore, if the *orans* represents the church, what, then, is the significance of the posture of prayer?[18] There are problems as well in the identification of the anonymous *orans* with the soul, especially with the claim that the female figure portrays the soul of a deceased male, since there are examples of male *orantes* identified by name representing deceased males.[19]

However, the greatest problems with these attempts to interpret the *orans* as a symbol is that they fail to synchronize the two most important features of the *orans*, that she is a woman and that she is praying. The symbolic or allegorical meaning of the figure must have some relationship to its literal meaning. What was so potent about women praying, or women's prayers, in the second century that generated the ubiquitous symbol of the *orans?* Why should the power, work, service, ministry, and authority of prayer be portrayed by a female figure? Although images may be universal in their appeal, they are not universal in their meanings. They "speak" to a viewer within the context of a lived world shaped by communal experience because they represent the symbols a particular historical community has generated and the meanings that it invests in them. Not only must images be contextualized historically; they must also be probed for the affective valences created by their historical context. An interpreter of historical images must press beyond their cognitive meanings, as Margaret Miles writes: "The image's universality rests not on its potential for abstraction—that is, on a 'detachable conclusion'—but on the capacity of the viewer to grasp in the concrete particularity of the image a universal affectivity. . . . The universality of an image thus depends on an act of recognition by each viewer."[20]

Most scholars have failed to ask two important historical questions: What did second-century viewers associate with the posture of prayer, and what was their experience with women's ministries? Prayer itself was recognized as a potent force: it established contact with the powerful world of the divine; it preceded miracles; it opened the worshipper for ecstasy, visions, and revelations and prepared the way for the gifts of wisdom; and it elicited the presence of the Spirit. How did such a powerful act come to be associated with women?

Does the symbol give any clue to the experience of women's authority in the early Christian communities? Did early Christian religious practice give women's prayer a prominent place? What was the social experience of the church that eventually led to the *orans* being a prominent symbol? What were the affective valences of women's prayer for second-century Christians? What are the earliest meanings of the figure of a woman praying? What did second-century Christians "see" in this image? What were the associations they made between woman and prayer? These historical and contextual questions must be asked first, before the symbolic meaning of the *orans* can be interpreted.

In the literary sources the posture of the *orans* is almost always mentioned in a context of Christian worship in connection with liturgical prayers, congregational prayers, prayers over baptism, and prayers over the Eucharist.[21] Occasionally martyrs in the arena assumed the posture of the *orans* by stretching out their arms to create the form of the cross, which was interpreted as an act of prayer and a witness to Christ.[22] However, it should be noted that prayer itself is a complex and fluid concept capable of multiple meanings, such as adoration, petition, prayer, prophecy, and piety.

The funerary context itself was also liturgical. Early Christians followed Roman burial customs and celebrated a eucharistic meal at the tomb, which included prayers of blessing over the bread and wine and prayers for the dead, as well as appeals to the deceased as intercessors. Many portrayals of this eucharistic meal are painted on the catacomb walls. Furthermore, women played an important role in Roman funerary rites; in public processions they acted as mourners, pronouncing the lament and calling on the dead. Their centrality is attested by the fact that both Greek and Roman legislators attempted to limit the power women exercised in funerary rituals.[23]

SECOND-CENTURY PRAYER: LITURGICAL PROPHECY

The iconography of the *orans* emerged during the period when Christian churches were still meeting in the homes of householders and celebrating the Eucharist with a communal meal, when women presided over house churches and served as presbyters (or priests) and deacons, when women's distinctive piety and their ministries on behalf of the church were institutionalized first in the office of widow and then in the office of virgin.[24]

During the first and second centuries, the order of worship was quite fluid; the elements of songs, psalms, readings, discussions, prophecy, prayers, and a communal meal created a loosely woven tapestry of worship.[25] In Paul's letter to the Corinthian church, praying and prophesying are closely linked. In fact, the terms *proseuchein* (to pray) and *prophaeteuein* (to prophesy) taken together refer to a wide range of liturgical activities, including singing, teaching, giving a revelation, speaking ecstatically, and interpreting. Ecstatic prayer itself is variously called speaking, praying, singing praises, blessing, and thanking. Even prophecy encompasses a wide range of liturgical expressions, including ecstatic speaking, blessing, teaching, and revealing.[26] A prophet speaking under inspiration and delivering a revelation also interjected exclamations of praise, blessing, and thanks. Prayer and prophecy were so fully integrated at Corinth that Antoinette Wire describes their worship as those endowed with the Spirit mediating "God's insight to each other in wisdom, revelation, knowledge, prophecy, and teaching and in turn responding to God in hymns, blessings and tongues."[27]

Prophecy was considered a natural role for women in antiquity, and women were the most prominent group among the Corinthian prophets. Even Paul acknowledged the authority and wisdom of the women prophets and their possession of the Spirit. Those who were inspired to pray and prophesy at Corinth stood to deliver their message and stretched out their arms, assuming the posture of the *orans*.[28] Second-century Christians familiar with the spirit-inspired worship of churches like that of Corinth would have associated the *orans* with women's "liturgical" prophecy. In making this connection their affective responses to the image drew on their own experiences of worship in a context of inspired teaching, revelation, exhortation, ecstatic prayer, adoration, praise, and above all a sense of the presence of the divine.

I have used the term *liturgical prophecy* to refer to prophetic instruction and revelation delivered in the setting of Christian worship. Using the adjective *liturgical* calls attention to the fact that it was a constituent element of early Christian worship. The many dimensions of liturgical prophecy— exhortation, revelation, and counsel—invested prophetic speech with considerable authority and gave the prophets a teaching role. Because it took place in the assembly setting, liturgical prophecy was both a "public" action and an exercise of authority.[29]

This was a matter of concern for Paul in the case of the women prophets at Corinth. Their authority over the congregation seemed to subvert their gender identity as women who were to be subordinate to men. Paul's solution was to require that they wear their veils to signal acknowledgment of their inferior status. The controversy over veiling itself is evidence of the authoritative liturgical character of women's praying and prophesying.[30] From the practice at Corinth we can also assume that the four daughters of Philip stood with their arms extended and eyes raised while praying and prophesying during the community worship of the house church at Caesarea.

The words of prophets were often written down and published as collections of oracles. So too were elements of this melding of prayer and prophecy, which were so characteristic of communal, inspired, and spontaneous worship. An early collection of hymns, the odes of Solomon, connects liturgical prophecy with the posture of the *orans* in a striking way. In the opening stanza of the ode the speaker introduces herself/himself by describing the posture of prayer that she/he assumes in this liturgical moment. "I extended my hands and approached my Lord, for the expansion of my hands is his sign, and my extension is the common cross that was lifted up on the way of the Righteous One." What began as a prayer moves directly into a prophetic voice in which Christ speaks: "And I became useless to those who knew me not because I shall hide myself from those who possess me not and I shall be with those who love me."[31] A fixed distinction between speaking to God (prayer) and speaking for God (prophecy) belongs to a later period. In the understanding of the early church, both prayer and prophecy participated in a "movement of divine reflexivity, a sort of answering to God in and through the one who prays. Prayer is participation in the divine life and both activities are moved and inspired by the Spirit."[32]

A second-century church order, the Didache, confirms that prophetic prayer was also a part of the eucharistic celebration. The Didache provides two simple blessings for the wine and bread, but stipulates that when a prophet presides over the eucharistic meal she or he should pray freely as inspired by the Spirit.[33] Even assemblies devoted to exhortation and instruction were led by inspired prophets speaking ecstatically. Christians familiar with the worship of these communities would also associate the posture of prayer with prophecy or inspired speech.

THE OFFICE OF WIDOW AND LITURGICAL PRAYER

Women's liturgical prophecy is one association evoked by the *orans* for second-century Christians. However, women also filled other liturgical roles that would have led early Christians to associate women and prayer. Very little has been written on the liturgical roles connected with the two church offices that were held exclusively by women—the office of widow and the office of virgin.

The letter to Timothy became the charter for the office of widow, whose work was to "pray without ceasing."[34] The potency of the prayers of the widows was greater than that of other Christians because their ascetic practices—renunciation of sexuality, fasting, prayer, and good works—endowed them with a superior piety.[35] Later in the second century, Polycarp proclaimed that the widow's service of prayer was an offering on the altar.[36] The office of widow became one of the orders within the clergy when the leadership roles of the second-century church were organized into the clerical orders of the third-century church. The widows were seated in front of the church with the rest of the clergy who officiated during the liturgy.[37] In Africa the penitents seeking readmittance into the church prostrated themselves before the widows at the front of the church.[38] In Egypt the widows were part of the clergy, and in Syria widows were entrusted with all the ministries to women.[39]

Because the widows' distinctive ministry was prayer and they were part of the clergy, we may well ask whether the widows' ministry of prayer was carried on in the context of Christian worship.[40] Did the widows' ministry include liturgical prayer? How was the widows' ministry of prayer distinct from the obligations laid on all Christians to pray? What was involved in the widows' prayers? intercession? adoration? petition? exhortation? revelation?

There are few clues to the roles women played during the worship of the Christian communities. On the rare occasions when they make a textual appearance, it is usually as the object of some prohibition. Nevertheless, some conclusions can be drawn about women's liturgical roles. *The Statutes of the Apostles,* a church order of the early third century regulating the ordination of bishops, presbyters, readers, deacons, and widows, explicitly assigns the work of prayer and prophecy to women in the order of widows: "Let them ordain three widows, two to continue together in prayer for all who are in trials and to ask for revelation concerning what they require, while the other is to be appointed to wait upon the women who are tried in sickness, ministering well, being sober, telling the presbyters of the things which happen, not a lover of shameful gain, not a drunkard, that she may be able to be sober so as to minister at night."[41] In this text the liturgical role of women prophets is confirmed by ordination and institutionalization. Two of the widows are to continue in the traditional work of prayer and prophecy. The innovation is that the third widow is ordained to attend women in sickness, a role that had traditionally been the responsibility of the deacons.[42]

The Statutes of the Apostles also contains some tantalizing clues about women's liturgical prayer. Although instructions on the ordination of bishops, presbyters, readers, deacons, and widows are given in paragraphs 16–30, ten of the *Statutes'* fourteen chapters are devoted to the issue of women's ministries. The opening lines establish the treatise as a dialogue between the apostles themselves, and therefore its regulations have apostolic authority.[43] Our Lord commanded us "to find the dignity of the bishops, the seating of the presbyters, the service of the deacons, the wisdom of the readers, and the sinlessness of the widows, so that the order of the earthly church might be a type of the heavenly worship." This apostolic authority is enlisted to restrict some of women's liturgical functions. Following directly on Peter's instructions on the ordination of widows, the apostle Andrew urges, "It is a good thing to set apart women to be made deacons"; and Peter replies, "We've already defined this, but concerning the oblations, the *prosphora* of the body, and the blood of the Lord, we shall declare the thing with certainty." The apostle John interrupts, "You have forgotten, O brethren, on the day when our master took the bread and the cup, he blessed them saying, 'This is my body and my blood.' You've seen that he gave not a place to the women to assist with them." Martha answered that it was because of Maria, because he saw her laughing. But Maria responds, "Not because of that I laughed, for he said to us in his teaching, the weak will be healed by the strong." Peter replies, "Some say that it is right for women to pray standing up and not to throw themselves upon the earth." And Jacob answered, "Where shall we be able to set apart women for ministry, except this ministry of this kind only, that they should help the needy?"[44]

Mary and Martha are among the cast of the apostles (the apostles are John, Matthew, Peter, Andrew, Philip, Simon, Jacob, Nathaniel, Thomas, Cephas, Bartholomew, and Judas, the brother of Jacob). Here the anonymous author portrays a debate among the apostles over whether the women should take part in the liturgical act of the blessing of the cup. Peter acknowledges that women are also deacons, but the question is, as deacons or as presbyters do they have a role in the eucharistic liturgy? Peter seems on the verge of declaring with certainty that the women can participate in the bringing of the oblation, in the ministry of the body and blood. But John interrupts to contradict Peter. He assumes first that Mary and Martha were both present at the Last Supper, that they were counted among the apostles, and that it would be natural for them, having received the body and blood, to carry out the apostolic ministry. But he wishes to remind the other apostles that at that critical moment the women were not included.

The anonymous author then attempts to provide a rationale for this anomaly that the women apostles were present at the Lord's Supper but not commissioned. He uses the Martha character, who explained, "It's because of Mary, because he saw her laughing." The implication is that women lack the necessary seriousness to be eucharistic ministers. But Mary responds, "Not because of that I laughed, for he said to us in his teaching, 'The weak will be healed by the strong.'" The Mary character provides a different rationale for this anomalous exclusion of women from the eucharistic ministry by saying, "The weak will be healed by the strong." The weak—that is, women—will be healed by the strong (male) eucharistic ministers. The debate is not concluded because then Cephas says, "Some say that it is right for women to pray standing up and not to throw themselves upon the earth, or to prostrate themselves." The question that this tantalizing passage raises is, What does it mean to assist in the ministry of the oblation? Does it have anything to do with Cephas's question about whether it is right for a woman to pray standing up?

The burden of the pseudo-apostolic message is that women may not assist at the eucharistic prayers and may not pray standing up. So Jacob concludes this section by saying, "Where shall we be able to set apart women for ministry?," meaning "What ministry can women have except this ministry, the

Figure 2.1 *Orans* and eucharistic altar. Reproduced by permission of Letouzey et Ané from *Dictionnaire d'archéologie chrétienne et de liturgie*, vol. 1, col. 3159.

ministry that they should help the needy?" The apostolic exhortation then concludes with Peter saying, "Brethren we are not having authority over anyone by compulsion but we have been commanded by God. I entreat you to keep the commandments of God without taking anything from them or adding to them. In the name of our Lord Jesus the Christ whose glory is for ever, Amen."[45]

The question provoked by this enigmatic text is whether women did in fact assist at the Eucharist and offer liturgical prayers. For a piece of supporting evidence we turn again to the art preserved in the catacombs. A catacomb painting from Rome (fig. 2.1) shows an *orans* in the typical posture, standing up and arms outstretched, assisting a presbyter/priest in the consecration of the Eucharist, with the eucharistic bread and wine presented on a small portable tripod altar.[46]

The very sources that reveal clues about women's liturgical roles also disclose the social forces that gradually led to their exclusion. As the domestic space of the house churches gave way to the more public space of the larger assembly hall, equipped with a raised podium and a bishop's chair, women's authority and liturgical leadership were challenged on the grounds that public roles, public speech, and public authority were male prerogatives.

During the third century, the leadership of Christian congregations in the larger cities passed from the prophets and teachers to the centralized authority of the bishop, except in churches where there was a revival of prophecy, and women who prayed and prophesied continued to be recognized leaders of Christian worship. Liturgical prophecy was displaced by preaching on the scriptural readings. In contesting the authority of the women prophets of the New Prophecy movement, Origen, the famous Alexandrian intellectual, claims that women's prophecy was private. "It was not in the assembly that the daughters of Philip spoke. . . . Nor did Debra address the people in the form of a public speech as did Isaiah and Jeremiah."[47] The prophet Mary did speak in an assembly, but it was an assembly of women.[48] By equating liturgical prophecy with public speaking, Origen invokes the image of a woman infringing on the masculine privilege of the podium. His rhetorical strategy is to reduce prophecy to public speaking in which the orator speaks in his own voice and claims the authority the podium conveys. However, a woman praying and speaking in the prophetic voice was neither speaking in her own person nor claiming the power of the female voice. In speaking to and for God she was claiming divine authority, an authority that the congregations were prepared to recognize. Origen even grants that women prophets might be capable of sound teaching: "A woman might even say admirable things or even saintly things." But for Origen, because the Greco-Roman gender system did not authorize women's public speech, neither did God.

THE ORDER OF VIRGINS: LITURGICAL SINGING

Women who had refused marriage and converted to an ascetic lifestyle exercised a spiritual authority in their second-century congregations. By the third century their ministries on behalf of the church were institutionalized in the order of virgins. Their liturgical roles were also associated with prayer. The virgins led community worship by reciting or singing the Psalms (the earliest collection of set prayers used by Christian communities). The role of women as singers in religious rites was already established. The practice of women's singing at a celebratory meal in the Roman cultural context created space for women's singing as an accompaniment to the Christian communal meal.[49] Just as women sang hymns in the Roman funerary rites, Christian women, again often the women in the order of virgins, sang during the funerary ritual and procession and at the rites performed over the body. Virgins also led the prayers and singing at the all-night vigils held at martyrs' shrines, one of the more popular of the church's services.[50] Thus early Christians might well have associated virgins praying and singing with the figure of the *orans*. However, beginning in the fourth century, ecclesiastical regulations attempted to silence the voices of women doing liturgical singing, and by the end of the sixth century the chorus of virgins was replaced by the boys' choir.[51]

Very few literary sources documenting women's preaching in the early church have survived; hence the recent turn of feminist scholars to epigraphic and artistic sources. One of the most popular figures in early Christian art, the *orans* gives mute testimony to the importance of women's prayer. By situating the *orans* in her historical context and asking what associations second- and third-century viewers would have with women and prayer, we can see in this image some of the earliest evidence for women's preaching. Because Christian worship took place in house churches, in domestic space, women's authority in teaching, preaching, prophesying, and administration was widely accepted. Again by focusing on the second-century context we discover that "liturgical" prayer in the second century encompassed prophecy, preaching, teaching, exhortation, and revelation as well as petition, praise, and adoration.

Once an iconographic tradition like the *orans* was established, it remained relatively stable over the succeeding centuries. Roman society did not value creativity or innovation, and artists were expected to recreate the symbols authorized by tradition, not invent new ones from their subjective experience. However, as the patterns of Christian worship changed over the next centuries, so did the meanings assigned to prayer and the roles allotted to women. Toward the end of the third century, as prophetic leadership was gradually eclipsed by a clerical hierarchy, Christians likely associated the *orans* with the prayers of women in the office of widow. Later, as widows were displaced by deaconesses, the *orans* was associated with liturgical singing and prayers of women in the order of virgins and the prayer of the deaconesses. After the fourth century, the strongest association evoked by the *orans* were the hours of prayer offered by women monastics living in religious communities. But for the first three centuries, wherever prayer and prophecy were forms of Spirit-inspired preaching and teaching, the figure of the *orans* was associated with women's liturgical praying and prophesying. As such, the many representations of the *orans* can be taken as evidence of the earliest tradition of women preachers.

NOTES

1. Karen Jo Torjesen, *When Women Were Priests: Women's Leadership in the Early Church and the Scandal of Their Subordination in the Rise of Christianity* (San Francisco: Harper San Francisco, 1993).

2. Ibid., pp. 111–34.

3. Bernadette Brooten, *Women Leaders of the Ancient Synagogue* (Chico, Calif.: Scholars Press, 1982), pp. 35–72; Ross Kraemer, *Maenads, Martyrs, Matrons and Monastics* (Philadelphia: Fortress Press, 1988), pp. 218–46.

4. Dorothy Irvin, "The Ministry of Women in the Early Church: The Archaeological Evidence," *Duke Divinity School Review*, no. 2 (1980): 76–86. See also Joan Morris, *The Lady Was a Bishop: The Hidden History of Women with Clerical Ordination and Jurisdiction* (New York: Macmillan, 1973).

5. The term *orans* derives from the Latin participle of *orare*, to pray, and has passed into French and German as *orante* and into English as *orant* or *orans*.

6. J. Sauer, *Lexikon für Theologie und Kirche*, vol. 7, pp. 742–43.

7. H. Leclercq, *Dictionnaire d'archaéologie chrétienne et liturgie*, pp. 2292–2324.

8. "The Three Children," Priscilla Catacombs, and "Susanna," Priscilla Catacombs, J. Wilpert, *Malereien der Katakomben* (Freiburg im Bresgau: Herder, 1903), catalogue table F13 and F14.

9. Mary as an *orans* is found on a marble bas relief in Berlin (O. Wulff, *Altchristlische und Mittelalterlichebildwerke*, vol. 1 [1909], p. 308, no. 1626); she is portrayed in the temple in Jerusalem and in the vestibule of St. Maximin in Nicea and the chapel of the archbishop's palace at Ravenna (*Dictionnaire d'archéologie chrétienne et liturgie*, pp. 1986 and 2308).

10. J. Sauer, *Lexikon für Theologie und Kirche*, p. 743.

11. Guillaume de Gerphanion, "Les caractéristiques et les attributs des saints dans la peinture Cappadocienne," *Analecta Bollandiana* 55 (1937): 4–6.

12. F. Zoepfl, *Lexikon für Theologie und Kirche*, vol. 7, 2d ed. (1957), pp. 1190–91.

13. See the Museum at Alexandria, no. 342 and no. 3113; British Museum, no. 821. An Egyptian inscription depicts three male *orantes* before Osiris; Sharp, *Egyptian Inscriptions*, p. 264; Sybel, *Paradise in Adoration*.

14. Cicero, *Ad Familiares* 7.5; Virgil, *Aeneas*, 687; Apuleius, *De Mundo*, 33. The Christian theologian Tertullian was well aware of the pagan use of the posture of prayer and struggles to differentiate the Christian posture from its pagan prototype by urging Christians to adopt an attitude of humility and raise their arms or eyes as high as the pagans. Tertullian, *De Oratione*, 14.

15. J. B. de Rossi, *Bull. di archaeol. Christ.* 1981, p. 63.

16. K. Wessel, "Ecclesia *oran*," *Archaeologischer Anzeiger* 70 (1955): 315–34. Enrico Jossi, "Orante," in *Enciclopedia Cattolica*, pp. 179–81. These scholars insist that the female *orans* represents the soul of the deceased, even when the deceased is a baby or an old man.

17. Leclerq, *Dictionnaire d'archéologie chrétienne et liturgie*, pp. 1488–97; H. Liell, *Die Darstellungen der allerseligsten Jungfrau and Gottesgebaerin Maria auf den Kunstdenkmalereien der Katakomben* (Freiburg, 1887); A. Stuiber, "Refrigerium interim: die Vorstellungen vom Zwischenzustand und de fruehcristlich Grabeskunst," in *Theophaneia*, vol. 11 (Bonn: Schwann, 1957); W. Neuss, "Die Oranten in der altchristlicher Kunst," in *Festschrift Paul Clemens* (Bonn: Schwann, 1926), pp. 130–49.

18. In the Roman basilicas of the fifth and sixth centuries the church is unambiguously portrayed allegorically as a woman (the female figure bears the inscription *Ecclesia*), but not in an attitude of prayer; rather she is presented in a formal pose similar to that found in paintings and statues of illustrious Roman women.

19. Further, artists do portray the soul leaving the body; but in those instances it has wings, wears no clothes, and appears genderless. Except in the catacombs of Domatilla, where a baby who died at three months is portrayed as a nude with wings (borrowing on the iconography of Icarus), none of these departing souls is depicted in the gesture of prayer. *Mélanges d'archéologie et d'histoire de l'École française de Rome*, t. 4, pl. 13 n. 1.

20. Margaret Miles, *Image as Insight* (Boston: Beacon Press, 1985), p. 30.

21. 1 Timothy 2:8; Justin, *Dialogue with Trypho* 90; Minucius Felix, *Octavius*, XXIX; Tertullian, *On Baptism*, XX; Origen, *On Prayer*, 31; Chrysostom, Homily III on Philippians.

22. Eusebius, *Church History*, bk. 8, para. 7. Several scholars have used this early Christian association with the cross to interpret the *orans*. D. Dplooij (*Expository Times* 23 [1912]: 199–203, 215–19) sees in the pre-Constantian *orans* a confession of Christ through the cruciform outstretched arms.

23. See Gail Horst-Warhaft, *Dangerous Voices: Women's Laments and Greek Literature* (London: Routledge, 1992); Nichole Loraux, *The Invention of Athens: The Funeral Oration in the Classical City* (Cambridge, Mass.: Harvard University Press, 1986).

24. Torjesen, *When Women Were Priests*, pp. 53–88; Elisabeth Schüssler Fiorenza, *In Memory of Her: A Feminist Theological Reconstruction of Christian Origins* (New York: Crossroad, 1983), pp. 41–67; Bonnie Thurston, *The Widows: Ministry of Women in the Early Church* (Minneapolis: Fortress Press, 1989); Ann Jensen, *God's Self-Confident Daughters* (Louisville, Ky.: Westminster/John Knox, 1996).

25. Pliny, Epistle, 111; Justin, *Apology*, 61; *Didache* 9, 10, 14.

26. It is Paul who attempts to dissociate prayer from prophecy, and ecstatic speaking from teaching. See Antoinette Wire, *The Corinthian Women Prophets* (Minneapolis: Fortress Press, 1989), pp. 140–41.

27. Ibid., p. 142; see also Cecil Roebeck, *Prophecy at Carthage* (Minneapolis: Fortress Press, 1993), p. 199.

28. Wire, *The Corinthian Women Prophets*, p. 147.

29. Ibid., pp. 135–58.

30. There are a number of interesting interpretations of Paul's desire that the Corinthian women prophets be veiled. See Schüssler Fiorenza, *In Memory of Her*, pp. 218–36; Cynthia Thompson, "Hairstyles, Head-coverings and St. Paul: Portraits from Roman Corinth," *Biblical Archaeologist* 51 (June 1988): 99–115; J. A. Fitzmyer, "A Feature of Qumran Angelology and the Angels of I Cor. XI.10," *New Testament Studies* 4 (1956–58): 48–58. I offer an interpretation of the issue of veiling based on Greco-Roman notions of female shame. See Torjesen, *When Women Were Priests*, pp. 135–52.

31. Ode 42, trans. James H. Charlesworth, *Old Testament Pseudepigrapha*, p. 145. See also Ode 27, in which the prayer is introduced in the same way but without moving into the prophetic voice. I am grateful to Don Harrison for calling my attention to the *orans* in the Odes of Solomon.

32. Sarah Coakley, "Why Three? Some Further Reflections on the Origin of the Doctrine of the Trinity," in *The Making and Remaking of Christian Doctrine*, ed. Sarah Coakley and David Pailin (Oxford: Clarendon Press, 1993), p. 37.

33. *Didache*, 9–11.

34. 1 Tim. 5:5.

35. See Jouette Bassler, "The Widow's Tale: A Fresh Look at I Timothy 5:3–16,"

Journal of Biblical Literature 103 (1984): 23–41; Dennis R. MacDonald, "Virgins, Widows and Paul in Second Century Asia Minor," in *Society for Biblical Literature 1979 Seminar Papers* (Missoula, Mont.: Scholars Press, 1979).

36. Polycarp IV.3.

37. Thurston, *The Widows*, p. 82. Tertullian, *On Modesty*, XIII; *Apostolic Constitutions* in *Ancient Nicene Fathers* 18:85; and Arthur Maclean, "Testament of the Lord," in *The Ancient Church Orders*, ed. Arthur J. Maclean (Cambridge: Cambridge University Press, 1910), pp. 17 and 83.

38. Tertullian, *On Modesty*, XIII.

39. Jean B. La Porte, *The Role of Women in Early Christianity* (Lewiston, N.Y.: Edwin Mellen Press, 1982), p. 126. For Syrian widows, see Maclean, "Testament of the Lord," in *The Ancient Church Orders*.

40. Widows were ordained to pray; see *The Apostolic Tradition*; *The Didascalia*; Maclean, "Testament of the Lord," in *The Ancient Church Orders*; Ambrose, *On Widows*; and Cyprian, *On Widows*.

41. G. Horner's *The Statutes of the Apostles* contains Sahidic, Arabic, Ethiopic, and Latin versions of the statutes. The Latin version is given by Hauler in *Didascaliae Apostolorum Fragmenta*. Francis Xavier Funk has produced a Greek reconstruction of this text, *Doctrine Duodecim Apostolorum*. The Sahidic version can be found in W. Til and J. Leipholdt, "Der Koptische Text der Kirchenordnung," *Texte und Untersuchungen* 58 (1954). The Arabic is in J. Perier and A. Perier, "Les 127 Canons," *Patrologia Orientalis*, vol. 8, fasc. 4, Statute 21.

42. The order of deaconesses eventually supplanted the widows, and their ministries were restricted to women.

43. Statute 1 (Sahidic text).

44. Statutes 24–28 (Sahidic text).

45. Statute 30 (Sahidic text).

46. See the catacomb painting in figure 2–1. A sermon from Chrysostom alludes to eucharistic ministers praying before the congregation and for the congregation, standing in the posture of the *orans*. Hom. III, Epistle to the Philippians, iv.

47. Origen, "Fragments on I Corinthians 74," *Journal of Theological Studies* 10 (1959): 41–42.

48. Origen designates this group as the disciples of Priscilla and Maximilla, two famous women prophets. The assembly of women that Origen has in mind was in the home of Elizabeth, but of course all second- and third-century house churches met in homes.

49. Rebecca Rollins, "The Singing of Women in the Early Christian Church: Why It Occurred, Why It Disappeared," D.M.A. diss., Claremont Graduate School, 1988.

50. Ibid., pp. 54–67.

51. Ibid., p. 98.

THREE

Maria Magdalena: *Apostolorum Apostola*

Katherine Ludwig Jansen

On December 9, 1279, an ancient sarcophagus in the crypt of the church of Saint-Maximin near Aix-en-Provence was opened and its contents inspected. The authorities convened by Charles of Anjou, the prince of Salerno, examined and duly confirmed that the relics contained in the tomb were those of Saint Mary Magdalene who, it was popularly believed, had evangelized southern Gaul. The Dominican Bernard Gui, a somewhat belated witness to the events, described in his chronicle the marvelous signs that accompanied the opening of the sarcophagus. Beyond the sweet fragrance ("as if an apothecary shop of sweet spices had been opened") that normally issued from saints' relics upon discovery, a further sign authenticated the finding: a tender green shoot was found growing from the saint's tongue.[1] A sign, however, is of little value without an interpretation, and that was duly supplied by Philippe of Cabassole, chancellor of the kingdom of Naples, when in 1355 he described the *inventio* in his *Libellus hystorialis Mariae beatissimae Magdalenae*. He suggested that the small palm frond issuing from the saint's tongue signified that as *apostolorum apostola*, apostle of the apostles, she announced (*nunciavit*) to the apostles that Christ had risen from the dead and, furthermore, that she preached (*praedicavit*) to the pagan people.[2]

Philippe's twofold analysis of this miraculous sign neatly encapsulates late medieval views of the Magdalene's vocation as *apostolorum apostola*. Scriptural authority, particularly John 20:1–18, asserted that as first witness of the Resurrection, Christ bade her announce the news to the apostles; legends, adding another layer of meaning to the epithet, claimed that after the Ascension she embarked on an apostolic career. Jacobus of Voragine and others maintained that the saint and some of her closest companions evangelized Gaul, preaching and converting the pagans to Christianity. Consequently, the title *apostolorum apostola* referred not only to her scriptural mandate but also to her missionary career in Provence.[3]

As is well known, preachers of the Middle Ages frequently turned to patristic authorities for exegetical guidance. To understand the late medieval conception of the Magdalene's double apostolate, let us first turn briefly to the writers of the Late Antique period, whose thought was instrumental in shaping that of subsequent generations.

THE LATE ANTIQUE LEGACY

The origins of the appellation *apostolorum apostola* are not entirely clear. Paul-Marie Guillaume finds a close approximation in the earliest commentary on *The Song of Songs* attributed to Hippolytus, bishop and martyr of Rome (d. 235?).[4] Hippolytus suggests that the Shulammite, or bride of the *Canticles*, who was seeking her beloved (Cant. 3:1), typologically prefigured Mary and Martha, who sought Christ in the sepulchre. Furthermore, he explains, the women represent the synagogue and in that capacity reveal the good news as apostles to the apostles (*quae apostoli ad apostolos*) sent by Christ. He maintains: "Lest the female apostles doubt the angels, Christ himself came to them so that the women would be apostles of Christ and by their obedience rectify the sin of the ancient Eve. . . . Therefore the women announced the good news to the apostles. . . . That the women not appear liars but rather truth-bearers. . . . Christ showed himself to the (male) apostles and said to them: . . . 'It is I who appeared to these women and I who wanted to send them to you as apostles.'"[5]

This commentary provided ample grist for the busy mills of later commentators. Exegetes such as Hilary of Poitiers, Ambrose of Milan, and Augustine of Hippo refined and clarified these notions to the point that they became cornerstones upon which much of the edifice of Western Resurrection theology was erected. The thematic elements of this commentary—woman as redeemer of Eve's sin; as first witness of the Resurrection; and as the bride/church/synagogue—became familiar motifs in Western exegetical tradition.

The theme of the female redeemer, the counterweight to Eve, is taken up by many biblical commentators. Augustine's *ordo in similitudine* is emblematic of this style of interpretation. He argued in an Easter homily that just as "humanity's fall was occasioned by womankind, humanity's restoration was accomplished through womankind, since a virgin brought forth Christ and a woman announced that He had risen from the dead." And in a celebrated concluding remark: *per feminam mors, per feminam vita.*[6]

Thus Mary, sometimes Martha and Mary, sometimes the three Marys, or sometimes just plain "woman" played a compensatory role in the history of salvation according to many authorities. By bearing the news of the Resurrection, any or all of these women, who symbolized the female sex, restored the order of creation that original sin and its consequences had destroyed. In other words, they brought about salvific symmetry. The lack of specificity about to whom—precisely—Christ had first shown himself and whom—precisely—he had designated to proclaim the good news of his Resurrection was not of course due to exegetical incompetence. Imprecision arose from the daunting task of trying to reconcile the evangelists' (apparently) inconsistent Easter narratives. A further difficulty with which the commentators had to contend was the "muddle of Marys" that populates the gospels.[7] Christ's immediate circle of female followers, in addition to the Virgin Mary, consisted of at least five other women called Mary: Mary mother of James the less and Joses, the "other Mary," Mary of Bethany, Mary Cleophas, and of course Mary Magdalene.[8] Theoretically, the place name Magdala should have been enough to distinguish at least one Mary from the next; but in practice it was not quite so simple. At one point, Ambrose, suffering the deleterious effects of an overdose of scriptural Marys, suggested that there were two Mary Magdalenes. In an act of exegetical desperation (possibly following Eusebius), he remarked: "Some of the women are not aware [of the Resurrection], others are. . . . One Mary of Magdala does not know according to John, the other Mary Magdalene knows according to Matthew; the same woman cannot know it at first and then not know it. Therefore if there were many Marys, there were perhaps many Magdalenes, because the latter is a surname, the former a placename."[9]

One might assume that the Virgin Mary, by virtue of her unique and exalted status as mother of Christ, stood apart from the exegetical difficulties posed by a surfeit of Marys and Magdalenes. This was not the case, however. The Alexandrine method of textual analysis used by Hippolytus (not to mention Origen and Bede) produced a certain amount of ambiguity in relation to Marian identity. The elaborate literary conceit employed by these commentators sometimes identified the Virgin as the church, sometimes the Magdalene as the church, and all three as brides of Christ. Consequently, the personae of the Virgin Mary and Mary Magdalene were not as entirely distinct as their individual biographies might suggest. Although Augustine had defined a clear division of labor in the history of redemption—one woman had brought Christ into the world while another had proclaimed the news of his Resurrection—such clarity did not always obtain, particularly in the East.[10] In a discourse traditionally attributed to Cyril of Jerusalem, the author claimed that the Virgin herself had told him, "I am Mary Magdalene because the name of the village wherein I was born was Magdala. My name is Mary of Cleopa. I am Mary of James the son of Joseph the carpenter."[11] Thus in one fell swoop the Virgin Mary assumed the identities of three other scriptural Marys, all witnesses to the Resurrection.

A later Coptic text, the apocryphal *Book of the Resurrection of Christ*, ascribed to the apostle Bartholomew, exacerbates the confusion. Here the Virgin Mary expropriates the role of *nunciatrix* that the evangelist John (20:16–18) had assigned to the Magdalene: "[The] Saviour came before them . . . and he cried out . . . 'Thou Mary, the mother of the Son of God.' And Mary, who understood the meaning turned herself and said, 'Rabonnei.'. . . And the Saviour said unto her, 'Go thou unto My brethren, and tell them that I have risen from the dead.' . . . Mary said unto her Son, 'Jesus, my Lord, and my only Son, bless Thou me . . . if indeed Thou wilt not allow me to touch Thee.'"[12] Not only does the Virgin speak one of the Magdalene's lines in the Johannine Resurrection drama ("Rabboni"), but evidently she had also been warned *"noli me tangere,"* and then sent off to bear the news of the Resurrection to the apostles. In the West this sequence of events always retained the same two players: Jesus and Mary Magdalene.[13]

Ephrem the Syrian's hymns also tended to fuse together the personae of the Virgin and the Magdalene. Robert Murray has suggested that this penchant for fusing the Virgin with the other Marys reflected a strong Eastern, particularly Syrian, devotion to the Virgin. Essentially it was a form of praise to endow the Virgin Mary with all the important female roles and laudable attributes of women who figured in the Gospels.[14] M. R. James scorned this Eastern tradition, dismissing it as "the reckless identification of the Virgin Mary with all the other Maries of the Gospels," which was "typical of the disregard of history" of such rhapsodies.[15] Whether or not we find this tendency as offensive as James evidently did, we cannot dismiss it as a Coptic eccentricity. We shall encounter these Eastern-style Mary Magdalene/Virgin Mary conflations again in the Latin West of the Middle Ages. But first we shall encounter another great confusion of identities, this time of Western origin: the figure of Saint Mary Magdalene herself.

THE MIDDLE AGES

On September 21, 591, Pope Gregory the Great preached a homily in the basilica of San Clemente in Rome that established for Western Christendom a new Magdalene, indeed a figure who would have been almost entirely unrecognizable to her colleagues in the primitive church.[16] In his thirty-third homily, which took as its theme the gospel pericope Luke 7:36–50, Gregory proclaimed: "We believe that this woman [Mary Magdalene] whom Luke calls a female sinner, whom John calls Mary, is that Mary from whom Mark says seven demons were cast out."[17] In other words, Gregory the Great cobbled together a Magdalene from three separate scriptural figures: an unnamed female sinner (Luke 7:37–50); Mary of Bethany, sister of Martha and Lazarus (John 11:1–45); and the demonically possessed Mary of Magdala (Mark 16:9). This was the composite saint that the West, from the Middle Ages onward, accepted as Mary Magdalene.[18]

In the soil of the Carolingian period we find that the notional seeds of

Gregory's Magdalene took root and indeed flowered, as Rabanus Maurus's *De rerum naturis* demonstrates. Dedicated to Louis the Pious (ca. 844), the text shows its debt to Gregory the Great, Jerome, and the Alexandrine school and offers something new as well. The abbot of Fulda twice interprets the Magdalene's mission figuratively, but with a rather different descriptive vocabulary. Rabanus suggests that the women who announced the Resurrection of the Lord to the apostles are to be understood as the law and prophecy, who as precursors preached (*praedicaverunt*) the glory of the Resurrection. In regard to Mary Magdalene, Rabanus suggests that the name Magdalene meant tower, the mystical sense of which was the faith and piety of the holy church, and that by her preaching (*praedicando*) she had filled the universe with the scent of the news of Christ.[19] Although he uses the verb *praedicare* to describe the mystical significance of her mission, nevertheless, I believe it is the first time that it is used in any way in relation to Mary Magdalene's role as herald of the Resurrection. For Rabanus's predecessors, *nunciare* (to announce) had been the word of choice.

In a Mary Magdalene homily once attributed to Odo of Cluny, one of the first texts for the office of the saint's feast day,[20] the author places the Magdalene's mission on equal footing with that of the apostles: "if the disciples were thus called apostles because they were sent by him to preach the Gospel to all creatures, not less was blessed Mary Magdalene chosen by the Lord for the apostles since she removed doubt and incredulity of his Resurrection from their hearts." He calls her *apostolorum consors*.[21]

Abbot Hugh of Semur (d. 1109), under whom Cluny flourished, brought devotion to the apostolic Magdalene to that great monastic foundation.[22] In a letter of instruction regarding the nuns of Marcigny, he refers to the Magdalene as the sinner who was so glorified that she was worthy to be called *apostolorum apostola* of the Resurrection. It should be noted that the appellation *apostola* has emerged as a Magdalenian title. The early twelfth century, then, seems to have been the birth date proper of the title, which is found in the works of many of the major figures of the period, including Peter Abelard and Bernard of Clairvaux.[23]

In a sermon for the Magdalene's feast day, a contemporary of Abelard's, the abbot Geoffrey of Vendôme (d. 1132), preached that the famous sinner of Luke's gospel was one and the same Mary Magdalene who afterward was made a glorious preacher.[24] What is remarkable about Geoffrey's text is his use of the word *preacher* (*praedicatrix*) in relation to the Magdalene; moreover, he refers to her activities as preaching. Geoffrey remarks that Saint Peter denied what Mary Magdalene preached (*praedicavit*) about the Resurrection, and, moreover, that she finished out her days preaching (*praedicans*) and testifying to the truth of his Resurrection.[25]

Significantly, the first Western pictorial representations of Mary Magdalene discharging her duty as *apostolorum apostola* also date from the twelfth

Figure 3.1 *Mary Magdalene, apostolorum apostola,* from Psalter of St. Albans, Hildesheim: Dombibliothek, MS St. God. 1 (property of the Parish St. Godehard Hildesheim); photo reproduced by permission of the Dombibliothek, Hildesheim.

Figure 3.2 *Mary Magdalene, apostolorum apostola,* from Gospel Book of Henry the Lion, Wolfenbüttel: Herzog August Bibliothek, MS Guelf. Noviss. 2°; photo reproduced by permission of the Herzog August Bibliothek, Wolfenbüttel.

century. The St. Albans Psalter (1120–30), made possibly for Saint Christina of Markyate, depicts Mary Magdalene heralding the good news to eleven rather astonished apostles (fig. 3.1).[26] Another twelfth-century manuscript, the Gospel Book of Henry the Lion, also represents this scene, but this time through the lens of an Easter trope. Seven apostles greet Mary Magdalene and (on their scroll) ask, "Tell us Mary, what did you see on the way?" She answers (also by means of a scroll), "I saw the sepulchre of the living Christ and the glory of the risen one" (fig. 3.2).[27] Susan Haskins has reproduced a lovely example of female devotion to the Magdalene venerated under the title of *apostola.* The donor page of the psalter of Jutta Tersina of Liechtenfels (ca. 1200) shows her kneeling at the feet of Mary Magdalene over whom the words *Sancta Maria Magdalena apostolorum apostola* are inscribed.[28] A manuscript dating from 1310–20, known as Queen Mary's Psalter, shows the Magdalene preaching to five rather doubtful apostles (fig. 3.3).[29]

Joseph Szövérffy, in his fine study of Magdalene hymns, finds that the emergence of the apostolic title for the Magdalene dates to approximately this same period. Of the twelve Magdalene hymns that refer to her as *apostola,* two date from the eleventh or twelfth century and two others from the twelfth century. Later periods also laud the *apostola,* but he finds no earlier examples of the title.[30]

Figure 3.3 *Mary Magdalene, apostolorum apostola,* from Queen Mary Psalter, London: British Library, MS K22827; photo reproduced by permission of the British Library.

Why then did veneration of the apostolic Magdalene not emerge until the twelfth century? A number of associated reasons can be posited. By the twelfth century there was almost unanimous acceptance of the Gregorian composite saint who had engaged in a sinful life until her lachrymose conversion at Christ's feet in the house of the Pharisee. To medieval exegetes, her tears symbolized contrition, the first part of the penitential obligation. Once Luke's *peccatrix* had been assimilated to her biography, the Magdalene became the paradigmatic repentant sinner, whose personal history of sin allied her with her sinful sister Eve. Divine symmetry demanded that a female penitent rectify the sin of her sinful predecessor.

A change in *mentalité* also contributed to reshaping the figure of the Magdalene. A new emphasis on the writing of history and biography emerged from the twelfth-century "rediscovery of the individual."[31] M.-D. Chenu has written that "the awakening of an active awareness of human history was one of the achievements of Latin Christendom in the twelfth century."[32] The high Middle Ages saw the proliferation of chronicles, and writers such as Abelard and Guibert of Nogent produced the first autobiographies since Late Antiquity. Without displacing the traditional approach to sacred texts—the figurative method of analysis—history and biography found a place in critical interpretation as well. Consequently, Peter of Celle could say that the Lord had made a saint from a sinner and an *apostola* from a whore, and no one batted an eye.[33] The preachers' treatment of Mary Magdalene reflects this new emphasis on historical rather than figurative analysis. Rather than representing the church of the Gentiles or the synagogue in the Resurrection drama, Mary Magdalene became a historical figure whose biography was not only of intrinsic interest but also crucial to the unfolding of salvation history. What then were the biographical facts of her life? Exegetes turned first to Gregory the Great's composite Magdalene, but by the twelfth century there were other sources as well. Stories and legends had been accumulating since at least the eighth century. These legends fleshed out the bare-boned Gospel accounts of her life and endowed her with both a preconversion and a post-Ascension life. In so doing they added another dimension to the title *apostolorum apostola*.

VITAE MARIAE MAGDALENAE

The tenth-century homily once attributed to Odo of Cluny is an extremely important document for the history of Mary Magdalene's cult in the West. It was both one of the first texts used for the saint's office and one of the first to stitch together all the scriptural passages about her life into one seamless narrative fabric. It also embellished the sketchy facts of her life. We learn from Odo, for instance, that Mary Magdalene was the scion of noble and wealthy parents and that during her adolescence, on account of her great wealth, she had succumbed to the temptations of sin.[34]

As Hans Hänsel, Victor Saxer, and others have demonstrated, between the years 875 and 900 legendary material about the saint was circulating in Europe. The two predominant legends took the form of *vitae* and are now known as the *vita eremitica* and the *vita apostolica*.[35] Scholars regard the *vita eremitica* as a literary conflation with the life of Mary of Egypt; the story traveled west to southern Italy in the cultural baggage of Byzantine monks fleeing the Iconoclasm controversy in the East. It took some time, but by the early twelfth century it found its way into Western homiletic accounts of the saint's life. Honorius Augustodunensis, whose Magdalene homily made up a part of his *Speculum Ecclesiae*, drew on the *vita eremitica* to enliven his sermon. In his account, after the risen Lord had appeared to the Magdalene and sent her as *apostola* to the apostles, she saw the Lord ascend to heaven and at Pentecost received the Holy Spirit with all the others. Finally she withdrew to the desert and lived for some years as a hermit in a cave.[36]

Not everyone accepted the eremitical facts of her life so easily, however. A contemporary of Honorius, an anonymous Cistercian who in the early twelfth century wrote a *vita* that was once ascribed to Rabanus Maurus,[37] dismissed the desert legend with this withering criticism:

> The rest of the tale—that after the ascension of the Saviour she immediately fled to the Arabian desert; that she remained there without any clothing in a cave; and that she saw no man afterwards until she was visited by I know not what priest, from whom she begged a garment, and other such stuff—is false

and a fabrication of storytellers drawn out of the accounts of the Penitent of Egypt [Mary of Egypt]. And these tale-spinners convict themselves of falsehood from the very beginning of their story, for they ascribe their account to Josephus, that most learned historian, though Josephus never mentions anything about Mary Magdalene in his books.[38]

However scornfully the Cistercian rejected the facts of the *vita eremitica*, he took up enthusiastically the motifs of the *vita apostolica*, yet another legend that began circulating in the eleventh century, probably in relation to the cult developing at Vézelay.[39] This legend described the evangelization of Gaul by Mary Magdalene and her companions and marks the turning point in conceptions of Mary Magdalene's office; for here at last we find evidence of her double apostolate. The Cistercian, drawing on the *vita apostolica*, describes in a familiar manner how Christ honored the Magdalene by appearing to her before all others, and how the Virgin and the Magdalene collaborated to atone for the sin of Eve.[40] The monk, however, adds a piquancy: the Magdalene was not just the herald of this news; she was also a prophet because she had announced the news of the Lord's forthcoming Ascension. He calls her the *ascensionis eius prophetissa* and compares her explicitly to John the Baptist: "She witnessed the ascension on the mountain; just as she announced to the apostles the first event as soon as it had taken place. . . . She showed she was equal to John the Baptist in being more than a prophet. . . . Her deeds are equal to his, write the four evangelists."[41]

He further represents her mission to the apostles as her *apostolate*, and when later he describes her preaching activities in Gaul he links them to her role as herald in salvation history: "Who among the apostles clung so firmly to the Lord?" he asks. "It was fitting, then, that just as she had been chosen to be the *apostle* of Christ's Resurrection and the prophet of his Ascension, so also she became an evangelist for believers throughout the world. . . . She preached to the unbelievers and confirmed the believers in their faith."[42]

The material of the *vita apostolica* quickly became *materia praedicabilis*, as is witnessed by a sermon already examined, at least in part. It will be recalled that Geoffrey of Vendôme remarked that the Magdalene preached and testified to the truth of the Resurrection until the end of her days. His account draws on the *vita apostolica* and narrates that after witnessing the Ascension and the advent of the Holy Spirit, the *venerabilis discipula veritatis* said farewell to her country and, for the love of her Creator, undertook the joy of exile and ended her days preaching.[43]

Inevitably some clever author came along and spliced together the *vita eremitica* and the *vita apostolica*, creating what scholars now somewhat ponderously call the *vita apostolico-eremitica*.[44] This, patched together with the pre-Ascension narrative of the Cluny sermon and various miracle stories, eventually formed the crazy quilt of a *vita* that Jacobus of Voragine included in

The Golden Legend.[45] Carlo Delcorno has masterfully demonstrated how legendary material was plundered by preachers hungry for *materia praedicabilis.*[46] The infusion of the Magdalenian legendary material into sermons both enlivened them and provided the raw material for late medieval preachers' reconceptualization of the Magdalene's apostolate. As such, we find a shift in focus in the sermons themselves. In the later Middle Ages, preaching on the Magdalene, although still mindful of her mission to the apostles, broadened its vision to consider also how her mission from Christ led inevitably to her apostolate in Provence.

How, then, did the image of a preaching female apostle accord with the Pauline injunction that women should not deign to teach (1 Tim. 2:12)?[47] It did not. Just at the time that the image of the apostolic Magdalene became a commonplace in the preachers' homiletic vocabulary, a debate emerged— not coincidentally—that turned on the question of whether or not women were allowed to preach. Responses to that question reverberated in what was preached about Mary Magdalene's apostolate.

THE DEBATE

In the fourth century, citing Paul as his authority, Saint Ambrose interpreted the words *noli me tangere*—the phrase the risen Christ uses to forbid Mary Magdalene to touch him (John 20:17)—to mean that women were forbidden to teach in church.[48] Ambrose's interpretation still obtained in the twelfth century: Peter Comestor and Peter the Chanter, Parisian masters both, taught that the moral sense of the *noli* was a prohibition against women preaching and administering the sacraments.[49] This moral interpretation also found its way into the mid-twelfth-century *Glossa ordinaria.* Echoing Ambrosian speech and sentiment, it declared that women were not to undertake important things (such as teaching in church), but to consult those who were more perfect.[50]

Gratian's *Decretum* (ca. 1140), which compiled centuries of ecclesiastical tradition into canon law, forbade women to baptize, to handle sacred objects, vestments, and incense, and to carry the consecrated host to the sick, and perforce prohibited teaching, even if a woman was *docta et sancta.*[51] Pope Innocent III, well versed in canon law and the moral theology with which it was suffused, expressed similar views on December 11, 1210, in a letter to two Spanish bishops:

> Recently certain news has been intimated to us, about which we marvel greatly, that abbesses . . . give blessings to their own nuns, and they also hear confessions of sins, and, reading the Gospel, they presume to preach in public. This thing is inharmonious as well as absurd and not to be tolerated by us. For that reason by means of our discretion from apostolic writing, we order that it be done no longer and by apostolic authority to check it more firmly, for, although the Blessed Virgin Mary surpassed in dignity and in excellence all the Apos-

tles, nevertheless, it was not to her but to them that the Lord entrusted the keys to the kingdom of heaven.[52]

Twenty-four years later Gregory IX cited this letter in full in his *Decretals*, which themselves had the force of law. Elsewhere he acted to prevent women from entering the sanctuary, serving at mass, reading the Gospels in public, acting as confessor, or preaching.[53] Contemporaneously, Thomas Aquinas in the *Summa Theologiae* adduced an argument against women's witness of the Resurrection, arguing, "it is preaching which makes this witness public and preaching is not a woman's function." Paul and Ambrose are his authorities.[54]

The *quodlibetal* questions of this period, adding yet another dimension to the debate, dwelled on whether the office of preaching had been given to *both* men and women. In her article on thirteenth-century Parisian preaching on the Magdalene, Nicole Bériou brought these important sources to our attention.[55] Masters such as Gauthier of Château-Thierry, Eustache of Arras, and Henry of Ghent, although parting ways on detail, agreed that female saints such as Mary Magdalene, Catherine, Lucy, and Cecilia had indeed preached but had done so by divine dispensation and in extraordinary circumstances, because the early church was bereft of preachers.[56] As such, their mandate from the Holy Spirit exempted them from the Pauline ban.

Unsurprisingly, manuals for preachers forbade women to discharge the office of preaching. Humbert of Romans (d. 1277) in *De eruditione praedicatorum* advanced four reasons for this: (1) women are lacking in sense; (2) they are bound by a subject condition; (3) if women preach, they provoke lust, just as the *Glossa* (*ordinaria*) says; and finally (4) in memory of the foolishness of the first woman, Bernard said "she taught [just] once and subverted the whole world."[57] The inquisitor's manual or *summa* condemned female preaching too. At least one polemist—the Dominican Moneta of Cremona—contended that Waldensian women justified their own claims to the pulpit by appealing to the Magdalene's role as *nuncia* in the Johannine Resurrection passages.[58] Finally, sermons themselves often included admonishments about women's preaching. In a sermon given on April 11, 1305, the Dominican Giordano of Pisa preached, "Non è commesso ad ogni uomo l'ufficio del predicare; chè, innanzi innanzi, a tutte le femine è vietato in tutto e per tutto." (The office of preacher is not permitted to just anyone; [and] is above all forbidden to women altogether and forever.)[59]

Now one might imagine that, surrounded on all sides by prohibitions against woman preaching—the unassailable authority of Saint Paul, the Parisian masters, the *Glossa ordinaria*, canon law, the *quodlibetal* questions, and preaching manuals and sermons themselves—any sensible preacher would omit references to Mary Magdalene's apostolate from his sermons. Yet this is not what happened. Instead, it remained a popular motif, and diffused as it was by the liturgy and sermons, it provided inspiration for representation in various other art forms. Fresco cycles depicted her missionary activities among the pagans in Marseilles, lauds sang the praises of her preaching, and sacred plays represented her as a preacher, going so far as to recreate the words of her sermon. Before we examine those sources, let us listen to what late medieval preachers, particularly friars, were preaching about the *apostolorum apostola.*

MENDICANT SERMONS

Late medieval preachers, unlike their predecessors, willingly accepted the Magdalene's role in the redemption drama. No longer was there an urgent need to explain why a woman had been commissioned as the herald of the Resurrection; but a new question emerged in its stead: Why, given everyone in his immediate circle, had Jesus chosen Mary Magdalene as his messenger? Some preachers still explained the episode in terms of gender similitude— a woman had to atone for the sin of the first woman—but more often than not it was explained in terms of the Magdalene's personal penance.[60] Christ himself proclaimed that he had come not for the righteous but for sinners; consequently he had shown his Resurrection first to a former sinner. The Dominican preacher Hugo of Prato Florido (d. 1322) exemplified this view when he preached: "great was the consolation to the woman who first was a sinner, because the first apparition of the Lord's Resurrection was manifested to her."[61] Anthony of Padua (d. 1231) expressed the same view when he represented the episode. He described the first witness only as a "penitent soul."[62] Another Franciscan, Servasancto of Faenza (d. 1300?), tells us the Lord wanted to show himself first to Mary Magdalene—a sinner—to demonstrate that he had died for the sake of sinners, while Ubertino of Casale, apologist for the Spiritual wing of the Friars Minor, asserted that the Lord chose the Magdalene—a former sinner—to announce the glory of his Resurrection to his beloved disciples.[63] But the closing lines of a sermon by the anonymous author whom the Middle Ages believed to be Saint Augustine put it best. They assert: "lest anyone despair, take the sinner Mary, lady of luxury, mother of vainglory, sister of Martha and Lazarus as an example, who after [her conversion] was worthy to be called Apostle of the apostles."[64]

Yet another theme that distinguished late medieval sermons from their predecessors, particularly Easter sermons, was the question of why Christ had not appeared first to his mother. As Marian devotion grew ever stronger in the later Middle Ages, this became a burning issue not only for the preachers but also for their audiences. We have already seen that in the Late Antique period, particularly in Eastern literature, the Virgin, through deft authorial maneuvering, frequently appropriated the role of first witness to the Resurrection.[65] The preachers of the late medieval period were not so audacious, but they could finesse the answer if so inclined. Giordano of Pisa, O.P. (d. 1331), gives voice to his Florentine parishioners' queries with this plaintive question: "Why did he not appear first to his mother?"[66] There was neither a stock response nor a party line; preachers had to follow their own inclinations. Some, despite scriptural evidence to the contrary, maintained the conviction that Christ had shown himself first to his mother. They had the authority of Saint Ambrose on this matter, even though he was very rarely cited.[67] Servasancto of Faenza preached that "the Magdalene saw his Resurrection first, after the appearance to his mother, about which fact," he says regretfully, "the Gospels are silent."[68] In a sermon for the Easter vigil, Jacobus of Voragine (d. 1298) pursued such logic to its end and constructed an elaborate apologia for the Virgin in the Easter drama. He argued that there was no reason for her to go to the tomb along with the other Marys because she knew already that her son's body was not there, that he had risen. Furthermore, the pious must believe that he had appeared to her before all others for three reasons: "(1) On account of authority: because the venerable doctor of the Church Sedulius had said so, (2) on authority of Custom: The pope always celebrates the first station on Easter Day at Santa Maria Maggiore, commemorating that Christ appeared first to his mother, and (3) On account of the moral reason: For God commanded 'Honor thy Father and thy Mother.'" The Genoese preacher further explained that honor would hardly be constituted by Christ's showing himself first to everyone else and then showing up finally at the doorstep of his "disconsolate mother."[69]

Popular devotional literature also inclined toward this view. Domenico Cavalca (d. 1342) told in his life of Mary Magdalene how Christ, having tarried too long in the task of harrowing hell, appeared to his mother in the company of those he had liberated from Limbo. He assures his anxious mother that his wounds no longer torment him, and presents no less than John the Baptist along with Adam and Eve to give her consolation. After narrating this marvelous event, the author, like Servasancto, registers a few misgivings: "I am content to think that she had this overwhelming consolation of sight and understanding . . . but I do not affirm it, because, for all I know, it is not to be found so in the Scriptures; but I delight to think that she should receive full consolation from her blessed Son."[70]

Northerners both, Birgitta of Sweden (d. 1373) and Jordanus of Quedlinburg (d. 1380) took similar positions. In her *sermo angelicus*, Saint Birgitta claimed that although Scripture says otherwise, it must be believed without doubt that the Virgin knew first and that Jesus had shown himself to her first.[71] Jordanus said that the Virgin Mary knew of Christ's Resurrection and therefore had no need to look for the living among the dead. Furthermore, he preached: "It must be believed that Christ appeared to her first, although Scripture is silent on this matter."[72] Eventually the Franciscan rosary incorporated this meta-scriptural visit to the Madonna among the joyful mysteries of the Virgin.[73]

This was not the prevailing opinion in late medieval sermons; in fact, it caused great consternation in certain quarters. Iohannes of Biblia (d. 1338), a Dominican preacher active in Bologna, disputed with no less an authority than Saint Ambrose when he argued (citing Augustine) that the Lord showed himself immediately after the Resurrection to Mary Magdalene, alone. Iohannes maintained that, despite Ambrose's arguments to the contrary, Jesus had not yet shown himself to the disciples or to his mother.[74]

Cardinal Eudes of Châteauroux (d. 1273) preached to the Orvietans that the "Lord privileged Mary Magdalene above the rest of the apostles and even the Blessed Virgin because he appeared to her first and so quickly." Her second privilege was the office that the Lord entrusted to no other woman and no other person. Eudes regarded it as a unique privilege and referred to her as both *apostola* and *praedicatrix veritatis*. Humbert of Romans in an *ad status* sermon to *omnes mulieres* argued that at the time of the Resurrection Christ appeared first to a woman—namely, Mary Magdalene.[75]

By the late thirteenth century the appellation *apostolorum apostola* was used almost reflexively in Mary Magdalene sermons. Bartholomew of Trent, O.P., who in the mid-thirteenth century produced a compendium of saints' legends for preachers that listed briefly the important facts of their lives, considered this designation so important that he referred twice to the fact that Christ made her apostle of the apostles. It is the closing remark in his "Mary Magdalene" entry.[76] The title was used even by men such as Innocent III, who did not countenance the notion of women wielding sacerdotal authority.[77] Preachers used other titles as well to designate this honor; they include *praedicatrix et annunciatrix fidei, praedicatrix privilegiata, doctrix, magistra, prenuncia, testis veritatis, seminatrix,* and *sapientiae schola*.[78]

Nunciare was the verb used most often to describe the Magdalene's mission to the apostles; when it came to describing what she did among the pagans of Marseilles, however, *praedicare* was the verb of choice.

Some preachers, such as Humbert of Romans and the Augustinian Alberto of Padova (d. 1282), upheld the view found in the *quodlibets* that indeed Mary Magdalene had preached after the Ascension, but only by special privilege.[79] Iohannes of Biblia held the same opinion but tried to normalize her preaching by placing it in its historical context; he observed that there were women prophets among the Jews and sibyls among the pagans.[80] Another Dominican, Giovanni of San Gimignano, mindful of the Pauline injunction, observed, "one reads that after Pentecost [Mary Magdalene] preached as an apostle to the people. But then it was prohibited to other women by the Apostle, who said: 'Let women keep quiet in Church.'"[81] Vincent of Beauvais found an ingenious solution to the problem by emphasizing the Magdalene's legendary obedience. He maintained that the saint, upon hearing the news of the Apostle's pronouncement, retired immediately from her apostolic career and gave herself over entirely to the contemplative life.[82]

Figure 3.4 *Mary Magdalene preaching from a pulpit,* from Francesco Laurana, *Lazarus Altar,* Marseilles: La Vieille Major; photo by author.

Caution did not mark the majority of preached narratives of the Magdalene's apostolic career, however. Most preachers were rather imperious in their presentation of this episode of her life. An anonymous Franciscan from Marseilles remarked that, thanks to her preaching the men and women of Marseilles were converted, and by her "mediation many more were saved than damned."[83] Although the canonist Huguccio had taught that women were not to ascend the pulpit, nonetheless that is just where artists envisioned Mary Magdalene preaching.[84] In a damaged fresco from the church of Sant' Antonio di Ranverso (near Turin) the Magdalene is shown preaching from a pulpit, just as she is in Francesco Laurana's altar made for La Vieille Major in Marseilles (fig. 3.4).[85] A fresco from the church of San Domenico in Spoleto shows how her mission in Provence was frequently epitomized: she is shown giving her benediction to the people of Marseilles.[86]

Franciscus of Meyronis (d. 1328), the famous Franciscan preacher and theologian from Digne, crowned the Magdalene with the golden aureola, which was normally reserved for preachers. He narrated how the saint disseminated the seed of the Word throughout the realm of Marseilles and how, having converted the prince and his wife, she then converted almost all of Provence to the faith of Christ. Furthermore, he maintained that she had earned the quadruple crown, one layer of which was the golden aureola—

the one reserved for the learned (*doctoribus*). "Because wisdom is noted in gold according to Gregory and she taught wisdom and knowledge of the Christian faith."[87] He made no mention whatsoever of the Apostle's injunction, or that she undertook her ministry by special privilege. In the normal way, the aureola was represented as a triple honor deriving from excellent deeds. The prior of the Dominican convent at Strasburg, Hugh of Ripelin (d. 1296), explained the triple crown in this way: "Whence it is clear that the aureola is due to virgins, martyrs, and preachers. Martyrs conquer the world, virgins the flesh, and preachers the devil whom they not only expel from themselves but also from the hearts of others."[88] In a miniature from a fourteenth-century German manuscript, the Magdalene is shown wearing the triple crown, the crown reserved for martyrs, virgins, and preachers (fig. 3.5).[89]

William Peyrault (d. 1281) and Nicholas of Dinkelsbühl (d. 1433) preached that Saint Catherine of Alexandria wore the triple aureola as well.[90] Catherine, like Mary Magdalene, was often represented in her missionary guise. Both were regarded as learned women who had converted pagans to Christianity: Catherine by her public disputation with the philosophers, the Magdalene by her preaching. Such images were disseminated widely. David d'Avray points out in relation to Saint Catherine that since her feast day was a solemn one— a holiday on which work stopped—the laity would have encountered the model of the female intellectual saint in her feast-day sermon. The same would obtain for the feast day of the Magdalene.[91]

Frequently the two saints are found paired in late medieval religious painting. A polyptych by Simone Martini made for the Dominican monastery of Santa Caterina in Pisa exemplifies this relationship (fig. 3.6) Mary Magdalene and Catherine are paired with saints from the Order of Preachers. Teaching is one of the central themes of this altarpiece.[92] The confessor-preachers Saints Dominic, John the Evangelist, and Mary Magdalene gaze on the Madonna and child from her right, while the martyr-preachers John the Baptist, Catherine, and Peter Martyr flank her on the left.[93] That the Dominican order, founded on the twin pillars of erudition and service, should show particular devotion to these two saintly intellectuals is hardly surprising.[94]

Like any righteous early Christian missionary, Mary Magdalene was affronted by pagan superstition and attempted to destroy it root and branch. Servasancto of Faenza directed those reading his model sermons to "say how for two years she preached in Marseilles and how the idols were destroyed." Peregrinus of Oppeln, O.P. (d. 1322), observed that Mary Magdalene's preaching was so effective that after hearing her the people of Marseilles destroyed all the idols in their city and built many churches.[95] In the *Leggendario Ungherese*, a lavishly illustrated catalogue of saints' lives made for an Angevin prince, Mary Magdalene zealously performs the deed herself (fig. 3.7).[96]

After preaching the faith, destroying pagan idols, and confirming people

Figure 3.5 *Mary Magdalene wearing the triple crown,* from London: British Library, MS Add. 15682; photo reproduced by permission of the British Library.

Figure 3.6 *Mary Magdalene and Catherine of Alexandria,* from Simone Martini, Dominican polyptych, Pisa: Museo Nazionale di S. Matteo (ex Convento di S. Caterina); photo by author.

in the faith, an early Christian missionary usually baptized people. Contrary to canon law, Mary Magdalene engaged in this activity as well. Pietro of Natali's legend described the Magdalene performing baptisms after destroying pagan temples.[97] The church of Saint Maurice in Angers preserves the font, donated by King René, in which she baptized the rulers of Provence.[98]

The liturgy too would have reminded the faithful of the Magdalene's designation as *apostolorum apostola* because the credo was recited on her feast day; she was the only female to merit this honor other than the Virgin Mary.[99] The antiphon *O apostolorum apostola* would have been yet another reminder.[100] Humbert of Romans took it for granted that the canonesses to whom he directed one of his *ad status* sermons were familiar with this antiphon. He reminded them that "once there were not only prophets, but prophetesses, and not only apostles but even apostlesses, as is sung about the Magdalene."[101]

Laude, that form of devotional poetry made famous by the Franciscan Jacopone of Todi, sang the praises of the apostolic Magdalene as well. One from Cortona chanted:

> sì ke sua discipula la fece,
> comme la scriptura el conta et dice.

Figure 3.7 *Mary Magdalene destroys the pagan idols*, from *Leggendario Ungheresse* (Hungarian Legendary), Vatican City: Biblioteca Apostolica Vaticana, MS Vat. lat. 8541; photo reproduced by permission of the Biblioteca Apostolica Vaticana.

Poi rimase apostola in sua vece
per lo suo vengelio predicare.[102]

[Thus he made her his disciple
as scripture recounts and tells.

Then she remained an apostle in his stead
in order to preach his gospel.]

Sacred drama, the genre that developed from the *laudesi* tradition, also celebrated the *apostolorum apostola*. In one *Rappresentazione di S. Maria Maddalena*, Saint Maximin, arriving in Marseilles together with the Magdalene, surveys the territory for a moment and then beseeches her: "And you Mary, you who are so eloquent, would you preach to these people first?" Without hesitation Mary Magdalene begins to preach the faith:

O benighted people, O ignorant people,
O people mired in error and sin . . .

And concludes:

Leave your pagan sect now
which is full of every false error
And come to the true and holy faith
which saves everyone who believes.[103]

Devotional literature also took up the theme of the Magdalene's apostolate and elaborated it. According to *The Golden Legend*, when she began to preach to the pagans, "all wondered at her, not only for her beauty but for her eloquence, which eloquence was not indeed a matter of surprise on lips that had touched the Lord's feet."[104] Cavalca's *vita* told of her evangelization in Gaul and also of how the Magdalene preached the faith even during Christ's lifetime. She preached the doctrine of the Lord so sweetly to the tenants of her estates (she was the wealthy landowner of the *castellum* of Magdala) that the people all wept for devotion, and they began to cry with one voice, saying: "Magdalene, do not leave us, for now we will be more faithful and better servants than ever before."[105] Their cries went unheeded, though. She left them, and like the other apostles she sold all she had and gave the profits to the poor. Servasancto of Faenza remarked the parallel between the Friars Minor and the Magdalene, observing that both, having been called to their apostolic vocation, renounced the world and themselves. A fifteenth-century fresco cycle in Cusiano shows the saint and her siblings distributing their worldly goods to the needy (fig. 3.8).[106]

Taking their cue from Acts 1:14, many writers also claimed that she was present when the Holy Spirit descended at Pentecost. One Italian legend maintained that the Holy Spirit descended "in the form of flaming tongues and it infused all those who were present, including the Madonna, the disciples, and the beloved hostesses Martha and the Magdalene and all the others."[107]

Ultimately the image of the *apostolorum apostola* was ubiquitous, indeed almost inescapable in the Middle Ages. The powerful image of a woman discharg-

Figure 3.8 *Mary Magdalene, Martha, and Lazarus distribute their worldly goods to the needy,* from Giovanni and Battista Baschenis de Averara, fresco cycle in the apse of Santa Maria Maddalena, Cusiano (Trentino); photo reproduced by permission of Beni Culturali della Provincia Autonoma di Trento.

ing the office of preacher was found in popular devotional literature, sacred poetry and drama, religious art, the liturgy, and sermons. And this image, which emerged in the eleventh century, only to bloom in the twelfth and succeeding centuries, was part of the common conceptual economy at least until the Council of Trent. Thus for a good five hundred years Mary Magdalene was represented as *apostolorum apostola.*[108]

Though some medieval commentators tried now and again to restrict the meaning of the image, ultimately they fought a losing battle. "Popular" interpretation had already taken possession of it. Or as Michael Camille has argued in relation to a different set of medieval images, ecclesiastical authority suffered a "loss of hegemony over representation."[109] In this case, however, "popular" representation did not stand outside the church. The paradox is that these images, whether contained in sermons, *laude*, liturgical drama, or on church walls, were produced in the service of the church and in the name of Christian piety, and most often—such as in the sermons of preachers—by representatives of the church itself.[110] They were not, as theologian Elisabeth Moltmann-Wendel seems to believe, the products of a heretical counter-church.[111] Nonetheless, the image of Mary Magdalene, *apostolorum apostola*, purveyed by some members of the church carried a potentially subversive discourse that countered the official rhetoric and teachings of the schools and the law. While some sermons may have come with disclaimers about the Magdalene's apostolate in France, other cultural forms honoring her did not. Certain cautious preachers may have issued caveats about Mary Magdalene's apostolic mandate, but given the evidence, they were not much heeded.

In the event, we must ask whether the image of the apostolic Magdalene influenced women to take up their own ministries. We know that Catherine of Siena was sensitive to visual images: she reported receiving a vision of Saint Dominic, who looked just as "she had seen him painted in the churches."[112] Catherine was sensitive to literary imagery as well, particularly the sort found in medieval hagiography and sermons. In a letter to Monna Agnese Malavolti, Catherine refers to Mary Magdalene as *apostola* and praises her preaching in Marseilles. Further, she invokes the Magdalene who "runs and embraces the cross," the cross being Catherine's metaphor for apostolic ministry, as she makes plain on a separate occasion when referring to the apostles at Pentecost who "climbed into the pulpit of the holy cross." Finally, in a letter of 1376 to her confessor, Raymond of Capua, Catherine describes a vision in which Christ gave her the cross and asked her to: "Tell them, I announce to you a great joy."[113] The Johannine commission to Mary Magdalene resounds in all of the words she chose to describe her vision.

As is well known, women's speech was fair game for moralists and satirists of the Middle Ages. The example of Mary Magdalene, *apostola*, however, stood in stark contrast to the caricatured garrulous and gossipy woman who inhabited much of medieval discourse. The image of the *apostolorum apostola* thus served as an antidote to such gendered constructs and even provided a counterargument to them. Robert of Sorbon (d. 1274) told his audience that the Magdalene was the *praedicatrix* of the Lord's Resurrection; therefore men should not disdain women's words.[114]

A certain female author who earned her living crafting words in the late

Middle Ages could not have agreed more. Appropriately, she shall have the last word. In 1405, Christine de Pisan maintained:

> If women's language had been so blameworthy and of such small authority, as some men argue, our Lord Jesus Christ would never have deigned to wish that so worthy a mystery as His most gracious Resurrection be first announced by a woman, just as He commanded the blessed Magdalene, to whom He first appeared on Easter, to report and announce it to His apostles and to Peter. Blessed God, may you be praised, who, among the other infinite boons and favors which You have bestowed upon the feminine sex, desired that woman carry such lofty and worthy news.[115]

NOTES

1. "Inventum est corpus sanctissimae Magdalenae . . . tanquam si aperta fuisset suavium aromatum apotheca, consequentibus signis, et multis miraculis gloriosis. Ex ejus lingua sacratissima, adhuc tunc suo capiti et gutturi inhaerente, radix quaedam cum ramusculo fernicli [sic] exibat"; *Flores chronicorum seu catalogus pontificum Romanorum* (ca. 1311–31), cited in E.-M. Faillon, *Monuments inédits sur l'apostolat de Sainte Marie-Madeleine en Provence*, 2 vols. (Paris: J.-P. Migne, 1859), vol. 2, pp. 777–78. *Bibliotheca Hagiographica Latina* (*BHL*), 2 vols. (Subsidia Hagiographica, vol. 6) (Brussels, 1898–1901), vol. 2, n. 5506. The date is from Thomas Kaeppeli, *Scriptores Ordinis Praedicatorum Medii Aevi* (*Scriptores*), 4 vols. (Rome: Istituto Storico Domenicano, 1970–93), vol. 1, p. 212. All translations are my own unless otherwise indicated.

2. "Repertis, igitur, sacratissimi corporis immenso praelibato thesauro, et signo tutissimo in eodem, videlicet virente ramusculo palmitis, progrediente de sacratissima lingua ejus, qua apostolorum apostola, Christum resurrexisse a mortuis, apostolis nunciavit, et gentibus praedicavit"; cited in Faillon, *Monuments*, vol. 2, p. 792. *BHL*, vol. 2, n. 5509.

3. For studies on the history of the cult of Mary Magdalene, see Helen Meredith Garth, *Saint Mary Magdalene in Mediaeval Literature* (Baltimore: Johns Hopkins University Press, 1950); Victor Saxer, *Le culte de Marie-Madeleine en occident dès origines à la fin du moyen-âge* (*Cahiers d'archéologie et d'histoire*, 3) (Auxerre: Publications de la Société des Fouilles Archéologiques et des Monuments Historique de l'Yonne; Paris: Librairie Clavreuil, 1959), the most comprehensive of his many studies on the saint; *Marie Madeleine dans la mystique, les arts et les lettres*, Actes du colloque international, Avignon, July 20–22, 1988, ed. Eve Duperray (Paris: Beauchesne, 1989); the recent volume of collected essays, *La Madeleine (viiie–xiiie siècle)*, published in the series *Mélanges de l'École Française de Rome: Moyen Âge* (*MEFRM*) 104, no. 1 (1992); Susan Haskins, *Mary Magdalen: Myth and Metaphor* (London: HarperCollins, 1994); and Katherine Ludwig Jansen, "Mary Magdalen and the Mendicants in Late Medieval Italy" (Ph.D. diss., Princeton University, 1995).

4. Paul-Marie Guillaume, "Marie-Madeleine" in *Dictionnaire de Spiritualité Ascétique et Mystique. Doctrine et Histoire* (*DS*), 16 vols. (Paris: Beauchesne, 1937–94), vol. 10 (1980), cols. 559–75.

5. "Vide hoc perfectum super Martham et Mariam; cum eis synagoga cum dili-gentia quaerebat Christum mortuum, quem vivum esse non cogitabant. . . . Et post hoc clamans confitetur synagoga per has mulieres; bonum testimonium nobis osten-dunt quae apostoli ad apostolos fiebant, missae a Christo. . . . Ut autem non ab ange-lis apostoli dubitarent, occurrit ipse Christus apostolis, ut mulieres Christi apostoli essent et defectum veteris Evae per oboedientiam implerent. . . . Propterea mulieres bonum-nuntium nuntiaverunt discipulis. . . . Ut non apparerent sicut deceptores, sed veritatem dicentes, in illo tempore Christus (fuit) manifestatus eis et eis dixit: . . . 'Ego qui mulieribus his apparui, et ad vos apostolos mittere volui'"; *Corpus Scriptorum Chris-tianorum Orientalium,* vol. 264 (1965), pp. 43–49. The commentary survived only in Georgian. The Latin edition is a translation made from the Georgian by Gérard Garitte.

6. "Quia per sexum femineum cecidit homo, per sexum femineum reparatus est homo, quia virgo Christum pepererat, femina resurrexisse nuntiabat"; Augustine, *Sermo 232, Patrologiae cursus completus: series latina* (hereafter *PL*), ed. J.-P. Migne, 221 vols. (Paris: J.-P. Migne, 1844–64), vol. 38, col. 1108. Augustine's predecessors had also taken this line. Commenting on Matthew 28:9, Hilary of Poitiers, following the evangelist, suggested that Christ had shown himself first to the three Marys: "Quod vero primum muliericulae Dominum vident, salutantur, genibus advolvuntur, nun-tiare apostolis jubentur; ordo in contrarium causae principalis est redditus: ut quia a sexu isto coepta mors esset, ipsi primum resurrectionis gloria et visus et fructus et nuntius redderetur"; in *Commentarius in Matthaeum, PL* 9, col. 1076.

Ambrose singled out one Mary for this honor: "Adoravit enim Christum Maria, et ideo praenuntia resurrectionis ad apostolos destinatur, solvens haereditarium nexum, et feminei generis immane delictum. Hoc enim operatus est in mysterio Dominus: *Ut ubi superabundaverat peccatum, superabundaret et gratia*" (Rom. 5:20); in *De Spiritu Sancto,* Lib. III, *PL* 16, cols. 826–27.

7. It is Marina Warner's phrase. See Marina Warner, *Alone of Her Sex: The Myth and Cult of the Virgin Mary* (New York: Vintage Books, 1983), p. 344.

8. Mary mother of James the less and Joses (Mark: 15:40, 47; 16:1); the "other Mary" at the tomb (Matt. 27:61; 28:1); Mary of Bethany (Luke 10: 39–42 and John 11:1–45; 12:1–8); Mary Cleophas (John 19, 25); and Mary of Magdala (Matt. 27:56, 61; 28:1; Mark 15:40, 47; 16:1, 9; Luke 8:2; 24:10; John 19:25; 20:1–18); Carla Ricci, *Maria di Magdala e le molte altre: Donne sul cammino di Gesù* (Naples: M. D'Auria, 1991), pp. 69–70; now translated by Paul Burns as *Mary Magdalen and Many Others: Women Who Followed Jesus* (Minneapolis: Fortress Press, 1994).

9. "Mulieres aliae nesciunt, aliae sciunt. . . . Nescit una Maria Magdalene, secun-dum Joannem (John 20:15); scit altera Maria Magdalena, secundum Matthaeum (Matt. 38:9); nam eadem et ante scire, et postea nescire non potuit. Ergo si plures Mariae, plures fortasse etiam Magdalenae, cum illud personae nomen sit, hoc loco-rum"; *Expositiones in Lucam,* Lib. X, *PL* 15, col. 1936.

Eusebius had previously developed the idea in *Questiones ad Marinum*: "Laudabil-ius tamen fiet, si ne mendum quidem in his locis esse causabimur, duasque potius Magdalenas censebimus, sicuti jam quatuor demonstravimus fuisse Marias. Certe nulla absurditas vetat, quominus duas Marias ab eodem castello Magdalo venisse dicamus: prorsus et nulla jam perplexitas relinquatur, sed altera sit illa quae sero Sabbatorum apud Matthaeum, altera rursus et ipsa Magdalena quae apud Joannem mane ad mon-umentum accedit"; *PG* 22, col. 947.

10. "Virgo Christum pepererat, femina resurrexisse nuntiabat"; *Sermo 232, PL* 38, col. 1108.

11. A Coptic text cited in Montague Rhodes James, *The Apocryphal New Testament Being the Apocryphal Gospels, Acts, Epistles, and Apocalypses* (Oxford: Clarendon Press, 1924), p. 87. See now *The Apocryphal New Testament: A Collection of Apocryphal Christian Literature in an English Translation*, ed. J. K. Elliott (Oxford: Oxford University Press, 1994). See also E. A. Wallis Budge, *Miscellaneous Coptic Texts in the Dialect of Upper Egypt* (Oxford: Oxford University Press, 1915), p. 630.

12. E. A. Wallis Budge, *Coptic Apocrypha in the Dialect of Upper Egypt* (Oxford: Horace Hart, 1913), pp. 221–24. James (*Apocryphal New Testament*, p. 183) dates the text between the fifth and seventh centuries. See also Ciro Giannelli, "Témoignages patristiques grecs en faveur d'une apparition du Christ ressuscité à la Vierge Marie," *Revue des Études Byzantines* (Mélanges Martin Jugie 11) (1953): 106–19, who notes that Chrysostom also gave this privilege to the Virgin Mary.

13. The words *noli me tangere* were so associated with the Magdalene in the West that the basilica at Saint-Maximin in Provence still retains a relic called by that name. It is said to be the piece of skin where Christ touched Mary Magdalene's forehead when he uttered those famous words in the garden. It was renowned in the Middle Ages, as Pietro de' Natali (d. 1400) attests: "caput in eodem loco habetur ex toto denudatum excepta parte frontis quam Christus sua manu tetigit post resurrectionem quando dixit ei noli me tangere: quam adhuc carnem et pellem habet que a Christo tacta fuit"; *Catalogus Sanctorum* (Venice: Nicolaus de Frankfordia, 1516), p. 258. The *noli* was removed from the skull in 1789 and placed in a separate reliquary that is still exhibited with her skull on her feast day.

14. Robert Murray, *Symbols of Church and Kingdom* (Cambridge: Cambridge University Press, 1975), pp. 146–48, 329–31. See also Giannelli, "Témoignages," pp. 106–19.

15. James, *Apocryphal New Testament*, pp. 88 and 186.

16. The *PL* provides the day and month; Victor Saxer proposes the year in "Les origines du Culte de Marie-Madeleine en Occident," in Duperray, *Marie Madeleine*, pp. 33–47.

17. "Hanc vero quam Lucas peccatricem mulierem, Joannes Mariam nominat, illam esse Mariam credimus de qua Marcus septem daemonia ejecta fuisse testatur. Et quid per septem daemonia, nisi universa vitia designatur?" *Homilia 33, Homiliarum in evangelia*, Lib. II, *PL* 76, col. 1239.

18. The Orthodox Church never accepted the Gregorian conflation. Its liturgical calendar marked separate feasts for distinct women: June 4 for Mary of Bethany, and June 30, July 22, and August 4 for Mary Magdalene. See Victor Saxer, "Les saintes Marie Madeleine et Marie de Béthanie dans la tradition liturgique et homilétique orientale," *Revue des sciences religieuses* 32 (1958): 1–37.

19. "Mulieres quae apostolis Domini resurrectionem annuntiant, lex et prophetia intelliguntur, quae gloriam resurrectionis Christi, antequam revelaretur, quasi praecursores praedicaverunt. . . . Haec a loco Magdalo Magdalene dicitur. Interpretatur enim Magdalene turris. Mystice autem significat fidem ac pietatem sanctae Ecclesiae, quae odorem notitiae Christi praedicando in universo spargit mundo"; *De rerum naturis*, Lib. IV, which appears under the title *De universo* in *PL* 111, col. 84.

Rabanus's Magdalene is Gregory's composite Magdalene: "Maria ergo Magdalene ipsa est soror Lazari et Marthae, de qua Dominus ejecit septem daemonia. Ipsa est autem non alia, quae quondam, ut Lucas scribit, peccatrix adhuc, veniens pedes Domini lacrymis poenitentiae rigavit"; ibid.

In the year 412 Jerome interpreted the name Magdala similarly: "Mary of Magdala, called 'of the tower' because of her earnestness and ardent faith, was privileged to see the rising Christ first even before the apostles." *Letter 127* (To Principia), *Select Letters of St. Jerome*, trans. F. A. Wright (London: G. P. Putnam's Sons, 1933), p. 451.

20. Victor Saxer thinks it comes from eleventh-century Cluny; see "Maria Maddalena," *Bibliotheca Sanctorum (BS)* 8 (1967), col. 1094. See also Saxer, *Le culte*, pp. 316–17. Dominique Iogna-Prat gives it a tenth-century date; see his "'Bienheureuse polysémie': La Madeleine du *Sermo in veneratione Sanctae Mariae Magdalenae* attribué à Odon de Cluny (xe siècle)," in Duperray, *Marie Madeleine*, pp. 21–31, and "La Madeleine du *Sermo in Veneratione Sanctae Mariae Magdalenae* attribué à Odon de Cluny," in *MEFRM* 104, no. 1 (1992): 37–67, an expanded version.

21. "Et si discipuli ideo apostoli vocati, quia missi sunt ab ipso ab [sic] praedicandum Evangelium omni creaturae, nec minus beata Maria Magdalene ab ipso Domino destinata est ad apostolos, quatenus dubietatem et incredulitatem suae Resurrectionis, ab illorum cordibus removeret"; *Sermo II* (*In veneratione Sanctae Mariae Magdalenae*) *PL* 133, col. 721. The hymn attributed to Odo says: "Surgentem cum victoria/Jesum vidit ab inferis/Prima meretur gaudia/Quae plus ardebit caeteris"; ibid., col. 715. "*Consors*: . . . sed apostolorum consors effecta, illis donata est Dominicae Resurrectionis nuntia"; ibid., col. 714.

22. Iogna-Prat, "La Madeleine," p. 40. The first mention of the feast at Cluny is found in the "Customary of Bernard," written about 1063. There were three readings taken from Gregory the Great's thirty-third homily. The first known martyrology from Cluny, that written for the nuns of Marcigny-sur-Loire between 1087/89 and 1095, also mentioned the feast. Finally, the second lectionary of Cluny dated about 1100 attests that the feast had grown in importance: there were now twelve readings from Gregory's thirty-third homily.

23. "Jesu bone, Jesu clementissime, qui Mariam illam peccatricem . . . ita honorasti, ita glorificasti, ut in resurrectione tua ipsa *apostolorum apostola* esse mereretur"; in *Commonitorium ad successores suos pro sanctimonialibus Marciniacensibus, PL* 159, col. 952.

In a sermon that drew a comparison between the honor bestowed on women at Passover in the Old Testament (Miriam) and at Easter in the New Testament (Mary Magdalene), Abelard remarked: "Illa quippe prophetes memoratur, haec *apostolorum apostola* dicitur. . . . *Apostolorum* autem *apostola* dicta est, hoc est legatorum legata: quod eam Dominus ad apostolos primum direxerit, ut eis resurrectionis gaudium nuntiaret"; *Sermo 13, PL* 178, col. 485. Miriam, tambourine in hand, makes an appearance in the Magdalene Chapel in the lower church at Assisi as well.

Bernard of Clairvaux uses the title in the plural for the three Marys: "Missae ab angelo opus faciunt *evangelistae;* factaeque *apostolae apostolorum,* dum festinant ad annuntiandum mane misericordiam Domini"; *Sermo 75, PL* 183, col. 1148.

24. "Istam peccatricem feminam nulli dubium est Mariam fuisse Magdalenam, quae prius quidem exstitit famosa peccatrix, sed postea facta est gloriosa praedicatrix"; *Sermo IX* (*In festivate b. Mariae Magdalenae*) *PL* 157, col. 271. He subsequently uses *nuntiavit* in the same sermon: "Huic Christus surgens a mortuis primum apparuit; et haec illum surrexisse apostolis prima nuntiavit" (col. 273). Cf. Peter of

Celle: "Talis apprehensio virtutis et vitii deprehensio, vel potius depressio, de aegra sanam, de leprosa mundam, de peccatrice sanctam, de meretrice apostolam constituit"; *Sermo 64 (in festo S. Mariae Magdalenae), PL* 202, col. 839.

25. "Sed postea fact est gloriosa praedicatrix. . . . Illum siquidem Petrus negat quem mulier praedicat"; ibid., cols. 271, 273, 274.

26. For the psalter, see Otto Pächt, C. R. Dodwell, and Francis Wormald, *The St. Albans Psalter (Albani Psalter)* (London: Warburg Institute, 1960), p. v. For the dating of the MS, see R. M. Thomson, quoted in *The Life of Christina of Markyate*, ed. C. H. Talbot (Oxford: Clarendon Press, 1959; reprint 1987), p.v; the stained glass at Chartres (1200–10), Notre Dame at Semur-en-Auxois (1225–30), and Auxerre (1230) all represent this scene. See Colette Deremble, "Les Premiers cycles d'images consacrées à Marie Madeleine," in *MEFRM* 104, no. 1 (1992): 187–208. Virginia Chieffo Raguin, *Stained Glass in Thirteenth-Century Burgundy* (Princeton, N.J.: Princeton University Press, 1982), reproduces the scene from Semur as fig. 136. For a listing of Magdalenian iconography, see M. Anstett-Janssen, "Maria Magdalena," in *Lexikon der Christlichen Ikonographie*, 8 vols. (Rome: Herder, 1968–76), vol. 7 (1974), cols. 516–41.

27. Miniature: MS Wolfenbüttel, Herzog August Bibliothek: Cod. Guelf. 105 Noviss. 2, f. 171r. The trope is from Wipo of St. Gall's *Victimae paschali*, written in the eleventh century. By the twelfth century it had been incorporated into the Easter drama, *Visitatio Sepulchri*. See Karl Young, *The Drama of the Medieval Church*, 2 vols. (Oxford: Clarendon Press, 1933), vol. 2, pp. 273–306. For the Gospel Book of Henry the Lion, see Franz Jansen, *Die Helmarschausner Buchmalerei zur Zeit Heinrichs des Löwen* (Hildesheim: August Lax, 1933).

28. Haskins, *Mary Magdalen*, pp. 220–21, 452 n. 78. Haskins notes that this scene also appears in the *Ingeborg Psalter*, made in the late twelfth century for the wife of Philip Augustus. Thirteenth-century miniatures of this scene are also found in the lectionary of S. Chapelle (B.N., MS Lat. 8892, f. 9r) and a miscellany at St. John's College, Cambridge (MS K21, f. 56v). See R. Branner, "Le premier évangéliaire de la Sainte-Chapelle," *Revue de l'art* 3 (1969): 37–48. Magdalen LaRow notes that there are four instances of this scene in the eleventh century, eight in the twelfth century (four of which are MS illuminations), and fourteen in the thirteenth century, half of which are miniatures; see Magdalen LaRow, "The Iconography of Mary Magdalen: The Evolution of a Western Tradition until 1300" (Ph.D. diss., New York University, 1982), pp. 219, 221, 224.

29. Miniature: MS British Library K22827, f. 301r. Scholars believe that it was made for Isabella, wife of Edward II of England. For the psalter, see George Warner, *Queen Mary's Psalter: Miniatures and Drawings by an English Artist of the Fourteenth Century* (London: Trustees of the British Museum, 1912); and Anne Rudloff Stanton, "The Queen Mary Psalter: Narrative and Devotion in Gothic England" (Ph.D. diss., University of Texas at Austin). I thank John Clarke for this last reference.

30. Joseph Szövérffy, "'Peccatrix quondam femina': A Survey of the Mary Magdalen Hymns," *Traditio* 19 (1963): 79–146.

31. For the debate concerning twelfth-century individualism, see Colin Morris, *The Discovery of the Individual, 1050–1200* (New York: Harper and Row, 1972); John F. Benton, "Consciousness of Self and Perceptions of Individuality," in *Renaissance and Renewal in the Twelfth Century*, ed. Robert L. Benson and Giles Constable (Cambridge, Mass., 1982), pp. 263–95; and Caroline Walker Bynum, "Did the Twelfth Century

Discover the Individual?" in *Jesus as Mother: Studies in the Spirituality of the High Middle Ages* (Berkeley: University of California Press, 1982), pp. 82–109.

32. M.-D. Chenu, *Nature, Man and Society in the Twelfth Century: Essays on Theological Perspectives in the Latin West*, trans. J. Taylor and Lester Little (Chicago: University of Chicago Press, 1968), pp. 162–201, esp. 162.

33. "de peccatrice sanctam, de meretrice apostolam constituit"; *Sermo LXIV (in festo S. Mariae Magdalenae)*, *PL* 202, col. 839.

34. *PL* 133, col. 714. "Fuit igitur secundum saeculi fastum clarissimis beatissima Maria natalibus exorta, quae, ut Patrum asserrunt traditiones, a Magdalo castello Maria Magdalene nuncupata est. Quam non solum germinis dignitas, verum etiam patrimonii jura parentum excessu splendidam reddiderunt: adeo ut duplicatus honor nominis excellentiam circumquaque diffunderet. . . . Sed quia rerum affluentiam, interdum voluptas comes sequitur, adolescentioris vitae tempora, lubricis supposuit discursibus, solutis pudicitiae frenis"; *BHL*, n. 5439.

35. The *Vita eremitica (BHL,* nn. 5453–56) was thought in the Middle Ages to have been written by Josephus Flavius. A version has been edited by Jean Misrahi, "A Vita Sanctae Mariae Magdalenae *(BHL,* n. 5456) in an Eleventh Century Manuscript," *Speculum* 18 (1943): 335–39. The *Vita Apostolica (BHL,* nn. 5443–49) has recently been edited by Guy Lobrichon, "Le Dossier Magdalénien aux xie–xiie siècle," *MEFRM* 104, no. 1 (1992): 163–80. The question of textual transmission of the *vitae* is a thorny one and beyond the scope of this essay. See Hans Hänsel, *Die Maria Magdalena Legende: Eine Quellen Untersuchung*, Greifswalder Beiträge zur Literatur und Stilforschung, XVI/ 1 (Greifswald, 1937). See also Saxer, "Maria Maddalena," cols. 1078–1107; David Mycoff, *The Life of Saint Mary Magdalen and Her Sister Martha*, Cistercian Studies Series, vol. 108 (Kalamazoo, Mich.: Cistercian Publications, 1989), pp. 5–6; for some interesting remarks about the fortunes of the *Vita eremitica* in Anglo-Saxon Britain, see Veronica Ortenberg, "Le culte de Sainte Marie Madeleine dans l'Angleterre Anglo-Saxonne," *MEFRM* 104, no. 1 (1992): 13–35.

36. "Unde et angelum videre meruit Dominusque resurgens primo omnium ei publice apparuit, eamque apostolam apostolis suis misit. . . . De ea etiam fertur quod postquam Dominum cum aliis discipulis coelum ascendere viderit, Spiritumque sanctum cum aliis acceperit; eius amore postea virum videre noluerit, sed in heremum veniens, in spelunca aliquot habitaverit"; *de Sancta Maria Magdalena* in *Speculum Ecclesiae, PL* 172, col. 981.

37. Victor Saxer, "La vie de sainte Marie Madeleine attribuée au pseudo-Raban Maur, oeuvre claravalienne du xiie siècle," *Mélanges Saint Bernard* [XXIVe Congrès de l'Association bourguignonne de Sociétés savantes (viiie centenaire de la mort de S. Bernard)] (Dijon, 1953), pp. 408–21. The vita has recently been translated by David Mycoff as *The Life of Saint Mary Magdalen*; I use his translation.

38. *PL* 112, col. 1496; Mycoff, *Life*, p. 98.

39. *BHL*, n. 5443.

40. *PL* 112, cols. 1474–75; Mycoff, *Life*, pp. 73–74.

41. *PL* 112, cols. 1495, 1474–75, 1484–85; Mycoff, *Life*, pp. 96, 73–74, 84. Among others who associate Mary Magdalene with prophecy are Rabanus Maurus, *PL* 111, col. 84; Peter Abelard, *PL* 178, p. 485; Iohannes de Biblia: MS BAV Borgh. 24, f. 63v; and Humbert of Romans, *de modo prompte cudendi sermones* in *De eruditione praedicatorum*, Lib. II, ed. Marguerin de La Bigne in *Maxima Bibliotheca Verum Patrum*, vol.

25 (Lyons: Anissonius, 1677), pp. 483–84. It is also significant that the Hebrew prophet Miriam appears in the Magdalene chapel in the lower church of Assisi. For the chapel decoration, see Lorraine C. Schwartz, "The Fresco Decoration of the Magdalen Chapel in the Basilica of St. Francis at Assisi" (Ph.D. diss., University of Indiana, 1980).

42. Apostolate, *PL* 112, cols. 1475, 1494–95; Mycoff, *Life*, pp. 73, 96.

43. "Pro sui Conditoris amore suscepit gaudens exsilium! Est itaque de propriis egressa finibus, Dominum Jesum Christum Deum verum assidue praedicans et eius resurrectionis testificans veritatem"; *PL* 157, cols. 273–74.

44. *Vita apostolico-eremitica, BHL*, nn. 5443–48. According to Mycoff, this happened sometime in eleventh-century Italy; Mycoff, *Life*, p. 6.

45. The *Vita evangelico-apostolica* (*BHL*, n. 5450) fuses together the Cluny homily (*BHL*, n. 5439) with the *Vita apostolico-eremitica* (*BHL*, nn. 5443–48). *Legenda Aurea vulgo Historia Lombardica dicta*, 3d ed., ed. Th. Graesse (Vratislaviae: 1890). I cite the English translation, *The Golden Legend*, 2 vols., trans. William Granger Ryan (Princeton, N.J.: Princeton University Press, 1993), vol. 1. For more on *The Golden Legend*, see Alain Boureau, *La Legende dorée: Le système narratif de Jacques de Voragine (+1298)* (Paris: Éditions du Cerf, 1984); Sherry Reames, *The Legenda Aurea: A Reexamination of Its Paradoxical History* (Madison: University of Wisconsin Press, 1985), p. 101; and Barbara Fleith, "*Legenda aurea:* Destination, utilisateurs, propagation: L'histoire de la diffusion du légendier au XIIIᵉ siècle," in *Raccolte di vite di sante dal XIII al XVIII secolo*, ed. Sofia Boesch Gajano (Fasano di Brindisi: Schena, 1990), pp. 41–48.

46. Carlo Delcorno, "Il racconto agiografico nella predicazione dei secoli XIII-XV," in *Agiografia nell'Occidente Cristiano secoli XIII-XV*, Atti dei Convegni Lincei 48 (Rome: Accademia Nazionale dei Lincei, 1980), pp. 79–114.

47. For the representation of male apostles and preachers, see Roberto Rusconi, "*Forma Apostolorum:* L'immagine del predicator nei movimenti religiosi francesi ed italiani dei secc. xiiᵉ e xiiiᵉ," *Cristianesimo nella Storia* 6 (1985): 513–42.

48. "Quid est igitur: *Noli me tangere* (Ioan. 20: 17)? Noli manum adhibere majoribus; sed vade ad fratres meos, hoc est, ad perfectiores. 'Quicunque enim fecerit voluntatem Patris mei qui in coelis est, ipse meus et frater, et soror, et mater est' (Matt. 12:50). Quia resurrectio non facile nisi a perfectioribus capi potest, fundatioribus huius fidei praerogativa servatur: 'Mulieribus autem docere in Ecclesia non permitto (1 Tim. 2:12); domi viros suos interrogent (1 Cor. 14:35).' Ad eos ergo mittitur qui domestici sunt, et accepit praescripta mandata."; *PL* 15, col. 1939.

49. Michel Lauwers, "'Noli me tangere' Marie Madeleine, Marie d'Oignies et les pénitentes du XIIIᵉ siècle," *MEFRM* 104, no. 1 (1992): 244 n. 183. See also Philippe Buc, "*Vox Clamantis in Deserto?* Pierre le Chantre et la Prédication Laïque," *Revue Mabillon*, n.s. 4, 65 (1993): 5–47.

50. Mystice, *Noli me tangere*, "Noli manum maioribus adhibere, sed vade ad perfectiores qui facile resurrectionem credant. Mulieribus enim in ecclesia docere non permittitur" (*Biblia sacra cum glossa interlineari ordinaria*, vol. 5 [Venice, 1588], p. 241); cited in Lauwers, "'Noli me tangere,'" p. 244.

51. Baptism: *Decreti tertia pars de consecratione*, dist. IV, C. XX; Sacred objects and vestments: *Decreti prima pars*, dist. XXIII, C. XXIV-XXV and cf. *tertia pars*, Dist. I. C. XLI; Host: *tertia pars*, dist. II, XXIX; *Docta et Sancta: prima pars*, dist. XXIII, C. XXIX,

and cf. *tertia pars,* dist. IV, C. XX, *Decretum magistri Gratiani,* in *Corpus Iuris Canonici,* ed., Aemilius Friedberg, 2 vols. (Graz: Akademische Druck und Verlagsanstalt, 1959), vol. 1. Cited in Lauwers, "'Noli me tangere,'" p. 244 nn. 184–86. Lauwers also reminds us that all these interdictions have their origins in late antiquity. Gratian himself cites the authority of the Fourth Council of Carthage, but in fact they originate in the *Statuta ecclesiae antiqua,* a fifth-century document drawing on third- and fourth-century sources. For Gratian's view of the condition of women, see René Metz, "Recherches sur la condition de la femme selon Gratien," in *Studia Gratiana* (*Collectanea Stephan Kuttner,* II) 12 (1967): 379–96.

52. Letter 187, *PL* 216, col. 356. I use the translation of E. Ann Matter, "Innocent III and the Keys to the Kingdom of Heaven," in *Women Priests: A Catholic Commentary on the Vatican Declaration,* ed. Leonard and Arlene Swidler (New York: Paulist Press, 1977), pp. 145–51. The abbess in question ruled the Cistercian house of Las Huelgas.

53. Lib. V, tit. 38, *De Poenitentiis,* cap. 10, *Decretalium Collectiones* in *Corpus Iuris Canonici,* ed. Aemilius Friedberg (Graz: Akademische Druck und Verlagsanstalt, 1959), vol. 2. See also Lauwers, "'Noli me tangere,'" p. 245.

54. *Tertia Pars, questiones* 53–59: "The Resurrection of the Lord," *Summa Theologiae,* 60 vols., ed. Blackfriars (Latin text and English translation) (London: McGraw-Hill, 1964–), vol. 55 (1974), ed. C. Thomas Moore, O.P., esp. pp. 36–40. See also Matter, "Innocent III," p. 148.

55. Nicole Bériou, "La Madeleine dans les sermons parisiens du XIIIe siècle," *MEFRM* 104, no. 1 (1992): 269–340.

56. Both texts are cited in ibid., pp. 301–2 nn. 106–7. Gauthier of Château-Thierry, *De officio predicandi. I: Utrum conveniat viris tantum vel viris et mulieribus* (ca. 1245): "Privilegia paucorum non faciunt legem communem. Vel dicendum quod non predicavit sed fuit prenuntia resurrectionis Christi. . . . Quondam indiguit vel licuit in ecclesia uti predicatione et magisterio virginum ut Catharine tempore et Magdalene et Cecilie et Lucie etc. Propter necessitatem fidei et ecclesie edificande que tunc novella erat, licuit feminis quod tamen non liceret eis si esset plantata sicut modo, et hoc propter defectum predicatorum."

Eustache of Arras, *Quodl.* II, q. 5 (ca. 1263–66): "beata Maria Magdalena et beata Catherina auctoritatem habuerunt a Spiritu sancto ipsis instigante et specialiter mittente, sicut apparuit per officium: ubi enim fides periclitatur, igitur a Spiritu sancto sunt missae, et quod dicit Apostolus, dicendum quod loquitur de mulieribus nuptis, quia sunt in statu communi mulierum, non autem de illis que omnino specialiter electae fuerunt et privilegiatae, et sic etiam intelligitur Glossa."

For an edition of Henry of Ghent and an anonymous *quaestio* on the same subject, see Alcuin Blamires and C. W. Marx, "Woman Not to Preach: A Disputation in British Library MS Harley 31," *Journal of Medieval Latin* 3 (1993): 34–63. See also Alcuin Blamires, "Women and Preaching in Medieval Orthodoxy, Heresy, and Saint's Lives," *Viator* 26 (1995): 135–52.

57. "Circa personam est notandum quod debet esse sexus virilis. 1 Tim. 2: Mulierem docere non permitto. Huius autem ratio est quadruplex. Prima est defectus sensus, de quo non praesumitur in muliere tantum sicut in viro. Secunda est conditio subjectionis quae inflicta est ei: praedicator autem tenet locum excellentem. Tertia est, quia si praedicaret, aspectu suo provocaret ad luxuriam, sicut dicit *Glossa,* hic. Quarta in memoriam stultitiae primae mulieris, de qua Bernardus: Semel docuit, et

totum mundum subvertit"; Humbert of Romans, chap. 12: *de persona praedicatoris*, in *De eruditione praedicatorum*, in *Opera de vita regularis*, ed. Joachim Joseph Berthier, 2 vols. (Rome: Typ. A. Befani, 1888–89), vol. 2, p. 406. For Humbert, see Edward Tracy Brett, *Humbert of Romans: His Life and Views of Thirteenth-Century Society* (Toronto: Pontifical Institute of Medieval Studies, 1984).

58. As Beverly Mayne Kienzle points out, we unfortunately have no evidence from the Waldensian side to support such a claim; see the chapter by Kienzle in this volume.

59. Giordano of Pisa [da Rivalto], *Prediche sulla Genesi recitate in Firenze nel 1304*, ed. Domenico Moreni (Florence: Il Magheri, 1830), p. 175. For Giordano, see Carlo Delcorno, *Giordano da Pisa e l'antica predicazione volgare* (Biblioteca di 'Lettere' Italiane, vol. 14) (Florence, 1975).

60. For the relation between the cult of the Magdalene and the preaching of penance, see Katherine Ludwig Jansen, "Mary Magdalen and the Mendicants: The Preaching of Penance in the Late Middle Ages," *Journal of Medieval History* 21 (1995): 1–25.

61. "Magna fuit consolatio mulieri que primo peccatrix fuit quod illi facta fuerit prima resurrectionis dominice apparatio vel representatio"; *Sermones de sanctis per annum* (Paris: O. Petit, 1542), p. 249. For Hugo of Prato, see André Rayez, "Hugues de Prato," *DS* 7 (1969), cols. 893–94.

62. "Primo apparuit Mariae Magdalenae: animae enim poenitenti prius quam ceteris apparet gratia Domini"; *In Pascha Domini, S. Antonii Pat. Sermones Dominicales et in Solemnitatibus quos mss. saeculi XIII Codicibus qui Patavii servantur*, ed. Antonius Maria Locatelli (Padua: Societas S. Antonii Patavini, 1895), p. 128. For Saint Anthony, see G. Sabatelli, "Antonio da Padova, santo," *Dizionario Biografico degli Italiani* (*DBI*) (Rome: Società Grafica Romana, 1960–), vol. 3 (1961), pp. 561–68.

63. "Voluit primo apparere beate Marie Magdalene ut ostenderet se esse mortuum pro peccatoribus"; MS Antoniana 490, f. 102r. Although many of Servasancto's sermons were published as Bonaventure's, *Sancti Bonaventurae ex ordine Minorum S.R.E. Episcopi Card. Albanen. eximii Ecclesiae Doctoris Operum Tomus. III. Sermones de Tempore ac de Sanctis complectens* (Rome: Vatican Typographia, 1596), this was not one of them. See V. Gamboso, "I sermoni festivi di Servasanto da Faenza nel codice 490 dell'Antoniana," *Il Santo* 13.1 (1973), pp. 55–56. Cf. Siboto: "Voluit autem suam resurrectionem primo omnium manifestare ei que peccatrix extiterat ut daret intelligi quia passus est et resurrexit pro peccatoribus"; MS BAV Vat. lat. 6005, f. 113r. For Siboto, see *Scriptores*, vol. 3 (1980), pp. 338–40. Ubertino: "nunc etiam ad nunciandum sue resurrectionis gloriam ipsismet dilectis discipulis magdalenam quondam peccatricem elegit"; Ubertino of Casale, *Arbor Vitae Crucifixae* (Venice: De Bonettis de Papa, 1485), book 4, chap. 29, unpaginated. Cf: "Quante enim pietatis fuit: & consolationis ad peccatores devotos: quod primo apparere voluit magdalene. Et ut huius pietatis exprimeretur affectio. . . . Vide quia qui propter peccatores mortuus est: peccatoribus sue resurrectionis gloriam conquisiuit. Unde & huic principali peccatrici primo apparuit"; ibid. For Ubertino, see Frédégard Callaey, *L'Idéalisme franciscain spirituel au xive siècle: Étude sur Ubertin de Casale* (Louvain: Bureau du Recueil, 1911); and D. L. Douie, *The Nature and Effect of the Heresy of the Fraticelli* (Manchester, England: University Press, 1932), pp. 120–52.

64. "Et ne aliquis desperet, Mariam illam peccatricem, dominam luxuriae, vanae gloriae matrem, sororem Marthae et Lazari in exemplum assumite, quae postmodum Apostolorum apostola meruit nuncupari"; Pseudo-Augustine, *PL* 40, col. 1298.

65. Eadmer of Canterbury (d. 1128) reminds us yet again how multiple variations on the theme of Marian identity were still possible in the Middle Ages. In his treatise on the Virgin Mary, he concludes his chapter on Prudence by observing that she is called both *apostolorum apostola* and *evangelistarum evangelista; PL* 159, col. 582.

66. *Sermo 88, Quaresimale Fiorentino 1305–1306*, ed. Carlo Delcorno (Florence: Sansoni, 1974), p. 420.

67. "Vidit ergo Maria resurrectionem Domini: et prima vidit, et credidit. Vidit et Maria Magdalena, quamvis adhuc ista nutaret"; *Liber de Virginitate, PL* 16, col. 283.

68. "Quintus est quia post resurrectionem suam primo Magdalena apparuit; videlicet post apparitionem matris de cuius apparitionem evangelia tacent"; MS Antoniana 490, f. 102r. Another Franciscan, Bernardino of Siena, would argue similarly: "La prima apparizione si deve credere che fosse alla sua diletta madre, la Vergine Maria. Non lo dicono gli evangelisti; non dicendolo però essi lo affermano più che se lo dicessero"; *Giorno di Pasqua, Prediche della Settimana Santa. Firenze 1425*, ed. Marco Bartoli (Milan: Figlie di San Paolo, 1995), p. 242.

69. "Primo per auctoritatem. Sedulius enim magnus & antiquus doctor ecclesiae, agens de Christi apparitione dicit. . . . Secundo per ecclesiae romanae antiquam & probatam consuetudinem. Summus enim pontifex ad S. Mariam maiorem in die Pasche primam stationem celebrat, per hoc iuveniens ad beatam Mariam primam factam fuisse apparitionem. Tertio per quandam moralem rationem. Deus enim praecepit. Honora patrem & matrem. Sed si esset aliquis filius in ultra marinis partibus constitutus, de quo mater intellexisset quod mortuus esset, & tandem sanus rediens personas extraneas visitaret & ad matrem tribulatam ultimo accederet, iste bonus filius non esset, nec matrem honorasset. Sic etiam Christus matrem non multum honorasse videretur, si prius alios de sua resurrectione laetificasset, & tandem matri desolatae apparuisset"; *Sermo I* (*in die Sancto Paschae*), *Sermones quadragesimales* (Venice: Ioannis Baptista Somaschis, 1571), p. 209. On Jacobus of Voragine, see Ernest C. Richardson, *Materials for a Life of Jacopo da Voragine* (New York: H. W. Wilson, 1935); and more recently, Carla Casagrande and Silvana Vecchio, "Cronache, morale, predicazione: Salimbene da Parma e Jacopo da Varagine," *Studi Medievali* 30 (1989): 749–88.

70. Domenico Cavalca, *Vite de' Santi Padri*, ed. Bartolommeo Sorio and A. Racheli (Milan: l'Ufficio Generale di Commissioni ed Annunzi, n.d.), p. 383. There is an incomplete English translation attributed to "Pseudo-Cavalca," *The Life of Saint Mary Magdalen, Translated from the Italian of an Unknown Fourteenth-Century Writer*, trans. Valentina Hawtrey (London: John Lane, Bodley Head, 1904), p. 284. In the introduction, Vernon Lee suggests that the provenance of this text is Franciscan. I would incline more to Carlo Delcorno's view, which attributes such *vitae* to Cavalca or at least to his "bottega." See the entry "Cavalca, Domenico" in *DBI*, vol. 22 (1979), pp. 577–86.

The Franciscan *Meditations on the Life of Christ* narrates a touching reunion of mother and son in which the Virgin examines her son's wounds and asks poignantly whether they still cause him pain. After an intimate conversation, Jesus asks permission to console the distraught Magdalene. "'My blessed Son, go in peace and console her,'" says the Virgin, "'for she loves you very much and grieves . . . at your death; but remember to come back to me,' and embracing Him, she let Him go"; *Meditations on the Life of Christ: An Illustrated Manuscript of the Fourteenth Century,* trans. and ed. Isa Ragusa and Rosalie B. Green (Princeton, N.J.: Princeton University Press, 1961), p. 362.

71. "Item quamvis eciam Scriptura dicat, quod Christi resurreccionem Magdalena et apostoli prius viderunt, sine dubio tamen credendum est, quod sua mater dignissima antequam illi veraciter hoc sciebat et priusquam illi eum viuum resurrexisse a mortuis vidit"; *Opera Minora II,* ed. Sten Eklund (Stockholm: Almquist and Wiksells, 1972), p. 129. My thanks to Stephan Borgehammar for supplying me with this text.

72. "Credendum est enim quod resurgens christus primo ei apparavit licet scriptura hoc taceat"; *Sermo 255, Opus Postillarum et Sermonum Iordani de Tempore* (Strasbourg, 1483), unpaginated.

73. Giovanni of Capistrano is credited with the "Corona Francescana." See *Chronica Fratris Nicolai Glassberger OFM, obs.* in *Analecta Franciscana 2* (1888): 34; and Leone Bracaloni, O.F.M., "Origine, evoluzione ed affermazione della Corona Francescana Mariana," *Studi Francescani* (1932): 257–95, esp. 274. I thank Massimo Ceresa for these references. The Franciscan rosary was one of the traditions invoked to explain John Paul II's statement on Easter Monday, 1994, when he shocked thousands of pilgrims gathered in the piazza of Saint Peter's by remarking, "Even if Scripture does not mention it, there is the conviction that the first announcement of the risen Christ was made to the Madonna." This pronouncement apparently caused so much consternation among the faithful that the pope in his next public address two days later corrected himself, saying, "The first person to whom the risen Christ appeared was Mary Magdalene"; *La Repubblica,* April 7, 1994, p. 22.

74. "Non se manifestaverat dominus adhuc discipulis nec ipsi genitrici. Ambrosius tamen quarto *de virginibus* dicit eum primo matri apparuisse per hec verba: 'Vidit Maria resurrectionem domini et prima vidit,' et statim adiungit 'vidit et Maria Magdalene quamvis adhuc ista nutaret'"; MS BAV Borgh. 24, f. 63r. Johannes Baptist Schneyer, *Repertorium der lateinischen Sermones des Mittelalters für die Zeit von 1150–1350* (*RLS*), 11 vols. (Münster-Westfalen: Aschendorffsche, 1969–1990), vol. 3, p. 91. On Iohannes, see *Scriptores,* vol. 2 (1975), pp. 385–86. A great number of hymns lauded the Magdalene's privileged position as first witness as well. See Szövérffy, "Peccatrix," p. 119.

75. "In hoc eam privilegiavit dominus pre ceteris apostolis et etiam beata virgine quod primo ei apparuit et quod tam cito. Secundum privilegium eius est quod de officio alicuius mulieris vel etiam alicuius alterius personae non legimus dominum tantum se commendasse"; MS AGOP XIV.35, f. 181r; *RLS,* vol. 4, p. 947. Cardinal Joannes Baptista Pitra printed excerpts of this sermon in *Analecta Novissima: Spicilegii Solesmensis Altera Continuatio,* 2 vols. (Frascati: Typus Tusculanus, 1883), vol. 2, pp. 341–42. For the title *predicatrix veritatis,* see his sermon, edited by Bériou, "La Madeleine," p. 336. For Eudes, see Marie-Madeleine Lebreton, "Eudes de Châteauroux," *DS,* vol. 4 (1960), cols. 1675–78. Humbert of Romans: "Item tempore resurrectionis, primo apparuit mulieri, scilicet, Magdalenae"; *de modo prompte cudendi sermones,* p. 503.

76. "Primo ei resurgens Christus apparuit et apostolorum apostola[m] fecit"; MS

BAV Barb. lat. 2300, f. 18r. The *Epilogus in Gesta Sanctorum* (ca. 1244) was composed mainly of Italian and Dominican saints; see G. Abbate, "Il 'Liber Epilogorum' di fra' Bartolomeo da Trento," in *Miscellanea Pio Paschini* I (Rome, 1948). For a critical edition, see *Bartolomeo da Trento: Domenicano e Agiografo Medievale*, ed. Domenicano Gobbi (Trent: Gruppo Culturale Civis, 1990).

77. "Et facta est apostolorum apostola per quam dominus resurrectionis sue gaudium nunciavit"; BAV MS Arch. Cap. S. Petri D. 211, f. 78r. This sermon, the *incipit* of which is *Rogabat Jesum quidam phariseus ut manducaret cum illo,* is not included in either of the two sixteenth-century editions of the *Opera Omnia,* nor is it found in Migne, *PL,* vol. 217, which is based largely on the two earlier editions. Nor does Schneyer include it in the *RLS.* Barthélemy Hauréau, however, published a partial transcript of it from a damaged MS in *Notices et extraits de quelques manuscrits latins de la Bibliothèque Nationale,* 2 vols. (Paris: Klincksieck, 1890), vol. 1, pp. 173–79. My edition of the full sermon is forthcoming in *Revue Mabillon.*

Because the title *apostolorum apostola* is ubiquitous in medieval texts, it is impossible to list its every appearance. It shall suffice to say that it is found in the writings of preachers, popes, and moralists such as Jacques of Vitry, Honorius III, Gregory IX, Franco Sachetti, Remigio of Girolami, Ubertino of Casale, Pseudo-Augustine, and Saint Antoninus Pierozzi, among many others.

78. *Praedicatrix et annunciatrix fidei:* Matteo d'Aquasparta, MS Assisi 682, 193r; *praedicatrix privilegiata:* Remigio de' Girolami, MS Flor. Naz. Conv. Sopp. D. 1. 297, f. 232r; *doctrix:* Iohannes de Biblia, MS BAV Borgh. 24, f. 61r; *doctrix apostolorum:* Siboto, MS BAV Vat. lat. 6005, 112v; *magistra:* Iohannes de Biblia, ibid.; *prenuncia:* Petrus de Palude, *Sermones Thesauri Novi de sanctis* (Strasburg: Martinus Flach, 1488), unpaginated (Sermo 105); *testis veritatis:* Siboto, MS BAV Vat. lat. 6005, 112v; *seminatrix:* anonymous, MS British Library, Add. 15682, f. 108r; *sapientiae schola:* Bernardino of Siena, *Sermo XLVI, Opera Omnia,* 9 vols. (Quaracchi: Typographia Collegii S. Bonaventurae, 1950–1965), vol. 3 (1956), p. 438. Similar titles show up in hymns: *Marsiliae apostola, vitae praedicatrix,* and *testis crucis Christi;* see Szövérffy, "Peccatrix," p. 92.

79. Humbert of Romans: "Ipsa tamen ex privilegio singulari hoc est officium executa. Predicavit enim Marsilie gentibus . . . sicut dicit historia"; *Liber de eruditione predicatorum,* ed. Simon Tugwell, O.P. (Oxford: Oxford University Press, forthcoming). I am indebted to Fr. Tugwell for providing me with his edition of the text.

Alberto of Padova: "Facta est autem Maria Magdalena resurrectionis Christi praenuncia, & verborum ipsius relatrix, cum tamen apostolus prohibeat mulierem docere & predicare. Quod speciale privilegium merita gratiarum beatae Mariae Magdalenae accumulant"; *Evangelia Totius Anni Dominicalia* (Turin: Antonius Ranotus, 1529), p. 172.

80. Iohannes de Biblia: "Licet enim secundum legem comunem mulieri docere non permittat apostolus, ex speciali tamen privilegio doctoris officium ei commisit spiritus sanctus. Unde etiam in populo iudeorum alique mulieres prophetie spiritum et officium habuerunt et apud gentiles sibelle . . . extiterunt"; MS BAV Borgh. 24, f. 63v; *RLS,* vol. 3, p. 91.

81. "Unde post pentecostem legitur tanquam apostola populis predicasse. Quod tunc aliis mulieribus ab apostolo prohibetur dicente (1 Cor. 14) 'Mulieres in ecclesia taceantur'"; MS BAV Barb. lat. 513, f. 98v; *RLS,* vol. 3, p. 377. For Giovanni, see *Scriptores,* vol. 2 (1975), pp. 539–43.

82. "Sancta Maria Magdalena cum diutius verbum Dei predicasset, maximeque cum ad eius notitiam pervenisset quod Apostolus 'mulieres in ecclesiis tacere precepisset,' contemplationi arctius vacare desiderans, monente Domino, ad eremum asperrimum se contulit"; *Speculum Historiale* (vol. 4 of *Speculum Maioris*) (Graz: Akademische Druck und Verlagsanstalt, 1965; reprint of Douai, 1624), book 9, chap. 102, p. 359.

83. "Massilia conversa sua predicatione ubi possimus dire quod quo tempore homines et mulieres de Massilia sunt salvati mediantibus suis meritis. Sunt salvati et sic incomparabiliter plures quam dampnavit"; MS BAV Borgh. 138, f. 145v; *RLS*, vol. 9, p. 96. I am grateful to Fr. L.-J. Bataillon for bringing this manuscript to my attention.

84. See Buc, "Vox," p. 15 n. 31: "Mulier [quamvis docta et sancta viros], usque in conventu [docere non presumat], publico, scilicet in ecclesia ascendendo pulpitum, et faciendo sermonem ad populum."

85. The fresco is one scene taken from a Trecento narrative cycle in a chapel dedicated to the saint. The painter has been tentatively identified as Pietro of Milano. See Enrico Castelnuovo, "Appunti per la Storia della pittura gotica in Piemonte," *Arte Antica e Moderna* 13/16 (1961): 97–111. He reproduces some of the frescoes as figs. 33b, 34a, 34b, 35a, and 35b. The predella of the altar of Saint Lazarus (1481) was commissioned by King René d'Anjou and depicts the life of Mary Magdalene and her brother Lazarus. One of the bas-reliefs represents Mary Magdalene in the pulpit preaching to the citizens of Marseilles. See the catalogue *Le Roi René en son temps (1382–1481)* (Aix-en-Provence: Musée Granet-Palais de Malte, 1981), pp. 158–62. Carla Ricci made the identification.

86. For a reproduction of this image, see George Kaftal, *Iconography of the Saints in Central Italian Painting* (Florence: Sansoni, 1965), p. 767. For the fresco cycle, see Roberto Quirino, "Un argomento di pittura spoletina fra tre e quattrocento: Il Maestro dei Cavalari," *Esercizi: Arte, Musica, Spettacolo* 5 (1982): 20–33.

87. "Et dicitur quod habuit quadruplicem coronam. . . . Secundo coronam auream quam datur doctoribus unde in auro notatur sapientia secundum Gregorium et ipsa docuit sapientiam et scientiam fidei christiane. De qua corona dicitur ecclesiasti"; *Sermones de Laudibus Sanctorum* (Venice: Pelegrinus de Pasqualibus, 1493), pp. 79–80.

88. "Unde patet quod virginibus, martyribus et predicatoribus debet aureola. Martyres enim vincunt mundum; virgines carnem; predicatores diabolum quem non solum de se sed etiam eum expellunt de cordibus aliorum"; MS Balliol 230, f. 97r. For Hugo, see *Scriptores*, vol. 2 (1975), pp. 260–69.

89. British Library, MS Add. 15682, f. 144r. For the significance of the triple aureola, see Antonio Volpato, "Il tema agiografico della triplice aureola nei secoli XIII–XV," in *Culto dei Santi Istituzioni e classi sociali in età preindustriale,* ed. Sofia Boesch Gajano and Lucia Sebastiani (Aquila: L.U. Japadre, 1984), pp. 509–26. See also Antonio Volpato, "*Corona Aurea* e *Corona aureola*: ordini e meriti nella ecclesiologia medioevale," *Bullettino dell'Istituto Storico Italiano per il Medio Evo* 91 (1984): 115–82.

90. Volpato, "Il tema," pp. 514, 521 n. 18. Despite the calendar reform of 1969, Catherine of Alexandria is still venerated as the patron saint of scholars, male and female.

91. "Katherine of Alexandria and Mass Communication in Germany: Woman as Intellectual," in N. Bériou and D. L. d'Avray, *Modern Questions about Medieval Sermons: Essays on Marriage, Death, History and Sanctity* (Biblioteca di Medioevo Latino, 11) (Spoleto: Centro italiano di studi sull'alto medioevo, 1995). I am grateful to David d'Avray for sharing this essay with me before its publication.

Mary Magdalene's feast became an obligation in Paris around 1268. See Bériou, "Marie-Madeleine," p. 274 n. 13. See also C. R. Cheney, "Rules for Observance of Feast Days," *Bulletin of the Institute of Historical Research* 34 (1961): 117–47. In a letter dated June 27, 1228, Gregory IX urged the prelates and clergy of Germany to celebrate the Magdalene with a solemn feast. See André Simon, *L'ordre des Pénitentes de Ste Marie-Madeleine en Allemagne au XIIIᵉ siècle* (Thèse, Fribourg: Imprimerie et Librairie de l'oeuvre de Saint-Paul, 1918), p. 26.

Haskins lists a number of retributive punishments for those who failed to honor Mary Magdalene properly on her feast day. One poor peasant was struck by lightning; two women were flogged; and the town of Béziers was attacked by crusaders. See Haskins, *Mary Magdalen*, p. 135.

92. See Joanna Cannon, "Simone Martini, the Dominicans and the Early Sienese Polyptych," *Journal of the Warburg and Courtauld Institutes* 45 (1982): 69–93. She does not, however, connect the Magdalene to this mission.

93. Enzo Carli, *Il Museo di Pisa* (Pisa: Pacini, 1974), pp. 51–52. He reproduces color plates of the Magdalene and Katherine as figs. XI and XII. He argues that the polyptych was completed by 1319 and precedes a similar one made by Simone Martini for the Dominicans in Orvieto in 1320.

94. The Dominican Order claimed Mary Magdalene as patron at the General Chapter of Venice in 1297. See William R. Bonniwell, *A History of the Dominican Liturgy, 1215–1945*, 2d ed. (New York: Joseph F. Wagner, 1945), p. 220; Daniel-Antonin Mortier, *Histoire des maîtres généraux de l'ordre des frères prêcheurs*, 7 vols. (Paris: Alphonse Picard et fils, 1903–14), vol. 2 (1904), p. 345. Mortier concedes that there is no official decree proclaiming the saint as patron of the Order; however, in their liturgical calendar the following words can be found: *Sanctae Mariae Magdalenae Protectricis Ordinis Nostri*. He observes: "Le corps de Madeleine est sous la garde des Prêcheurs, l'ordre des Prêcheurs, sous la garde de Madeleine." The royal convent at Saint-Maximin still remembers the Magdalene as *apostolorum apostola*. In the old chapel (now used for conferences) there is a fresco by Jean Martin-Roch that depicts Mary Magdalene announcing the good news to the new apostles, the Dominican Order. It dates from 1940–41.

The great Dominican convent at Pisa that produced the likes of Domenico Cavalca and Giordano of Pisa was under the patronage of Santa Caterina. For its history, see *Cronica antique conventus sanctae Catharinae de Pisis*, ed. Francesco Bonaini, in *Archivio storico italiano*, ser. 1, vol. 6, fasc. 2 (1845), pp. 399–593.

95. Servasancto: "Sed dic quomodo per duo annos predicavit in Marsilia et quomodo destructa sunt omnia ydola"; MS Antoniana 490, f. 103r. Peregrinus: "Tunc in civitate et in terra sua omnia ydola destruentes multas ecclesias eo struxerunt"; *RLS*, vol. 4, p. 147, MS BAV Pal. lat. 465, f. 156r. For Peregrinus, see *Scriptores*, vol. 3 (1980), pp. 211–21.

A chapel dedicated to Mary Magdalene beside la Vieille Major in Marseilles commemorated her evangelization. It was supposedly built on the ruined temple of Diana of Ephesus (against whom Saint Paul preached in Acts 19:23–40). At this church the canons recited a little "cantinella" in Provençal during an Easter vespers procession that went from la Vieille Major to the chapel. Verse 14 commemorated her role as apostle of the apostles:

> En prêchant les louanges du Christ,
> Elle convertissait les païens
> Et arracha Marseille à l'erreur
> Ceux qui l'entendaient prêcher
> Se convertissaient avec amour.

Bernard Laluque, *Marseille fut-elle evangelisée par une femme?* (Marseilles: Le Comité du Vieux Marseille, 1986), pp. 350, 368.

96. BAV MS Vat. lat. 8541, f. 103v. For the legendary, see *Heiligenleben Ungarisches Legendarium Cod. Vat. lat. 8541,* facsimile ed, and commentary (Zürich: Belser, 1990). Bergamo: *Pittura a Bergamo dal Romanico al Neoclassicismo,* ed. Mina Gregori (Milan: Silvana Ed. d'Arte, 1991), pp. 9, 74, 226; *I Pittori Bergamaschi dal XIII al XIX secolo,* 13 vols. (Bergamo: Bolis, 1975–1992), vol. 1: *Le origini,* ed. Miklós Boskovits, pp. 408–14. My thanks to Lester Little, who unearthed the Bergamo references.

97. "omniaque idolorum templa destruens cum omni populo baptisma suscepit"; *Catalogus Sanctorum,* p. 257.

Thomas Aquinas argued that in exigent cases a woman could perform a baptism if no man could be found. See Kari Elisabeth Børresen, *Subordination and Equivalence: The Nature and Role of Woman in Augustine and Thomas Aquinas,* trans. Charles H. Talbot (Washington, D.C.: University Press of America, 1981), p. 39.

98. Laluque, *Marseille,* p. 404.

99. Josef A. Jungmann, *The Mass of the Roman Rite,* 2 vols. (New York: Benziger, 1950–55), vol. 1, p. 470 n. 55. According to Jungmann, some medieval liturgists advised that the Credo be said on Mary Magdalene's feast day because of her designation as *apostolorum apostola.* It was recited for all feasts of the Lord from Christmas through Pentecost, the feasts of the Virgin Mary, the feasts of the apostles, and on All Saints' and All Souls' Days.

100. At the convent for repentant prostitutes dedicated to Mary Magdalene in Avignon, according to the statutes of 1367, the antiphon was sung daily after matins, mass, and vespers. See P. Pansier, *L'oeuvre des repenties à Avignon du XIIIe au XVIIIe siècle* (Paris: Honoré Champion and J. Roumanille, 1910), p. 114.

101. "Notandum quod sicut olim fuerunt non solum prophetae, sed etiam prophetisse . . . et non solum Apostoli, sed & Apostolae, ut cantatur de Magdalena"; in *de modo prompte cudendi sermones circa omne hominum genus* in *De eruditione praedicatorum,* p. 484.

102. No. 40 in *Laude Cortonesi dal secolo XIII al XV* (Biblioteca della Rivista di Storia e letteratura religiosa. Studi e testi, vol. 5), ed. Giorgio Varanini et al. (Florence: Leo S. Olschki, 1981), p. 280.

103. *Sacre Rappresentazioni dei secoli XIV, XV e XVI,* ed. Alessandro d'Ancona, 3 vols. (Florence: Successori le Monnier, 1872), vol. 1, p. 404.

104. Jacobus of Voragine, *The Golden Legend,* p. 357.

105. "Pseudo-Cavalca," *The Life of St. Mary Magdalen,* pp. 100–102.

106. "Et hac vocatione vocati sunt apostoli (Matt. 4). . . . Hac vocatione sunt fratres

minores qui relinquerunt mundum et se ipsos. Hac vocatione vocavit Magdalenam";
MS Antoniana 490, f. 101r.

107. *Il Libro di Lazero & Martha & Magdalena* (Florence: Francesco Buonaccorsi,
1490), unpaginated. Among other sources, the Dominican hagiographer Bartholomew of Trent, O.P., in his *Epilogus in Gesta Sanctorum*, said that Mary Magdalene
"*spiritum sanctum cum aliis recepit*"; MS BAV Barb. lat. 2300, f. 18r. See also Geoffrey
of Vendôme, *PL* 157, pp. 273–74; and Pseudo-Rabanus Maurus, *PL* 112, p. 981. Hymns
also told of her presence at Pentecost; see Szövérffy, "Peccatrix," p. 100.

108. Susan Haskins misrepresents the historical record when she speaks of the
"brief resurgence" of the title in the Middle Ages; see Haskins, *Mary Magdalen*, p. 67.

109. Michel Camille, *The Gothic Idol: Ideology and Image-making in Medieval Art* (Cambridge: Cambridge University Press, 1989), p. 211.

110. The conception of "popular religion" that seeks to distinguish between "high"
and "low" culture or lay and clerical cultures has had its share of critics; see Natalie
Zemon Davis, "Some Tasks and Themes in the Study of Popular Religion," in *The
Pursuit of Holiness in Late Medieval and Renaissance Religion* (Studies in Medieval and
Renaissance Thought), ed. C. Trinkhaus and H. Oberman (Leiden: E. J. Brill, 1974),
pp. 307–36; J.-C. Schmitt, "'Religion populaire' et 'culture folklorique,'" *Annales E.S.C.*
31 (1976): 941–53; and Leonard Boyle, O.P., "Popular Piety in the Middle Ages: What
Is Popular?" *Florilegium* 4 (1982): 184–93.

111. Elisabeth Moltmann-Wendel, *The Women around Jesus* (New York: Crossroad,
1986), pp. 80–81. There is no evidence to support the theory that Cathar women
were proponents of the cult of the Magdalene, particularly the apostolic Magdalene.
Indeed, one of their alleged blasphemous beliefs was that she was Christ's concu-
bine. See Carolus du Plessis d'Argentré, *Collectio Judiciorum de Novis Erroribus, qui ab
initio duodecimi seculi post Incarnationem Verbi, usque ad annum 1713*, 3 vols. (Paris: Lam-
bertus Coffin, 1724–36), vol. 1, p. 172.

112. Cited in Millard Meiss, *Painting in Florence and Siena after the Black Death* (Princeton, N.J.: Princeton University Press, 1951), pp. 105–6. Of related interest is Jeffrey
F. Hamburger, "The Use of Images in the Pastoral Care of Nuns: The Case of Hein-
rich Suso and the Dominicans," *Art Bulletin* 71, no. 1 (1989): 20–46.

113. Letter 61 in *Le lettere di S. Caterina da Siena*, ed. Niccolò Tommaseo, 4 vols.
(Florence: G. Barbèra, 1860), vol. 1, pp. 264–68. Karen Scott has argued that Catherine's own mission as *apostola* was at least partially shaped by recourse to the Magdalene's apostolic career; see Scott, "St. Catherine of Siena, 'Apostola,'" *Church History*
61, no. 1 (1992): 34–46, esp. 42; and Scott, "*Io Catarina*, Ecclesiastical Politics and
Oral Culture in the Letters of Catherine of Siena," in *Dear Sister: Medieval Women and
the Epistolary Genre*, ed. Karen Cherewatuk and Ulrike Wiethaus (Philadelphia: University of Pennsylvania Press, 1993), pp. 87–121, esp. 111–12. Pulpit: cited in Scott, "*Io
Catarina*," p. 111. To Raymond: Letter 65, *Epistolario*, ed. Eugenio Dupre Theseider,
vol. 1 (Rome: Tipografia del Senato, 1940), p. 275.

114. "Magdalena predicatrix fuit apostolis resurrectionis dominice. Ideo non debet
homo negligere verba mulieris"; cited in Bériou, "La Madeleine," p. 279 n. 33.

115. She concluded: "Some foolish preachers teach that God first appeared to
a woman because He knew well that she did not know how to keep quiet so that this
way the news of His resurrection would be spread more rapidly. [But they are] fools
who said this. It is not enough for them to attack women. They impute even to Jesus

Christ such blasphemy, as if to say that He wished to reveal this great perfection and dignity though a vice. I do not know how a man could dare to say this, even in jest, as God should not be brought in on such joking matters." Christine de Pisan, *The Book of the City of Ladies,* trans. Earl Jeffrey Richards (New York: Persea Books, 1982), pp. 28–29.

PART TWO

The Middle Ages

FOUR

The Prostitute-Preacher

Patterns of Polemic against Medieval Waldensian Women Preachers

Beverly Mayne Kienzle

Geoffroy of Auxerre (d. 1188?), secretary and later successor to Bernard as abbot of Clairvaux, included in his writings various first- and secondhand accounts of historical events. One of his reports from around 1180 concerns two women from the French city of Clermont who were disciplined by their local bishop after he found them preaching in his diocese. The bishop reportedly compelled the women with threats and arguments to renounce their sect. At some later point, according to Geoffroy, the women confronted the same bishop in public, hurling insults at him and shouting blasphemous statements. One of their comments was taken down as evidence of their licentious behavior, that they deserved to be called prostitutes and merited comparison with the woman prophet Jezebel denounced in the Book of Revelation.[1] The accusations made against the women of Clermont because of their public preaching link them to women of other centuries and reveal disturbing patterns of rhetoric that are analyzed in this essay.

Although no other known source records the event recounted by Geoffroy of Auxerre, the fact that the women preached agrees with what we know of the early followers of Peter Valdes. Waldensianism began in 1173 as a primarily lay apostolic movement when Peter Valdes, inspired by the conversion story of Saint Alexis, decided to follow Matthew 19:21 literally: He sold his possessions, renounced his worldly life and his family, and gathered followers who joined him in practicing voluntary poverty and preaching the Gospel. A group of Waldensians journeyed to Rome, presenting themselves at the Third Lateran Council (1179) to seek approval for their way of life and permission for their preaching. Pope Alexander III affirmed their way of life but cautioned them not to preach without authorization. But the Waldensians, who asserted that obedience was owed to God alone and not to human authorities (Acts 5:29), continued to preach.[2] To ensure that the good news could be told by all, they had the Scriptures and certain patristic texts translated into the vernacular.[3] The Waldensians' preaching was reportedly simple, a repetition of gospel passages in the vernacular augmented by the denunciation of sin and exhortation to repent. Yet unauthorized preachers were seen as threats to the established church.[4] Their evangelizing led to their expulsion from the city of Lyons and eventually to their condemnation in the 1184 decree, *Ad abolendam,* issued jointly at Verona by Pope Lucius III and the emperor Frederick Barbarossa, who was reconciled with the papacy after several years of schism (1169–77).[5] The proliferation of literature directed against heresy, from the late twelfth century onward, repeatedly condemned the Waldensians for the unauthorized preaching they advocated for all believers, including women.

Until recently, historians of the medieval Waldensians have not devoted much attention to the material about women's participation in the movement. A groundbreaking study was done in 1962 and was followed by an article in 1980; recently two reexaminations of the material have appeared, and the role of Waldensian women in the later Middle Ages has also been reconsidered.[6] Thus far no new sources for the early women followers of Valdes have been discovered; instead the same materials have been read from different perspectives, but primarily with regard to their merits as historical evidence and not within the context of polemics against women preaching.

Like the report from Geoffroy of Auxerre, information about the early Waldensians comes primarily from their opponents. The appearance of the Waldensians and other dissenting religious movements spurred the production of polemical literature: first treatises and sermon collections, and then inquisitors' manuals designed to assist with identifying heretics, preaching against them, and interrogating them. These works were directed first to an audience that was already convinced of their correctness. However, because members of that audience were also preachers, the argumentation provided models for persuading a larger public. There are of course problems inherent in using polemical literature to reconstruct history, but for this period we do not have other texts to provide a balance and so use what we have with caution. The sources fall into two broad categories: (1) texts of various genres that incorporate reports of what is seen as deviant religious behavior; and (2) theological arguments based on Scripture or patristic sources. Passages in the first category range in length from a line or two to a paragraph embedded in a longer work and provide a glimpse, albeit biased, of what was actually or reportedly happening; those of the second type can be used to determine what biblical and other texts the Waldensians used to justify their preaching. The earliest such polemical sources we have are the account cited from Geoffroy of Auxerre, which is included in a collection of sermons on the Apocalypse, and a treatise written in the late twelfth century, the *Adversus Waldensium sectam liber* by Bernard, Premonstratensian abbot of Fontcaude.[7] Because of limitations on space, this essay draws primarily on these important writings and discusses one other work: the *Summa adversus Catharos et Valdenses* (ca. 1241) of Moneta of Cremona. Brief reference is made to other texts that confirm the preaching activity of Waldensian women.

Proposed here is a rereading of the sources with the aim of establishing links to Christian women in other centuries who encountered opposition to their preaching. The available sources are examined chronologically with a view to answering two questions: (1) What attitudes, textual authorities, and language were used to condemn women's preaching? (2) What were the authorities—role models and texts—that these twelfth-century women saw as justification for their spreading the word of God? The analysis in this study incorporates R. I. Moore's insights on fear and persecution but extends them to investigate different texts and to focus on attacks aimed at women. Those attacks reveal a deeply rooted fear that allowing women a voice of authority in matters of religion would subvert a social and religious structure grounded in their lack of power and convinced of their fundamental subordination, sinfulness, and propensity for seduction. Examination of the arguments of the polemical texts draws on Perelman and Olbrechts-Tyteca's *New Rhetoric*.[8]

GEOFFROY OF AUXERRE

Looking first to Geoffroy of Auxerre's account and its context, we see that his denunciation of the women preachers is preceded by a general condemnation of lay preaching within the Waldensian movement.[9] Yet women are more severely condemned than their male counterparts because of the close association Geoffroy makes between preaching women and Jezebel, queen of Israel and prophet in the Book of Revelation. Through Saint Jerome's explanation of her name as flowing blood and excrement, she represents abundant iniquity and impurity.[10] No wonder that Geoffroy remarks: "Paul spoke well when he forbade women from speaking in churches and said they should ask questions of their husbands at home." He adds his own emphasis: "at home," he says, "not outside"; "'they should ask questions,' not presume to teach." The questions are not to be asked "of each other," but "of husbands"; and finally, "not any husbands whatsoever," but "their own."[11] Next Geoffroy's offensive turns to the women followers of Valdes, described in the words of 2 Timothy 3:6: "wretched little women, burdened with sins," "curious and verbose, forward, shameless, and impudent," who "enter the houses of other people."[12] The Latin word *mulierculae* accurately translates the Greek *gynaikária*, a derogatory diminutive, and biblical scholars see in the background of 1 and 2 Timothy controversies over women's teaching in the early church. Thus Geoffroy has recourse to a passage that is perfectly suited for his position.[13] We recall also that his larger context is a commentary on the Apocalypse. The activity of women preachers is a sign that the social reversal signaling the end of the world could be at hand. He argues from the reality of the biblical text but also constructs a new reality, forcing the events of his day into the mold of the authoritative text and threatening divine retribution for this deviant behavior.[14]

As Geoffroy turns to the two women of Clermont, the text takes a narrative form.[15] He reports that the bishop of Clermont was passing through a crowd of wicked followers (of Valdes) and encountered the two women who reproached him as gravely as they could and upbraided him because he had forced them with threats and arguments to renounce their sect after he found them preaching in his diocese. They hurled insults at him, uttered shameless blasphemies, and made a public statement, which Geoffroy reports in Latin:

> Post praedicationem cotidie lautius epulantes, noctibus pene singulis novos nobis eligebamus amasios, nullius obnoxiae, sine sollicitudine, sine labore, sine ullo vitae periculo tempora transigentes, in quibus nunc ancillae dominorum cotidie mori periclitamur, et variis miserae subiacemus aerumnis.[16]

An approximate English translation reads:

> After the preaching every day [we were] feasting splendidly; almost every night we were choosing new lovers for ourselves; bothersome to no one, without care, without toil; passing time without any danger to life; now as servants of masters we are in danger of death every day, and wretched, we will be subject to various hardships.

To Geoffroy, this statement demonstrated the women's sinfulness. Historians have noted rightly both its stereotypical accusation of promiscuity and its use of folkloric motifs—the world upside down and the land of plenty ("le pays de cocagne").[17] More can be said about the passage, however, in analyzing how elements of truth might have been distorted by the attitude and the language of polemic.

The first part of the statement can be divided into seven units: We preached (or someone preached). We feasted splendidly. We had new lovers every night. We obeyed no one. We had no worries. We did not work. We passed our time out of danger. A contrast in time and circumstance signaled by *nunc*—"now"—joins these seven units to the next three: We are subject to masters; we risk death; we will subject ourselves to various hardships. The contrast between then and now describes the difference between great freedom with high living and subjection with hardship. That contrast marked by *nunc* is expressed with the opposition of the Latin imperfect tense and the present and future.

Examining the components of the accusation, we find that three of the seven are consonant with the Waldensian model of piety, two are not, and two refer to changes in circumstances. Specifically, preaching, not working (except at preaching), and obeying no one (if no one is ecclesiastical authorities) could describe Waldensian practices seen from Geoffroy of Auxerre's point of view. Having no worries and not being in danger could also be apt ways to describe the Waldensians' status before persecution. The two units that do not conform to Waldensian piety are splendid feasting and taking new lovers every night. Here lies the greatest potential distortion. Feasting would be directly contrary to the austere life espoused by Valdes and his fol- lowers. Promiscuity was a common charge, broadly made against heretical movements and their adherents, male and female, but especially female. The association between heresy, women, and promiscuity was already centuries old at this point.[18]

Leaving aside for now some of the questions posed by this text, we prefer not to simply discard it as a biased piece of evidence. It is possible to point to threads of truth that have become exaggerated and distorted within the negative framework of polemic. The contrast between the discursive past and present probably reflects the reality of life before and after persecution. Only two elements of the reported statement—feasting and promiscuity—when stripped of their polemical shading, would probably have been objection- able to a twelfth-century Waldensian. These two accusations belong to the rhetorical baggage of social institutions that denounce those whom they per- ceive as threats.[19] They probably also reflect the suspicions raised by secret meetings, which are mentioned in other sources as gatherings to discuss the Scriptures and celebrate the Eucharist.[20] Perhaps too there was in the orig- inal statement some reference to a eucharistic meal, or to Christ as a lover— common in the literature of the day—which was misunderstood because of linguistic differences or simply distorted.[21]

After the reported statement, Geoffroy returns to his broader apocalyp- tic context and exclaims: "Who has brought that Jezebel back to life, a young woman after 1,000 years, so that she may run through the streets and squares like a prostitute preacher?" Hence Jezebel serves as an anti-model for the argumentation, and these associations of pollution are transferred from the biblical Jezebel to the unauthorized woman preacher of the twelfth century.[22] Geoffroy and his text soon jump to the common misogynist observation that women are more talkative and less cautious in their speech. He subsequently praises Mary, mother of Jesus, for her silence because she bore many things in her heart but uttered few with her lips (Luke 2:19).[23] Thus Mary serves as the perfect model and Jezebel as the anti-model for female behavior.[24]

BERNARD OF FONTCAUDE

The essential elements of Geoffroy's condemnation of women preachers are also found in the polemical treatises. Among those, the earliest, the *Adver- sus Waldensium sectam liber* by Bernard of Fontcaude, also has the most to say about the issue of women's preaching.[25]

The denunciation of women preachers rests on some general assumptions about obedience to the Roman Church and the order of the priesthood (I.i–ii, cols. 795–96), arguments based on the authority of the texts and of institutional practice. An unauthorized layperson is labeled a heretic, a disobedient usurper of the priestly office who should be treated as the Antichrist and a diseased person—that is, shunned in public and not admitted into one's home.[26] An unauthorized female preacher is to receive the same treatment as well as criticism particular to her gender.

A transitional phase in Bernard's condemnation comes when he argues by association, likening the heretical preachers to deceitful women.[27] Then he accuses these men, comparable to the devil, of deceiving sinful women, calling to mind Eve, Job's wife, and Pilate's wife, who voiced the devil's will to prevent Christ's passion so that he would not lose his dominion.[28] Bernard explains this in connection with the warning in 2 Timothy 3:6 against false teachers who enter houses and take in sinful women.[29] Through these women, men are ensnared; and they in turn are considered weak and sinful.[30] The next step in condemning the Waldensians is to address the identity and role of the sinful women who deceive others. Bernard devotes a whole chapter to why women should not be allowed to teach and preach (VIII, pp. 825–28).

The treatise allows for some reconstruction of the Waldensians' arguments in favor of permitting women to preach. Bernard states that the Waldensians rely on Titus 2:3 to affirm that women ought to teach.[31] The key phrase here is, "they are to teach what is good, and so train the young women" ("bene docente; ut prudentiam doceant adolescentulas"). The abbot counters that Paul does not say that older women should teach men, but that they should teach young girls in private.[32]

The Waldensians also are said to call upon the example of the prophet Anna, who received Jesus in the temple, as reported in Luke 2:36–38, where verse 38 states: "And coming up at that very hour she gave thanks to God, and spoke of him to all who were looking for the redemption of Jerusalem." To that Bernard responds that Anna prophesied and did not preach, which leads him to the general conclusion that prophesying is an acceptable activity for women.[33]

The arguments Bernard of Fontcaude makes against preaching by women are based on expected biblical texts (1 Cor. 14:35; 1 Cor. 11:5; Gen. 3:16; Eph. 5:23 and 1 Cor. 11:3, 9; 1 Tim. 2:11–14; and 1 Peter 3:1–2) with the warning that one must take care that the ancient enemy does not fall back on old methods and use the word of women to lead men astray.[34] The abbot also draws on the example of Job's wife, reproached by her husband for speaking like a foolish woman (Job 2:9–10), and he echoes Gregory the Great's opposition to women preaching voiced in the *Moralia* 3.8.[35] Earlier the abbot used Gregory's typological interpretation, casting Job as the figure of the orthodox church and his friends as heretics.[36] In the context of Eve's beguilement of Adam, Job's comment to his wife demonstrates that women are foolish and seductive and therefore should not speak.[37]

Women of the New Testament also serve as models for the Premonstratensian abbot's arguments against women preaching. He asserts that Mary Magdalene and the other women followers of Jesus did not preach. Furthermore, like Geoffroy of Auxerre, he praises the example of Mary, mother of Jesus, as the perfect model. Mary's silence is associated with the purity of her virginity in Bernard's observation: "The glorious mother of God and Virgin, who 'kept all the words' revealed to her, 'pondering them in her heart,' is not reported to have preached."[38]

Following the treatise by Bernard of Fontcaude, several other twelfth- and thirteenth-century witnesses refer to women and lay men preaching. Although they add little new information for this study, they do confirm the preaching activity of Waldensian women. Among the authors and texts are Alan of Lille's *Summa quadrapartita* (1190–94), letters written by Innocent III (1199), Joachim of Fiore's *De articulis fidei* (1193–94), Ermengaud of Saint Gilles's list of errors (1200–1210), the 1210 profession of faith by Bernard Prim, the *Anonymous of Passau* (ca. 1260), David of Augsburg's *De inquisitione haereticorum*, Anselm of Alessandria's *Tractatus de hereticis* (ca. 1266), Etienne of Bourbon's *De septem donis spiritus sancti*, and Bernard Gui's *Manuel de l'inquisiteur* (1323–24).[39] Inquisition records, which remain to be fully studied, also refer to Waldensian women preaching.[40]

MONETA OF CREMONA

Another author who brings material to our discussion is Moneta of Cremona, a Dominican whose *Summa adversus Catharos et Valdenses* (ca. 1241) provides evidence that the Waldensians appealed to the example of Mary Magdalene to justify preaching by women.[41] At the conclusion of a section of the *Summa*, in which he explains with abundant scriptural references the knowledge and wisdom necessary for a preacher, he says: "Still it must be known that just as the office of preaching is not for all men, so also it is completely forbidden to women." Moneta cites 1 Corinthians 14:34 and 1 Timothy 2:12, explaining that the Waldensians go against the latter. "Their women preach in church," he says, "if their assembly should be called the church, which in truth it is not. They have said in response to this that Christ sent Mary Magdalene to preach when he said in John 20:17: 'Go to my brethren and say to them: I am ascending to our Father and your father, to my God and your God.' Mary Magdalene went and said to the disciples, 'I have seen the Lord.'" Moneta explains that the interpretation that Jesus sent her to preach should be ascribed to the distorted understanding of a heretic, because the Gospel author says only that she announced to the disciples, not that she preached. The Dominican author asks, "Now, whenever a woman is sent to announce something good to a church, should it be said that she preaches to that church?" His answer of course is "Non."[42] The association between women and heresy is again reinforced when Moneta interprets Revelation 2:20 as an injunction to prohibit preaching by heretics, represented by the figure of Jezebel.[43]

CONCLUSION

In summary, twelfth- and thirteenth-century sources that provide information on the preaching of Waldensian women are polemical works that present arguments designed for use by other preachers and writers in the campaign against heresy. Occasionally they also contain anecdotal information and in one case—the Apocalypse commentary of Geoffroy of Auxerre—the words attributed to two women followers of Valdes are used to accuse them of sexual promiscuity, and the women preachers are likened to Jezebel. Familiar arguments are presented against women teaching or preaching in public, but some sources mention private gatherings where men and women read and commented together on the Scriptures.

As far as models and authorities for this preaching are concerned, one source, Bernard of Fontcaude, reports that the Waldensians looked to the prophet Anna as a model; another, Moneta of Cremona, cites their reliance on Mary Magdalene. Several scriptural passages reportedly were used to justify lay preaching, and Titus 2:3 as well as the examples of Anna and Mary Magdalene directly support the question of women preaching.[44]

The text most frequently cited against the preaching of women is 2 Timothy 3:6, a verse that encapsulates views of woman's inferiority, sinfulness, and inability to know the truth. Both 1 and 2 Timothy and Titus reflect controversies over women's teaching in the early church, and the other texts adduced by the polemicists belong to the stock resources of the continuing controversy. Noteworthy is the use of Gregory the Great's works both to support lay preaching and to denounce women's preaching.[44]

Arguments advanced by the polemicists are generally based on standard medieval methods of appealing to authoritative texts and typological models. What gives added force and persuasive power to the arguments, however, is the extension of the typological model to construct a reality that fits the mold described in the authoritative text. The biblical text is seen as the forerunner of the contemporary situation.

All the polemical sources studied here reflect the fear and contempt of their authors. Disparaging remarks against lay men preachers were prompted by their disobedience, while comments against women reflect what the polemicists believed to be their fundamental inferiority, unalterable sinfulness, and proclivity for seduction. Any preaching woman was cast as Jezebel, the quintessential representative of impurity and deceit. In contrast to the perfect model of Mary's purity and silence, Jezebel was the anti-model for defining norms of holy preaching and acceptable behavior for women.

The combination of subordination, sinfulness, and seduction has deep roots in the history of biblical interpretation. It also belongs to a broader cultural pattern, what Mary Douglas, based on observations of different cultures, has called the Delilah complex—the idea that women weaken and then betray men.[45] Feminist theologians have often pointed out the biblical underpinnings of misogyny in Christian cultures and demonstrated how certain scriptural passages have been used to justify discrimination and violence toward women.[46]

R. I. Moore asserts that twelfth-century Europe, like the societies studied by the anthropologist Mary Douglas, gave women high value as currency but low status—the mark of a society that fears females could subvert a social structure founded on their lack of power.[47] Yet in the area of religion it seems that most women were assigned both low value and low status. For the most part, a woman's preaching—that is, the expression of her voice about religious topics and in particular the Scriptures—was seen as a threat to the social order and to the clerical hierarchy, a violation of her God-given condition of subordination, sinfulness, and seductiveness.

NOTES

1. The text from Geoffroy of Auxerre was first published with others in Jean Leclercq, "Le témoignage de Geoffroy d'Auxerre sur la vie cistercienne," *Analecta Monastica*, 2d ser., *Studia Anselmiana* 31 (Rome: Herder, 1953): 174–201. Geoffroy's commentary was later edited in full by Ferruccio Gastaldelli and published with an introduction by Jean Leclercq: Goffredo di Auxerre, *Super Apocalypsim, Temi e testi* 17 (Rome: Edizioni di storia e letteratura, 1970); the passage appears on pp. 179–80. The bishop was probably Ponce of Polignac, former Cistercian abbot of Clairvaux and Grandselve, who was chosen bishop of Clermont in 1170; *Dictionnaire des auteurs cisterciens*, ed. E. Brouette, A. Dimier, and E. Manning, *La documentation cistercienne* 16, t. 2 (Rochefort: Abbaye de Notre-Dame de St-Remy, 1979), col. 576.

2. The early years of the movement are discussed in various histories; see, e.g., Malcolm Lambert, *Medieval Heresy*, 2d ed. (Oxford: Basil Blackwell, 1992), pp. 62–77; and R. I. Moore, *The Origins of European Dissent* (Oxford: Basil Blackwell, 1985), pp. 228–31. The sources are reviewed by Giovanni Gonnet in "Le cheminement des vaudois vers le schisme et l'hérésie (1174–1218)," *Cahiers de Civilisation Médiévale* (1976): 309–45. Recent scholarship is discussed in *Les vaudois des origines à leur fin (xiie–xvie siècles)*, ed. Gabriel Audisio (Turin: A. Meynier, 1990). Philippe Buc underscores the participation of some secular clergy in the movement and the sympathy of some learned clergy for it; "*Vox clamantis in deserto?* Pierre le Chantre et la prédication laïque," *Revue Mabillon*, n.s. 4 (=t.65) (1993): 33.

3. For general background, see Lambert, *Medieval Heresy*, pp. 73–74. The translations, in particular those reported in Metz in 1199, and the church's attitude toward them, are discussed in Leonard E. Boyle, "Innocent III and Vernacular Versions of

Scripture," in *The Bible in the Medieval World: Essays in Memory of Beryl Smalley*, ed. Katherine Walsh and Diana Wood, SCH Subsidia 4 (Oxford: Basil Blackwell, 1985), pp. 97–107. The role of literacy in Waldensianism is discussed in Alexander Patschovsky, "The Literacy of Waldensianism from Valdes to c. 1400," in *Heresy and Literacy, 1000–1530*, ed. Peter Biller and Anne Hudson (Cambridge: Cambridge University Press, 1995), pp. 112–36, and their existing texts surveyed and analyzed in the same volume by Anne Brenon, "The Waldensian Books," pp. 137–59.

4. Lambert, *Medieval Heresy*, p. 72; R. I. Moore, *The Formation of a Persecuting Society* (Oxford: Basil Blackwell, 1987), p. 104.

5. The text of *Ad abolendam diversarum haeresium pravitatem*, November 4, 1184, is given in Giovanni Gonnet, *Enchiridion fontium Valdensium*, I (Torre-Pellice: Claudiana, 1958), pp. 50–53. G. Gonnet considers arguments for and against the historicity of the condemnation in his "Le cheminement," pp. 311–29. Historians of heresy include the decree in the development of the process of inquisition. Edward Peters terms it the "most elaborate juridical statement concerning the treatment of heretics made to that date by the Latin Church," and says that it has been called "the founding charter of the Inquisition." See Edward Peters, *Inquisition* (Berkeley: University of California Press, 1988), pp. 47–48; and Moore, *Formation of a Persecuting Society*, pp. 6–9.

6. Gottfried Koch, *Frauenfrage und Ketzertum in Mittelalter* (Berlin: Akademie Verlag, 1962), pp. 156–80; Giovanni Gonnet, "La donna presso i movimenti pauperistico-evangelici," in *Movimento religioso femminile e francescanesimo nel secolo XIII*, Società internazionale di studi francescani—Convegni, VII (Assisi: La Società internazionale di studi francescani, 1980), pp. 103–29; the two recent reexaminations are Giovanni Gonnet, "La femme dans les mouvements paupéro-évangéliques du Bas Moyen Age (notamment chez les vaudois)," *Heresis* 22 (1994): 27–41; and Grado Merlo, "Sulle 'misere donnicciuole' che predicavano," in G. Merlo, *Valdesi e valdismi medievali II. Identità Valdesi nella storia e nella storiografia* (Turin: Claudiana, 1991), pp. 93–112. I am grateful to Roberto Rusconi for calling Merlo's essay to my attention. On later Waldensian women, see Peter Biller, "The Preaching of the Waldensian Sisters," in *La prédication sur un mode dissident: laïcs, femmes, hérétiques . . . (xie–xive)*, Actes de la 9e Session d'Histoire Médiévale organisée par le C.N.E.C./René Nelli, 26–30 août 1996, sous la présidence de Beverly Mayne Kienzle (Carcassonne, forthcoming 1998); and "What Did Happen to the Waldensian Sisters? The Strasbourg Testimony," in F. Giacone, ed., *Mélanges Giovanni Gonnet* (forthcoming). I am grateful to Peter Biller for prepublication copies of these essays.

7. *Adversus Waldensium sectam liber*, PL 204, cols. 793–840. According to Christine Thouzellier, the dispute took place around 1185–87. Bernard Gaucelin, archbishop of Narbonne, called it together; Raymond de Daventrie arbitrated and then pronounced the poor of Lyons as heretics; see Christine Thouzellier, *Catharisme et Valdeisme en Languedoc à la fin du xiie et au début du xiiie siècle* (Paris: Presses Universitaires de France, 1966), pp. 50–51. Wakefield and Evans date the debate around 1190 and Bernard's death no later than 1193; see Walter L. Wakefield and Austin P. Evans, *Heresies of the High Middle Ages: Selected Sources Translated and Annotated* (New York: Columbia University Press, 1969), p. 211. See also Libert Verrees, "Le traité de l'abbé Bernard de Fontcaude contre les Vaudois et les Ariens," *Analecta Praemonstratensia* 31 (1955): 5–35. According to G. Gonnet, Bernard of Fontcaude's treatise, along with the *Summa*

quadrapartita of Alan of Lille, inaugurates the genre of the polemical treatise in this period. Gonnet, "Le cheminement," p. 321, states: "dans le but expressément formulé de combattre d'une façon systématique les hérétiques de leur temps ils ont inauguré par là-même la grande littérature polémique des xiiᵉ et xiiiᵉ s."

8. Moore, *Formation of a Persecuting Society*; Chaim Perelman and L. Olbrechts-Tyteca, *The New Rhetoric: A Treatise on Argumentation* (Notre Dame, Ind.: University of Notre Dame Press, 1969). I was introduced to this work by Antoinette Clark Wire's *The Corinthian Women Prophets: A Reconstruction through Paul's Rhetoric* (Minneapolis: Fortress Press, 1990).

9. The twelfth-century debate on lay preaching is examined in John M. Trout, "Preaching by the Laity in the Twelfth Century," Studies in Medieval Culture 4.1, ed. John R. Sommerfeldt, Larry Synergaard, and E. Rozanne Elder (Kalamazoo, Mich.: Medieval Institute Publications, 1975), pp. 92–108; J. B. Schneyer, "Die Laienpredigt im Mittelater," *Münchener Theologische Zeitschrift* 18, no. 3 (1967): 206–18; and R. Zerfass, *Der Streit um die Laienpredigt* (Freiburg im Breisgau: Herder, 1974). Moore, *Formation of a Persecuting Society*, esp. pp. 135–140, discusses the hostility of the twelfth-century literate elite toward the unlettered.

10. Geoffroy cites Jerome's interpretation of Jezebel's name (*Liber interpretationis hebraicorum nominum* 80.20, CC72:160): "In eo quoque quod Iezabel fluens sanguinem vel sterquilinium interpretatur, de abundantia iniquitatis et immunditiae eadem appellatione notatur." Jerome states: "Iezabel fluxus sanguinis vel fluens sanguine. Sed melius ubi est sterquilinium."

11. *Super Apocalypsim*, p. 179: "Bene Paulus mulieres in ecclesiis loqui prohibens, ait: 'Domi viros suos interrogent.' 'Domi,' non foris; 'interrogent,' non docere praesumant; nec se invicem, sed 'viros'; non quoscumque, sed 'suos.'"

12. Ibid.: "In quibus non desunt miserae etiam mulierculae oneratae peccatis, quae domos penetrant alienas, curiosae etiam et verbosae, procaces, improbae, impudentes."

13. For a summary of scholarship on the Pastoral Letters, see Ralph P. Martin, "1, 2 Timothy and Titus," in *Harper's Bible Commentary*, ed. James L. Mays (San Francisco: Harper and Row, 1988), pp. 1237–44; and Robert A. Wild, "The Pastoral Letters," in *The New Jerome Biblical Commentary*, ed. Raymond E. Brown, Joseph A. Fitzmyer, and Roland E. Murphy (Englewood Cliffs, N.J.: Prentice-Hall: 1990), pp. 891–902. Merlo, "Sulle 'misere donnicciuole,'" p. 104, rightly points out that a distorted mirror is used when the Waldensian women are associated with the *mulierculae* of 2 Timothy, but he does not examine the Greek text or the view of the passage in New Testament scholarship.

14. On argument from authority, see Perelman and Olbrechts-Tyteca, *New Rhetoric*, pp. 305–10.

15. *Super Apocalypsim*, pp. 179–80: "sicut duae earum ante hoc ferme quinquennium in exercitu quodam satellitum nefandorum venerabilem Arvenicae urbis episcopum, quod eodem postmodum referente multis innotuit, transeuntem quam gravissimis poterant contumeliis impetebant, improperantes ei quod in sua dioecesi praedicantes olim reperiens, minis et persuasionibus eidem sectae abrenuntiare compulerit. Propter quod improbe blasphemantes, convicia iaculabantur in eum et publice proclamabant."

16. Ibid., p. 180.

17. See Roberto Rusconi, *Predicazione e vita religiosa nella società italiana da Carlo*

Magno alla Controriforma, Documenti della storia, 30 (Turin: Loescher Editore, 1981), p. 90; and Merlo, "Sulle 'misere donnicciuole,'" pp. 99–100.

18. Moore, *Formation of a Persecuting Society,* pp. 100–101, discusses fear of sexual pollution and fear of social change, relying on the analysis of Mary Douglas, *Purity and Danger* (Boston: Ark Paperbacks, 1966), esp. pp. 140–58. A clear association between women, heresy, and sexual immorality is made in Tertullian, *De praescriptione haereticorum* XXX; Eusebius, *Historia Ecclesiastica* V.18.3; and Timothy of Constantinople, *De iis qui ad ecclesiam accedunt, PG* 86:20. I am grateful to Karen King for these references.

19. See Moore, *Formation of a Persecuting Society,* pp. 100–101.

20. Secret meetings involving preaching are discussed in the letters of Innocent III concerning the 1199 events in Metz. See note 42 below. Evidence about the sacraments first appears in a letter from late-twelfth-century Piacenza, attributed to Ardizzo, bishop of that city (1192–99); see text in A. Dondaine, "Durand de Huesca et la polémique anti-cathare," *Archivum Fratrum Praedicatorum* 29 (1959): 274: "Et quod sine habundanti lacrimarum torrente a quoquam fidelium dici non potest, non solum laici eorum, licet otiose, venerandi Dominici corporis sacramenta facere presumpserunt, verum etiam et eorum mulieres hoc ipsum presumpsisse cognoscuntur."

21. I am grateful to my students at Harvard Divinity School, Marcia McCall and Charles Gilley, who suggested these possibilities when we discussed the text in a course on twelfth-century preaching. They, Sasha Swetland, and Chris Ruddy commented on an earlier version of this essay.

22. Moore, *Formation of a Persecuting Society,* p. 95, cites L. L. Otis, *Prostitution in Medieval Society: The History of an Urban Institution in the Languedoc* (Chicago: University of Chicago Press, 1985), p. 16, on the use of word *meretrix,* so common that in the twelfth century it was necessary to qualify it with *publica* in order to differentiate a prostitute from a woman whose behavior was considered merely scandalous. Geoffroy's use of the word clearly includes an accusation of promiscuity if not actual prostitution. On the anti-model in argumentation, see Perelman and Olbrechts-Tyteca, *New Rhetoric,* pp. 366–68.

23. *Super Apocalypsim,* p. 180: "In omnibus nempe sacrorum libris Evangeliorum verba eius nonnisi septem invenisse se comendabat. Erat enim plurima conferens in corde suo, pauca proferens ex ore suo."

24. On the perfect model in argumentation, see Perelman and Olbrechts-Tyteca, *New Rhetoric,* p. 371.

25. See note 7 above on approximate date of this work, edited in *PL* 204, cols. 793–840. References to the section of the work and the column in Migne will be given in parentheses except when specific passages are cited. Philippe Buc, "*Vox clamantis,*" pp. 5–47, argues convincingly that Bernard of Fontcaude's treatise represents a conservative view in the church at that time; a more open view was supported by Peter the Chanter and Huguccio. Buc discusses lay preaching in general and only briefly refers to women's preaching.

26. VI.x, *PL* 204, col. 820C: "Haec sacrarum Scripturarum verba, quasi commonitoria salutis fidelibus Christi cogitanda, memoriterque retinenda excerpsimus; ut aperte sciant, non esse participationem, seu societatem habendam cum perfidis haereticis, nec audiendos, quasi anathematizatos, sed vitandos quasi perditos et manifeste incorrigibiles, nec eis commiscendum esse, quasi inobedientibus, nec salutandos, aut in domum recipiendos, quasi antichristos, sed quasi profanos et inaniloquos devi-

tandos. Trahunt nempe ad impietatem et more cancri, paulatim sana membra, id est fideles, corrumpunt, atque quasi fermentum eos, qui sibi participant, quasi massam similae, amissa naturali dulcedine Catholicae unitatis inflant ad superbiam, et acidos reddunt, id est conformes mente, sed et mente corruptos, ut ait Apostolus, et qui veritate privati sunt, existimantes quaestum esse pietatem, dum pro quaestu, non pro futuris praedicant."

27. VII.ii, *PL* 204, col. 821B: "Seducunt ergo mulieres, viros, non viriliter sed muliebriter agentes."

28. VII.ii, *PL* 204, col. 821BC: "Seducunt mulieres prius, per eas viros; ut diabolus prius Evam, et per eam Adam. Sic et Job per ejus uxorem subvertere voluit dicentem: 'Adhuc permanes in simplicitate tua? Benedic Deo, et morere' (Job 2:9). Sic et per uxorem Pilati dicentem ei: 'Nil tibi et justo illi: multa enim passa sum hodie per visum propter illum' (Mt. 27:19). Mysterium passionis Domini voluit impedire, ne per ejus mortem, amitteret imperium." The statement by Job's wife is repeated in *PL* 240, col. 826AB.

29. VII.ii, *PL* 204, col. 821C: "Hinc Apostolus de pseudochristis et haereticis ait Timotheo: 'Habentes quidem speciem pietatis, virtutem autem ejus abnegantes; et hos devita. Ex his enim sunt, qui penetrant domos; et mulierculas ducunt captivas, oneratas peccatis, quae ducuntur variis desideriis'" (2 Tim. 3:6).

30. VII.iii, *PL* 204, col. 821C: "Ecce patet, quia seducunt non firmos, sed mulieres seductibles, dignas seduci, utpote oneratas peccatis. Seducunt et viros femineae debilitatis." Others who are deceived are listed through chapter VII (*PL* 204, cols. 821–823) with scriptural citations as supportive evidence: the "imperitos," "innocentes" or "simplices," "infirmos et inscios," and so on.

31. "Sed, dicunt inimici veritatis, mulieres debere docere; eo quod Apostolus dicat ad Titum" (VIII.v, *PL* 204, col. 826).

32. VIII.v, *PL* 204, cols. 826D–827B: "Ad quod notandum est, Apostolum non dicere, ut publice viros anus doceant, sed private adolescentulas, ita tamen ut eas prudentiam illam doceant quam consequenter subdit. . . . Repellunt igitur, ne doceant mulieres haeresim sapientes, secundum praedicta autem verba, ne doceant, nisi sint anus moribus et aetate, et ne doceant, nisi adolescentulas: imo, omnino interdicitur eis, ne doceant; ideo scilicet quia non sunt sanae in fide, sine qua esse convincitur, quisquis obediens non est, ut superius monstratum est." Robert Wild places this verse in the context of duties of the members of a Christian household, while the author of the Pastoral Epistles generally "did not want women teaching men in a worship context"; see Wild, "Commentary on Titus," in *The New Jerome Biblical Commentary*, p. 895.

33. VIII.vi, *PL* 204, col. 827B: "Item hunc errorem confirmare nituntur exemplo Annae prophetissae, quae Evangelio teste in ipsa hora, qua Dominus oblatus est in templo, superveniens confitebatur Domino et loquebatur de illo omnibus, qui exspectabant redemptionem Israel. . . . Nec dicitur hic, quia praedicavit vel docuit; sed 'locuta est de Christo omnibus, qui exspectabant redemptionem Israel.' Non est idem, praedicare et loqui. . . . Cum igitur aliud sit donum prophetiae, aliud sermo doctrinae, secure concesserim, Annam, seu quasdam mulieres prophetasse; nec tamen consequenter dicendum erit, easdem docuisse; alioqui male posuit Apostolus eadem quasi diversa."

34. (1 Cor. 14:35) VII.i; *PL* 204, col. 825D: "Praeter errores jam dictos, graviter

errant; quia feminas, quas suo consortio admittunt, docere permittunt, cum hoc sit
apostolicae doctrinae contrarium. Scriptum est enim: 'Mulieres in ecclesiis taceant. . . .'
ecce Apostolus jubet, ut mulieres taceant in ecclesiis materialibus, vel in congregationibus fidelium, non quidem ab oratione vel laude Dei, sed a doctrina; et ne quae
in ecclesia aliquid interrogent sub occasione docendi, sed domi viros suos."
    (1 Cor. 11:5) In VIII.iii; *PL* 204, col. 826C, Bernard remarks "Qua ergo temeritate
praesumat mulier verba Dei publice docere, quae ipsum Deum orare, aut prophetae
non debet, nisi velata?"
    (Gen. 3:16, Eph. 5:23, and 1 Cor. 11:3, 9) After citing 1 Corinthians 11:3, the abbot
asks: "Et si caput mulieris est vir, qua fronte audeat docere virum, scilicet caput suum?"
PL 204, col. 826C.
    (1 Tim. 2:11–14) VIII.i; *PL* 204, col. 825D: "Ecce aperte Apostolus dicit, ut mulier,
etiam cum discit sileat, nec doctorem Ecclesiae interroget. Docere quoque non permittitur, vel dominari in virum duabus de causis: tum scilicet, quia post virum for-
mata est; tum etiam, quia seducta fuit in praevaricatione Dominici praecepti, quasi
diceret: Et non vir."
    In VIII.ii; *PL* 204, col. 826, after citing 1 Peter 3:1–2, Bernard remarks: "Ecce, hic
dicitur aperte, quomodo fideles mulieres debent lucrifacere viros infideles, scilicet
exemplo sanctae conversationis, sine verbo praedicationis."
    VIII.i; *PL* 204, col. 826A: "Timendum est enim, ne hostis antiquus arte pristina
utens, per mulieris verbum virum seducat."
    35. *PL* 204, col. 826B; *Moralia in Job*, ed. M. Adriaen, CC143 (Turnhout: Brepols,
1979), I, 3.8.12: Gregory speaks of a wife's ability to influence her husband, concluding:
"Unde bene et per Paulum dicitur: Docere autem mulieri non permitto."
    36. *PL* 204, col. 817D; *Moralia in Job*, II, 17.20.11.
    37. VIII. ii, *PL* 204, col. 826B.
    38. VIII.iv; *PL* 204, col. 826D: "Praeterea gloriosa Dei mater et Virgo, quae 'con-
servat omnia verba' sibi ostensa, 'conferens in corde suo (Luc 2:19),' non legitur
praedicasse. Sed nec Maria Magdalena, aut aliqua de mulieribus, quae secutae sunt
Dominum."
    39. Bernard Gui, *Manuel de l'inquisiteur*, V, I, ed. Guillaume Mollat (Paris: Librairie
Honoré Champion, 1926), p. 34. The other sources are identified in full and reviewed
briefly by Gonnet, "La femme," pp. 29–37.
    40. Two references are cited by G. Gonnet: one from Toulouse, MS 609, f. 321,
and the other from the inquisitor Pierre Sellan, who reported seeing a Waldensian
woman explaining the Lord's passion. Gonnet, "La femme," p. 36.
    41. Moneta, a professor at the University of Bologna, joined the Dominican order
there in 1218 or 1219. See Wakefield and Evans, *Heresies*, p. 307.
    On Mary Magdalene, see the article by Katherine Jansen in this volume. Alcuin
Blamires comments on the paradox that Mary Magdalene and Catherine of Siena,
whose preaching is recounted in the *Legenda aurea*, presented for medieval women:
"As for women who felt inspired to emulate them, only two alternatives seemed open.
They could teach within the cloister, discreetly, if they became abbesses: or they could
become heretics"; Alcuin Blamires, "Women and Preaching in Medieval Orthodoxy,
Heresy and Saints' Lives," *Viator* 26 (1995): 151. I am grateful to Barbara Newman
for bring Blamires's article to my attention.
    42. "Adhuc sciendum, quod sicut officium praedicationis non est universale viris,

ita etiam ex tot prohibetur feminis; unde 1 Cor.14.v.34. 'Mulieres in Ecclesiis taceant, non enim permittitur eis loqui,' id est praedicare. Item 1 Timoth.2.v.12. 'Docere autem mulieri non permitto.' Contra hoc praeceptum Apostoli veniunt Valdenses: Mulieres enim eorum praedicant in Ecclesia; Si tamen Ecclesia debet dici eorum congregatio, quod verum non est. Ad hoc autem dixerunt, quod Christus Mariam Magdalenam misit praedicare dicens Johannis 22.v.17. Vade autem ad fratres meos, et dic eis: Ascendo ad patrem meum, et Patrem vestrum: Deum meum et Deum vestrum. (v.18) Venit Maria Magdalene annuncians discipulis: Quia vidi Dominum. Sed pravae intelligentiae haeretici est adscribendum; non enim praedicasse, sed tantum nuntiasse dicitur discipulis, id quod Evangelista dicit. Nunquid quandocumque aliqua mulier mittatur aliquod bonum nuntiare Ecclesiae alicui, debet dici praedicare ei? Non." *Adversus Catharos et Valdenses libri quinque*, ed. Thomas A. Ricchini. (Rome, 1743; rpt. Ridgewood, N.J.: Gregg Press, 1964), p. 442.

43. "Praeterea, si non est haereticus prohibendus, quodmodo stabit illud, quod legitur Apocal.2.v.20. ubi Dominus ait Angelo Thyatirae: 'Sed habeo adversus te pauca: quia permittis mulierem Jezabel, quae se dicit prophetem, docere, et seducere servos meos?' Per Jezabel intelliguntur haeretici, quia sicut Jezabel uxor Achab contraria erat doctrinae Domini, et prophetarum ejus, ita es isti." *Adversus Catharos*, p. 443.

44. See pp. 104–105 and notes 35–37, above. Reconstructing the Waldensian arguments, also from Bernard of Fontcaude's treatise (IV, *PL* 204, cols. 805–12), one finds that among their statements in favor of lay preaching were two citations from homily 6.6 of Gregory the Great's *Forty Homilies on the Gospels* and an appeal to the lay preachers Honoratus and Equitius, who figure in his *Dialogues* (1.1, 4; II. 15). For further discussion, see Beverly Mayne Kienzle, "La prédication: pierre de touche de la dissidence et de l'orthodoxie," in *La prédication sur un mode dissident* (forthcoming 1998), and "Holiness and Obedience: Denouncement of Twelfth-Century Waldensian Lay Preaching," in *The Devil, Heresy, and Witchcraft in the Middle Ages: Essays in Honor of Jeffrey B. Russell*, ed. Alberto Ferreiro (Leiden: E. J. Brill, forthcoming 1998).

45. Douglas, *Purity and Danger*, p. 154.

46. See, for example: Margaret Miles, "Violence against Women in the Historical Christian West and in North American Secular Culture: The Visual and Textual Evidence," in *Shaping New Vision: Gender and Values in American Culture*, ed. Clarissa Atkinson, Constance Buchanan, and Margaret Miles, Harvard Women's Studies in Religion Series, vol. 2 (Ann Arbor, Mich.: UMI Research Press, 1987), pp. 11–29; Elisabeth Schüssler Fiorenza, "Introduction," in *Violence against Women*, ed. Elisabeth Schüssler Fiorenza and M. Shawn Copeland (London: SCM Press; Maryknoll, N.Y.: Orbis Books, 1994), pp. vii–xxiv; and Rosemary Radford Ruether, "The Western Religious Tradition and Violence against Women in the Home," in *Christianity, Patriarchy and Abuse*, ed. Joanne Carlson Brown and Carole R. Bohn (Cleveland: Pilgrim Press, 1989), pp. 31–41.

47. Moore, *Formation of a Persecuting Society*, pp. 100–101.

FIVE.

The Voice of the Good Women

An Essay on the Pastoral and Sacerdotal Role of Women in the Cathar Church

Anne Brenon

This holy baptism in the Holy Spirit, the Church of God has kept it from the apostles down to the present day, and it has been handed down this far from Good Man to Good Man, and [the Church of God] shall do so until the end of the world.

OCCITAN CATHAR RITUAL OF LYONS[1]

So that this power may be handed down from Good Man to Good Man and from Good Woman to Good Woman. For there are Good Women as well as Good Men, and these Good Women have this power, and may console men and women upon their deathbeds—so long as there are no Good Men present; and those that are received into death by Good Women are saved as if they had been received by Good Men.

GUILHEM BÉLIBASTE[2]

These two quotations illustrate the relevance of an essay on Cathar women to the theme of this volume. The first shows how, far from deriving from a miscellany of oriental religious beliefs, Catharism was a Christian sect, with Christian origins and Christian rites; it considered itself to be *the* true Church of God, as opposed to the false Catholic Church. The second quotation confirms the active participation of women in Cathar religious life:[3] although the Cathar communities of ordained sisters, variously called Christians or Good Women, had been wiped out by the mid-thirteenth century, Guilhem Bélibaste, a Cathar minister in the first quarter of the fourteenth century, took it for granted that women, like men, had received from Christ and the apostles the power not only to absolve sinners by baptism in the Holy Spirit but also to confer it upon others—which was very nearly a sacerdotal function.[4]

Bélibaste adds, however, that women might perform this sacrament "only in the absence of Good Men." In this essay, I assess the consequences of this de facto restriction on the religious role of women, which is also the starting point for many of the questions I raise.

Drawing on eleventh- and twelfth-century sources, I review the reasons why, theoretically and theologically (which here amount to the same thing),

Catharism might appear to have been a relatively egalitarian Christian counter-church. After tracing the main historical landmarks of a feminine clergy's active involvement in the church, I attempt to define the Good Women's sacerdotal and pastoral functions, focusing on the Cathar churches of Languedoc. Indeed, the archives of the Inquisition from southern France offer historians ample and detailed information about the daily life of this dissident clergy, which was openly tolerated over a wide geographical area, from Quercy to Carcassès, for several generations of the twelfth and thirteenth centuries. It was thus given to the Cathar Church to practice the lifestyle and religious beliefs it preached. Source material reveals a substantial, and in places massive, presence of women among preachers and believers alike.

Working from witnesses' recorded experiences, and without neglecting the possible weight of traditional Christian misogyny on Cathar beliefs, I highlight the position and function of consecrated women both within the Cathar Church organization and in relation to a population of believers (*credentes*), at a time when the Catholic Church generally confined its nuns to the silence of cloisters; but the voice of the Good Women remains elusive on the background of Cathar preaching.

What we do know is that until the annexation of Languedoc by the French kings, these nuns without enclosure lived in the heart of Occitan society. They set an apostolic example that was visible to all in the streets of the villages, and thereby implicitly helped to spread the message of a new spirituality, which made them precursors of the Mendicant orders' practice of establishing convents in the towns.

THE *ELECTAE* OF THE CHURCH OF GOD

The Two Churches

References to heresy appear in medieval Greek and Latin texts in the years preceding and following A.D. 1000. Recently discovered historical sources now make it possible to consider many of the religious movements that sprang up in Europe in the eleventh century as very probably pre- or proto-Cathar.[5] Certainly they already bore most of the distinctive features of Catharism, which was the main religious dissidence of the Middle Ages: Docetism, defiance of the papal hierarchy, a refusal to venerate the cross and holy pictures, a rejection of all the Catholic sacraments, a simple blessing of bread instead of the Eucharist, and the practice of a single sacrament: baptism in the Holy Spirit by the laying on of hands. Some early eleventh-century texts even suggest the existence of a dissident clergy.[6]

The evangelical communities that sprang up on the fringes of the Catholic Church, claiming to follow the *lex* and *disciplina* of the apostles, included men and women as indiscriminately as they attracted monks, clerics, and lay people. Taboos were broken: there was no worship of relics encased in gold and silver, no practice of what they considered abuses of sacraments such as baptism for infants too young to argue or weddings. It was in an apparently rationalist, mockingly anticlerical atmosphere that these "textual communities"[7] coalesced around "the devil's heretical ministers."[8]

Rich, plentiful, and detailed source material dating from the twelfth and thirteenth centuries provides a good picture of the extent to which Catharism was a Christian counter-church. Some time around 1143, Evervin, the Premonstratensian prior of Steinfeld, wrote to Bernard of Clairvaux for advice on some heretical communities that had just been discovered in the region of Cologne and promptly eradicated. From this letter, to which I shall return, it appears that their members insisted on calling their church the true Church of God, as opposed to the worldly Catholic Church. In effect, they were contrasting the Church of God and the church of this world, just as the Gospels and the First Epistle of John contrast God and this world. They also stood on its head the position of Catholicism at the time, which claimed to be the one and only authorized Christian church, and denounced it as the wicked church of false prophets, ministers of evil, and the Antichrist, the wicked church of heretics.

> This is their heresy. They claim that they are the true Church, because the heritage of Christ survives in them alone. They are the true followers of the apostolic life, because they do not seek the things of this world, houses or land or any other sort of property. . . . Of themselves they said: . . . We live thus because we are not of this world; you are lovers of the world, at peace with the world because you are worldly (John 15: 19). False apostles have corrupted the word of Christ for their own ends, and have led you and your fathers astray. We and our fathers, the successors of the apostles, have remained in the grace of Christ, and will remain so until the end of the world. To distinguish between you and us, Christ said "By their fruits you shall know them" (Matthew 7: 16). Our fruits are the following in the footsteps of Christ.[9]

Cathar dualism, which is often misunderstood, finds its roots here: in the New Testament, where God and the world are presented as opposed, and in the medieval religious context; at the time, worshiping, especially of the Cluniac kind, tended to be devil-haunted and obsessed with the struggle between the forces of good and evil, which eventually gave rise to the Crusades. Cathar dualism can no longer be considered a dogmatic emanation of non-Christian Eastern beliefs. Even more insistently than their eleventh-century precursors, twelfth-century dissenters stressed everything in their faith that corroborated their Christian affiliation: their apostolic way of life; the exclusively Christian tradition that their theology rested on; and the paleo-Christian nature of their sole sacrament, baptism by the laying on of hands, which they traced back to the Acts of the Apostles. There is no need to refer to Zoroaster or Manes to explain Catharism or, for that matter, Bogomilism.[10]

The Presence of Women

From the moment heresy is first described, around A.D. 1000, by the chroniclers and clerics of Latin and Greek Catholic Christendom, the presence of women in their ranks is mentioned. In *Discours contre les Bogomiles* (Discourse against the Bogomils), written around 970, the Bulgarian priest Cosmas condemned the fact that the heretics, who used faith as a pretext to brainwash simple souls, included mere women who took it upon themselves to administer penance—that is, to remit sins. What, he asks, can be more contemptible? He goes on to cite the Epistles of Paul, on which the medieval church founded its traditional mistrust of women.

In Western Europe, the religious dissenters of the first millennium evidently welcomed women in their midst as "utopian sisters," to use the phrase coined by Georges Duby. The evangelical dissident communities that claimed their *lex* and *disciplina* from the apostles included religious and lay women. Marriage was mocked. So were the Catholic Church's other sacraments. Whether men or women, Christians were equal.[11]

However, until the early twelfth century, Western sources do not mention the role of women in these breakaway movements as explicitly as Greek sources; the same texts also define Catharism as being in every respect the Western, Christian version of Bogomilism.

There were autos-da-fé as early as 1135, in the Rhineland, in the archbishopric of Cologne, and in the see of Liège. Those who were burned in 1163, the poor of Christ, or apostles, belonged to one of three ranks: auditors, believers or *credentes,* and Christians or *Electi;* they claimed to be members of the true Church of God and to be baptized in the Holy Spirit by the laying on of hands. Furthermore, "These apostles of Satan have women among them who are—so they say—chaste, widows or virgins, or their wives, both among the *credentes* and among the *Electi,* alleging that they follow the apostles who permitted them to have women among them."[12]

Among the Women: The Elect and the Believers

Before commenting on the women, Evervin of Steinfeld outlined the threefold structure of the Rhineland communities. The *auditor* who lent a sympathetic ear to their ministers' preaching could, if he or she wished, move up to the rank of *credentes* after a first catechesis and a first imposition of hands. A believer who wished to become an Elect or Christian had to submit to a second period of novitiate and instruction, which was followed by a second sacrament. This twofold laying on of hands, which was both baptism and ordination, clearly foreshadows the Cathar *consolamentum;* by the end of the twelfth century, it had become a single ceremony, at least in Western Europe. The twofold ritual described by Evervin in the first half of the twelfth century resembles the Bogomils' ordination in two stages, which the Swedish scholar Ylva Hagman has identified.[13] Clearly, we find here an early form of these dissident communities' ritual and organization. In his letter to Bernard of Clairvaux, Evervin also expounded on the significance of the heretics' sacramental gesture of the laying on of hands: "They take whatever references to the laying-on of hands are to be found in the Acts of the Apostles or the Epistles of Paul. Anyone who is baptized among them in this way is called *Electus,* and has the power to baptize others who are worthy of it."[14]

Thus Evervin clearly included women among the sacerdotal group of the Elect as well as among the believers of the Rhineland Cathar communities he observed and described. Like the men, these women could administer the sacrament of baptism through the imposition of hands. This was the only sacrament recognized by the dissenters because, in their view, it was textually founded on Scripture and not instituted by the Catholic Church, which they considered a human creation, not God's: as John the Baptist, after baptizing in water, said of Christ, "He shall baptize you in the Holy Ghost and in fire" (Matt. 3:11).[15] Thus women, mere women, were practicing the same hand movement as Christ. Already in the second half of the tenth century, the Bulgarian priest Cosmas had been outraged to see Bogomil women remit sins—which was one essential purpose of the sacrament, along with baptism, initiation, ordination, marriage, and confession.[16]

Women who had attained the rank of Elect thus had the power to loose and to bind that Christ had conferred upon his church and which, the Cathars claimed, made theirs the true Christian church. Thus women participated in the holy ministry. The three surviving Cathar rituals of the *consolamentum* give the text of a central formula used for absolution—and in the Dublin ritual, this Christological power is listed as an attribute of the true Church of God: "This Church of God of which we speak has received such power from Our Lord Jesus Christ that sins are remitted by its prayers, as Christ says in the Gospel according to Saint John: 'Receive the Holy Spirit: If you forgive the sins of any, they are forgiven; and if you retain the sins of any, they are retained'" (John 20:22–23).[17]

During the mid-thirteenth-century inquest, believers of Languedoc overwhelmingly testified to having been convinced that the Cathars they had approached were Good Men and Women who had the power to save souls. The *Electae*, whether Christians or Cathar Good Women, were considered to be repositories of the power to cleanse from sin and save souls.

Christian Dualism and the Native Equality of Souls

Twenty years after Evervin, another Rhineland cleric, Eckbert of Schönau, who was canon of Bonn, had the opportunity to examine some heretics before they were burnt. In 1163 he wrote a series of sermons on the subject, in which we learn that they called themselves Cathars—this was probably an invention of Eckbert's—and that they were dualists, preaching that the world had been created not by God but by a fallen angel, probably Lucifer.[18]

The Cathars' Christian dualism originated in the apocalyptic myth of the fight below the walls of heavenly Jerusalem, in which the archangel Michael battled with the dragon, the old serpent that embodied evil, and hurled him into outer darkness. In its fall, the dragon used its tail to pull down one-third of the heavenly stars. Expanding on the Christian myth of the fallen angels, which was popular in eleventh- and twelfth-century Christendom, Cathar theologians gradually developed an evolutive and vague dualism, according to which human souls were fallen creatures of God who had accidentally become prisoners of the flesh. John of Lugio, a kindly scholastic theologian and an Italian Cathar bishop who lived in the first half of the thirteenth century, argued that original sin and free will did not enter into the debate. He was the author of the *Book of Two Principles* and the theoretician of absolute dualism.[19]

The starting point of this theological reflection, which the Catholic Church condemned as "Manichaean" dualism, was founded on the Gospels and the First Epistle of John (on the central tenet of Jesus' teaching: "My kingdom is not of this world . . . you are not of the world," variously worded in John 15:18–20, 16:1–3, 16:28, 16:33, 18:36; 1 John 2:15–16; 1 John 3:1; 1 John 4:4–5; and elsewhere). Hence the notion of two churches, used by Catholics and Cathars alike.

Fallen angels of God trapped in the bondage of the flesh, human souls were "all equal and good," to quote the phrase used again and again by believers brought before the Inquisition; in the early fourteenth century, a shepherd, Pierre Maury, expounded on this native equality of souls for the benefit of Jacques Fournier, an inquisitor whose interest in the Cathar sect was more thorough than that of his predecessors fifty years earlier: "I have heard those heretics say that men and women's souls are identical, that there is no difference between them, that the only difference between men and women is in their flesh, which is the work of the devil. So that, when the souls of men and women leave their bodies, there is no difference between them."[20]

Pierre Maury also told Fournier, however, that Guilhem Bélibaste, one of the last heretics he had long talks with, preached somewhat inconsistently that women who were Good Christians when they died became men just

before reaching the kingdom of God—a detail that Jean Duvernoy has identified as a specific survival of Origenism.[21]

Albeit mitigated, this theoretically equal footing on which Catharism put
the two sexes no doubt accounts for the fact that its clergy included men
and women. It may also explain, if only indirectly, why sources show women
to have been actively involved, as believers and Good Women, wherever the
Cathar Church was free to spread.

Richard Abels and Ellen Harrison have noted that, according to the records
of the inquiries carried out by inquisitors Bernard de Caux and Jean de Saint-
Pierre (MS 609 of Toulouse), 45 percent of the heretical ministers cited in
the early thirteenth century for the Lauragais, the region between Toulouse
and Carcassonne, were women, which is an impressive proportion, especially
if one compares this with the Catholic clergy.[22]

THE GOOD WOMEN IN THEIR COMMUNITY HOUSES

Confined to the Lower Ranks of the Hierarchy

Scholars agree that the early conversion to Catharism of the landowning nobil-
ity, and more especially of its female members, contributed decisively to the
sect's flourishing success in Languedoc.

Almost everywhere in Europe, Catharism had been ruthlessly persecuted
from the early twelfth century onward and stamped out in regions such as
Flanders, Champagne, the Rhineland, and Burgundy; the main exception
was the area of Languedoc, which stretches from Carcassonne across to
Toulouse and up to Agen and Albi. Swayed perhaps by their vassals, its territorial princes tolerated Cathar preaching and the setting up of bishoprics
and religious communities. Thus Catharism virtually became an established
church in the Midi, until the social and political upheaval that followed the
Albigensian Crusade (1209–29) and the ensuing conquest of the region by
the French king, with the arrival of the Inquisition (after 1233). As long as
the Cathars were tolerated, they stood for a form of ordinary Christianity
that authorized women as well as men to cleanse people of sin and to save
souls, perhaps even to preach. As such, Catharism first attracted the active
support of noblewomen, who were soon followed by the artisans' and peas-
ants' wives of their *castra*.

This said, to our knowledge, no woman ever attained the higher ranks of
the secular hierarchy, despite a relatively tolerant social environment that
enabled Catharism to flourish as early as the second half of the twelfth century: the church had four bishoprics, to which a fifth was added, each with
its ordained bishop, his two coadjutors, and deacons. No name of a woman
bishop or deaconess has survived. The status of a Good Woman—or *Perfecta*
(so called by the Inquisition)—thus seems to have remained similar to a nun's,

with the most senior Good Women becoming mother superiors in the religious communities they led.

The Cathar Nuns

The Cathar clergy was a regular clergy, organized like any religious order of its time. Its members took their vows (by receiving the *consolamentum*), kept observances, and were bound to specific sequences of prayers. Outward-looking, its members were entrusted with a twofold mission: to go out into the world to preach and administer the sacrament. In this respect, they competed directly with Catholic priests and clerics. Above the Good Men and Women the secular hierarchy of bishops, coadjutors, and deacons preached, administered the sacrament, and supervised the running of the community houses.

Good Women lived in sisterhoods known as the "houses of the *Perfectae*," which sprang up alongside those set up for men in the towns of Languedoc before the Crusade.[23] On entering a community house, they ritually vowed "to devote themselves to God and the Gospels."

Whether male or female, members of the Cathar religious communities were bound to the vows they had taken of chastity, poverty, and abstinence. They observed the "rule of the Gospel" and followed the "way of righteousness and truth" of the evangelical precepts. They prayed at ritual hours, repeating the *paternoster* and the *adoremus;* they exchanged the ritual kiss of peace and ate only after one of them had blessed bread. They abstained from all meat, survived on bread and water three times a week, and observed longer fasts three times a year. Their vow of chastity forbade Good Women even to sit on the same bench as men. In their community houses, Good Women probably owed obedience to their mother superiors, who seem to have exerted a fair amount of authority. Good Women never went out alone: each was assigned a companion (*socia*), because it was important never to break the rule of community life.

Uncloistered Sisters

Unlike Catholic nuns, however, these sisters were free to come and go, to receive visitors in their establishment, to meet members of the laity. The absence of enclosure made these medieval sisters exceptional and enabled them to have a pastoral mission.[24] Their intramural life was not restricted to contemplation, fasting, and long hours of prayer; because the Cathar clergy were bound to work, in the tradition of Christ's disciples they also performed manual labor. In this they differed significantly from the new Mendicant orders; the Cathars were poor, but they were not beggars.

Depending on the tasks they carried out, Cathar establishments frequently resembled genuine workshops, with each community doing its best to harmonize its members' activities. The Good Christians sewed, wove (using yarn supplied by villagers), tooled leather, and worked wood and horn. In the *castrum* of Montségur, Marquesia de Lanta, a former Toulouse noblewoman and the mother of Corba de Pereille, the castellan's wife, worked as a seamstress with her fellow community members. In the course of the long siege, and not long before dying in the auto-da-fé of March 16, 1244, she gave her grand-daughter Philippa de Mirepoix a veil, gloves, and shirts.[25] Statements made in depositions frequently recalled that Good Women went on working even when they were forced into hiding after the French conquest. Sheltering on the outskirts of *castra* or in huts in the forests, they untiringly spun flax or wool supplied by followers who, while helping them, turned their presence to their own advantage.[26]

Unlike Catholic convents, Cathar community houses kept open board— and perhaps lodging too. Some seem to have been run as hospices or almshouses. In the upper-class circles of the Lauragais and its dependent fief-doms, it was considered fashionable to be seen having a meal at the house led by the former lady of the *castrum*, Blanche, who had become a Good Woman with her daughter, Mabilia.[27] On a humbler level, Pierre Magis, a mason of Montauban, met Waldensian women preaching in public and got into the habit, while working in town, of taking his meals at a sisterhood of "heretical" women—"Cathar" women, according to the terminology used by the Inquisition—who took advantage of his presence to indoctrinate him.[28]

Sisters on a Mission

As long as Catharism was freely tolerated, and before persecution forced the Good Christians to disband and go into hiding, community houses were not cut off from the outside world. Visitors came and went, bringing orders and supplies for the workshops, seeking board, sharing the bread, nuts, or apples they brought for their perfected relatives, and no doubt exchanging edify-ing thoughts with them the while.[29] Conversely, nothing seems to have pre-vented Good Men and Women from visiting family and friends or traveling for other purposes, although we have no means of knowing whether they did so on their own initiative or at the request of their superiors. Statements made before the Inquisition suggest that Good Women were sent on reli-gious missions. Abels and Harrison have noted that the names of the 318 *Perfectae* cited in the Inquisition records of Bernard de Caux and Jean de Saint-Pierre recur less often than those of their male counterparts: they were sighted less frequently, and seem to have been less active outside their estab-lishments.[30] They were not cloistered, however.

They went out to nurse the sick, often no doubt at the request of rela-tives, whereas it may have been on the instructions of their superiors that they watched by the bedsides of the dying who, once they had received the deathbed *consolamentum*, had to live out their last hours accordingly to prevent the defilement of the sacrament. Occasionally, a Good Woman visited someone on her own initiative if we are to believe the statement of Guillelmette de Quiders, sister of the coseigniors of Le Mas Saintes-Puelles; she may, however, simply have been trying to deflect attention from her own Cathar sympathies when she claimed that her mother, Garsende du Mas, the former lady of Le Mas who had been perfected like so many of her rank, burst into her home one day and carried off her ailing little boy, Othon de Quiders, to have him nursed and baptized in the community house where she lived.[31]

In peacetime, a group of Good Women might be seen going down the street in a ritual procession, as they escorted one or more novices to be ordained by a member of the hierarchy—bishop, coadjutor, or deacon. The ceremony, described in detail in the Cathar Ritual, was public and collective.

From what witnesses told the Inquisitors, Good Women were frequently sighted outside their houses during the period when the Cathar Church was tolerated, though it is not always clear whether their activities were prompted by private or religious considerations: Barssalone of Brugairolle, a noblewoman of Villepinte, said that when she was a child living at Fanjeaux her father, Jean de Couffignal, frequently offered Good Women hospitality. (The Inquisition records contain many other similar depositions.)[32]

In 1233, Barssalone's father played host to a party of distinguished Cathars. Although their church had come under increasing pressure, it was still tolerated in places like Fanjeaux, which, having come under the protection of the count of Toulouse in 1229,[33] was spared the Inquisition until the late 1230s. The guests were two Good Men: Pierre Bordier, who was probably the deacon of Fanjeaux, and his *socius;* and two Good Women, Guillelma and her *socia*. A prayer meeting of sorts was held, not unlike those secretly organized by members of the French Reformed Church after the Edict of Nantes was revoked. Neighbors and trusted friends were present, as well as the Couffignal family, to ask for the Christians' blessing, hear them preach, and receive the kiss of peace. *Praedicaverunt,* Barssalone declared, without going into details. Should one infer from this that the Good Men preached, not the Women—or did they preach jointly? As for the kiss of peace, the Good Women would have received it symbolically through the Holy Book, which their brothers placed on their shoulders according to the Cathar rite, and then shared it in turn mouth-to-cheek with all the women believers present.

The Good Women's Ministry

Although they lived in communities more frequently than their brothers, Good Women were not cut off from the outside world once they had been ordained, and they continued to lead a social as well as a consecrated life.

As we have seen, this outward-looking attitude implied a genuinely religious function. Theoretically endowed with the power to remit sins and save souls, they insisted on their right to use it. Yet before the onset of persecution, Good Men took precedence over Good Women in sacramental ceremonies.

Good Women were present during *consolamenta*, they carried the kiss of peace among women believers, and they offered prayers aloud with their brothers, but nothing indicates that their right hands mingled with the men's over the open book that was held above a postulant's head during the baptism in the Holy Spirit. This would have been ruled out also by the prohibition against men and women touching. A collective imposition of hands was either all male or all female.

The peacetime administering of the sacrament seems therefore to have been a predominantly male function, reserved to members of the church hierarchy.

Like his Catholic counterpart, the Cathar bishop seems to have represented the holy fountainhead of his church: by ordaining the members of his church, be they Good Men or priests, he conferred upon them the duties of the holy ministry and the power to loose and to bind. It probably was a matter of keeping the succession of the Holy Spirit as impeccable and therefore as valid as possible—a succession that in the Cathar view had been preserved by the Church of God since the apostles and had to be maintained until the end of time by avoiding a multiplication of "sowers" of the Holy Spirit that would eventually get out of hand. It is interesting to note that in the thirteenth century the Italian Cathar churches fell apart over rumors about their founding bishops' private lives: questioning their moral conduct amounted to questioning the legitimacy of the long line of *consolamenta* that could be traced back from them.

As persecution gained ground in Languedoc, the hierarchy crumbled, and the de facto equality between the male and female Elect of "the persecuted Church of Christ" (to use the Cathars' own phrase) resurfaced. The pressure of events led rank-and-file Perfects to "receive [believers] into the sect of the heretics" (to use the inquisitors' language)—in other words, to confer the *consolamentum* not only on the dying but also on postulants. And these self-appointed ordinants included women as well as men.

If the sight of a Good Woman baptizing someone by the laying on of hands remained exceptional, the mere fact that a few cases are recorded confirms that this was theologically possible. In Inquisition sources I have found five instances of Good Women conferring the ordination *consolamentum*. This suggests that other examples are almost certain to be found elsewhere in the mass of records—even though we shall probably never find a great many. The best known is the case of Arnaude de Lamothe, who gave Friar Ferrer a long, pathetic account of her existence, on the run and in constant anguish, before being captured and recanting.

Another example, more dramatic in its urgency and spiritual despair, is that of a Good Woman living alone and hiding in a woodsman's hut in the Lauragais; she saw her son, Raimon Raseire, arrive one day in the company of her daughter—his own sister—so that the Good Woman would baptize her and take her as a *socia*. Mother and daughter lived together, helped by Raimon and a few trusted friends, presumably until they were captured and burned.[34] Until the Crusade, this Good Woman had led a devout, apostolic, and hardworking but somewhat effaced life in the midst of the *castrum;* hardship had restored her to the concrete practice of her holy ministry, to the sacramental power she had to save souls.

THE GOOD WOMEN'S VOICES

Catechists in Their Community Houses

Even though in peacetime Good Women were virtually never ministers, could they more openly preach? In their community houses, they were entrusted catechumens who hoped to be perfected. From what a great number of deponents told the Inquisition, we can reconstruct these probationary periods, which lasted at least two years. The first stage included learning the daily ritual gestures and offering prayers and being gradually introduced to the Perfects' ascetic way of life: total chastity, permanent vegetarianism, and repeated periods of Lent and fasting. We know that at least one young novice, Dulcie Faure, of Villeneuve-la-Comtal in the Lauragais, was not ordained in the end because she found the austere life too difficult.[35]

Yet, before giving up, Dulcie had already embarked on the second stage of her novitiate, in which she received religious instruction. She confessed that initially she had gone of her own free will to Gailharde, a Good Woman in her village, and told her she wished to take the vows. Gailharde escorted her to a community house at Castelnaudary run by Blanche de Laurac. Dulcie spent a year there, learning the gestures and rites of the Good Women: "I ate bread with them which they had blessed and adored them several times, genuflecting three times [the rite of the *melhorier*], and several times I heard them preach."

She had therefore been given a first level of religious education. From there she entered a community house at Laurac, run by a mother superior, Brunissende, where she spent another year observing rites and hearing preaching. Only after that was she finally allowed to begin the novitiate proper with the same sisterhood. The preaching or catechesis took on a more theological bent. Understandably, Dulcie was at pains to convince the inquisitor examining her that she had not been taken in by the heretics' preaching: "I was not ordained because, owing to my youth, I could not do what the heretics do or teach others to do. I heard them talk of the visible world . . . but believed nothing of this."

Descriptions of novitiates abound and agree.[36] Good Women were in charge of personally training and instructing the novices entrusted to them. The deacon visited each community once a month to hear confessions, a ceremony known as the *apparelhament;* he may have taken the opportunity to lecture the novices on theology, but mention of this has not surfaced in any of the inquisitorial sources. What seems more probable is that some establishments specialized more than others in catechism and served as seminaries. Judging from what Dulcie told the inquisitor, the religious teaching at the house led by Brunissende seems to have been more advanced than in those run by Gailharde and Blanche. Some Good Women must have been more educated and better exegetes than others and therefore preached and taught in their houses according to their abilities.

This teaching was, however, a catechistic rather than a truly pastoral function. Evidence that some of the Good Women addressed lay assemblies of believers would be needed to prove that they really were allowed to preach. The community houses were not self-enclosed, and visitors came and went, sharing meals with the whole sisterhood or, more frequently, with a specific Good Woman, who might be a relative or former neighbor. Unfortunately, we do not learn much from witnesses examined by the Inquisition. It is hard to tell whether visits were prompted simply by personal affection or by religious considerations. Was it moral support or religious guidance one sought from one's perfected friends and relatives?

The Good Christians' Way of Preaching

Similarly, Good Women do not seem to have left their community houses without a religious purpose: until the persecutions began, such was the display of religious solemnity when they visited close or distant relatives that one feels they must have been on a mission—probably a proselytizing mission.

Occitan Catharism was a Christianism of proximity. It relied on close contact between clergy and believers and on the shining, tangible example the Perfects set, living as they did among the laity, in houses set up for them in the towns and *castra*. Believers could see for themselves whether they practiced what they preached; they could visit them and verify that the evangelical message they carried was not belied by their way of life, which was modeled on that of the apostles. The Cathars set great store in this. Similarly, Good Men and Women could visit believers in their homes to rekindle their faith and loyalties when necessary. Unlike the Waldensian preachers and apostolic friars, Cathar ministers did not preach in public places; they did not harangue crowds. There are a few reports of solemn occasions when great dignitaries of the church preached before large assemblies: Guilhabert de Castres, for instance, did so at Fanjeaux and Montségur Castles. Many accounts tell of intimate gatherings in private homes, around the hearth, with a Perfect preaching for the benefit of just a few relatives and friends or perhaps for one believer whose flagging faith needed reviving.

Cathar theologians produced high-level treatises and are known to have been excellent debaters and skillful exegetes of Scripture. In contrast, everyday preaching was closer to believers' concerns. Scripture was cited to convince listeners that they were *the* true Christians, that "they had the greatest power to save souls." Catechesis was elaborated especially for novices as an introduction to the rationalist-symbolic interpretation of the New Testament that characterized Catharism,[37] to teach of "things visible and invisible" and give them "the understanding of Good."

Inquisition records for the early fourteenth century offer vivid reminiscences of the Good Men's simple, direct, and colorful preaching. While this did not rule out humorous touches, it was always based on Scripture.

> I will tell you the reason why we are called heretics. It is because the world hates us, and it is not surprising the world hates us (1 John 3:13), for it also hated Our Lord, whom it persecuted, and his apostles too. We are hated and persecuted because of his law, in which we walk without faltering. . . . For there are two churches: the one flees and forgives (Matthew 10:22–23), the other possesses and scourges.[38]

Those were the words with which Good Man Pierre Authié greeted a young shepherd, Pierre Maury, on their first meeting in 1303 or 1304: he argued in the same way as the Rhineland heretics, quoted by Evervin of Steinfeld two centuries earlier. Cathar preachers never indulged in pulpit rhetoric. They were chatty and confidential; they relied on mutual trust, expected listeners to argue, and could quote the appropriate scriptural references to bolster their own arguments. Some witnesses also recalled Good Men reading aloud from the New Testament or getting a literate member of the congregation to do so in their place, to show that they were not fabulating, that the main tenets of their faith were there for all to check, in the Holy Scriptures.[39]

Women Preachers

In this context, the significance of Good Women's visits to the homes of friends or relatives becomes clearer. Although they acted more discreetly and were less frequently sighted than Good Men, they were probably out on pastoral missions keeping the faith of Cathar believers alive. It is difficult, however, to infer much more than this from what witnesses told their inquisitors. More often than not they were referring to male ministers when they used the words *praedicatio* and *praedicaverunt*. Whether in peacetime or during the persecutions, the Good Women mentioned in the depositions seem to have been silent. Believers performed the ritual *melhorier*, asked for their blessing, and ate bread they had blessed. No one ever describes them book in hand. But it is hard to imagine that Good Women who taught novices in their establishments had nothing to tell the believers they met.

A few witnesses did testify to hearing Good Women discuss their religion. Guillelma Faure, from the hamlet of Camplong, near Saint-Martin-Lalande, was, with her *socia*, the sole representative of persecuted Catharism in that part of the Lauragais between 1233 and 1240. Nearly all the inhabitants questioned by Bernard de Caux and Jean de Saint-Pierre in 1245 admitted to having seen the two women in some of the villagers' homes. Lady Ermessen, wife of Bernard Mir Arezat, one of the coseigniors of the place, recalled having seen Guillelma with the wife of another coseignior, Lady Cerdane, who was a relative, in the home of Melia, wife of Pierre Déjean; after hearing the Good Woman and her companion "preach," they asked for their blessing. This was around 1233.[40] There were no men present.

Another woman, Lady Biverne Golairan of Avignonnet, revealed during the same inquest that sometime around 1230 she had sheltered Good Woman Bérengère de Sègreville and her *socia*. She had not asked for their blessing, but she had heard them "preach."

The most vivid instance of female preaching was provided by another woman, who was herself a former Good Woman, Arnaude de Lamothe. Captured after a long period of hardship and constant flight, she was thrown in a Toulouse prison, where she finally recanted. Brought before Friar Ferrer in the summer of 1244, she described in detail how she had been perfected, even though religion had never really been her vocation, and the ensuing life she led. Her tragic tale begins in 1207, in Montauban:

> Under oath, she declared that one day two heretical women, whose names she did not know, arrived at Montauban at the house of her mother, Austorgue. These heretical women preached there, in her, Arnaude's, presence, and in the presence of her sister, Peirone, her mother, Austorgue, and Lombarde, the widow of her uncle Isarn d'Aussac. And at the end of this preaching, Austorgue and Lombarde adored the heretical women three times, genuflecting in front of them and every time saying in turn: "Lady, bless me, pray God for the sinner that I am, that he make me into a good Christian and that he lead me to a good end." And to each of these *Benedicite* the heretical women replied, "God bless you." And after the last *Benedicite* they added: "Pray God that he makes you into a good Christian and that he leads you to a good end." After that, the two heretics left the house and went on their way.[41]

Arnaude is here referring to the Cathar Church's flourishing years, which is why her statement is so important. It is one of the rare occasions on which Good Women are described as being on a pastoral round, as missionaries of their church. The two visitors preached, and the adult believers performed the ritual *melhorier*. But the purpose of their visit does not seem to have stopped there. Shortly afterward, two members of the Cathar hierarchy were sent to fetch the two sisters, Arnaude and Peirone, and take them to the house run by Good Woman Poncia at Villemur, to begin their novitiate.[42] The previous preachers had probably been sent by their community, at the request of the girls' mother. A similar story occurred some fifteen years later, around 1222, when, assuming that persecutions were a thing of the past, the women of the Lamothe family chose to re-enter the weakened Cathar Church and start a new novitiate; the first coadjutor of the Toulousain church sent them the mother superior of a sisterhood at Linars, in Quercy, whose members had survived persecution by living under the habits of Catholic nuns. She and her *socia* came to Montauban to meet Arnaude, Peironne, and their mother, Austorgue, and escort them to Linars.[43]

Cathar nuns therefore participated actively in their church. Their establishments were part of the Cathar pastoral strategy. Again, the story of Arnaude de Lamothe casts light on this point. Once the mother and daughters had been perfected, the hierarchy of the Toulousain church set up a house for them in a village of the Lantarès, in the heart of the region the Cathar Church tried hard to reconquer in 1220–25.[44] Good Women were apparently preferred to Good Men when it came to curing the souls of, and preaching to, the feminine population of believers. This was probably true in the Waldensian movement too. Until persecution forced them into hiding and a life on the run, Good Women almost certainly never traveled without good and precise reasons; visits paid to the homes of relatives and friends were also discreet but efficient pastoral missions.

Before the Inquisition finally wiped out their last surviving communities, Good Women were numerous in the ranks of the Cathar clergy. In the region of Toulouse, in the Albigeois and the Lauragais, they may well have been as numerous as Good Men. Less visible than their spiritual brothers, less likely to carry out sacerdotal and pastoral missions, they nonetheless rightly held and exerted a far more important function than Catholic nuns.

They fully accepted the twofold nature, regular and secular, of their church, which for all purposes was like a religious order. Ordained, they were also present on the secular front, even if they were kept out of the hierarchy. Authorized to administer the sacrament in an emergency, they brought salvation; they also preached to spread God's message, mainly among women believers, who represented a substantial proportion of the laity in Occitan towns and *castra*. When visiting relatives, friends, or members of their lineage (if they were noblewomen), they were de facto emissaries of the male hierarchy of their church. All these roles made theirs a valued presence within the ranks of their church. By carrying Catharism into the heart of family clans, they provided their church with some of its most devoted and ardent followers. This explains the impressive resistance of Cathar convictions in Languedoc during a century of ruthlessly efficient persecutions.

As to what these Good Women actually preached, we know practically nothing. Did their preaching have a markedly feminine slant, in contrast with the Good Men's preaching? One voice remains memorable, in a distinctive, though unfortunate way: it is that of a Good Woman telling a pregnant young woman that she bears a "devil" in her womb. Another voice is that of a Good Woman seeking to console a bereaved mother, clumsily telling her that her nextborn will replace the baby that has just died. Neither is really enlightening, and neither carries any weight when one knows how ambiguous some of the records of the Inquisition can be.

More likely than not, the Good Women's voices echoed the Men's: aimed at small gatherings, their preaching eschewed all rhetorical effects but knew when to be emphatic. What mattered above all was the *example* they set, the apostolic *exemplarity* of their way of life: they referred constantly to the Scriptures, which were more often than not learned by rote rather than actually read in the text; they used simple, popular, and jolly *exempla* similar to those used by Mendicant preachers in the same period. Theirs was homespun preaching spoken round the hearth, adapted to those present and all the more effective because of the speaker's self-effacement and powerful convictions.

It might be going too far to claim to hear in the preaching of those heretical women a "new pastoral" according to the pattern proposed by Jean-Claude Schmidt and Jacques Le Goff. Good Women were talking about salvation and God's forgiveness at a time when the ideology of pontifical theocracy was gaining ground, the Christian community was increasingly seen as severely circumscribed, and doctrinal orthodoxy was developing a rigid framework under the successive pressures of the Inquisition and Thomism. There was no Cathar kissing of lepers at a time when Franciscan mysticism was profoundly renewing Catholic spirituality in the greatness of God the Man. Male and female Cathar preachers invariably preferred simple, straightforward Christian practices on which believers could model themselves: "Those who call themselves Good Men, who lie not and kill not, nor have commerce with women, who turn the other cheek when struck, who offer their cloaks if their tunics are removed, who also say there are two Churches, one good, the other sinful. . . . "[45]

Over two centuries, Cathar Christians remained astonishingly faithful to their earliest practices, which were inherited from the monastic and austere eleventh century and might have appeared antiquated in the fourteenth century. Yet the new Mendicant orders modeled their lifestyle on the Cathars'; and Dominic may have had Cathar sisterhood houses in mind when he set up establishments for women Dominicans alongside those for his preachers— starting at Prouilles, which he founded in the valley just below Fanjeaux.[46]

Several generations after the last *Perfectae* had been hounded out of existence, the inquests of Geoffroy d'Ablis (1308) and Jacques Fournier (1318–25) show that there were still a great many determined women, ardent in their attachment to the doomed Cathar Church, among the last devoted *credentes*.

Witness the example of the sentence passed against Stephana de Proaudes of Toulouse by Inquisitor Bernard Gui, who covered the city from 1307 to 1323. She was released to the secular arm to be burned alive, "Since it appears . . . that [she] commends the life, sect, and faith of the said heretics, that [she] encourages, defends and supports it, claiming that there is no Salvation for anyone except for those received in their sect."[47]

NOTES

This essay was translated by Janice Valls-Russell.

1. Occitan Cathar Ritual of Lyons, "3) Receiving the consolamentum." For a French translation of this early-thirteenth-century text, see René Nelli, *Ecritures cathares* (Paris: Denoël, 1959), reedited and expanded by Anne Brenon (Paris: Le Rocher, 1995), p. 232.

2. Testimony of Arnaud Sicre, of Ax. For a French translation, see Jean Duvernoy, *Le registre d'Inquisition de Jacques Fournier (1318–1325) traduit et annoté*, 3 vols. (Paris: Mouton, 1978), vol. 3, p. 774.

3. For a general study on this subject, see Anne Brenon, *Les femmes cathares* (Paris: Perrin, 1992).

4. On the extinction of the last communities of Good Women around the mid-thirteenth century as a result of a dangerous underground existence and persecution, and more generally on the part played by women in the Cathar Church, see ibid.; for statistics, see Richard Abels and Ellen Harrison, "The Participation of Women in Languedocian Catharism," *Mediaeval Studies* 41 (1979): 215–51.

5. For a survey of these new sources and the departures they provide, see Richard Landes, "La vie apostolique en Aquitaine en l'An Mil: Paix de Dieu, culte des reliques et communautés hérétiques," *Les Annales, Economie, Société, Civilisation* 3: *Les "hérésies" du début du xie siècle; de nouveaux documents* (May–June 1991): 7–9. See also Guy Lobrichon, "Le clair-obscur de l'hérésie au début du xie siècle en Aquitaine," in *Essays on the Peace of God: The Church and the People in Eleventh Century France*, ed. Thomas Head and Richard Landes, *Historical Reflections/Réflexions historiques* 14 (Waterloo, Ontario, 1987), pp. 441–43; and more especially Pierre Bonnassie and Richard Landes, "Une nouvelle hérésie est née en ce monde," in *Les sociétés méridionales autour de l'An Mil* (Paris: Éditions du CNRS, 1992), pp. 435–59.

6. A good synthesis is provided by Jean Duvernoy, *Le catharisme*, 2 vols., *L'histoire des cathares* (Toulouse: Privat, 1978, 1990), vol. 1, pp. 99–100. For a more recent appraisal, see Anne Brenon, "Les hérésies de l'An Mil: nouvelles perspectives sur les origines du catharisme," *Heresis* 24 (1995): 21–36.

7. Richard Landes, "La vie apostolique en Aquitaine en l'An Mil: Paix de Dieu, culte des reliques et communautés hérétiques," p. 9. Landes cites the model proposed by Brian Stock.

8. These words of Adémar de Chabannes, spoken in his sermon on the Eucharist, have just been discovered and published in Bonnassie and Landes, "Une nouvelle hérésie est née en ce monde," pp. 454–57.

9. The Latin text of Evervin of Steinfeld's letter is available in *PL* 182, cols. 676–80 (appendix to Saint Bernard's letters, letter CDLXXII). Translated into English by

Robert I. Moore, *The Birth of Popular Heresy* (Toronto: University of Toronto Press, 1995), pp. 74–78; see specifically pp. 75–76.

10. This departure in medieval studies on Catharism was first expounded in detail by Jean Duvernoy in *Le catharisme.*

11. See Georges Duby, *Le Chevalier, la femme et le prêtre* (Paris: Hachette, 1981).

12. Ervin of Steinfeld's letter to Saint Bernard, in Moore, *The Birth of Popular Heresy*, p. 78.

13. Ylva Hagman, "Le rite d'initiation chrétienne chez les cathares et les bogomiles," *Heresis* 20 (1993): 13–31.

14. Ervin of Steinfeld's letter to Saint Bernard, in Moore, *The Birth of Popular Heresy*, p. 76.

15. Ibid.

16. See Anne Brenon, "Les fonctions sacramentelles du *consolament*," *Heresis* 20 (1993): 33–50; and Hagman, "Le rite d'initiation chrétienne," p. 26.

17. Occitan Cathar Ritual of Dublin, French translation by Anne Brenon in her edition of René Nelli, *Ecritures cathares*, p. 276.

18. "Eckberti Schonaugiensis Sermones adversus . . . Catharorum . . . haeresim"; *PL* 195, cols. 11–103.

19. For a French translation and a good commentary on this Cathar treaty, see René Nelli, *Ecritures cathares* (1995 ed.), pp. 73–188.

20. Testimony of Pierre Maury in Duvernoy, *Le registre d'Inquisition de Jacques Fournier*, vol. 3, p. 999.

21. Ibid.; see also Brenon, *Les femmes cathares*, pp. 109–10.

22. Abels and Harrison, "Women in Languedocian Catharism," p. 225. Of the 719 Cathar ministers cited, 318 were women.

23. On Cathar nuns, see Anne Brenon, "L'hérésie en Languedoc au XIIe–XIIIe siècles: une religion pour les femmes?" in *La femme dans l'histoire et la société méridionales* (IXe–XIXe siècles), Proceedings of the Sixty-sixth Congress of the F.H.L.M.R. (Montpellier: F.H.L.M.R., 1995), pp. 103–16.

24. Abels and Harrison ("Women in Languedocian Catharism," p. 219) tend to see Cathar and Catholic sisters as similar, however. On the Cathar establishments, see Anne Brenon, "La maison cathare: une pratique de vie religieuse communautaire entre la règle et le siècle," in *Europe et Occitanie, les pays cathares*, Proceedings of the Fifth Session of Medieval History of the Centre d'Etudes Cathares (Carcassonne: Heresis, 1995), pp. 213–32.

25. Testimony of Philippa de Mirepoix, MS Paris, B.N. Doat 24, f. 196b–204a. See Brenon, *Les femmes cathares*, p. 252.

26. Ibid., pp. 195, 206, 268.

27. Ibid., pp. 143, 163–64. See also the testimonies of Pierre de Cornélian, knight of Montgey, MS Paris, B.N. Doat 24, f. 19b–24a, and of Bernard Mir Arezat, coseignior of Saint-Martin Lalande and knight of Laurac, MS Toulouse, B.M. 609, f. 30a.

28. Brenon, *Les femmes cathares*, p. 214. Testimony of Pierre Magis, MS Paris, B.N. Doat 21, f. 275a.

29. See, for instance, the testimony of Berbéguèira de Loubens, wife of a knight of Puylaurens, in MS Paris, B.N. Doat 24, f. 131b–144. The convivial worldliness of aristocratic establishments is covered in Brenon, *Les femmes cathares*, esp. pp. 167–72.

30. Abels and Harrison, "Women in Languedocian Catharism," p. 226.

31. Brenon, *Les femmes cathares,* pp. 182–83.

32. The details that follow are taken from the testimony of Barssalone (Barcelona) de Brugairolles before Inquisitors Ferrer and Pons Garin in 1244, MS Paris, B.N. Doat 23, f. 121a–125a. See Brenon, *Les femmes cathares,* pp. 195–96.

33. See Michel Roquebert, "Un exemple de catharisme ordinaire: Fanjeaux," in *Europe et Occitanie, les pays cathares,* Proceedings of the Fifth Session of Medieval History of the Centre d'Etudes Cathares (Carcassonne: Heresis, 1995), pp. 169–211; see esp. 189–90.

34. Testimony of Martin de Caselles, a former priest of Auriac, MS Toulouse, B.M. 609, f. 237b–238a. See Brenon, *Les femmes cathares,* p. 270.

35. Testimony of Dulcie Faure, MS Toulouse, B.M. 609, f. 184b. See Brenon, *Les femmes cathares,* pp. 131–33.

36. Examples are given in Brenon, *Les femmes cathares,* esp. pp. 15–17 and 210–15.

37. For a detailed analysis of this, see Anne Brenon, "La catéchèse cathare: une pastorale de l'Evangile," in *Catéchismes et professions de Foi,* Proceedings of the Colloque Jean Boisset 1994, Centre d'Histoire des Réformes et du Protestantisme (Montpellier: C.H.R.P., 1995), pp. 99–131.

38. Testimony of Pierre Maury in Duvernoy, *Le registre d'Inquisition de Jacques Fournier,* vol. 3, p. 924.

39. See, for instance, the testimony of Guilhem Bernard, knight of Vaudreuilhe, in MS Toulouse, B.M. 609 f. 232b. Brenon, *Les femmes cathares,* pp. 210–15.

40. Testimony of Ermessen, wife of Bernard Mir Arezat of Saint-Martin-Lalande, MS Toulouse, B.M. 609, f. 35b.

41. Arnaude de Lamothe gave Inquisitor Ferrer a long and detailed testimony in 1244 (MS Paris, B.N. Doat 23, f. 1–49b [f. 2b–3a for the extract given here]), which was followed by a shorter testimony before Bernard de Caux in 1245 (MS Toulouse, B.M. 609, f. 201b–203b). I have attempted to reconstruct the story of her life in Brenon, *Les femmes cathares,* pp. 13–57.

42. MS Paris, B.N. Doat 23, f. 3b.

43. Ibid., f. 7b.

44. Ibid., 13a–b.

45. Analysis, in an eighteenth-century inventory, of a lost register of testimonies gathered between 1305 and 1309 before the bishop of Béziers. Text published by A. C. Germain, *Inventaire inédit concernant les archives de l'Inquisition de Carcassonne* (Montpellier: Publications de la Société archeologique, 1855), vol. 4, no. 24 (1855), pp. 287–308, esp. 304. Cf. Anne Brenon, "Mort et effacement du catharisme," *Etudes théologiques et religieuses* 69 (1994): 67–79.

46. See Père M. H. Vicaire, O.P., "L'action de saint Dominique sur la vie régulière des femmes en Languedoc," *La femme dans la vie religieuse du Languedoc* (XIIIᵉ–XIVᵉ), *Cahiers de Fanjeaux* 23 (1988): 217–40, esp. 227–28.

47. Sentences passed by Bernard Gui; see *Historia Inquisitionis,* ed. Philippe a Limborch (Amsterdam, 1692), pp. 5–6. On the last Cathar believers and more generally on the place of women in the last years of Catharism, see Brenon, *Les femmes cathares,* pp. 319–84, esp. 325–26.

SIX

The Right of Women to Give Religious Instruction in the Thirteenth Century

Nicole Bériou

In contrast to the early Christian practice of instructing catechumens prior to baptism, almost everyone from the early Middle Ages onward was baptized shortly after birth. Consequently, those who were given religious instruction received it after baptism. No formal catechism or catechesis existed, and children were supposed to get the rudiments of faith and morals from their parents, if possible.[1] They also were expected to commit to memory two or three prayers[2] and recite them, and to attend church, where their individual participation in liturgical rituals played a greater role than listening to sermons. No doubt the influential *Liber Pastoralis*, written by Gregory the Great about 591 and widely diffused among clerics, reminded priests of their duty to teach. Indeed, the pope's remarks were so pertinent that Gratian, about 1140, quoted them at length in the *distinctio* of his *Decretum*, which was devoted to this question.[3] Unfortunately, most priests were unable to carry out these teaching duties, but other people, such as those in monastic communities and families, also bore some of the responsibility for religious instruction.

One of the most famous examples of a woman's personal involvement in the task of educating is provided by the relationship between Blanche of Castille and her children, especially her elder son, Louis. The Spanish princess had been married to Philip Augustus's son when she was twelve, and twenty-six years later she had to assume the regency of the kingdom of France when her husband, Louis VIII, died after a reign of only three years (1223–26). In 1226 their son Louis was twelve, and we may conjecture that both parents had shared the responsibility of his religious instruction. According to John of Joinville, the close friend and confidant of Saint Louis, Blanche of Castille played the main role in the king's education: "God kept him, thanks to his mother's good teachings. She taught him how to believe in God and how to love him, and she made many religious people come around him, and when he was a young boy, she made him have regard for the prayers of Hours and hear sermons on feast days. He remembered that once his mother made him understand that she would prefer him dead than having committed a mortal sin."[4]

At first glance, this testimony seems to give evidence only of the prince's religious instruction by his mother. In fact, Joinville also emphasizes the connection between home and church and between two ways of teaching, engaging in conversation and listening to sermons. In private, Blanche de Castille showed her son how to behave well and how to cultivate the sense of a religious link with God. And we can assume that she did so particularly when she taught him to read in the psalter.[5] She also got him into the habit of reciting the Hours every day. Clerics and friars did the rest, especially the preachers. Their sermons formed part of the child's familiar world.[6] From this standpoint, Louis's religious instruction depended on preachers as much as on a woman, his mother.

In this essay, I show that the example given by Joinville reflects a new attitude toward religious instruction, which fits with a new context in the thirteenth century. First, we know that women provided religious instruction before the thirteenth century, but not all of those women were mothers or teaching in private. Second, during the thirteenth century, the topic of teaching doctrine became an important subject of discussion in the Parisian schools, in connection with other theological debates on the right to preach and on the nature and the function of prophecy in the church. Third, since the prevailing opinion in those debates was that women and preachers had to play complementary parts, at two different levels of religious instruction, I examine how this idea was disseminated among clerics and laypeople.

We have little direct information on the private teaching of children by their mothers. The most fascinating example comes from a book dictated by Dhuoda to an anonymous secretary between 841 and 843. This high-ranking lady had given two sons to William of Septimania. Because her elder son, who was fifteen, had been living far from her for years, at the Carolingian imperial court, she wanted to prepare for him "a mirror where he might contemplate his soul's salvation."[7] Such a summary of the Christian faith, made by a woman who was not reluctant to quote and to interpret the holy Scripture, is unique.[8]

Documents concerning oral teaching by mothers do not go beyond the aristocracy until the end of the thirteenth century. In this milieu, at least, thanks to their sons' memories, we know of some women who played an important part in their children's education at home within the family. Guibert of Nogent (1053–1124), who was eight months old when his father died, received all his education from his mother. In the anecdotes and sayings he retained, her teaching about prayer prevails. Through her gestures and the moments she chose for praying, this illiterate woman inculcated faith in her young son.[9]

Another charming testimony comes from Saint Anselm of Canterbury (1033–1109), who told his companion Eadmer many memories from his long life. When he was a very young child, Anselm had heard from his mother that God was in heaven, from where he embraced and governed the whole world. Thus, in a dream, Anselm saw himself climbing up the mountain close to his house. There he met this great king in his court, and he received a wonderful piece of bread that satisfied him totally. When the child woke up he told everyone that he had gone to heaven and eaten the bread of God.[10]

Between the lines, we can perceive his mother's teaching, which was certainly founded on the two main Christian prayers in the eleventh century, the Our Father ("Give us this day our daily bread") and the Creed ("I believe in God the Father Almighty, Creator of heaven and earth").

It is impossible to evaluate the extent of mothers' involvement in religious instruction; but it is clear that some were able to teach their children and that all of them were expected to do so. In the twelfth century, a secular romance gives corroborative evidence of this. According to Chrestien de Troyes, Perceval's first education included his mother's introduction to faith and to religious behavior on the day before he left the familial manor house. Like Guibert's mother, but with words only in her case, she recommended prayer in churches; like Anselm's mother, she insisted on faith in God the Creator of all things, and on the Eucharist. She also added a summary of the central part of the Creed, about Christ's Passion, death, and descent into hell.[11]

Clerics and monks admitted and probably appreciated this involvement. Until the thirteenth century, they did not criticize the role of nuns either. Religious instruction in their monasteries was normal for the children of the aristocracy, who were often brought up there. Héloïse, for example, was first educated in the monastery of Argenteuil. But in the mid-thirteenth century, the archbishop of Rouen, Eudes Rigaud, did not appreciate this "custody," which had been extended to the burghers' daughters. He repeatedly ordered the convents of Normandy to dismiss the few young lay girls he found within them.[12] Other clerics, monks, or mendicant friars were better prepared to accept children's attendance at schools run by women, where they probably received an initiation to reading and to Christian doctrine simultaneously. Beguines opened some of these schools; others existed in parishes, as the Dominican Thomas of Cantimpré incidentally tells us in an *exemplum*.[13]

Even public teaching, in the form of solemn sermons delivered to various audiences, if not usual, was not inconceivable. Between 1158 and 1170, Hildegard's public preaching in monasteries and outside, at the end of her life, did not rouse opposition or censure from the clergy.[14] During the same period, several anonymous hagiographies underlined the part played by women in converting people to faith in earlier times.[15] And Mary Magdalene herself, whom the liturgy worshiped as "apostle of the apostles," was famous for her preaching in Provence. This legendary part of her life was well known in the twelfth century. Stained-glass windows represented Mary Magdalene as a preacher, and in Auxerre she was even represented preaching from the pulpit.[16]

From the end of the twelfth century, the right to preach had become one of the questions of the moment. In the south of France, in Italy, in Flanders, and in certain parts of the Rhine valley, laypeople desired to live their faith in a more personal, thoughtful, and committed way. And they felt the need to give public testimony of their belief, in deeds and in words. Men and women who followed Valdès in Lyons around 1179 were especially determined to preach, but it is unlikely that among the Cathars women did the same publicly: the rare testimonies that tell us of women in the act of "preaching" show them speaking to other women, and this certainly did not create the same scandal as the public preaching by Waldensian women.[17] In any case, was it possible to let laypeople and, among them, women speak on religious matters everywhere and in any circumstances without control?[18] Confronted with this problem, the papacy answered more or less rigidly, and Innocent III is well known for negotiating with converted Waldensians, Humiliati, and others and for tolerating certain forms of public speech, which he preferred to call *exhortatio* instead of *predicatio*.[19] After him, Pope Gregory IX finally decided to forbid preaching by laypeople. This interdiction, which he first expressed in a letter to the bishop of Milan in 1228, was entered into the Book of Decretals in 1234.[20]

During the whole period from 1180 to 1235, and even later, during the 1260s, theologians also addressed the question of the right to speak in the church in a more comprehensive way than before. The communication of divine revelation required its oral transmission, but the multiplication of speakers and speeches had given rise to an emergency situation. In this context, *Summae* and debates gradually provided a more lucid account of the relationships between preaching, teaching doctrine, and expounding the Scriptures; a more accurate distinction among various types of speaking: preaching, exhorting, curing a bad habit, reproaching, and in another field, prophesying;[21] and finally, a more precise assignment of these types of speech according to circumstances and people. Among the scholars who tried to clarify the ecclesiastical position on these matters, and to support it using the pronouncements of authorities and rational arguments, two of them addressed the main ideas then under discussion.

The first was Gauthier of Château-Thierry, a secular master who was to become chancellor of the University of Paris. In 1245 he debated on the *questio:* Did anybody, either a woman or a man, have the right to preach—that is (according to his formulation), to teach Christian doctrine?[22] Or was it an exclusive right of men? If so, did it belong to any of them or only to those who had received holy orders? In his conclusions, the master distinguished among three types of religious teaching. Anybody might "recite" the articles of the Creed, teach children their prayers, and "exhort" them to behave well. This suited old women, as Saint Paul advised them to educate young girls in his epistle to Titus (2:3–4); mothers too had to teach their children *verbo et exemplo* (that is, to exhort them and to teach them how to behave well). Neither were laymen exempted from the duty of "exhortation" by charity. But only the clerics were allowed to give the other two types of religious teaching he mentioned: to read the word of God publicly, in a loud voice, which was the first way of "expounding" it according to its literal sense, and to interpret it according to the three other senses of the Scripture (allegorical, anagogical, and moral). Actually, this was their religious duty, and the third type of teaching concerned not only the bishops and the priests but also the mendicant friars, the secular masters in theology,[23] and, if their superior "sent" them or if a prelate in charge of souls asked them to do so, the monks and the canons.[24] Gauthier echoed the recent papal interdiction of "preaching" for the whole laity (in the year 1234), and he contributed to imposing a more precise use of the word in a sense that was implicit in the papal text. For him, "to preach" meant to perform the privileged office of teaching doctrine, which was done by giving relevant explanations of the Scripture.[25]

Twenty years later (about 1263–66), a Franciscan again discussed the question of "preaching and teaching" by women, from another angle.[26] Could one maintain the opinion that women might preach by virtue of a mission or by virtue of an office? Eustache of Arras knew the classical arguments used to oppose such a claim. The most usual came from Saint Paul in the first Epistle to Corinthians (14:34): "Let women be silent in church, for it is not permitted for them to speak." But the friar had also meditated on the examples of holy women. He observed that Saint Catherine and Saint Mary Magdalene had given evidence of their faith by teaching openly. Gauthier of Château-Thierry had reduced these examples to the minimum: at the beginning of the history of the church, these women and a few others (Saint Lucy and, with Saint Paul's agreement, Saint Thecla) had preached because men who were capable of preaching were too rare—in a sense, it had been a temporary expedient. And according to the secular master, even if Mary Magdalene was called "apostle of the apostles," this special privilege could not be extended to other women. Eustache of Arras took a more cautious position. In his opinion, the Holy Spirit inspired these women and gave authority to their teachings. Saint Paul's interdiction did not concern them, but it was directed against married women only. The friar implicitly stated that virgins were allowed to speak in public, when the Holy Spirit inspired them. He probably had in mind the crucial spread of mysticism among women during his time. In place of the right to preach, a certain right to speak authoritatively might be recognized for women who had the special gift of prophecy.[27]

Theological debates dealt with the real problems that confronted the church. Their conclusions help us to grasp the complexity of these problems and the variety of possible solutions. But when clerics fulfilled their pastoral duties, they avoided providing arguments for controversy. When clerics taught the laity, they focused only on their own right and duty to preach, in the sense of "teaching doctrine." At the same time, they also insisted that it was parents' duty to bring their children to church, where they would receive religious instruction. According to the synodal statutes, this was required especially in areas where heresy had been widespread, such as the diocese of Béziers (1247). And the requirement concerned both fathers and mothers. In fact, in his commentary on 1 Corinthians 7:1, Saint Thomas noted that some animal species have to bring up their offspring together—that is, in pairs. In the same way, among humans, the male is an essential element in providing the right education, which consists in nurturing not only the body but also the soul.[28]

Such an insistence on fathers' involvement does not mean that the theologian's expectation was fulfilled. More probably, women still played the largest part in private religious instruction. Jacques of Vitry implicitly acknowledged it in his *ad status* collection (about 1230), grounded on a perceptive observation of society in his time. In the chapter on sermons to married people, Jacques kept silent on the matter of religious instruction. But he dealt with it copiously in the two chapters on sermons to widows. In one of them he recalled that women have to attend churches and sermons. In the other he invited women to bring children to church with them and to apply their minds to their children's education. Then he explained the sense of the *Pater Noster* and of the *Credo* at length. He also added a long warning about the wrong beliefs of old women and the spells they could cast over people. By doing so, he invited the preachers who would use his handbook to worry about the right faith of women themselves, before worrying about their children's faith.[29]

In the mid-thirteenth century, Robert of Sorbon undertook the defense of women, whose right to repeat at home what they had heard during sermons was being challenged. He asserted that when Saint Monica returned home after listening to Saint Ambrose's preaching she told her son Augustine and his fellow students what she had committed to memory in order to convert all of them to the Christian faith.[30]

But in a sermon delivered in 1273 at Paris, in a parish church, a Franciscan proclaimed that laypeople were wrong to pray "O Lord God, honor and a good life!" if they did not understand the true meaning of honor, the honor in heaven. And he added: "If I had been as learned in the past as I am now, I should have told my mother off, when I was a young boy, for praying in that way in her garden."[31]

Here, the mother's authority was gently disturbed by the *Alma mater,* through the words of her grown-up son the preacher. This friar was anxious to redress the common practice of spontaneous prayers. Hence the complicity between the mother and the preachers, which Joinville also suggested when he wrote about Blanche de Castille, could change into a censure.[32]

Finally, the image that preachers conveyed themselves integrated the maternal role that they claimed. In treatises and sermons where they dealt with women's duties, clerics never linked the two roles of feeding children and giving them religious instruction. But when they described their own duty of preaching, they drew upon the ancient metaphor used by Augustine, Gregory, Caesarius of Arles, and others: namely, that the preacher is "the mother of souls." Peter of Rheims saw preachers as the breast of the Church.[33] And according to Hugh of Saint Cher, himself a Dominican, since the members of his order lived both the active and the contemplative life, they associated the fecundity of the mothers, when they preached, with the purity of the virgins, when they devoted themselves to meditation.[34] This appropriation of maternity by clerics was probably another way to exclude women from the ministry of preaching.[35]

To conclude, during the thirteenth century, the new surge in preaching and its prevailing definition as the *officium docendi* settled women in a subordinate position for a long time. Mothers continued giving elementary instruction to their children and helping them improve their faith. But their words had to be disciplined, supervised, and even prompted by preachers. Moreover, any word uttered by a woman, married or not, might be looked upon with suspicion by many clerics, and women mystics were soon submitted to their confessors' censure.

This change was neither sudden nor radical. Pious clerics and laymen worshiped women such as Saint Catherine of Siena, and they drank in their every inspired word. And mothers' authority firmly lasted in the minds of their children. At the beginning of the fifteenth century, Joan of Arc still asserted to her judges that her mother had taught her the *Pater,* the *Ave,* and the *Credo,* and that no one but her mother had taught her religious beliefs.[36] In the courts and in the towns, however, preachers were so influential that the roles were redistributed for their benefit.

Even far from the courts and the towns, the preeminent place of preachers in religious instruction could be admitted. At the beginning of the fourteenth century, in Montaillou, a Cathar "redoubt" not far from the Pyrenees, adult men who asserted that their mothers had taught them their prayers echoed the usual testimonies. One of them, Guillaume Aussatz, further explained that he also had his opinions from his mother, Guillelma. She had persuaded him of the reality of metempsychosis and dissuaded him from believing in the resurrection of bodies. But how did Guillelma come to such convictions? According to her son, she had merely listened to the "perfect" Peter Autier, when he delivered sermons in their country. So, in this man's mind, Guillelma's teaching gained authority from the preacher's assertions, which she retained and quoted.[37]

NOTES

For an earlier treatment of this issue, see N. Bériou, "Femmes et prédicateurs: La transmission de la foi aux xIIe et xIIIe siècles," in *La religion de ma mère: Le rôle des femmes dans la transmission de la foi*, ed. J. Delumeau (Paris: Éditions du Cerf, 1992), pp. 51–70.

1. According to Thomas Aquinas, among Christians, parents are supposed to teach their children zealously, which excuses godfathers and godmothers from taking on this responsibility (*Summa theol.* III, qu. 67, a. 8).

2. The *Ave* was added to the *Pater* and *Credo* in the twelfth century. Teaching prayers seems to have been the godfathers' and godmothers' special duty, in the opinion of clerics, who probably refer to a promise made during the baptism: see, for example, Jean Beleth, *Summa de ecclesiasticis officiis* 110 r and t, ed. H. Douteil, CCCM 41–41A (Turnhout: Brepols, 1976); Peter the Chanter, *Summa de sacramentis et anime consiliis* III (2b), ed. J.-A. Dugauquier (Louvain: Nauwelaerts, 1967) (Analecta mediaevalia Namurcensia, 11), pp. 501–2, made this interesting comment: "Non solvit patrinus promissum si doceat filiolum suum symbolum sicut puella docet gabionem vel picam loqui. Immo tenetur eum instruere in lingua propria, ut intelligat aliquantulum explicite articulos fidei, quia nullus potest salvari nisi credat trinum et unum." On the *Ave Maria*, see *Prier au Moyen Age: Pratiques et expériences (ve–xve siècles)*, ed. N. Bériou, J. Berlioz, and J. Longère (Turnhout: Brepols, 1991).

3. *Decreti Prima Pars, dist.* xLIII, c. 1: *de discretione predicationis et silentii* (source: Gregory the Great, *Pastoralis* II, c. 4), Friedberg I, pp. 153–55. The introduction to this text by Gratian himself insists on three aspects: first, the classic rule of teaching *verbo et exemplo;* second, the necessity of giving oral instruction for priests, where he uses the metaphor of barking dogs that chase wolves away from the flock; third, the useful art of discretion (*discretio*), which tells people when they should talk or keep silent.

4. Jean de Joinville, *Vie de Saint Louis*, para. 71, ed. J. Monfrin (Paris, 1995), pp. 33–35 (my translation). This testimony is confirmed by the other biographers. On Blanche and her children's education, see J. Richard, *Saint Louis* (Paris, 1983), pp. 27–36; J. le Goff, *Saint Louis* (Paris: Gallimard, 1996).

5. On teaching reading and doctrine at the same time, see D. Alexandre-Bidon, "Des femmes de bonne foi: La religion des mères au Moyen Age," in *La religion de ma mère*, pp. 91–122. The psalter from which Saint Louis was taught to read has been kept: see A. Lecoy de la Marche, *Saint Louis* (Paris, 1893), p. 194.

6. When he was older, his interest in sermons was well known. King Henry III,

who was more familiar with liturgical services, mentioned the difference in behavior between them in a nice way, when he said that "he [Henry] preferred to see a good friend, instead of hearing good news about him" (according to the chronicler William Rishangler, quoted by L.-K. Little, "Saint Louis' Involvement with the Friars," *Church History* 33 [1964]: 125–48, at p. 129).

7. Dhuoda, *Manuel pour mon fils*, ed. P. Riché (Paris: Éditions du Cerf, 1975) (Sources chrétiennes no. 225; 2d ed., 1991, no. 225bis); English trans. Carol Neel (Lincoln: University of Nebraska Press, 1991). See P. Riché, "L'éducation religieuse par les femmes dans le haut Moyen Age: le 'Manuel' de Dhuoda," in *La religion de ma mère*, pp. 37–49.

8. Texts written or dictated by mothers (even letters) are very rare, too: see Alexandre-Bidon, *La religion de ma mère*, p. 38 (for the seventh century), and p. 51 (Jean Gerson's mother, end of the fourteenth century). On writing made available to women during the Middle Ages, see P. Dronke, *Women Writers in the Middle Ages: A Critical Study of Texts from Perpetua to Marguerite Porete* (Cambridge: Cambridge University Press, 1984); J. W. Thompson, *The Literacy of the Laity in the Middle Ages* (Berkeley: University of California Press, 1939), esp. p. 132.

9. Guibert de Nogent, *Autobiographie*, introduction, ed., trans. E. R. Labande (Paris, 1981), pp. 11, 15, 25–27, 77, 79, 87, 93, and 97. On the influence of Saint Augustine's *Confessions*, which did not prevent Guibert from a personal testimony on his life, see J. F. Benton, *Self and Society in Medieval France: The Memoirs of Abbot Guibert of Nogent* (New York: Harper and Row, 1970); and *A Monk's Confession: The Memoirs of Guibert of Nogent*, trans. and introd. Paul Archambault (University Park: Pennsylvania State University Press, 1990), pp. xxv–xxvi.

10. *Vita sancti Anselmi* I, 1, para. 1–2, *PL* 158, cols. 49–51. See R. W. Southern, *Saint Anselm and His Biographer: A Study of Monastic Life and Thought (1059–ca. 1130)* (Cambridge: Cambridge University Press, 1966).

11. *Le Conte du Graal ou le Roman de Perceval*, lines 469–562.

12. *The Register of Eudes of Rouen*, ed. J. F. O'Sullivan and trans. S. M. Brown (New York: Columbia University Press, 1964), pp. 656, 658, 729, quoted by D. Herlihy, *'Opera muliebra': Women and Work in Medieval Europe* (Philadelphia: Temple University Press, 1990), p. 65.

13. In the countryside, a little girl wanted to get a psalter and to learn to read, but her father was not able to buy the book. Then he decided to put her in the parish school, where the schoolteacher gave her lessons on Sundays and feast days. Her reading quickly improved. Other children put their resources together and offered her a psalter (*Bonum universale de apibus*, I, 23, quoted by A. Lecoy, *L'esprit de nos aïeux* [Paris, n.d.], pp. 296–97). On women schoolteachers, see C. Jourdain, *Mémoire sur l'éducation des femmes au Moyen Age* (Paris, 1874), pp. 49–50. On the Beguines' school attended by Béatrice of Tirlemont (1200–1268) at the beginning of the thirteenth century, see *Vita Beatricis* I, 3, ed. L. Reypens (Antwerp, 1964), pp. 24–25.

14. A famous canon in the *Decretum* (*Prima Pars, distinctio* 23, c. 29, ed. Friedberg I, p. 86) warned women that they had to refrain from teaching (*docere*) men in an assembly. The exception made for the abbess was founded on her gift of prophecy: Hildegard herself proclaimed that the Holy Spirit inspired her and compelled her to speak. See B. Newman, "Divine Power Made Perfect in Weakness: Saint Hildegard on the Frail Sex," in *Medieval Religious Women*, ed. L. T. Shank and J. A. Nichols, t. 2,

Peaceweavers, CS72 (Kalamazoo, Mich.: Cistercian Publications, 1987), pp. 103–22, at pp. 118–19; B. Newman, *Sister of Wisdom: Saint Hildegard's Theology of the Feminine* (Berkeley: University of California Press, 1989); and Carolyn Muessig, "Prophecy and Song," in this volume.

15. F. Lifshitz, "Des femmes missionnaires: L'exemple de la Gaule franque," *Revue d'Histoire ecclésiastique* 83 (1988): 5–33.

16. See V. Saxer, *Le culte de Marie-Madeleine en Occident des origines à la fin du Moyen Age* (Paris: Clavreuil, 1959); "La Madeleine (viiie–xiiie siècle)," *Mélanges de l'École française de Rome, Moyen Age (MEFRM)* 104, no. 1 (1992): 7–340, especially the contributions by Colette Deremble, Michel Lauwers, and Nicole Bériou, pp. 187–340; and in this volume see Katherine Ludwig Jansen, "Maria Magdalena: *Apostolorum Apostola.*"

17. The right of women to teach other women in monasteries, for example, did not become controversial before the thirteenth century, when various positions were adopted on this matter: in 1210, Pope Innocent III forbade the abbesses of Burgos and Palencia from preaching openly, saying that they claimed the right to do so because they were allowed to read the Gospel (*Decretalia* l.V, tit. 38 *De penit.,* c. 10, ed. Friedberg II, pp. 886–87); around 1220, Thomas of Chobham wrote, "possunt tamen abbatisse et priorisse in capitulis suis moniales suas instruere et vitia reprehendere, sed non licet eis sacram Scripturam predicando exponere" (*Summa de arte praedicandi* III, ed. F. Morenzoni, CCCM 82 [Turnhout: Brepols, 1988], p. 58). However, later on, according to Adele Simonetti, who recently edited the sermons of Umiltà da Faenza (1226–1310), this abbess used Saint John's Gospels and the Book of Revelation intensively when she preached to the nuns under her direction inside the walls of her monastery (Adele Simonetti, *I sermoni di Umiltà da Faenza* [Spoleto: Centro italiano di studi sull'alto medioevo, 1995], pp. xxxvi and liii). On the Waldensians, see G. Merlo, *Eretici ed eresie medievali* (Bologna: Il Mulino, 1989), pp. 49–56; on preaching by the Cathars, see R. Abels and E. Harrison, "The Participation of Women in Languedocian Catharism," *Mediaeval Studies* 41 (1979): 215–51; and in this volume see Beverly Mayne Kienzle, "The Prostitute-Preacher," and Anne Brenon, "The Voice of the Good Women."

18. To this question, Gratian had provided negative answers in advance; see the canons in which he dealt with the right of women to teach men publicly: "Mulier quamvis docta et sancta viros in conventu docere non praesumat. Laicus autem presentibus clericis (nisi ipsis rogantibus) docere non audeat" (*Decreti Prima Pars, Distinctio* 23, c. 29, ed. Friedberg, I, p. 86); and with the foundation of the right to preach admitted for priests: "praeter Domini sacerdotes nullus audeat praedicare sive monachus sive laicus sit" (canon *Adicimus, Decreti Secunda Pars,* XVI, q. 1, c. 19, ed. Friedberg I, p. 765).

19. On the influence that Huguccio and Peter the Chanter exerted on the pope for such distinctions, see P. Buc, "*Vox clamantis in deserto?* Pierre le Chantre et la prédication laïque," *Revue Mabillon,* n.s. 4 (= t. 65) (1993): 5–47.

20. Texts in R. Zerfass, *Die Streit um die Laienpredigt: Eine pastoralgeschichtliche Untersuchung zum Verständnis des Predigtamtes und zu seiner Entwicklung im 12 und 13 Jahrundert* (Freiburg im Bresgau: Herder, 1974), pp. 254–55.

21. On these distinctions, see Buc, "*Vox clamantis*"; in this volume see Darleen Pryds, "Proclaiming Sanctity through Proscribed Acts"; on prophecy, see J.-P. Torrell,

Recherches sur la théorie de la prophétie au Moyen Age (xiie–xive siècles): Études et textes (Fribourg: Editions Universitaires Fribourg Suisse, 1992); N. Bériou, "Saint François premier prophète de son ordre," *MEFRM* 102, no. 2 (1990): 535–56.

22. "Queritur hic de officio predicationis et doctrine, et primum, utrum conveniat viris tantum vel viris et mulieribus." This transcription is given by M. Peuchmaurd, *Sacerdoce et prédication,* unpublished thesis for the degree of Reader, Paris, 1961, t. 2, annexe 2. In his answers, Gauthier partly follows Alexander of Hales (before 1236), *Quaestiones disputatae antequam esset frater,* q. 29, *De officio praedicationis* (Florence: Quaracchi, 1960), I, pp. 516–27.

23. Following Peter the Chanter, Gauthier recalls that these masters' duties are to expound the Scripture, to debate upon theological questions, and to preach ("ratione dignitatis, quia officium eorum est in tribus, scilicet in lectione, disputatione et predicatione"). On the friars' involvement, the secular master's tolerance is noticeable, at a time when strong tensions had already appeared between secular clerics and the friars. Around 1236, the Dominican Hugh of Saint-Cher denounced the hostile attitude of other secular clerics when the friars tried to preach in parish churches or in cathedrals: "Vade, dicunt ipsi, et predica in claustro tuo, *et in Bethel,* id est in parochia mea, *non adicies ultra ut propheta,* id est ut predices, *quia sanctificatio regis est et domus regni est* (Amos 7:13), quasi: 'ego sum rex vel dominus ibi.' Vel quia ecclesia cathedralis est, ecce *domus regni,* et non est consuetudo quod pauperes predicent ibi" (first *Postilla* on the Book of Revelation, quoted by R.-E. Lerner, "Poverty, Preaching and Eschatology in the Commentaries of Hugh of Saint-Cher," in *The Bible in the Medieval World: Essays in Memory of B. Smalley,* ed. K. Walsh and D. Wood, Studies in Church History, Subsidia 4 (Oxford: Basil Blackwell, 1985), pp. 157–89, at p. 175.

24. On this important notion of canonical mission, see M. Peuchmaurd, "Mission canonique et prédication: Le prêtre ministre de la parole dans la querelle entre Mendiants et Séculiers au xiiiᵉ siècle," in *Recherches de Théologie ancienne et médiévale* 30 (1963): 122–44 and 251–76.

25. Ten years later, in his model collection, the Franciscan Guibert of Tournai published a sermon on Saint Francis in which the duty of the saint's disciples is described in similar words (*"predicatio et doctrina," "officium docendi"*); see N. Bériou, "Saint François prophète," p. 554. The distinction between *"praedicatio officiosa"* and *"praedicatio caritativa"* had been previously used by Peter the Chanter in his *Verbum abreviatum,* chap. 7, *PL* 205: 39C.

26. Text in Dom J. Leclercq, "Le magistère du prédicateur au xiiiᵉ siècle," *Archives d'Histoire doctrinale et littéraire du Moyen Age* 15 (1946): 105–47, at p. 121. See also A. Blamires, "Women and Preaching in Medieval Orthodoxy, Heresy, and Saints' Lives," *Viator* 26 (1995): 135–52, at pp. 147–49.

27. It is important to remember that one of the usual senses of the word *prophetare* is "to interpret the holy Scripture," in order to reveal what is secret or hidden; see, for example, Thomas de Chobham, *Summa de arte praedicandi* I et III, ed. F. Morenzoni, CCCM 82, p. 17 ("dicitur etiam praedicatio quandoque prophetia . . . prophetare est ea que dicuntur ad populum exponere, et istud est utile, et secundum hoc prophetare est predicare") and pp. 58–59 ("prophetare vocat apostolus scire mentem sacre lectionis et eam populis exponere, et hoc pertinet ad maiores in ecclesia . . . omnes enim qui curam animarum susceperunt debent intelligere saltem superfi-

cialiter sensum et sententiam sacre lectionis quam legunt, ut eam sciant populo exponere"). In 1245, Gauthier of Château-Thierry distinguishes between two types of prophecy: "denuntiatio veritatis," which suits anybody, and "interpretatio veritatis," which requires that one be good and is reserved to men.

28. See Bériou, "Femmes et prédicateurs," pp. 66–67. And on the "natural" subordination of women to men in the field of teaching doctrine, according to Thomas Aquinas, see his *Summa*, II^a II^{ae}, q. 177.

29. MS Paris, B.N.F. Lat. 3284, f. 185–88. Old women are mentioned in the second text as *vetulae*, which also means "witches." This word might be implicitly opposite to the word *anus* used in Ep. to Titus 2:3–4: "anus in habitu sancto . . . bene docentes ut prudentiam doceant." On this second sermon, see also J.-C. Schmitt, "Du bon usage du *Credo*," in *Faire croire: Modalités de la diffusion et de la réception des messages religieux du xiie au xve siècle* (Rome: École française de Rome, 1981), pp. 337–61.

30. Text in MS Paris, B.N.F. Lat. 15971, f. 76ra (March 7, 1260). Husbands might also be "preached to" at home and in private by their wives, as Thomas of Chobham had recommended in his *Summa confessorum;* see S. Farmer, "Persuasive Voices: Clerical Images of Medieval Wives," *Speculum* 61 (1986): 517–43.

31. Text in MS Paris, B.N.F. Lat. 16481, f. 234r–237v. The preacher was John of Mons, a Franciscan who had been the confessor of Saint Louis and his daughter Isabelle.

32. In his *Summa*, IIIa pars, q. 71 (*De catechismo et exorcismo*), art. 4, *ad tertium*, Thomas Aquinas distinguishes between four types of instruction and attributes each one to particular "teachers": "Multiplex est instructio: conversiva ad fidem, quam Dionysius attribuit episcopo (*Hist. ecc.* 2, II, 1), et potest competere cuilibet predicatori, vel etiam cuilibet fideli; instructio qua quis auditur de fidei rudimentis, et qualiter se debent habere in susceptione sacramentorum, pertinet secundariter ad ministros, principaliter autem ad sacerdotes; instructio de conversatione christiane vite, et hec pertinet ad patrinos; instructio de profundis mysteriis fidei et perfectione christiane vite et hec ex officio pertinet ad episcopos." On godfathers, see also *Summa* III, q. 67, a. 8, quoted in note 1 above.

33. *Sermo de communi virginum*, edited among the works of Saint Anthony of Padua (Lyon, 1651), pp. 362–63.

34. *Postille* on the Bible, on John 2:12, quoted by B. Smalley, *The Gospels in the Schools, c. 1100–c. 1280* (London: Ronceverte, 1985), p. 137.

35. See C. Walker Bynum, *Fragmentation and Redemption: Essays on Gender and the Human Body in Medieval Religion* (New York: Zone Books, 1991), esp. chap. 5.

36. *Le procès de condamnation de Jeanne d'Arc*, ed. P. Tisset et J. Lanhers (Paris: C. Klincksieck, 1960), t. 1, p. 41 (February 21, 1431).

37. Text in J. Duvernoy, *Le Registre d'Inquisition de Jacques Fournier, évêque de Pamiers (1318–1325)* (Toulouse: Privat, 1965), vol. 1, pp. 203–4.

SEVEN

Prophecy and Song

Teaching and Preaching by Medieval Women

Carolyn Muessig

The notion of woman's natural inferiority was incessantly expounded upon in theological treatises from patristic times through the Middle Ages.[1] Woman's secondary creation and consequent subservience, elaborated in commentaries on Genesis, made her an unlikely model of a teacher or a preacher.[2] Even preachers who were known to be great supporters of female piety taught that women were subordinate to men. The influential preacher Jacques of Vitry (d. 1240) championed the spiritual aspirations of holy women, especially Marie of Oignies (d. 1213), while other men criticized such women.[3] Yet in his *Sermones feriales et communes,* a collection of twenty-five sermons on the first three chapters of Genesis, he expounds on woman's inferiority to man. In Sermon 12, which is based on Genesis 1:26–27, he states that man is directly created by God and is thus in the image of God, but that woman, because she is created through man, is in the image of man. Moreover, just as God is the beginning of all things, so man is the beginning of all men and women. Finally, because man is made in God's image, he has stronger intellectual powers than woman.[4] Jacques of Vitry's summary of woman's place in the order of creation was a dominant perception in the twelfth and thirteenth centuries.

The notion of women teaching and preaching was deemphasized in favor of women's educating privately within the family or a cloister.[5] However, examples of women preaching and teaching publicly were found in biblical stories and legends. Mary Magdalene offered a biblical example of a woman preaching in her announcement of the "Good News" to the apostles.[6] But this biblical model was often portrayed by theologians as an exception and not the rule. An example of this kind of interpretation can be found in a thirteenth-century collection of anonymous sermons contained in a manuscript in Paris, B.N.F. Lat. 15963.[7] This collection of model sermons supplied preachers with many examples to use in composing their own pastoral texts. In a sermon for the feast of Mary Magdalene it is written: "And this glorious sinner, just like the star of the sea, illumined the world with the joy of the dominical resurrection." However, the implication of this feminine exemplar of preaching is quickly restricted and defined: "And although it is prohibited for other women to preach, this woman had dispensation from the highest pope, therefore, she is called the apostle of the apostles, for she taught not only the simple but also the doctors."[8] The implication of Mary Magdalene as a precedent for female preaching is underscored by the statement of why her pastoral activity was more an anomaly than an exemplar.

Catherine of Alexandria is also an example of a preaching woman.[9] The legends about Catherine relate that she was martyred at the age of eighteen, but not before she converted philosophers and doctors to the Christian faith. In fact, she has been venerated as, among other things, the patron of maidens, female students, philosophers, and preachers.[10] The above-mentioned Parisian collection contains a sermon for the feast of Catherine that describes her silencing of the learned: "But moreover, in the preaching of truth she above all women, with the exception of the *Genetrix,* preached the truth rather keenly, since she silenced the doctors . . . and philosophers."[11]

The examples of Mary Magdalene and Catherine are exceptional because they preached and they are depicted as intelligent and wise women who teach "not only the simple but also the doctors." The assertion of intellectual keenness as an attribute of women was very rare in the Middle Ages. Therefore, it is not surprising that these paradigms of perspicacious female preachers did not erase the fundamental instruction of theologians, that women were inferior to men and therefore should not be permitted to teach or preach publicly.

Despite this pervasive belief, women's voices were not silent; women did teach and preach in and outside the cloister. However, unlike Mary Magdalene and Catherine of Alexandria, when a teaching or preaching woman is encountered in twelfth- and thirteenth-century medieval sources her ability to speak about divine matters is generally attributed to a charism of prophecy rather than to intelligence. The Benedictine nun Hildegard of Bingen (d. 1179) is perhaps the best example of this. Hildegard, unlike the most respected male scholars of her age, was not traditionally educated; she explained and understood her ability to preach as a gift of prophecy.[12] Although the power of prophecy was also claimed for some men who preached, such as Francis of Assisi,[13] clerics emphasized the academic side of pastoral formation more than the prophetic. In fact, male preachers in the thirteenth century were expected to go through a period of rigorous education before they received permission to preach.[14] For female preachers, however, prophecy is the recurrent explanation of their teaching capabilities. Thus, a woman's ability to instruct was connected with divine inspiration; schooling played no role in explaining her skill to communicate theology and biblical knowledge.

Two women from thirteenth-century Italy—Rose of Viterbo (d. 1252) and Umiltà of Faenza (d. 1310)—preached in public and in the cloister respectively; both were hailed as prophets.[15] Rose of Viterbo was a young girl when she preached publicly. Her preaching is also recounted as a miracle of prophecy; moreover, since she was never formally educated, Rose's purity of mind and body are credited with enabling her to be filled with the spirit of prophecy.[16] Umiltà of Faenza, a Benedictine nun whose sermons have come down to us, became a great educator of her congregation through her preaching and reading of Scripture.[17] Her hagiographer describes her ability to teach as a miracle:

> It was a thing marvellous in all respects, to see the blessed Umiltà, who had never learned letters, not only reading at table . . . but even discoursing and speaking in the Latin language, as if she had studied much in it, dictating sermons and lovely tractates on spiritual things, in which there appeared profound doctrine, very skilled verbal expression, even when speaking of the more sublime mysteries of sacred theology.[18]

In her sermons she discusses her ability to preach and teach, again as a gift of prophecy: "The divine words that I speak are not mine, but come from the Father and God most high."[19]

The pastoral abilities of Hildegard of Bingen, Rose of Viterbo, and Umiltà of Faenza are described as being derived purely from prophecy. Prophecy did not challenge the belief that women were intellectually inferior because their learning was not perceived as originating from a rational process such as the education mendicant preachers received in *studia*.[20] The abilities of these successful female preachers were understood and accepted as miraculous.[21] Nevertheless, although the gift of prophecy was cited to justify the preaching of Hildegard, Rose, and Umiltà, such women were rare.

Another kind of teaching available to women had perhaps more powerful effects than preaching: teaching in song. Again turning to Hildegard, we see the significance and importance of song in allowing women a vehicle for expressing their spiritual learning. Hildegard claimed to receive the power of song through the charism of prophecy. In regard to her musical abilities, Hildegard wrote: "untaught by anyone, I composed and chanted plainsong in praise of God and the saints, although I had never studied either musical notation or any kind of singing."[22] Hildegard said that she did not acquire her musical talent through any human intelligence but through God.[23]

Hildegard's understanding of spiritual music was shared by her contemporaries; it was an understanding inherited through Boethius's *De institutione musica*.[24] The correlation between body and soul was reflected in musical harmony. Boethius identified three kinds of music, *musica mundana, musica humana,* and *musica instrumentalis. Musica mundana* was the music of the spheres, which was produced through the movement of celestial bodies. *Musica humana* joined the soul's rational and irrational parts together and then joined them to the body. *Musica instrumentalis* was music that was created by humans. The human being is tuned to the cosmos, and thus the music that humans produce reflects the person's relationship to the *musica mundana.* Depending on the moral quality of the individual, music could either comfort or disturb the soul.[25] Monastic musical theorists introduced another aspect to the three sorts of music defined by Boethius: the *musica celestis,* which was described as the singing of the angels in heaven.[26] The angels were perceived as pure song because they were pure spirit.[27] Within the monastic context, the singing of the divine office with an attentive mind was thought of as being similar to the activity of the angels, who incessantly sing the Lord's praises.[28]

The mystical view of music held by Hildegard and her contemporaries found a wider audience in the later twelfth and early thirteenth centuries, when the *vita apostolica* movement took hold in Western Europe. People who followed this movement, the laity and clergy alike, led a life committed to the evangelical precepts of poverty, chastity, and preaching. Sermons and hagiographical literature, which both shaped and reflected the *vita apostolica* movement, reveal much about the role of music in the lives of individuals and communities. Four *vitae* of thirteenth-century holy women, sermons by Jacques of Vitry, as well as the sermons contained in Paris, B.N.F. Lat. 15963, offer an array of examples of images associating virginity, song, and preaching. References to bodily purity are related to bestowing upon women the power of singing and preaching.

The *Sermones de sanctis* of Jacques of Vitry contain 115 sermons that offer examples to the faithful of how the saints ought to be imitated.[29] In sermons for the feast days of the virgin martyrs, occasionally the relationship between chastity and singing is discussed. Virgins sing a song that no one else can sing because of their likeness to Christ.[30] Virgins are like Christ in their integrity of body and soul;[31] the implication is that since a virgin is similar to Christ in her flesh and mind, she is united to him and demonstrates this special union through her song. Similarly, in the Paris manuscript, the aforementioned sermon for the feast day of Catherine of Alexandria provides a demonstration of the implications of the relationship between preaching and purity of body. It is first stated that Christ did three things in the flesh: he preserved his cleanness, he preached the truth, and he died through charity. Catherine was assimilated to Christ through the integrity and cleanness of her body, in the preaching of truth, and in dying through charity.[32] It is through her union of the flesh with Christ that she is enabled to preach the truth. This union opens her mind, allowing it to be infused with knowledge.

The theme throughout these sermons is that a woman's bodily and moral purity bestows her with a gnosis that is articulated sometimes in preaching but more often in song. This theme is also contained in the four *vitae* to be considered here, which describe songs as tools of spiritual learning and edification. The subjects of these *vitae* received knowledge of the divine either through singing or through the hearing of a song. Like the example provided in the sermons for virgin martyrs, these women practiced chastity, thus disposing their minds toward a reception of spiritual knowledge. Moreover, sometimes when they sang, their voices were described as angelic or heavenly. The first two *vitae* to be examined are those of Marie of Oignies, composed by Jacques of Vitry shortly after her death in 1213, and of Christina of St. Trond (d. 1224), written around 1232 by the Dominican friar Thomas of Cantimpré.[33]

Marie of Oignies came from a wealthy family living in Nivelles. Her family objected to her desire to lead a religious life. Married at fourteen, she soon converted her husband to a life of chastity and apostolic simplicity. She eventually became a lay sister in the Augustinian priory of Saint Nicholas in Oignies, where she attracted many supporters who greatly admired her extraordinary pursuit of the *vita apostolica*.[34] Christina's life was dedicated to teaching people the torments of Purgatory and the importance of doing penance. Her *vita* is full of miracles, extraordinary even for a saint. For example, Thomas relates instances of Christina suffering in fiery ovens and frigid rivers but always emerging unscathed. These remarkable miracles underline the theme of Christina's *vita*—to avoid suffering the pains of Purgatory, people should do penance in this world.[35]

The *vitae* of Marie of Oignies and Christina of St. Trond emphasize that they did not preach or, in the case of Christina, did not feel comfortable expounding on the Bible.[36] Nevertheless, Marie and Christina did comment on the Bible and theological issues. Some of these explications were carried out through the medium of song. For example, Marie sang rhymed verses in French containing theological subtleties. Jacques of Vitry presents a description of the song that Marie sang on her deathbed, a song rich in biblical imagery and learning, similar perhaps to the religious poetry found in Liège psalters used by Beguines.[37] Jacques describes Marie's last wondrous song:

> When the promised time was near which she had so tearfully anticipated . . .
> behold, a sound was suddenly made and the *voice of the turtle was heard in our
> land* (Song 2:12). . . . She thus began to sing in a high clear voice and for three
> days and three nights did not stop praising God and giving thanks: she rhythmically wove in sweet harmony the most sweet song about God, the holy angels,
> the blessed Virgin, other saints, her friends and holy scriptures. She did not
> have to compose it or discover the meaning or have to ponder the rhythmical
> arrangement, but the Lord gave it to her just as if it had been written out before
> her at exactly the same time as it was spoken. She rejoiced with a continuous
> cry and did not have to deliberate over it, nor did she have to interrupt her
> song in order to arrange its parts. It seemed to her that one of the seraphim

was stretching his wings over her breast and with his help and sweet assistance, she was inspired to sing without any difficulty.[38]

Marie's theologically complex singing is identified, explained, and understood by Jacques of Vitry as being entirely miraculous. Like the preaching of Hildegard, Rose, and Umiltà, it is not the product of logical reasoning, for as Jacques relates, it seemed to Marie "that one of the seraphim was stretching his wings over her breast." The song is woven with rich learning.[39] Marie expounded upon the unity of the Trinity, she gave subtle explanations of the Scriptures, and she uttered much about the humanity of Christ, the Virgin, the angels, and the apostles. Jacques suggests that she sang about refined theories, such as how angels receive their understanding, the glorified body of the Virgin, and issues related to the resurrection of the human body.[40] Although Jacques makes it clear that Marie did not preach, he portrays her without hesitation as singing aloud about the Trinity, the humanity of Christ, and other theological issues.[41]

Christina is depicted singing more frequently than Marie. Whereas the only song recounted by Jacques is Marie's final one, Christina's singing is a common occurrence:

> She later became very familiar with the nuns of St. Catherine's who lived outside the town of Saint-Trond. Sometimes while she was sitting with them, she would speak of Christ and suddenly and unexpectedly she would be ravished in the spirit and her body would roll and whirl around like a hoop. . . . Then a wondrous harmony sounded between her throat and her breast which no mortal man could understand nor could it be imitated by any artificial instrument. Her song had not only the pliancy and tones of music but also the words—if thus I might call them—sounded together incomprehensibly. The voice of spiritual breath, however, did not come out of her mouth or nose, but a harmony of the angelic voice resounded only from between the breast and the throat.
>
> While all this was happening, all her limbs were quiet and her eyes were closed as if she were sleeping. Then after a little time, restored to her former self, she rose up like the one who was drunk—indeed she was drunk—and she cried aloud, "Bring the nuns to me that together we might praise Jesus for the great liberality of his miracles." Shortly thereafter the nuns of the convent came running from all sides and greatly rejoiced in Christina's solace and she began to sing the *Te Deum laudamus* and all the convent joined in and she finished her song.[42]

Christina's wondrous song is described as incomprehensible, and it stirred the listeners to great rejoicing and ultimately to communal singing. But sometimes her songs reflect an absorption of learning, although this too is presented as a miraculous event. When she was residing in Germany to be near a holy woman named Iutta, Christina sang in Latin, a language, according to Thomas of Cantimpré, she was never taught to read.[43] How Christina learned these Latin songs is never explained; instead, her Latin singing is treated as a miraculous gift:

> Christina went to the vigils of Matins every night after everyone had left the church and the doors were locked. Then, walking on the church pavement, she would utter such sweet songs that they seemed to be the songs of angels and not of human origin. The song was so marvellous to hear that it surpassed the music of all instruments and the voices of all mortals. . . . This song, I say, was in Latin and wondrously adorned with harmonious oratorical devices.[44]

Marie's and Christina's singing is described as originating from divine inspiration, which grants them a status similar to teachers and preachers. Because Marie is prophetic, she sings with authority about theological issues that she would not be permitted to preach. In Christina's case, Thomas of Cantimpré makes it clear that she has the capacity to discuss all aspects of the Bible. In addition to this aptitude, she spiritually refreshes the sisters of Saint-Trond with ethereal songs and dazzles holy women such as Iutta with her sophisticated Latin phrasing. The influence that these women could have on the spiritual formation of others is evident. But can their singing be likened to a form of preaching?

The eminent preacher Alain of Lille (d. 1203) defined preaching as such: "Preaching is an open and public instruction in faith and behavior, whose purpose is the forming of men; it derives from the path of reason and from the fountainhead of the 'authorities.'"[45] On the basis of this definition, one could argue that these women were not preaching, because their audiences were limited to their followers and admirers, and thus their instruction was not public. Moreover, their theological knowledge was described as emerging from their prophetic powers rather than from their rational abilities; thus, they were not properly trained to preach and therefore were not equipped to be preachers. Furthermore, their hagiographers never identify these women as preachers. However, preaching was also meant to develop faith and to encourage spiritual progress,[46] and the songs performed by Marie and Christina did edify others. Through their own distinctive instruction, these women inspired and assisted others in their spiritual development. Thus, although their enlightened lessons are described as singing, the effects of their songs on the listener equal or surpass the desired effects of preaching. This role of song as a type of communal teaching and edification is indicated in the third and fourth *vitae*.

Turning to two other holy women from the Low Countries, the Cistercian nuns Lutgard of Aywières (d. 1246) and Ida of Louvain (d. 1290), we see that song in the daily life of women was a fundamental tool in their spiritual formation.

Lutgard's singing demonstrates the perception of woman as vessel, wherein the divine intones its harmonies. When Lutgard sang the liturgy of the day it seemed to her that "Christ, with the outward appearance of a lamb, was positioning Himself on her breast in such a manner that one foot was on her right shoulder and the other on the left. He would place his mouth on her mouth and by thus sucking, would draw out from her breast a melody of wondrous mellowness."[47] This union with Christ also had its influence on the community: "Nor could anyone doubt that a divine miracle was taking place in this chanting, for it was only at that verse alone that her voice was heard to be measurelessly more filled with grace than usual and, in like manner, so too were the hearts of all who heard her marvellously moved to devotion."[48]

Ida of Louvain's reaction to singing and music illuminates the function of song as a highly emotive and educational form of religious instruction. At one time Ida had had a beautiful singing voice but lost it to an incurable hoarseness of the vocal cords.[49] Nonetheless, her inability to sing did not stop her from harmonizing with her fellow nuns in heart and mind. On the eve of the feast of the archangel Michael, she entered the convent church to hear her sisters singing the Psalms. While listening, she was overtaken by God's grace and lifted into the choir of the seraphim. Enabled to reflect with a clearness of mind beyond reason, she was thus led into the mystical realm.[50]

Her hagiographer emphasizes that although Ida was not learned in Latin and the fundamentals of education, through divine grace she was able to understand the words that the nuns in her community sang and read in Latin. This was true especially during the Lenten season; when the Holy Gospel was recited in Latin, she repeated it in the vernacular.[51] Thus, for Ida the hearing of songs led her both to the heights of mysticism and to the practicalities of biblical learning.

The female preachers and singing teachers examined in this study were described by their contemporaries as not receiving any systematic training in theology and biblical studies. Their insight was given to them from God, who wrote their words. They were perceived as vessels that could instruct and inspire through prophecy and song. Their genius was understood to be solely the result of divinely infused knowledge. This understanding created a platform upon which women could discuss theological lessons while not appearing to do so. But these women's voices were indeed heard. Since medieval women were often silenced at the pulpit, perhaps it is from the choir that we will hear the distant echoes of the intelligence and eloquence of women's voices.[52]

NOTES

I would like to thank the Social Sciences and Humanities Research Council of Canada and the Newman Fellowships Trust for their support of my research. I am grateful to the Rutgers Center for Historical Analysis for funding that allowed me to participate in this project. I am also grateful to Beverly Mayne Kienzle and George Ferzoco for their helpful suggestions.

1. Ambrose (d. 397) wrote on this theme in his commentary on Luke: "Just as woman was the author of man's sin in the beginning, and he the follower in error, so now she who had previously tasted death had first sight of the Resurrection, and in turn was first in the remedy for sin. So as not to endure the opprobrium of man's perpetual blame, she transmitted grace too, and compensated for the misery of the original fall by her disclosure of the Resurrection. Through woman's mouth death had proceeded: through woman's mouth life was restored. But since she is too inferior in steadfastness for preaching, and her sex is weaker in carrying things through, the evangelical role is assigned to men." In Alcuin Blamires, ed., *Woman Defamed and Woman Defended: An Anthology of Medieval Texts* (Oxford: Clarendon Press, 1992), p. 62. The Dominican preacher Humbert of Romans (d. 1277) offers an excellent example of the continuation of this thought. In his preaching manual, he indicates a variation on the theme of why a woman should not preach: "First is lack of judgement, for a woman has less than a man. Second is the condition of servitude that was inflicted on her. . . . Third, if she were to preach, her appearance would provoke lascivious thoughts. . . . Fourth, in remembrance of the foolishness of the first woman." Humbert of Romans, *De eruditione praedicatorum* (Rome, 1607), p. 31, as cited in Larissa Taylor, *Soldiers of Christ: Preaching in Late Medieval and Reformation France* (Oxford: Oxford University Press, 1992), p. 176.

2. Cf. Elisabeth Gössmann, "The Construction of Women's Difference in the Christian Theological Tradition," *Concilium* 6 (1991): 50–59.

3. Jacques of Vitry, Augustinian canon, preacher, hagiographer, and ultimately cardinal-bishop of Tusculum, was a dedicated supporter of the holy women of Liège. The best studies on his life are Philipp Funk, *Jakob von Vitry, Leben und Werke*, Beiträge zur Kulturgeschichte des Mittelalters und der Renaissance, vol. 3 (1909; reprint, Hildesheim: H. A. Gersternberg, 1973); John Frederick Hinnebusch, ed., *The Historia Occidentalis of Jacques de Vitry: A Critical Edition*, Spicilegium Friburgense, 17 (Fribourg: University Press, Switzerland, 1972), pp. 3–67; Monica Sandor, "The Popular Preaching of Jacques de Vitry" (Ph.D. diss., University of Toronto, 1993).

4. "Et hac racione dicit Apostolus quod uir ymago est Dei uel factus ad ymaginem Dei, non mulier. Vir enim inmediate factus est a Deo, mulier uero mediante uiro, iuxta illud: *Faciamus ei adiutorium simile sibi*. Et insuper sicut Deus principium est omnium rerum, ita uir, et non mulier, principium est omnium uirorum et mulierum, et quia uir naturaliter perspicaciora habet naturalia quam mulier." Carolyn Muessig, "The *Sermones feriales* of Jacques de Vitry: A Critical Edition," 2 vols. (Ph.D. diss., Université de Montréal, 1993), vol. 2, pp. 221–22. For further discussion of this theme, see Kari Børresen, "God's Image, Man's Image? Patristic Interpretation of Gen. 1, 27 and I Cor. 11, 7," in Kari Børresen, ed., *Image of God and Gender Models in Judaeo-Christian Tradition* (Oslo: Solum Forlag, 1991), pp. 188–207; cf. Gössmann, "The Construction of Women's Difference," pp. 50–59.

5. Thomas Aquinas (d. 1274) addressed the question whether or not a woman had the charism of wisdom in speech and knowledge such as pertains to man. Citing Proverbs 4:3, *I was an only-begotten in the sight of my mother; she taught*, he replies: "Speech can be used in two ways. In one way privately, to one or a few, in familiar

conversation. In this way the grace of speech becomes a woman. The other way publicly, addressing oneself to the whole Church. This is not conceded to women. First and principally, because of the condition of the female sex, which must be subject to man, according to *Genesis*. But to teach and persuade publicly in Church is not the task of subjects but of prelates. Men, when commissioned, can far better do this work, because their subjection is not from nature and sex as with women, but from something supervening by accident. Secondly, lest men's minds be enticed to lust. Thus *Ecclesiasticus*, 9:11: *Many have been misled by a woman's beauty. By it passion is kindled like a fire.* Thirdly, because generally speaking women are not perfected in wisdom so as to be fit to be entrusted with public teaching." Roland Potter, trans. and ed., "Prophecy and Other Charisms, 2a2ae. 171–178," in *St. Thomas Aquinas, Summa Theologiae*, 61 vols. (London: Blackfriars, 1964–1981), vol. 45, p. 133. For discussion of women's role in transmitting religious teaching in private settings, see Nicole Bériou's essay in this collection and her article, "Femmes et prédicateurs: La transmission de la foi aux xiie et xiiie siècles," in Jean Delumeau, ed., *La religion de ma mère: Les femmes et la transmission de la foi* (Paris: Éditions du Cerf, 1992), pp. 51–70.

6. See John, 20:18. For further discussion of Mary Magdalene as paradigm of female preacher, see Katherine Ludwig Jansen's "Maria Magdalena: *Apostolorum Apostola*" in this volume; see also Taylor, *Soldiers of Christ*, pp. 174–77; and Bériou, "Femmes et prédicateurs," p. 65.

7. The *Sermones de sanctis* collection has been attributed to the Parisian master of theology Robert of Sorbon (d. 1274) by Johannes Baptist Schneyer. See Johannes Baptist Schneyer, *Repertorium der lateinischen Sermones des Mittelalters für die Zeit von 1150–1350*, 11 vols., Beiträge zur Geschichte der Philosophie und Theologie des Mittelalters, 43 (Münster/Westphalia: Aschendorff, 1969–1990), vol. 5, pp. 312–28. Nicole Bériou tells me that these sermons were not written by Robert of Sorbon, although he probably read them.

8. "Et gloriosa peccatrix, quasi stella maris, mundum illuminauit gaudio dominice resurrectionis. Et cum aliis mulieribus sit prohibitum predicare, ista dispensationem habuit super hoc a summo pontifice, unde ipsa dicitur apostolorum apostola, docuit enim non solum simplices sed etiam doctores." Paris, B.N.F. Lat. 15963, f. 23ra–23rb. In regard to the foliation of this manuscript, I have not been able to use the manuscript itself but I have worked from a microfiche; therefore, please note foliation with care. To facilitate referencing the sermons that I have cited in this manuscript, the *incipits* from Schneyer are provided. *Incipit*: "Nigra sum sed formosa (Cant. 1, 4)." See Schneyer, *Repertorium*, vol. 5, p. 323, no. 193.

9. For further information on Catherine of Alexandria see Roberto Rusconi's essay in this volume. For a discussion of Catherine of Alexandria as an intellectual, see David d'Avray, "Katherine of Alexandria and Mass Communications in Germany: Woman as Intellectual," in Nicole Bériou and David d'Avray, eds., *Modern Questions about Medieval Sermons: Essays on Marriage, Death, History and Sanctity*, Biblioteca di Medioevo Latino, 11 (Spoleto: Centro italiano di studi sull'alto medioevo, 1994), pp. 401–8.

10. Herbert Thurston and Donald Attwater, eds., *Butler's Lives of the Saints*, 4 vols. (London: Burns and Oates, 1956), vol. 4, pp. 420–21.

11. "Sed etiam predicatione ueritatis que super omnes mulieres, excepta Dei gen-

itrice, ueritatem acrius predicauit, quia doctores . . . et philosophos confutauit." Paris, B.N.F. Lat. 15963, f. 110rb. *Incipit:* "Media nocte clamor factus est (Matth. 25,6)." See Schneyer, *Repertorium,* vol. 5, pp. 327–28, no. 270. This sentence implies that the Virgin preached; however, there is no further mention of this in the sermon.

12. Sabina Flanagan discusses twelfth-century educational conditions and their implications, particularly for women, whose standard of learning was inferior to that of men. See Sabina Flanagan, *Hildegard of Bingen, 1098–1179: A Visionary Life* (London: Routledge, 1989), pp. 54–55. Hildegard of Bingen's *Expositiones evangeliorum* is being edited by Beverly Mayne Kienzle and Carolyn Muessig, with the assistance of Monika Costard and Angelika Lozar, for the series *Corpus Christianorum, Series Latina, Continuatio Mediaevalis,* published by Brepols, and being translated by Fay Martineau and Beverly Kienzle for Cistercian Publications.

13. See Thomas of Celano, *First Life,* in Marion A. Habig, ed., *St. Francis of Assisi, Writings and Early Biographies,* 3d rev. ed. (Chicago: Franciscan Herald Press, 1973), pp. 249–51. Like the accounts of the hagiographers of women preachers, Thomas of Celano, in the *Vita secunda,* points out Francis's lack of learning; see pp. 105–6; Habig, ed., *St. Francis,* p. 446. Other examples of male preachers who claimed to preach through a charism of prophecy can be found among those who preached "The Devotion of the Alleluia" in northern Italy in 1233. See Augustine Thompson, *Revival Preachers and Politics in Thirteenth-Century Italy: The Great Devotion of 1233* (Oxford: Clarendon Press, 1992), pp. 118–26.

14. For example, the *Constitutiones Narbonenses,* compiled in 1260, indicates the Franciscan order's stress on education; no one was to be received into the order without being fully instructed in grammar and logic. *Constitutiones Generales Narbonenses,* Rubric 1 in *Doctoris Seraphici S. Bonaventurae S.R.E. Episcopi Cardinalis Opera Omnia,* 10 vols. (Quaracchi, 1882–1902), vol. 8, pp. 449–67 and 450b. See also Rubric 6 (vol. 8, p. 456a).

15. For more details about these women's lives, see Darleen Pryds's "Proclaiming Sanctity through Proscribed Acts," in this volume.

16. Rose's ability to preach is discussed in her canonization process, which was composed in 1457. *Processus pro Canonizatione s: Rosae,* in *Acta Sanctorum, Septembris,* II (Antwerp, 1748), pp. 442–45 (see p. 443).

17. *Vita s. Humilitatis Abbatissae Ordinis Vallumbrosani Florentiae,* in *Acta Sanctorum, Maii,* V (Venice, 1746), pp. 203–22 (henceforth *VH*). Catherine Mooney is translating the sermons of Umiltà into English. Her sermons are found on pp. 1127–37 in the same volume.

18. As cited and translated in Elizabeth Petroff, "The Analects of St. Umiltà," *Vox Benedictina* 7 (January 1990): 31–52 (see p. 37); cf. *VH,* p. 213.

19. See Petroff, "The Analects of St. Umiltà," p. 38; cf. *VH,* p. 213.

20. See Flanagan, *Hildegard of Bingen,* pp. 14–15. See also Elisabeth Gössman, "*Ipsa enim quasi domus sapientiae:* The Philosophical Anthropology of Hildegard of Bingen," in Elisabeth Gössman, *Hildegard of Bingen: Four Papers* (Toronto: Peregrina, 1995), pp. 5–16 (see pp. 6–7).

21. Ibid., pp. 158–78.

22. *Vita S. Hildegardis,* in J.-P. Migne, ed., *Patrologia Latina* 197 (Paris, 1882), cols. 91–130; see col. 104a, as cited and translated in *Saint Hildegard of Bingen: Symphonia. A Critical Edition of the "Symphonia armonie celestium revelationum" ["Symphony of the Har-*

mony of Celestial Revelations"], ed. Barbara Newman (Ithaca, N.Y.: Cornell University Press, 1988), p. 17 (henceforth Newman, *Symphonia*).

23. Newman, *Symphonia*, pp. 17–18.

24. Gottfried Friedlein, ed., *Boetii de institutione arithmetica, libri duo: De institutione musica, libri quinque* (Leipzig: B. G. Teubner, 1867), pp. 175–371.

25. Newman, *Symphonia*, p. 19.

26. Ibid., p. 20.

27. Ibid., p. 21.

28. Ibid., p. 20.

29. For further discussion of these sermons, see Carolyn Muessig, "Paradigms of Sanctity for Thirteenth-Century Women," in Beverly Mayne Kienzle, ed., *Models of Holiness in Medieval Sermons*, Proceedings of the International Symposium (Kalamazoo, Mich., May 4–7, 1995), Textes et Études du Moyen Âge, 5 (Louvain-la-Neuve: Fédération Internationale des Instituts d'Études Médiévales, 1996), pp. 85–102.

30. "Virgines enim cantant canticum quod nullus alius cantare potest: hoc est singulare gaudium de conformitate quam habunt cum Christo." *Sermo s. Cecilie*, Douai, Bibliothèque municipale 503, ff. 158v–160v (f. 158v).

31. Expounding on Revelation 14:2–4, Jacques of Vitry explains how chaste women are similar to Christ, the Virgin, and the holy angels in body and mind: "Et cantare canticum nouum quod nullus aliter cantare potest, quod est incomparabile gaudium cordis de similitudine expressa quam habunt cum Christo et Matre eius, et insuper cum angelis sanctis." *Sermo de uirginibus*, Douai, Bibliothèque municipale 503, ff. 217v–220r (see f. 219v).

32. "Et nota quod in carne Dominus tria fecit: seruauit mundiciam; predicauit ueritatem; mortuus est per caritatem. Assimilata est ei in carnis integritate et mundicia . . . predicatione ueritatis . . . per caritatem mortua est." *Sermo s. Katerine*, Paris, B.N.F. Lat. 15963, f. 110ra–110rb. See note 8 above for *incipit*.

33. Thomas of Cantimpré (d. 1270?), at first an Augustinian canon and then a Dominican friar, knew Jacques of Vitry and was greatly influenced by his preaching.

34. Sandor, *The Popular Preaching of Jacques de Vitry*, p. 107.

35. *Vita Christinae Mirabilis*, in *Acta Sanctorum*, 5 (Antwerp, 1727), pp. 637–60 (henceforth *VCM*). English translation taken from Margot King, trans., *The Life of Christina Mirabilis by Thomas de Cantimpré* (Toronto: Peregrina, 1995).

36. Jacques underlines Marie's awareness of the inappropriateness of her preaching: "With many tearful sighs, prayers and fasts she insistently asked and obtained from the Lord that he recompense her in some other person for the service and office of preaching which she could not herself exercise, and that the Lord give her one preacher for herself as a great gift." See *Vita Mariae Oigniacensis*, in *Acta Sanctorum Iunii*, 5 (Antwerp, 1727), pp. 630–66 (see esp. pp. 654–55) (henceforth *VMO*); English translation taken from Margot King, trans., *The Life of Marie d'Oignies by Jacques de Vitry* (Toronto: Peregrina, 1995), p. 97. Christina expounded upon the Bible, but only reluctantly: "Although she had been completely illiterate from birth, yet she understood all Latin and fully knew the meaning of Holy Scripture. When she was asked very obscure questions by certain spiritual friends, she would explain them very openly, but she did this most unwillingly and rarely, for she said that to expound Holy Scripture belonged to the clergy and not to the ministry such as her"; *VCM*, pp. 657; King, *Christina Mirabilis*, p. 29.

37. Judith Oliver, "Devotional Psalters and Beguine Spirituality," in *On Pilgrimage: The Best of Vox Benedictina 1984–1993*, ed. Margot King (Winnipeg: Peregrina, 1993), pp. 210–34 (see p. 225).

38. *VMO*, pp. 662–63; King, *Marie d'Oignies*, pp. 121–22. Francis of Assisi also sang in rhymed verses; see Habig, ed., *St. Francis*, p. 467.

39. *VMO*, p. 663; King, *Marie d'Oignies*, pp. 122–23.

40. *VMO*, p. 663; King, *Marie d'Oignies*, pp. 123–24.

41. See John Coakley, "Gender and the Authority of Friars: The Significance of Holy Women for Thirteenth-Century Franciscans and Dominicans," *Church History* 60 (1991): 445–60. This article indicates ways in which clerics perceived the prophetic powers of women. Moreover, it discusses the implications of ecclesiastical authority and how this influenced the relationship between clerics like Jacques of Vitry and female mystics like Marie of Oignies.

42. *VCM*, p. 656; King, *Christina Mirabilis*, pp. 26–27. King has interpreted Christina's singing in the following manner: "[H]er body is entirely taken over by God and in her worship her song is united with the music of the spheres, that expression of the identification of the sacramental universe with its Creator. Thus does Christina's material and spiritual life mirror the eternal cosmic order which obeys those 'laws of equality, unity and order' found in music: 'as God unites all things in the universe, so too does number, the basis of music' (Augustine, *De Musica* 6, 16, 53). Thus should human action reflect the cosmic order of 'the poem of the universe' which obeys 'the laws of equality, unity and order (ibid. 6, 2, 29)'" (King, *Christina Mirabilis*, pp. 45–46, note 29). For a discussion of saints' bodies in states of rapture, see Walter Simons, "Reading a Saint's Body: Rapture and Bodily Movement in the *Vitae* of Thirteenth-Century Beguines," in Sarah Kay and Miri Rubin, eds., *Framing Medieval Bodies* (Manchester: Manchester University Press, 1994), pp. 10–23.

43. King, *Christina Mirabilis*, p. 29.

44. *VCM*, p. 657; King, *Christina Mirabilis*, pp. 28–29.

45. Gillian Evans, trans., *Alan of Lille: The Art of Preaching*, CS 23 (Kalamazoo, Mich.: Cistercian Publications, 1981), pp. 16–17.

46. For this definition of preaching, see Pryds's "Proclaiming Sanctity," in this volume.

47. *Vita S. Lutgardis*, in *Acta Sanctorum Junii*, 3 (Antwerp, 1727), pp. 231–63 (see p. 241); Margot King, trans., *The Life of Lutgard of Aywières by Thomas de Cantimpré* (Toronto: Peregrina, 1991), p. 38.

48. Ibid.

49. See Daniel Papebroeck, *Vita Venerabilis Idae Virginis Cisterciensis*, in *Acta Sanctorum, Aprilis*, II (Antwerp, 1675), pp. 156–89 (see pp. 161 and 174). There exists an English translation of this life: Martinus Cawley, trans., *Ida of Louvain* (Lafayette, Ore.: Our Lady of Guadalupe Abbey, 1986), as cited in King, *Marie d'Oignies*, p. 134.

50. Papebroeck, *Vita Venerabilis Idae*, p. 188.

51. Ibid.

52. I am unaware of a comprehensive study of the use of music in the education of medieval women. In regard to the early modern period, however, Craig A. Monson has unearthed material that demonstrates the vital role music played in the lives of nuns; see Craig A. Monson, *Disembodied Voices: Music and Culture in an Early Modern Italian Convent* (Berkeley: University of California Press, 1995).

EIGHT

Proclaiming Sanctity
through Proscribed Acts
The Case of Rose of Viterbo

Darleen Pryds

Do not preach to anyone. . . . St. Paul forbade women to preach: Mulieres non permitto docere (1 Tim. 2:12). Do not criticize any man, nor blame him for his vices unless he is over-familiar with you. Holy old anchoresses may do it in a certain way, but it is not a sure thing, nor is it proper for the young: it is the business of those who are set over others and have to guard them, as teachers of Holy Church.

RULE FOR ANCHORESSES[1]

This admonition was written for a group of English women recluses in the early thirteenth century, but it summarizes much of ecclesiastical legislation on the subject of women's public apostolate in medieval Europe. Women—especially young women—were not to take or be given the responsibility of educating men in matters of faith either by preaching or by teaching.[2]

Roughly contemporary with the anchoress's warning, a teenage laywoman in Italy was gaining a reputation for holiness as she walked through the streets of Viterbo carrying a cross and exhorting large crowds of followers to live virtuously. Rose of Viterbo was born around 1233 and died in 1252, before she turned twenty.[3] Her life and her posthumously embellished reputation for sanctity compel us to reconsider the role of women's public apostolates in late medieval Europe.[4] Rose did not receive a license from ecclesiastical authorities to preach,[5] nor do the *vitae* written to promote her pious reputation portray her as having limited her teaching to groups of women in private settings. Instead, the case for her sanctity included her public announcement of the Word of God—an activity officially regulated by conciliar legislation on preaching.

Rose stands within a small but significant tradition of women who preached without ecclesiastical censure in the medieval period.[6] The majority of these preaching women were nuns or clearly affiliated tertiary (lay) members of an order.[7] Rose represents a different case: never allowed to enter the convent, Rose took a habit and wore a cord but was not clearly affiliated with a tertiary order or religious community.[8] As a charismatic, independent street preacher, Rose of Viterbo earned a reputation for saintliness. This reputation rested in large part on her public apostolate.

This study examines how a woman's public oratory was depicted by focusing on the two *vitae* that circulated during the official canonization processes instituted in the mid-thirteenth and the mid-fifteenth centuries. Both *vitae* portray Rose as speaking publicly; in the fifteenth century, her public oratory was described by a variety of speech acts, including preaching.

The significance of finding preaching in late medieval *vitae* written to promote saintly reputations of women has more to do with religious ideals and hagiographical tradition than with the women themselves. Hagiographical sources are by their nature works of religious propaganda intended to convince readers of the subject's special holiness. It follows that historians use these sources to measure general views toward the holy and holy people more than they use them to study the biography.[9] Thus, by focusing on the development of the theme of public speaking in the *vitae* of one woman, we can see evidence of interest in a public apostolate for women as a religious *ideal* in late medieval Europe.[10]

The case of Rose of Viterbo illustrates one of the critical problems involved in studying public apostolates of women and of the laity in general. A variety of words were used to describe her speech. The opening passage taken from the anchoress's Rule alludes to one blurry distinction: the difference between teaching and preaching. The biblical passage supporting the Rule's prohibition of preaching refers to Paul's interdict on women's teaching: "Women are not allowed to *teach*" (1 Tim. 2:12; emphasis added). What is the difference between teaching and preaching?[11] In addition, Rose's *vitae* reveal an even more varied thesaurus to refer to these related oratorical performances. It is a thesaurus that changes and becomes richer over time.

The purpose of this study then is twofold. First I draw attention to a special case of preaching said to have been performed by a laywoman who was neither censured nor condemned as a heretic but was promoted as a model of saintliness. As such, Rose was intended not to be imitated by other women but to be admired by them.[12] Within this context I set the groundwork for exploring the variety of terms used to refer to this woman's public acts of oratory, with the goal of beginning to establish the broad scope of a public apostolate attributed to saintly women in the late Middle Ages.

THE LEGAL STATUS OF WOMEN PREACHERS

Although the anchoress's directive on preaching is explicit, the legal status of lay preaching in general and of the preaching by women more specifically in the late medieval church is not plain for two reasons. First, by the late medieval period the preaching act encompassed a variety of public pronouncements in addition to what we normally associate with preaching: clerical oratory from the pulpit in a church. Even before the founding of the mendicant orders in the early thirteenth century, itinerant preachers—both clerical and lay, both authorized and heretical—had increased the opportunities to hear both ecclesiastically sanctioned preaching and unauthorized preaching and the locations where preaching took place. This allowed for an array of oratorical styles to be heard.[13] Because preaching was not limited to the pulpit in a church, it is important to determine whether the speech acts performed in the streets by women would have been recognized by their contemporaries as a form of preaching. Second, there are ambiguities in the wording of both ecclesiastical legislation and prescriptive literature on preaching that seem to allow for the inclusion of women lay preachers without encouraging such a practice.

A Definition of Preaching

What did it mean to preach in thirteenth- and fourteenth-century Europe? In *La prédication médiévale,* Jean Longère has offered this definition of sacred oratory: "to preach is to give a public discourse/oration founded on divine revelation in the context of organized society, seeing to the birth or development of faith and religious understanding and related to the conversion or spiritual progress of the listeners."[14] This definition echoes medieval definitions. Around 1200, Alain of Lille composed a treatise on preaching. His definition of the subject became the standard formulation for subsequent preaching manuals: "Preaching," he wrote, "is the public and open instruction in faith and morals or good conduct."[15] Later, he distinguishes between teaching, preaching, prophesying, and speech-making, but he does so not by the office held by the speaker but by the nature and size of the audience and the topics treated. Of these, only preaching involved a public audience and concerned their faith and morals, with the purpose of reform.[16]

These definitions allow for a rather broad range of oratorical acts to be considered preaching. In keeping with these definitions, Simon Forde has compiled a list of speech acts to be incorporated into our understanding of medieval preaching.[17] Included in his list are those who exhort others concerning morals and those who speak in public places about the faith. Medieval women preachers fall into these categories, for they exhorted groups of people on issues of faith and morals. The discussion below on the *vitae* of Rose amplifies the list of speech acts to be included in general discussions on lay preaching.

Prescriptive Literature

Legislation and prescriptive literature reveal a greater concern for the context of a woman's role in the instruction of faith than for her authority to offer it. The Council of Carthage issued the formulation echoed in the anchoress's Rule: "A woman, even one who is learned and holy, should not presume to teach men *in conventu*," that is, in a public assembly.[18] Later in the twelfth and thirteenth centuries there was an active debate over the right of lay*men* to preach, with proponents including Peter the Chanter, the canonist Huguccio, and Hugh of Saint Cher,[19] but these discussions did not extend to women, perhaps because the subject did not seem to warrant attention.[20] Preaching women tended to be introduced into antiheretical legislation directed against groups promoting lay preaching, such as the Waldensians and the Humiliati.[21] Comments concerning women preaching made their way into general preaching manuals, but the formulation is not always explicit. In the influential handbook *Summa de arte praedicandi,* written between 1233 and 1236, Thomas of Chobham devoted one section to "who can and ought to preach." Concerning the laity, Thomas writes, "Generally, it is true that neither a layman nor a woman can preach publicly, *namely in the church.*"[22] He continues with an account of a layman named Reginald who on the authority of the Lord *commended virtues and renounced vices outside the church.* He was not allowed to expound the *Sacra Pagina,* nor was he given a license to preach.[23] While Thomas makes no mention of women in the same capacity, women were doing the same kind of preaching. Even if Thomas's intention was not to endorse lay preaching, his handling of the subject offers a description of precisely the kind of speech acts attributed to Rose of Viterbo in the *vitae.*

ROSE OF VITERBO

Not much is known with certainty about the life of Rose of Viterbo, though more can be said about the environment in which she lived. When Rose was born around 1233, Viterbo was a city in which passionate conflicts of politics and religion raged. Ghibelline supporters of Emperor Frederick II, the papal archenemy, ruled Viterbo and clashed continually with papal forces.[24] Mendicant friars, having recently arrived in the city, offered public disputations to champion fidelity to the church against Frederick.[25] In addition, they preached in the streets and piazzas against their Ghibelline enemies and the heresies found in the city. But the friars were not the only preachers in Viterbo; they shared the streets with Waldensians and Humiliati, who found protection with the Ghibelline ruling class and preached sermons supporting their cause.[26] The two anonymous *vitae* written about Rose for the two canonization processes initiated to determine her sanctity give the impression that Rose would have witnessed this disparate preaching activity and that she was influenced by it.

Vita I was written soon after her death in 1252 for the process begun by Pope Alexander IV in 1253. *Vita II* was written at the beginning of the fifteenth century and was used for a process initiated by Pope Calixtus III in 1457.[27] Both reflect contemporary expectations concerning sanctity and point to the role of a public apostolate in establishing Rose's special capacity for holiness.[28] The following discussion highlights those passages dealing with Rose's speech.[29]

Vita I is the more conservative of the two. Although the verb "to preach" (*praedicare*) does not appear, Rose's public apostolate takes on significant forms. Chapter 5[30] describes Rose's role as a religious teacher to various groups of women. Having attracted a loyal group of followers, she instructed them to meet *outside* the house (one assumes this means in public), because her vision of the Virgin Mary had shown Mary outside. Then Rose sat among them and "began to speak," basing her authority to do so on her own vision of the bride of Christ, a sight not seen by the others.[31] Rose led this group of faithful women to church, attracting others along the way and instructing them to pray for all Christians.[32] After experiencing a vision of the crucified Christ, Rose lamented (*plorabat*) with great devotion and castigated herself. Still rapt with the vision of her crucified Lord, Rose had herself carried to church, where she lay prostrate in front of the crucifix and said to Christ while weeping (*dicebat ei plorando*), "Who crucified you, Father?" Afterward, she was led home, where she tortured herself (*se martyravit*) for three days, wailing or lamenting (*plorabat*) the entire time.[33]

After these events, Rose began her processions through the city's streets, with a cross in her hands, praising (*lauderet*) the names of Jesus Christ and the Blessed Virgin Mary.[34] Having thus alienated the Ghibelline forces in Viterbo, she and her family were exiled.[35] While in exile, Rose continued her public apostolate, this time based on her ability to prophesy. She proclaimed (*coepit dicere*) what an angel had made known to her: an announcement of good news. Within days, news arrived that the emperor had died.[36] The *vita* trails off mid-sentence soon after this.

Important themes that will reappear in amplified form in *Vita II* are already present in this fragment of *Vita I*. A variety of speech acts are attributed to Rose. In the first *vita*, speech is limited to talking (*dicere*), crying openly (*plorare*), and praising (*laudare*). What makes these acts resemble preaching is the context.[37] Rose speaks to groups of people, at times gathered in the private sphere at home. Whether designated as groups of women or not, it is significant that Rose leads them out of this domestic sphere into public space. Again, the public space is sometimes specified (church) and sometimes not ("out of the house," meaning the streets?); but it is clearly public. When she speaks, Rose instructs her audience to pray and she reveals prophecies to them. When no audience is specified, she cries out or sings praises (*laudare*), while moving in procession.

Equally important are the two themes of her authority and inspiration to speak and her exile. Like other women religious leaders, Rose received her inspiration and authority to speak from supernatural visions and her ability to prophesy.[38] Her vision is given as the reason for her female audiences to listen to her. Her prophecy of the emperor's death adds a political component to her speech. In addition, the theme of religio-political exile, which is significantly elaborated in *Vita II*, appears in the first *vita*. Expelled from Viterbo through the influence of heretics, Rose continues her public apostolate and attracts crowds of people with her politically charged prophecies. Whereas other women preachers were condemned as heretics because of their preaching, Rose preaches against heretics and political enemies of the church, and thus becomes a spokesperson for the church.

The theme of preaching becomes much more prominent in *Vita II*, which was written in the early fifteenth century when the growth of confraternities had added to the opportunities available to hear street preachers, including lay street preachers.[39] The anonymous author depicts Rose as a pious girl, attending church with her mother and frequently listening with devotion to the preaching of Franciscans and to the Word of God.[40] After experiencing a horrific vision of Christ crucified, Rose carried images of Christ and Mary at her breast. Agitated by her pious ardor, she would proceed through the neighborhoods and streets of the city singing (*decantando*) praises.[41]

Chapter 7 of the *vita*[42] is devoted completely to the speech acts of Rose. With a simple heart she preached (*praedicabat*) Jesus Christ daily to the people, announcing (*praenuntiando*) the eternal Good News to the good and eternal punishment to the evil. She raged fiercely (*saeviebat*) against heretics and refuted (*confutabat*) their heresies with reasonable arguments. She made known (*ostendebat*) and exposed (*replicabat*) their false arguments with frank reason. And she spoke (*loquebatur*) with faith in the Word of God against the heretics.[43]

Exiled from the city by these heretics, Rose and her parents left Viterbo. After experiencing a vision of an angel, Rose announced in public (*in populis dicens*) the prophecy of the emperor's imminent death.[44] While still in exile, Rose earned great popularity, attracting groups of both men and women to hear her exhort (*exhortabatur*) them to leave behind their vices and lead a moral and saintly life. Daily they would hear her and receive from her admonitions of salvation. Rose was also sought after for her powers of prayer. The parents of a blind girl asked Rose to pray for their daughter to gain the sight she had never had. Rose, overcome with emotion, began to pray (*in orationem dedit*); afterward, she laid her hands on the girl, and the girl acquired sight.[45]

And finally in another town, still in exile from Viterbo, Rose found herself in conflict with a heretic, who resisted the words of the young saint with snarls. Rose fought against the heretic with argumentation and disputation (*altercando et disputando*) and was successful in restraining the heretic with lucid reason. When reason and words were insufficient to convert the heretic,

Rose resorted to more spectacular means, such as fasting (which was not effective) and throwing herself into a fire in front of crowds of people. After the flames died down, Rose withdrew unhurt, crying out and saying (*clamans et dicens*), "Forthwith, lay aside your infidelity and submit with devoted spirit to Divine Law." Stupefied and silenced by the saint's reason and dramatic displays, the heretic was converted.[46] In this case, Rose used a combination of spectacle and speech to suppress and convert a heretic.

Vita II depicts Rose performing a wider variety of speech acts. Many of the situations are similar to those in *Vita I*, but the words used to describe the speech have changed. Most significantly, she preached daily (*praedicare*) to the people and announced (*praenuntiare*) the Good News. In confrontations with heretics, she raged (*saevire*) and actively debated against them by arguing (*altercare*) and disputing (*disputare*). In addition she revealed (*ostendere*) and exposed (*replicare*) their errors and refuted (*confutare*) them. When words alone were not effective, she used miraculous events and concluded the spectacle by crying out (*clamare*) and talking (*dicere*). Miracles could also occur as a result of her prayer.

Thus we see a picture of Rose addressing large groups of people—both men and women—in a variety of ways. Because of the legal restrictions placed on women's public preaching, this rich thesaurus may have been used to disguise Rose's speech acts. Such variety, however, is found in other examples of nonclerical preaching, including that performed by laymen.[47] Only in reference to elite lay preachers, such as kings and lawyers, do we find the consistent use of the verb "to preach" used to describe their speech.[48] The variety of speech acts, then, does not appear to be linked to the gender of the preacher exclusively, but rather to his or her clerical status. What does appear gendered, however, is the basis of Rose's authority to speak. As in *Vita I*, her claim to preach came from her special access to the divine through visions or miraculous events.

Although not linked directly to her speech acts, one final episode from *Vita II* is worth noting to complete the theme of exile in Rose's life. Upon her return to Viterbo after her political exile ended with the emperor's death, Rose sought to enter the order of Saint Clare, an enclosed order. The sisters refused her request, saying they had already reached their capacity. Rose responded that she knew with certainty that this was not true and that they despised in her what God loves in everybody. And in particularly biting words, Rose said: "Wisdom of this world is foolishness to God. Let this be known: [She] whom you despise to have living [among you], you will rejoice to have dead, and you will have her."[49] A few years after her death, the body of Rose was transferred to the Clariss church at the instigation of Alexander IV. One may surmise that the enclosed Clariss community would have been severely disrupted by the entrance into its fold of a young woman who was so used to speaking and preaching to crowds of men and women. Ironically, by keeping Rose outside the convent walls, the community allowed her to continue her preaching career.

CONCLUSION

The saintly reputation of the young laywoman from Viterbo known as Rose developed around several themes. In addition to performing miraculous cures and spectacular conversions, Rose excelled in holiness through her public speech. Her image as a preacher was not promoted by ecclesiastical officials for imitation by other girls but to showcase the rare example of an orthodox woman who functioned as the church's spokesperson against heresy and political enemies. Exiled for a period from her home for political reasons, Rose remained committed to her public calling and extended her influence beyond Viterbo. Exiled from the convent, the traditional religious life for a woman, Rose remained in the public's eye within the city walls of Viterbo. In both cases exile allowed her to continue her public apostolate.

The case of Rose of Viterbo, then, offers an important exception to legislation restricting a woman's public apostolate; she was certainly tolerated if not officially sanctioned. In the voices of women whose piety was judged so special as to be considered examples of sanctity, there was occasional acceptance by the late medieval church of a public apostolate for women. In addition to the better-known traits of female saintliness, often characterized by extreme asceticism, we can hear women's voices—and they are preaching.

NOTES

I would like to thank members of the Newberry Library Fellows' Seminar, Beverly Mayne Kienzle, Eric Leland Saak, and Elizabeth D. Weber, for reading earlier versions of this article.

1. *Ancrene Wisse*, as translated by A. Savage and N. Watson in *Anchoritic Spirituality* (New York: Paulist Press, 1991), p. 75. All other translations are my own unless otherwise indicated.

2. On the legislation directed against lay preaching in general, see R. Zerfass, *Der Streit um die Laienpredigt* (Freiburg: Herder, 1974).

3. Recent studies and compilations of documents regarding Rose include: G. Abate, *S. Rosa di Viterbo, Terziana Francescana: Fonti Storiche della Vita e loro Revisione critica* (Rome, 1952), orig. pub. in *Miscellanea Francescana* 52, fasc. 1–2 (Jan.–Jun. 1952): 112–278, which endeavors to decipher the historical Rose from the hagiographical legend (all page references are to the monograph version); A. Vacca, *La menta e la Croce* (Rome: Bulzoni, 1982), which fills out the legends of Rose with historical context, again to get a closer picture of the "real" Rose; E. Piacentini, *Il Libro dei miracoli di Santa Rosa di Viterbo* (Viterbo: E. Piacentini, Union Printing, 1991), which documents the thriving cult of the saint through the date of publication; and J. Weisen-

beck and M. Weisenbeck, "Rose of Viterbo: Preacher and Reconciler," in *Clare of Assisi: A Medieval and Modern Woman,* Clarefest Selected Papers, ed. I. Peterson, Clare Centenary Series, vol. 8 (St. Bonaventure, N.Y.: Franciscan Institute, 1996), pp. 145–55. Also see M. d'Alatri, "Rosa di Viterbo: La santa a voce di popolo," *Italia Francescana* 44 (1969): 122–30.

4. The primary sources for Rose's biography are hagiographical and thus pose difficulties in establishing the details of Rose's life. The earliest *vita,* dating from the thirteenth century shortly after her death, exists only in a single manuscript fragment. The second dates from the early fifteenth century. Both are anonymously composed and edited in Abate, *S. Rosa di Viterbo;* also see *Acta Sanctorum,* Sept. II, pp. 414–79.

5. While there is no evidence that Rose received a formal license to preach, this is a significant modern addition to her legend. The information that she had such a license may have entered the tradition of her life in the seventeenth century with P. Coretini's efforts to add legitimacy and authorization to Rose's preaching in order to promote the celebrity of a fellow Viterbo citizen; see P. Coretini, *Historia di S. Rosa Viterbese, raccolta dal suo Processo, a da altre memorie autentiche* (Viterbo, 1638) lib. 2, c. 15; lib. 3, c. 12. Cf. *Acta Sanctorum,* Sept. II, p. 433, note a; and Abate, *S. Rosa di Viterbo,* p. 91. That Rose did receive a license to preach is still frequently repeated in the secondary literature; see L. Taylor, *Soldiers of Christ: Preaching in Late Medieval and Reformation France* (Oxford: Oxford University Press, 1992), p. 176.

6. I am working on a larger study on lay preaching that will include women known to have preached as well as women preachers in the hagiographical tradition.

7. Other women with reputations for sanctity who preached include but are not limited to: Hildegard of Bingen, whose sermons were copied for distribution; Umiltà of Faenza, a fourteenth-century nun whose sermons to her fellow sisters are extant; and Catherine of Siena, the fourteenth-century Dominican tertiary whose public speeches are at times referred to as preaching. The research on these women is extensive; among the pertinent studies on Hildegard, see Barbara Newman, *Sister of Wisdom: St. Hildegard's Theology of the Feminine* (Berkeley: University of California Press, 1987). I am grateful to Professor Newman for allowing me to read a forthcoming work on the hagiographical tradition of Hildegard, which touches on her preaching. On Umiltà, see P. Zama, *Santa Umiltà: La Vita e i Sermones* (Faenza: Fratelli Lega, 1974); and A. Simonetti, *I sermoni di Umiltà da Faenza: Studio e edizione* (Spoleto: Centro italiano di studi sull'alto medioevo, 1995). And on the preaching of Catherine of Siena, see Karen Scott, "St. Catherine of Siena, 'Apostola,'" *Church History* 61, no. 1 (1992): 34–46.

8. Rose may have belonged to the lay Franciscan order called the Penitentials, but this is still debated on different accounts. It is questioned whether a lay order even existed at this time. It is noteworthy that the *vitae* do not emphasize her participation in a preexisting community but rather highlight her tendency to attract people around her. Arguments supporting her tertiary status are based on passages in the *vitae* in which Rose takes a habit and cord from a woman named Sita (Abate, *S. Rosa di Viterbo,* p. 120, para. 3); cf. M. d'Alatri, "*Ordo Paenitentium* ed Eresia in Italia," in *L'Ordine della Penitenza di S. Francesco d'Assisi nel secolo XIII* (Rome: Istituto storico dei Cappuccini, 1973), pp. 181–97, at pp. 194–95 n. 51; and A. Vauchez "L'Idéal de sainteté dans le mouvement féminin franciscain aux xiiie et xive siècles," in *Movi-*

mento religioso femminile e francescanesimo nel secolo xiii (Assisi: La società internazionale di studi francescani, 1980), pp. 317–67, at pp. 333, 352.

9. Considerable research has recently focused on medieval sanctity. On the use of hagiography as a historical source, see R. Kieckhefer, *Unquiet Souls: Fourteenth-Century Saints and their Religious Milieu* (Chicago: University of Chicago Press, 1984), pp. 3–4. Other important studies on medieval sanctity include A. Vauchez, *La sainteté en occident aux derniers siècles du moyen âge d'aprés les procès de canonisation et les documents hagiographiques* (Rome: École française de Rome, 1981); D. Weinstein and R. Bell, *Saints and Society: The Two Worlds of Western Christendom, 1000–1700* (Chicago: University of Chicago Press, 1982); M. Goodich, *Vita Perfecta: The Ideal of Sainthood in the Thirteenth Century* (Stuttgart: A. Hiersemann, 1982); T. Heffernan, *Sacred Biography: Saints and Their Biographers in the Middle Ages* (Oxford: Oxford University Press, 1988); and the various studies in R. Blumenfeld-Kosinski and T. Szell, eds. *Images of Sainthood in Medieval Europe* (Ithaca, N.Y.: Cornell University Press, 1991).

10. On the use of saints' *vitae* in constructing arguments specifically about women, see Jane Tibbetts Schulenburg, "Saints' Lives as a Source for the History of Women, 500–1100," in *Medieval Women and the Sources of Medieval History*, ed. Joel Rosenthal (Athens, Ga.: University of Georgia Press, 1990), pp. 285–320. Schulenburg's discussion of *vitae* as a source for female nonconformity is relevant to late medieval women preachers.

11. On the medieval use of *docere* (teaching) as an inclusive verb embracing *praedicare* (preaching), see Blamires, "Woman and Preaching," p. 139.

12. On the gap between imitating and admiring a saint's actions, see Kieckhefer, *Unquiet Souls*.

13. For a brief overview of preaching in this period, see C. Delcorno, *La predicazione nell'età comunale* (Florence: Sansoni, 1974). A classic study remains M.-D. Chenu, "The Evangelical Awakening," in *Nature, Man, and Society in the Twelfth Century* (Chicago: University of Chicago Press, 1968), pp. 239–69. On early examples of itinerant preaching performed by laymen who were not censured, see J. M. Trout, "Preaching by the Laity in the Twelfth Century," in *Studies in Medieval Culture*, 4, vol. 1, Selected Papers from the Fourth Conference (1968), ed. J. R. Sommerfeldt et al. (Kalamazoo, Mich.: Medieval Institute, 1973–74), pp. 92–108.

14. Jean Longère, *La prédication médiévale* (Paris: Études augustininenes, 1983), p. 12.

15. "Summa de arte praedicatoria," *PL* 210, col. 111.

16. It is noteworthy that Alain does not take up the issue of lay preaching in his treatise on preaching but does so only in his invectives against heretics. In keeping with the tone of these works, he had no tolerance for preaching by nonclerics: "Praedicare autem laico non licet, et ei periculosum est, quia non intelligit quod dicit, nec Scriptura intelligit quas exponere praesumit" (*PL* 210, col. 382).

17. See S. N. Forde, "Late Medieval Lay Preachers' Use of the Bible," *Medieval Sermon Studies Newsletter* 32 (1993): 44–50, esp. 45–46, 49–50.

18. D.23, c.29: "Mulieri in conuentu uiros docere non permittitur. Item ex concilio Cartagin. IV [c. 99 et 98] Mulier, quamvis docta et sancta, uiros in conuentu docere non presumat. Laicus autem presentibus clericis (nisi ipsis rogantibus) docere non audeat."

19. On Peter the Chanter and Huguccio, see Philippe Buc, "*Vox clamantis in deserto?*

Pierre le Chantre et la prédication laïque," *Revue Mabillon* n.s. 4, 65 (1993): 5–47. Note that Huguccio's discussion of lay preaching in his commentary on the *Decretum* stresses preaching as a duty of the sacerdotal office but allows for laymen to exhort (*exhortare*) and admonish (*admonere*) when a cleric was not available; see Buc, pp. 14–15 n. 31. On Hugh of Saint Cher, see M.-D. Chenu, *Nature, Man and Society*, p. 156. His discussion is based on Hugh's disputed questions over benefices; see F. Stegmüller, ed., "Die neuegefundene Pariser Benefizien-Disputation des Kardinals Hugo von St. Cher, O.P.," *Historisches Jahrbuch* 72 (1953): 176–204. Hugh discusses lay preaching in answering the first *quaestio*, "Quibus dari possit, utrum videlicet laicus sicut est clericis."

20. The subject of women preachers entered academic debates by the last quarter of the thirteenth century; see Alcuin Blamires, "Women and Preaching in Medieval Orthodoxy, Heresy and Saints' Lives," *Viator* 26 (1995): 135–52. Blamires analyzes academic disputations on the gift of preaching and its application to women. Also see the essay by Nicole Bériou in this volume.

21. On heretical women preachers, see the essays by Beverly Mayne Kienzle and Anne Brenon in this volume.

22. "Generaliter autem, uerum est quod nec laicus nec mulier predicare potest publice, scilicet in ecclesia." See Franco Morenzoni, ed., *CCCM*, vol. 72 (Turnhout: Brepols, 1988), p. 57.

23. "Vidimus tamen Parisius quendam laicum Reginaldum nomine, qui auctoritate domini, *in publicis congregationibus extra ecclesiam poterat uitia reprehendere et uirtutes commendare*. Sed sacram paginam non poterat exponere, nec ad hoc habuit licentiam domini pape" (ibid.; emphasis mine).

24. On Viterbo within broader papal-political strife, see P. Partner, *The Lands of St. Peter* (Berkeley: University of California Press, 1972).

25. Franciscans are specifically mentioned in Rose's *vitae;* on the Friars Minor in general, see J. Moorman, *A History of the Franciscan Order* (Oxford: Clarendon Press, 1968).

26. For a general introduction to heretical preachers, see M. Lambert, *Medieval Heresy*, 2d ed. (Oxford: Basil Blackwell, 1992); R. I. Moore, *The Formation of a Persecuting Society: Power and Deviance in Western Europe, 950–1250* (Oxford: Basil Blackwell, 1987). On heretics and their protection in Viterbo, see Abate, *S. Rosa di Viterbo*, pp. 94, 100.

27. Neither process ended with the official canonization of Rose. On the issue of abandoned canonization processes, especially those related to women, see A. Vauchez, *La sainteté;* on Rose, see pp. 61, 80–81, 297, 311, 427.

28. The connection between Rose's saintly reputation and preaching continued to be made; for example the seventeenth-century Franciscan chronicle by Luke Wadding furthers Rose's preaching reputation and indeed enriches the thesaurus of speech acts attributed to her. See Luke Wadding, *Annales minorum*, ed. J. M. Fonseca (Quaracchi: Tipografia Barbera Alfani e Venturi Proprietari, 1931), vol. 3, pp. 319–24.

29. The complete legend of Rose has been retold in various modern accounts; see especially the fluid narrative mixed with contextual additions in A. Vacca, *La Menta e la Croce.*

30. The chapter division referred to here is taken from Abate's edition. The sections of the *vitae* are divided differently in the various editions.

31. "Tunc omnes mulieres surrexerunt, et venerunt ad ipsam Virginem. Et Virgo dixit mulieribus: 'Venite omnes extra domum, quia beata Virgo Maria venit extra.' Et exiverunt post ipsam, et coeperunt omnes sedere; et Virgo sedebat in medio ipsarum, et incoepit dicere mulieribus: 'Audite, quia ego video Sponsam Christi speciosissimam, quam nemo vestrum videt'" (Abate, *S. Rosa di Viterbo*, pp. 120–21).

32. "Et continuo mulieres veniebant ad domum Virginis. Et ipsa accessit cum illis, quae secum fuerunt, ad ecclesiam, et dicebat ad alias: 'Quaelibet vestrum quamprimum vadat ad ecclesiam, et oret pro toto populo christiano'" (ibid., pp. 121–22).

33. "Praeterea, cum tunc Dominus noster Iesus Christus in cruce eidem Virgini apparuerit, et ipsa Virgo incontinenti incoepit extrahere sibi capillos . . . et plorabat cum magna devotione, et fecit se portari ad ecclesiam, et prostravit se ante Crucem, et dicebat ei plorando: 'Pater, quis te crucifixit?' Et, dum ita plorabat, surrexit quidam dominus G., et traxit ipsam de ecclesia, et duxit ad domum suam. Quae Virgo, cum ducta esset ad domum, tribus diebus se martyravit, semper plorans" (ibid., p. 122).

34. "Postmodum vero cum beata Virgo Rosa pergeret per civitatem Viterbii assidue, cum cruce in manibus et laudaret nomen Domini nostri Iesu Christi et beatissimam Virginem Mariam" (ibid.).

35. "quidam, qui tunc pro Imperatore Frederico praesidebat civitati Viterbii, rogatus a quibusdam haereticis, qui in eadem civitate publice tunc temporis morabantur, quod eam extra civitatem expellerent" (ibid.).

36. "Et iverunt ad quoddam Castrum, quod Serianum nomine appellatur. Et cum pervenirent ad dictum Castrum, beata Virgo Rosa coepit dicere, sicut ei ab Angelo fuerat nunciatum, quod antequam sint multi dies, amici Dei habebunt magna nova. . . . Quae cum dixisset, venerunt nova Viterbii non post multos dies, quod Imperator Fredericus debitum naturae exsolverat" (ibid., p. 123).

37. See Alain de Lille's definition of preaching based on content and audience, discussed above at nn. 15 and 16.

38. For the connection between prophecy and women's authority to speak, see, for example, Karen Scott, "Urban Spaces, Women's Networks, and the Lay Apostolate in the Siena of Catherine Benincasa," in *Creative Women in Medieval and Early Modern Italy: A Religious and Artistic Renaissance*, ed. E. Ann Matter and John Coakley (Philadelphia: University of Pennsylvania Press, 1994), pp. 105–19, at 109; Sabina Flanagan, *Hildegard of Bingen: A Visionary Life* (London: Routledge, 1989); and the essay by Carolyn Muessig in this volume.

39. The literature on confraternities is immense. See, for example, J. Henderson, *Piety and Charity in Late Medieval Florence* (Oxford: Clarendon Press, 1994); on lay preaching within confraternities, the standard study remains G. Meersseman, *Ordo Fraternitatis: Confraternite e Pietà dei Laici nel Medioevo*, 3 vols. (Rome: Herder, 1977).

40. "In pupillari autem aetate coepit haec Virgo dum devota matre sua ad ecclesiam pergere, praedicationes autem Fratrum Minorum frequenter audire et verbum Dei cum intentione mentali devota percipere" (Abate, *S. Rosa di Viterbo*, p. 127).

41. "apparuit ei Jesus Christi veluti cruci fixus. Ad cuius visum et crudele spectaculum commota sunt viscera eius, et tam ingentis doloris et compassionis aculeus pertransivit animam eius. . . . Ex tunc autem crucifixi Jesu et Virginis gloriosae imagines semper in suo pectore deferebat; et quia amor mentem amantis quiescere non permittit, de lectulo surgebat de nocte et per vicos et plateas civitatem circuibat, laudes divinas modulatis vocibus decantando" (ibid., p. 129).

42. Cf. chap. 3 in *Acta Sanctorum*, pp. 437–39.

43. "In simplicitate nempe cordis Christum Iesum quotidie gentibus praedicabat, bonis bona praenuntiando aeterna et malis supplicia sempiterna. Contra haereticos autem horribiliter saeviebat et eorum haereses argumentis sensibilibus confutabat. Argumenta enim illorum falsa replicabat, et, cunctis audientibus, dictorum argumentorum falsam apparentiam apertis rationibus luce clarius ostendebat. . . . Haeretici autem, qui tunc in Viterbio . . . contra hanc Virginem ut canes rabidi fremere coeperunt et a verbis obmutesceret. . . . Virgo autem Christi, in Dei amore et Fidei fulcimento firmata, comminationibus spretis et terroribus cunctis depulsis, loquebatur contra eos cum fiducia verbum Dei, asserens, se paratam pro favore Fidei Catholicae et defensione mortem libentissime sustinere" (ibid., pp. 131–32).

44. "virgo Rosa ibidem, et de nocte in visione per angelum recepto divino oraculo, de mane vaticinata est in populo, dicens: 'Audite, Christi fideles, et laetamini confidentes, quia usque ad paucos die habebitis nova trophea'" (ibid., p. 133).

45. "Mares et mulieres castri illius, audientes famam sanctitatis illius, susceperunt eam laetabundo animo et devoto; et illa, ut simplex erat, simplici confabulatione exhortabatur illos ad depositionem vitiorum et ad susceptionem bonorum morum et sanctarum virtutum. At illi cum devotione audiebant eam, et cotidie recipiebant ab ea monita salutis. Interea . . . erat quaedam virgo, nomine Delicata, quae ab ipsa sua nativitate caruerat virtute visiva. Quam quidem parentes eius ad virginem Rosam adduxerunt, supplicantes obnixe ut dignaretur pro ea orare atque suis humilibus precibus et Deo caris, virtutem, que carebat, visivam ei recuperaret. Virgo autem Rosa, precibus eorum commota, sese in orationem dedit: facta autem oratione, surrexit, et imponens manum lumen illis recuperavit optatum" (ibid., p. 134).

46. "Praeterea autem in eodem, quod diximus, castro Vitorclani erat quaedam haeretica perfida, quae contra Fidem Catholicam cotidie horrenda latrabat et verbis virginis Rosae, quantum poterat, obsistebat; sed virgo fidelis Rosa dictam haereticam veritatis iaculis feriebat, et, altercando et disputando, claris rationibus confutabat. . . . Cum nec sic acquiescere vellet, cogitavit virgo sanctissima Rosa convertere eam per virtutem Fidei sibi infusam, videlicet per jejunia prolixi temporis spatio tracta . . . fecit magnum ignem parari, et rogavit sacerdotes, ut pulsarent campanas ad hoc, ut populus conveniret ad tale spectaculum: et confidens de Dei clementia, pro cuius Fide et Lege certabat, in medium prosiluit eiusdem, et, hinc inde pluries se revolvens flammarum globis vallata undique, tandiu ibidem moram contraxit, quandiu ignis ille totaliter fuit extinctus. Finaliter inde exiens et sospes coram haeretica gradiens, dicti castri plebe astante, absque ustione vestimentorum et corporis sic illaesa apparuit, asci inter flores roridos commorata fuisset, clamans et dicens: 'Iam depone infidelitatem tuam et devota mente subde te Legi divinae.' Ad cuius stupendum miraculum prava illa haeretica stupefacta, infidelitate deposita, ad Fidem Christi totaliter se convertit" (ibid., pp. 134–35).

47. The clearest comparison is to the mid-fourteenth-century lay preacher Giovanni Colombini of Siena. The early-fifteenth-century *vita* written about him also uses a variety of verbs to describe his speech. See Feo Belcari, *Vita del Beato Giovanni Colombini da Siena*. ed. R. Chiarini (Lanciano: R. Carraba, 1914). On the use of *exhortatio* and *praedicatio* and their relationship to clerical hierarchy, see Buc, "*Vox Clamantis in Deserto?*" esp. pp. 18–24.

48. The tradition of royal preaching is limited; see D. Pryds, "*Rex Praedicans:* Robert

d'Anjou and the Politics of Preaching," in *De l'homélie au Sermon: Histoire de la prédication médiévale* (Louvain-la-Neuve: Université Catholique de Louvain, 1993), pp. 239–62, and "The Politics of Preaching in Fourteenth-Century Naples: Robert d'Anjou (1309–1343) and His Sermons" (Ph.D. diss., University of Wisconsin, Madison, 1994). Cf. P. Boyer, *"Ecce Rex Tuus:* Le roi et le royaume dans les sermons de Robert de Naples," *Revue Mabillon* n.s. 6, t. 67 (1995): 101–36. For an example of a preaching lawyer, see J. Powell, *Albertanus of Brescia: The Pursuit of Happiness in the Early Thirteenth Century* (Philadelphia: University of Pennsylvania Press, 1992), esp. pp. 90–106; and D. Pryds, "Monarchs, Lawyers, and Saints: Juridical Preaching on Holiness," in *Models of Holiness in Medieval Sermons,* ed. Beverly Mayne Kienzle et al. (Louvain-la-Neuve: Fédération Internationale des Instituts d'Études Médiévales, 1996).

49. "Sacra Virgo ait: 'Scio, namque scio, quod non ista est causa, sed quia despicitis in me, quae Deus acceptat in omnibus, ut scilicet propter Ipsum sapientes mundi sint stulti, ut fiant sapientes. Nam sapientia huius mundi stultitia est apud Deum. Sed hoc vobis notum sit, quia quam contemnitis habere viventem, gaudebitis habere defunctam; quam et habebitis'" (Abate, *S. Rosa di Viterbo,* p. 136).

NINE

Women's Sermons
at the End of the Middle Ages
Texts from the Blessed and Images of the Saints

Roberto Rusconi

"Mal sont les gens en doctrines / quant par feme sont le sermones" ("The people are poorly instructed when the sermons are by a woman"). So reads a caption in a French manuscript, under an illustration that portrays a woman preaching outdoors, from a pulpit, to an exclusively male audience.[1] The writer clearly rejects the possibility that a woman could preach in an effective manner.

Whenever a female figure is depicted in preacher's robes, medieval culture's outlook on this matter is essentially ambiguous. Several miniatures in the manuscript tradition of "Le Pèlerinage de la vie humaine" by Guillaume de Deguileville, for example, display "Reason" as a woman who addresses her listeners from a pulpit, with a preacher's gestures. Her left hand is raised with the palm open, and her right hand is shown with the index finger pointing upward, while she delivers a true sermon: "Quant fuy ainsi reconforte / De Grace qui m'ont avise, / Tantost au prone vi aler / Dame Raison pour sermonner" ("I was consoled by Grace, who advised me; then I saw Lady Reason go to the pulpit and preach").[2]

Within the Roman church, however, the practice of women's preaching was not unknown. Evidence transmitted in writing makes clear the particular importance of a woman's role within an ecclesiastical institution (notably that of an abbess in a female monastic community), and her reputation for holiness.[3] In the late Middle Ages, the issue of sermons given by women was raised in relation to twelfth-century religious movements, such as the Poor of Lyons. There are also references to sermons by women who belonged to the Cathar Church and by *mulieres religiosae* (religious women) connected to the new Mendicant orders.[4]

The ban on women's preaching, however, which derived from regulations in the *Decretum Gratiani,* compiled around 1140 at Bologna, remained in effect. Consequently, the late medieval devotional iconography on panel paintings for altars and in fresco cycles depicts a passive role for women—they are in the audience. However, there is one relevant exception, that of female saints who preached to pagans during Christianity's first centuries; and one ambiguous exception, that of some personages living primarily in the fourteenth century. Altar panels and frescoes were placed inside churches in order to promote devotion through the figure of a saint or blessed one. It would have been difficult for such artworks to reflect a practice, such as preaching by women, that was not officially recognized, or at least tolerated, by ecclesiastical institutions. (Similar conclusions can be drawn from illuminations of liturgical and devotional manuscripts.) The iconography of saints and blessed ones generally derived its inspiration and guidance for choosing subjects and themes from hagiographical literature, particularly from legends and canonization proceedings.

MULIERUM DEVOTA TURBA
(A DEVOTED THRONG OF WOMEN)

Normally, women are depicted in illustrations of preaching as listeners. They occupy a separate place in the audience, to reflect the physical separation between the sexes that was dictated by legislation and by preachers. Following a Byzantine-inspired formality in iconographic representation of preaching, women in the audience are portrayed crouched on the ground near the pulpit, with the men standing at their shoulders (as one sees, for example, in the scene of Saint Nicholas of Bari's conversion during an outdoor sermon, on a predella painted by Fra Angelico [fig. 9.1]).[5]

In fifteenth-century Italian art, contemporary preachers, who were officially canonized by the Roman church or venerated by the faithful through their reputation for holiness, are depicted preaching outdoors, still before an audience carefully divided between men and women. The sexes might be simply divided on the sides of a churchyard, as for a sermon held at the piazza of L'Aquila by the Friar Minor of the Observance Giovanni of Capestrano (d. 1456). This event is represented on a panel of a polyptych (fig. 9.2) commissioned to an Abruzzi master in order to promote the preacher's cult and canonization.[6] Men and women might even be separated by a length of cloth extended across the piazza, as for sermons held in the birthplace of Saint Bernardino of Siena (d. 1444). This is shown in Sano di Pietro's paintings (fig. 9.3), which were executed before the canonization of this most famous Friar Minor of the Observance.[7] At the century's close, sermons by the Dominican friar Girolamo Savonarola were also held inside the cathedral church of Santa Reparata in Florence; men in the central nave were separated from women in the lateral naves by curtains stretched

Figure 9.1   Fra Angelico, *The young Nicholas listening to a bishop preaching*, Rome: Vatican Museums; reproduced by permission.

between the pillars. This practice was frequent enough to appear on a frontispiece in a 1496 Florentine edition of Savonarola's *Compendium revelationis* (fig. 9.4), which was published by the friar before his death at the stake in 1498.[8]

These images have a common iconological element. The subordinate position of the female group is emphasized at the same time as their devotion in hearing the words pronounced from the pulpit.

Another element enters the scene when the group of veiled women listening to the sermon is scattered apart by a possessed woman with disheveled hair, who leaps to her feet. Sometimes particular emphasis is given to this event, as in the fresco executed for the little church of Macello, in Piedmont not far from Turin, relating to a sermon by the Dominican friar Vincent Ferrer (d. 1419); the fresco was painted a few years after his death. Sometimes such evidence of demonic possession constitutes only one small detail, as in a panel of a polyptych commissioned by Ferrer's brothers from the Erri workshop, for the Church of St. Dominic at Modena. This panel depicts the sermon preached by Ferrer in the piazza at Perpignan in 1415; the event is narrated in a hagiographical legend written after his canonization in 1458.[9] According to the proceedings for his canonization, one type of miracle accomplished by Vincent Ferrer in connection with effective preaching is the curing of women possessed by the devil. This power of a preacher's word was immediately and promptly captured in devotional iconography.[10] In an exceptional case, during a sermon by Giovanni of Capestrano in the piazza

Figure 9.2 Master of San Giovanni of Capestrano, *Giovanni of Capestrano in a pulpit outside the Cathedral of L'Aquila*, L'Aquila: Museo del Castello; reproduced by kind permission of Ministero per i Beni Culturali e Ambientali, Soprintendenza ai B.A.A.A.S. per l'Abruzzo, L'Aquila.

Figure 9.3 Sano di Pietro, *Bernardino's sermon in the Piazza del Campo in Siena*, Siena: Museo del Duomo; reproduced by permission of Opera della Metropolitana.

¶COMPENDIO DI REVELATIONE DELLO
INVTILE SERVO DI IESV CHRISTO
FRATE HIERONYMO DA FERRA
RA DELLORDINE DE FRA
TI PREDICATORI

¶IESVS   MARIA

ENCHE Lungo tempo in molti modi per
inspiratione Diuina lo habbia predecte mol
te chose future:nientedimeno considerando
lasententia del nostro saluatore christo Iesu
che dice. Nolite sanctum dare canibus:nec mittatis mar
garitas uestras ante porcos:ne forte conculcent eas pedi
bus:& couersi dirumpant uos:Sono sempre stato scarso
nel dire: & non misono exteso piu che misia parso essere
necessario alla salute degli huomini (in modo che le con
clusione nostre sono state poche/aduengha che molte sie

Figure 9.4 Frontispiece to Girolamo Savonarola da Ferrara's
Compendio di revelatione, Florence, 1496; reproduced by permission of Biblioteca Nazionale Centrale di Firenze.

of L'Aquila, a man possessed by a demon also appears and is miraculously cured by the preacher (fig. 9.2).

INDUXIT AD BAPTISMUM
(SHE LED THEM TO BAPTISM)

The value placed on preaching in late medieval Italian society was such that great power was also attributed to women's words. To circumvent the canonical regulations, and in the absence of an officially recognized practice, only female saints, from Christian antiquity if possible, could be considered for devotional representations.[11]

The controversy with pagan philosophers is one central theme in the hagiographical tradition concerning Catherine of Alexandria, who was believed to be the daughter of a king of Cyprus. She was martyred in the early fourth century C.E. The subject of the dispute appears in representations of her in the eleventh and thirteenth centuries in France; it becomes particularly common in fifteenth-century Italy.[12] In a chapel painted by Masolino da Panicale, in the church of San Clemente at Rome, for Cardinal Branda Castiglioni, probably around 1429–32, Saint Catherine of Alexandria is represented in a formal dispute with pagan philosophers.[13] She counts her arguments on her fingertips, with the gesture of the *computatio digitorum* (fig. 9.5). This subject is related in an organic way to another scene on the chapel wall (fig. 9.6), in which Catherine stands preaching against the cult of idols (on the front wall, episodes from the life of Saint Ambrose, the anti-Arian bishop of Milan, are depicted). The theme of the dispute with philosophers concerning the error of their faith, along with the *computatio digitorum,* was also common in the iconography of Christ, particularly in the scene involving the boy Jesus, who disputes with learned rabbis in the temple. A second theme, preaching against pagan idols, begins to appear more often in cycles of stories about apostles and saints from early Christianity. In fifteenth-century Italy, vernacular preaching to the people, in fact, explicitly promoted the ideal of a new Christianization of society.[14]

During the fifteenth century, the theme of Saint Catherine of Alexandria's dispute appears also to have been widespread in other European countries, particularly on the Iberian peninsula. There the *reconquista* against the Arabs led them to deduce from this iconographical subject an even more accentuated propagandistic appeal. (This occurred also in devotional representations of other saints.) However, the iconological significance of the church's triumph over paganism, to the schismatic Greco-Byzantine churches, and to Islam, appears fully expressed in a fresco executed by Bernardino di Betto, called Pinturicchio, in 1492–94, commissioned for the Borgia apartment by Pope Alexander VI (especially if it is true that in this fresco [fig. 9.7], the Byzantine emperor Andreas Paleologus and Djem, the son of the Turkish

Figure 9.5 Masolino da Panicale, *Saint Catherine of Alexandria disputing with the philosophers*, Rome: S. Clemente, chapel Brancacci; reproduced by permission of Ministero per i Beni Culturali e Ambientali, Soprintendenza per i Beni Ambientali e Architettonici, Rome.

Figure 9.6 Masolino da Panicale, *Saint Catherine of Alexandria refusing to worship the idols*, Rome: S. Clemente, chapel Brancacci; reproduced by permission of Ministero per i Beni Culturali e Ambientali, Soprintendenza per i Beni Ambientali e Architettonici, Rome.

Figure 9.7 Pinturicchio (Bernardino di Betto), *Saint Catherine of Alexandria disput-*
ing before the emperor, Rome: Vatican Palaces, Appartamento Borgia, Sala dei Santi,
reproduced by permission.

sultan Mahomet II, are portrayed among the audience when the learned
scholars are defeated by Catherine's arguments).[15]

In the sacristy chapel of the Church of Santa Maria del Carmine in Florence, belonging to the Mendicant order of Carmelites, Lippo di Andrea,
probably in the fourteenth century's final decade, frescoed the story of a
Roman martyr, Saint Cecilia. As the Latin inscription under the fresco panel
explains, this saint, after having distributed her wealth to the poor, expounds
fidei monita (admonitions of faith) from a kind of pedestal, and she leads
her listeners to baptism, administered to them by Pope Urban.[16] The
painter reproduced the iconography of a panel executed between 1300 and
1320 for the same Florentine church by an anonymous master.[17] Lippo di
Andrea further emphasizes the connection between baptism of converts to
the new faith and Cecilia's preaching; she is portrayed in the capacity of an
apostola (female apostle).[18] (Very similar to this is the iconographical scheme
used for the sermon to the population at Jerusalem, and for the dispute with
doctors of the law in Saint Stephen the Protomartyr's story, frescoed around

1450–57 by Fra Angelico in the Vatican Palaces' chapel and commissioned by Pope Nicholas V.)[19]

Mary Magdalene's preaching to the population at Marseilles, in southern France, promptly recorded also in the *Legenda Aurea* (Golden Legend) by the Dominican friar Jacopo da Voragine, provides the starting point for numerous paintings in various European countries.[20] However, with respect to Italy, it is very interesting to note that the wooden panel with the Magdalene's figure and stories about her life, executed by an anonymous master around 1280 (fig. 9.8), explicitly reproduces the model of the historical panel, a genre introduced in Italian art in the thirteenth century in connection with the cult of Saint Francis of Assisi. This saint started the Mendicant order of Friars Minor, dedicated in large measure to a preaching apostolate in late medieval Italy.[21] At the painting's center, the penitent Magdalene, clothed solely by her own hair, raises her right hand in a gesture that is simultaneously a testimony and an address. It is an exhortation to be converted, recalled from a text that, written in capital letters, is easily read on a scroll that is unrolled from her left hand. The penitential content in her preaching as the "evangelist of Provence" is rendered explicitly in a little scene to the right of the same hand. There the saint, standing on a platform base, with her right hand's index finger pointing up, addresses a packed and attentive audience. Revivals of this theme were numerous in the fifteenth century, both in Italian art and in that of the Iberian peninsula, along with a particular variant in sermon representations, shown in the open countryside instead, in some early sixteenth-century Flemish works (fig. 9.9).[22]

In the syncretistic hagiography that characterizes the late Middle Ages, the Magdalene's evangelical mission is joined by the figure of Martha from Bethany in, for example, a *retablo* (altarpiece) painted by R. Destorrents for the church named for the saint at Iravalls in Catalonia and in a stained-glass window (1407) in the Church of Saint Martha at Nuremberg in southern Germany.[23] Even more interesting is an altarpiece panel containing stories about Saint Martha that was executed toward the end of the fifteenth century by an anonymous Ligurian painter for the Church of San Martino at Briga Marittima (in France). At the predella's center, from the height of a coarse wooden pulpit erected outside a city's walls, the saint, portrayed in a nun's robes, or the robes of a *mulier religiosa*, raises her right hand to address an audience for her sermon (fig. 9.10). In this era, besides the preaching by other saints, Christ's sermons also might be represented as being delivered outside from a pulpit.[24]

SCRIBE

(WRITE)

No major differences appear between fifteenth-century iconography portraying the evangelical preaching of various saints from early Christianity and

Figure 9.8 Master of the Magdalene, *Mary Magdalene Altarpiece*, Florence: Academy; reproduced by permission of Ministero per i Beni Culturali e Ambientali, Soprintendenza per i Beni Artistici e Storici delle Provincie di Firenze e Pistoia.

Figure 9.9 Master of the Magdalene Legend, *Mary Magdalene preaching in a wood*, Philadelphia: Philadelphia Museum of Art, the John G. Johnson Collection; reproduced by permission.

Figure 9.10 Ligurian school (late fifteenth century), *Saint Martha preaching*, Briga Marittima: Church of San Martino; photo copyright Michel Graniou, Conseil Général des Alpes-Maritime.

the frescoed cycle of stories about Saint Rose of Viterbo (d. 1252), produced by the painter Benozzo Gozzoli around 1453. This cycle was located in the church named for the saint in her native city, shortly before canonization proceedings ended in 1457.[25] As it appears from a copy executed in 1632, before the frescoes' destruction, following an apparition of the cross, Saint Rose addresses the people outdoors, standing on a pedestal, and positioning her hands in a gesture similar to that of the apostles when they are preaching (fig. 9.11).[26]

A difference is evident, however, in a polyptych executed by the Sienese painter Pietro Lorenzetti and his workshop shortly before the mid-fourteenth century for the monastery of Saint John the Evangelist in Florence, of which the blessed Umiltà of Faenza (1226–1310) became abbess.[27] The stories about this blessed woman, placed in the same narrative order that is traced in the hagiographical legend written in 1332, record two prominent yet typical moments in the abbess's activity:[28] although illiterate, she is reading to nuns in the refectory (fig. 9.12) and dictating to the sisters the text of her own sermons, according to inspiration from the dove of the Holy Spirit (fig. 9.13).

In the mid-fourteenth century, moreover, two remarkable visionary figures emerge in Western church history: the Swedish princess Birgitta of Vadstena (d. 1370) and the Sienese *mantellata,* Catherine Benincasa (d. 1380).

Figure 9.11 Benozzo Gozzoli, *After the vision of a crucifix, Saint Rose of Viterbo preaches to the gathered people* (destroyed frescoes, reproduced in 1632), Viterbo: Museo Civico; reproduced by permission.

Immediately after her death, particularly in illustrations drawn in the voluminous manuscripts in which her *Revelationes* were recorded, Birgitta is represented primarily as a nun who puts in writing the content of the celestial visions she witnessed. (In several early-sixteenth-century English prints, her writing's spiritual nature is emphasized by the sending of the dove of the Holy Spirit and by assistance from an angel at her shoulder.[29] However, sources insist that the *Revelationes* were actually written down by Birgitta's confessors.)

Catherine of Siena was a visionary, a prophet, and also an author. She was often depicted, especially in miniature initials in the manuscripts of her writings, in the habit of an inspired nun who is dictating to her secretaries.[30] It thus proves difficult to claim that in a polyptych panel executed by the Sienese painter Giovanni di Paolo around 1463 (immediately after the saint's canonization) the scene of Catherine before the pope represents a sermon preached (fig. 9.14).[31] Still, in the early sixteenth century, between 1518 and 1524, in one chapel of the Roman Church of San Silvestro al Quirinale, the Dominican friar Mariano "del piombo" arranged for the painter Polidoro Caldara da Caravaggio to fresco stories about Saint Catherine of Siena.[32] In this era there were harsh criticisms in various circles favoring religious reform

Figure 9.12 Pietro Lorenzetti, *The illiterate Umiltà of Faenza reads in the refectory*, Florence: Uffizi; reproduced by permission of Ministero per i Beni Culturali e Ambientali, Soprintendenza per i Beni Artistici e Storici delle Provincie di Firenze e Pistoia.

Figure 9.13 Pietro Lorenzetti, *Umiltà of Faenza dictates her sermons inspired by the Holy Spirit,* Florence: Uffizi; reproduced by permission of Ministero per i Beni Culturali e Ambientali, Soprintendenza per i Beni Artistici e Storici delle Provincie di Firenze e Pistoia.

Figure 9.14 Giovanni di Paolo, *Saint Catherine of Siena "preaching" before the pope,* copyright © Fundación Colección Thyssen-Bornemisza, Madrid.

against the popes, while numerous female figures became influential as "living saints" who were elevated to fame as prophets.[33] In this context, the Sienese *mantellata,* who died in 1380 and was canonized in 1462, came to be portrayed while "preaching" outdoors before the pope, who sits centered in the portico of an imposing ecclesiastical edifice.

CONCLUSION

With the shattering of ecclesiastical unity in the West, iconography concerning Christian preaching by women, portrayed indirectly and ambiguously in the late Middle Ages, also encountered new challenges. In accord with preaching's growing importance in Italian society, starting from the early fifteenth century, the role of women who preached also had its own specific place within artistic representations.[34]

Indeed, women, like men, had begun to be incorporated into representations of the audience for preaching. In certain ways, the iconography is marked by women's devotional attitude, which is presented in a kind of dialectical juxtaposition with miraculous effects from male preachers' words; specifically, certain women who attend their sermons, namely, demonically possessed females, are cured within the context of preaching.

Otherwise, the iconographical conventions apply in an analogous manner to whomever fulfills the preacher's role, whether man or woman, on pedestal or pulpit, outdoors or in a church, for either saintly male or saintly female preachers (and the same applies to Jesus Christ). The female preacher is depicted using the same gestures as the males: the raised hand and pointing finger, as well as at times the *computatio digitorum*, indicating dispute.

The religious woman also comes to be represented in an author's robes, emphasizing, moreover, especially with regard to fourteenth- and fifteenth-century female visionaries and prophets, the supernatural character of the composition of her writings.[35] This can happen while she, like other monastic (male) authors, is dictating her own texts to scribes.

Frequent representation of female saints from Christian antiquity in the capacity of evangelists was already familiar in iconography from the twelfth century onward. However, in an era like the fifteenth century, such representation finally discovered an ulterior motive in the intention, among those who commissioned paintings and frescoes, to underscore saints' actions against pagans and heretics. In this era, a comprehensive program to reinvigorate Italian society with Christian ideals was activated. In the late fifteenth and early sixteenth centuries, to judge from the ample testimony of illustrations in the first printed books, all Europe was in the course of a profound transformation in the realm of religious experience. Women's religious and ecclesiastical status appeared to be different, and the change was reflected also in modifications to the iconography of female saints, to which was added, albeit for the most part in an indirect manner, the activity of preaching.[36]

NOTES

This essay was translated by Fay Martineau.

Because of the topic's immensity, this article focuses primarily on paintings and frescoes produced in Italy in the fifteenth century. References to the art-historical bibliography do not pretend to be complete; in particular, they do not venture to discuss attributions and datings of individual works in the principal repertory. They indicate therefore only essential studies and color reproductions.

1. Reproduced in Adriana Valerio, *La questione femminile nei secoli X–XII: Una rilettura storica di alcune esperienze in Campania* (Naples: M. D'Auria, 1983), between p. 48 and p. 49.

2. See Guillaume de Deguileville, *Le Pèlerinage de la vie humaine,* ed. J. J. Sturzinger (London, 1893), opposite p. 34, in relation to verses 1059–62.

3. See Beverly Mayne Kienzle, "The Typology of the Medieval Sermon and Its

Development in the Middle Ages: Report on Work in Progress," in *De l'homélie au sermon: Histoire de la prédication médiévale*, ed. Jacqueline Hamesse and Xavier Hermand (Louvain-la-Neuve: Université Catholique de Louvain, 1993), pp. 99–101; and Roberto Rusconi, "Afterword: Sources for the History of Religious Women in Late Medieval Italy," in *Women and Religion in Medieval and Renaissance Italy*, ed. Daniel E. Bornstein and Roberto Rusconi (Chicago: University of Chicago Press, 1996); see also in this volume the letter of Innocent III cited in Katherine Ludwig Jansen, "Maria Magdalena: *Apostolorum Apostola.*"

4. See Beverly Mayne Kienzle, "The Prostitute-Preacher: Patterns of Polemic against Medieval Waldensian Women Preachers," in this volume.

5. Reproduced in color in William Hood, *Fra Angelico at San Marco* (New Haven, Conn.: Yale University Press, 1993), fig. 83, p. 85.

6. See Roberto Rusconi, "Giovanni da Capestrano: iconografia di un predicatore nell 'Europa del '400," in *Predicazione francescana e società veneta nel Quattrocento: committenza, ascolto, ricezione*, 2d ed., Atti del II Convegno internazionale di studi francescani, Padua, March 26–28, 1987 (Padua: Centro studi antoniani, 1995), pp. 25–53.

7. The sermon at the Piazza del Campo is reproduced in color, for example, in *Dizionario degli Istituti di Perfezione*, vol. 7 (Rome, 1983), between col. 552 and col. 553. On the two paintings, see Michael Mallory and Gaudenz Freuler, "Sano di Pietro's Bernardino Altarpiece for the Compagnia della Vergine," in the *Burlington Magazine* 133, no. 1056 (1991): 186–92.

8. See Elisabetta Turelli, "Gli incunaboli con xilografie di fra Girolamo Savonarola nella Biblioteca Nazionale Centrale di Firenze," in *Immagini e azione riformatrice: le xilografie degli incunaboli savonaroliani nella Biblioteca Nazionale di Firenze*, ed. Elisabetta Turelli (Florence: Alinari, 1985), pp. 61–68, and fig. 62.

9. A color reproduction is in Daniele Benati, *La Bottega degli Erri e la pittura del Rinascimento a Modena* (Modena: Artioli, 1988), p. 134.

10. See Roberto Rusconi, "Vicent Ferrer e Pedro de Luna: sull'iconografia di un predicatore fra due obbedienze," in *Conciliarismo, stati nazionali, inizi dell'Umanesimo*, Atti del XXV Convegno storico internazionale, Todi, October 9–12, 1988 (Spoleto: Centro italiano di studi sull'alto medioevo, 1990), pp. 213–33.

11. See the *quaestio* of Gauthier de Château-Thierry (ca. 1245), "Utrum conveniat viris tantum vel viris et mulieribus," cited in Nicole Bériou, "La Madeleine dans les sermons parisiens du XIIIe siècle," *Mélanges de l'École Française de Rome: Moyen Age* 104 (1992): 301 n. 106: "Propter necessitatem fidei et ecclesie edificande que tunc novella erat, licuit feminis quod tamen non liceret eis si esset plantata sicut modo, et hoc propter defectum predicatorum" (On account of the necessity of faith and for edifying the church, which was new at that time, women were allowed to do what they would not be allowed if the church were well established as it is now, and this was due to the lack of preachers), referring explicitly to Catherine of Alexandria, Mary Magdalene, Saint Cecilia, and Saint Lucy. On this topic see also the more recent contribution by Alcuin Blamires, "Women and Preaching in Medieval Orthodoxy, Heresy, and Saints' Lives," *Viator* 26 (1995): 135–52.

12. Besides the general information in Peter Assion, "Katharina von Alexandrien," in *Lexicon der christlichen Ikonographie*, vol. 7 (1974), cols. 289–97, there are interesting notations in Chiara Frugoni, "La donna nelle immagini, la donna immaginata,"

in *Storia delle donne in Occidente*, vol. 2: *Il Medioevo*, ed. Christiane Klapisch-Zuber (Rome and Bari: Laterza, 1990), p. 453; English trans. (Cambridge, Mass.: Harvard University Press, 1992). See also, in this volume, some passages in Carolyn Muessig, "Prophecy and Song: Teaching and Preaching by Medieval Women."

13. Reproduced in color in Paul Joannides, *Masaccio and Masolino: A Complete Catalogue* (London: Phaidon Press, 1993), plates 139–41, pp. 190–93. It is even on the cover of Helen Solterer, *The Master and the Minerva: Disputing Women in French Medieval Culture* (Berkeley: University of California Press, 1995). The different iconographical interpretations of the chapel's frescoes are recorded in Perri Lee Roberts, *Masolino da Panicale* (Oxford: Clarendon Press, 1993), pp. 110–11 (the bibliography is indicated in notes 83–84).

14. See Roberto Rusconi, "I 'falsi credentes' nell'iconografia della predicazione (secoli XIII–XV)," in *Cristianità ed Europa: Miscellanea di studi in onore di Luigi Prosdocimi*, ed. Cesare Alzati (Rome: Herder, 1994), pp. 313–37.

15. Reproduced in color in Carlo Pietrangeli, ed., *Il Palazzo Apostolico Vaticano* (Florence-Nardini, 1992), pp. 100–101.

16. Reproduced in color in Luciano Berti, ed., *La chiesa di Santa Maria del Carmine a Firenze* (Florence: Nardini, 1992), table 10.

17. Currently preserved in Florence, at the Uffizi.

18. In the early fourteenth century, on an altarpiece of the Florentine school, there appeared a scene of another saint from early Christianity, who preaches aboard a boat; it is preserved at Livorno by the archconfraternity of Santa Giulia; the scene is reproduced in George Kaftal, *Saints in Italian Art: Iconography of the Saints in Tuscan Painting* (Florence: Sansoni, 1952), fig. 674 (2). See Gabriela Kaster, "Julia von Korsika (von Karthago?)," in *Lexicon der christlichen Ikonographie*, vol. 7 (1974), cols. 224–25.

19. A color reproduction is in John Pope-Hennessy, *Angelico* (Florence: Becocci, 1981), p. 61.

20. See Marga Anstett-Janssen, "Maria Magdalena," in *Lexicon der christlichen Ikonographie*, vol. 7 (1974), cols. 516–41. Reproduced in color in Marilena Mosco, ed., *La Maddalena tra Sacro e Profano (Da Giotto a De Chirico)* (Florence: Casa Usher, 1986), p. 213. See also the fuller discussion in the article by Katherine Ludwig Jansen, "Mary Magdalen and the Mendicants: The Preaching of Penance in the Late Middle Ages," *Journal of Medieval History* 21 (1995): 1–25; see also the essays in this volume, Jansen, "Maria Magdalena," and Muessig, "Prophecy and Song."

21. See Jeryldene Wood, "Perceptions of Holiness in Thirteenth-Century Italian Painting: Clare of Assisi," *Art History* 14 (1991): 301–28, specifically 308.

22. See Max J. Friedländer, *Early Netherlandish Painting*, vol. 12 (Leyden, 1975), plates 7–9, no. 10: pp. 13ss and 133–34. The polyptych is actually divided among several museums: see Jeanne Tombu, "Un triptyque du maître de la légende de Marie-Madeleine," *Gazette des Beaux Arts* 69, no. 1 (1927): 299–310.

23. See Marga Anstett-Janssen, "Martha von Bethanien," in *Lexicon der christlichen Ikonographie*, vol. 7 (1974), cols. 565–68.

24. See, for example, among many wood engravings, the sermon by Christ to Mary Magdalene in Giovan Pietro Ferraro, *Tesauro spirituale*, Milan, Guillaume le Siguerre, 1499, reproduced in Max Sander, *Le livre à figures italien depuis 1467 jusqu'à 1530* (Milan: Hoepli, 1943), no. 2700, plate 13.

25. See the essays in this volume by Darleen Pryds, "Proclaiming Sanctity through

Proscribed Practice: The Case of Rose of Viterbo"; and Carolyn Muessig, "Prophecy and Song."

26. See Gerlach van's Hertogenbosch and Oktavian Schmucki, "Rosa von Viterbo," in *Lexicon der christlichen Ikonographie*, vol. 8 (1976), cols. 287–88. See in particular Stefania Preti, "Lo scomparso ciclo di affreschi di S. Rosa da Viterbo di Benozzo Gozzoli e la sua influenza nel Viterbese: gli affreschi dell'isola bisentina," in *Il Quattrocento a Viterbo* (Rome: De Luca, 1983), pp. 159–78 and fig. 138; reproduced in color in Ernesto Piacentini, *Il Libro dei Miracoli di Santa Rosa da Viterbo* (Viterbo, 1991), pp. 90–91, no. 3. Beneath the fresco dated "Benotius de Florentia MCCCCLIII," the following inscription could be read: "Christus crucifixus apparet B. Rosae, quae commota compassionis decapillavit se, maxima cum devotione, et fuit ita inflammata, et repleta gratia, quod exivit de domo, et praedicabat de rebus divinis, adeo, quod unusquisque credebat suae praedicationi" (The crucified Christ appeared to Blessed Rose, who, moved with compassion, cut off all her hair, with greatest devotion; and she was so inflamed and filled with grace that she went out from her home and preached about divine things, to such an extent that everyone believed her sermons [Piacentini, *Il Libro dei Miracoli*, p. 170]).

27. See a brief mention also in Muessig, "Prophecy and Song." See Friedericke Werner, "Humilitas von Vallombrosa," in *Lexicon der christlichen Ikonographie*, vol. 6 (1974), col. 556. For more recent information on this personage, see Maria Adele Simonetti, ed., *I sermoni di Umiltà da Faenza: Studio ed edizione* (Spoleto: Centro italiano di studi sull'alto medioevo, 1995).

28. Reproduced in color in Maria Antonia Frías, "La mujer en el arte cristiano bajomedieval (ss. XIII–XV)," *Anuario Filosófico* 26 (1993): 573–98, figs. 14 and 16. See also Carlo Volpe, *Pietro Lorenzetti*, ed. Mauro Lucco (Milan: Electa, 1989), nos. 141–64, pp. 174–84.

29. See the indications supplied by Vincent Mayr, "Birgitta von Schweden," in *Lexicon der christlichen Ikonographie*, vol. 5 (1973), cols. 400–404, and in particular fig. 1 at col. 402 (Topler-Marstall-Epitaph, ca. 1500, Nürnberg, Germanisches Nationalmuseum): an image at the center of an extensive tradition. According to some interpretations, in the stories about Saint Birgitta of Sweden executed for the predella of a painting (now at the Gemälde Galerie of Berlin) originally from the Church of San Domenico at Camposanto in Pisa, and paid for by a relative of Chiara Gambacorta, the scene in which the saint is represented as standing on a column while flowers issue from her mouth has been a metaphor for preaching by a woman: see the reproduction in Miklós Boskovits, *Frühe Italienische Malerei* (Berlin: Gebr. Mann, 1988), Abb. 159.

30. See in general Lidia Bianchi and Diega Giunta, *Iconografia di S. Caterina da Siena*, vol. 1: *L'Immagine* (Rome: Città nuovo editrice, 1988); and Lidia Bianchi, "Caterina da Siena, santa," in *Enciclopedia dell'Arte Medievale*, vol. 4 (1993), pp. 486–92. On her dictation, see Sara F. Matthews Greco, "Modelli di santità femminile nell'Italia del Rinascimento e della Controriforma," in *Donne e fede: Santità e vita religiosa in Italia*, ed. Lucetta Scaraffia and Gabriella Zarri (Rome and Bari: Laterza, 1994), p. 318 (English translation forthcoming from Princeton University Press); on her reputation as a preacher, see Frugoni, "La donna nelle immagini," pp. 452–53.

31. See Henk W. Van Os, "Giovanni di Paolo's Pizzicaiuolo Altarpiece," *Art Bulletin* 53 (1971): 289–302. A color reproduction is in Keith Christiansen, Laurence B.

Kanter, and Carl Brandon Strehlke, *Painting in Renaissance Siena, 1420–1500* (New York: Metropolitan Museum of Art, 1988), p. 237.

32. A color reproduction is in Lanfranco Ravelli, *Polidoro a San Silvestro al Quirinale* (Bergamo: Edizioni dell'Ateno di scienze, lettere ed arti, 1987), tables 4 and 5. The identification of the scene is discussed in Diega Giunta, "La presenza di S. Caterina in Roma, cenni storico-iconografici," *Urbe* 42 (1979): fasc. II, pp. 15–19.

33. See Gabriella Zarri, "Le sante vive: Per una tipologia della santità femminile nel primo Cinquecento," *Annali dell'Istituto Storico Italo-Germanico in Trento* 9 (1980): 371–445, translated into English in Bornstein and Rusconi, ed., *Women and Religion in Medieval and Renaissance Italy*, pp. 219–303.

34. For considerations of a more general nature, see Roberto Rusconi, "'Predicò in piazza': politica e predicazione nell' Umbria del '400," in *Signorie in Umbria tra Medioevo e Rinascimento: l'esperienza dei Trinci* (Perugia: Deputazione di storia patria per l'Umbria, 1989), pp. 113–41; and Roberto Rusconi, "'Trasse la storia per farne la tavola': immagini di predicatori degli ordini mendicanti nei secoli XIII e XIV," in *La predicazione dei frati dalla metà del '200 alla fine del '300*, Atti del XXII Convegno internazionale di studi francescani (Spoleto: Centro italiano di studi sull'alto medioevo, 1995), pp. 405–50.

35. See a wood engraving representing the Blessed Veronica of Binasco writing her book of devotions in Isidorus de Insulis, *Gesta Beatae Veronicae*, Milan, 1518, reproduced in Irving Lavin, *Passato e presente nella storia dell'arte* (Turin, 1994; English ed., Berkeley: University of California Press, 1993), fig. 114.

36. For example, in the vernacular German edition of the legend of Saint Catherine of Siena, published at Augsburg in 1515, the saint is represented in the formal attitude of a preacher who turns to an audience of monks; the engraving is reproduced in Maria Consuelo Oldenbourg, *Die Buchholzschnitte des Hans Schäufelein: Ein bibliographisches Verzeichnis ihrer Verwendungen* (Baden-Baden: Heitz, 1964), p. 95, no. 582.

PART THREE

Sixteenth through Eighteenth Centuries

TEN

Feminine Exemplars for Reform

Women's Voices in John Foxe's *Acts and Monuments*

Edith Wilks Dolnikowski

In volume 3 of his *Acts and Monuments*, John Foxe records the deposition of Joan Cliffland against Margery Backster, who was brought before the bishop of Norwich in 1429.[1] In the course of Margery's trial, Joan made the following remarkable statements:

> Also this deponent saith, that the said Margery desired her, that she and Joan her maid would come secretly, in the night, to her chamber, and there she should hear her husband read the law of Christ unto them, which law was written in a book that her husband was wont to read her by night: and that her husband is well learned in the christian verity. Also that the same Margery had talked with a woman named Joan West, and said that a woman is in a good way of salvation. Also that the said Margery said to this deponent, "Joan, It appeareth by your countenance, that you intend to disclose this that I have said unto you. . . . If thou do accuse me unto the bishop, I will do unto thee, as I once did unto a certain friar, a Carmelite of Yarmouth, who was the best learned friar in all the country." Then this deponent desired to know what she had done to the friar. Unto whom Margery answered, that she had talked with the said friar, rebuking him because he did beg, saying that it was no alms to give him any good thing, except he would leave his habit, and go to the plough, and so he should please God more, than following the life of some of those friars. Then the friar required of the said Margery, whether she could teach him or tell him any thing else. Then the said Margery (as she affirmed to this deponent) declared to this friar the gospel in English; and then the friar departed from her. After this the said friar accused the said Margery of heresy.[2]

The deposition also reports that Margery considered the church's eucharistic theology idolatrous, repudiated fasting during Lent, and condemned auricular confession.[3]

By including such figures as Margery Backster in his catalog of martyrs and allowing them to express Protestant ideals, John Foxe defined the parameters of women as role models for the reformed church. Though clearly lacking clerical authority, Foxe suggested that women like Margery could contribute to the mission of the church as teachers, theologians, and evangelists in addition to performing their traditional duties as housewives and mothers. His open commendation of women who stepped out of the private sphere of home and family to proclaim their faith, even at the risk of ridicule or martyrdom, underscores his conviction that public testimony is a vital component of Christian life, regardless of gender. Foxe used stories about women throughout the history of the church to accentuate one of the central tenets of the English Reformation: the right of all Christians to read, study, and proclaim the Gospel in the vernacular. In this essay, I explore Foxe's use of female role models to promote a Reformation agenda by examining briefly its roots in the theology of Foxe's predecessor, John Wyclif.[4] Then I outline Foxe's use of both traditional and unconventional female role models to emphasize his Protestant theological convictions.

Foxe's devotion to the study of martyrs grew out of his experience as a young man of the persecution of English Protestants during the reign of Mary I (1553–58). His graphic depictions of the suffering of martyrs stirred the imagination of contemporary audiences and ensured a wide readership in succeeding generations. So popular was the *Acts and Monuments* that it was published in four separate editions in Foxe's lifetime (1516–87)[5] and was reissued numerous times from the seventeenth to the twentieth century. Like the Bible, Foxe's work served an increasingly literate population both as a source of entertainment and as an instructional book. Foxe's stories about martyrs dramatically conveyed two central tenets of reformed theology: the preeminence of the authority of the individual Christian believer and the necessity of all believers to learn and preach the Gospel in the vernacular language.

Both of these tenets can be traced directly to the thought of the controversial fourteenth-century theologian John Wyclif. Foxe devoted a large portion of his work to the life, writings, and persecution of Wyclif,[6] recording many stories about people like Margery Backster to demonstrate the compelling truth of Wyclif's views. The content of her views and her manner of expressing them suggest that Margery was a Lollard, trained in Wyclif's theological perspectives.[7] Although Wyclif was not the founder of the Lollard movement and in fact disavowed any connection with his more radical followers, his writings influenced the agenda of English reformers, including John Foxe, for three centuries.[8] Wyclif's academic treatises and sermons contain, of course, extensive references to many of the abuses that Margery associated with the late medieval church: superstitions with respect to the sacraments; the arrogance and false poverty of the friars; and the profusion of unnecessary rites and ceremonies.[9] These specific criticisms of the late medieval church were hallmarks of Protestant reform. More important than any of the particular complaints, however, was Wyclif's concern that the church consistently denied lay people the right to read, study, discuss, and proclaim the Gospel in their own language.[10] Throughout his writings Wyclif was unequivocal about the right of all baptized Christians to proclaim the Gospel in word and deed.[11] He asserted that it was the chief duty of the clergy to teach the laity holy Scripture so that they could proclaim the Gospel for themselves.[12]

Despite his strong advocacy of lay learning and preaching, Wyclif's extensive writings were directed more toward clergy than toward laity. His interest in lay preaching appears to have been somewhat theoretical and rooted in his theological views, rather than in his direct experience of lay education or spiritual witness. He certainly had little to say about the capacity for women to study Scripture and preach the Gospel in spite of his frequent assertion that all Christians should be engaged in this holy work. In contrast, Wyclif's followers were quick to put his theoretical construct of lay preaching into practice. Inspired by biblical models of itinerant prophetic preaching, they challenged the authority of the church hierarchy to restrict access to theological education and to prohibit public preaching by the laity. Margery Backster and her circle reflect quite clearly the Lollard imperative to empower the laity, both male and female, for theological discourse. By studying the Gospel in English at home, teaching the "law of Christ" to others, and publicly disputing theological matters with a friar, Margery exemplified Wyclif's ideal of a knowledgeable, preaching laity.[13] Thus Foxe used Margery's story and the stories of other theologically sophisticated women and men to express Wyclif's theoretical vision much more concretely. Foxe described a real person, from a specific time and place, who risked her family, her reputation, perhaps her life, to defend the truth she had discerned through the study of Christian doctrine and Scripture.[14] By offering examples of women like Margery, Foxe effectively defined and significantly expanded the spheres of influence in which women could act for the good of the church. Such examples also enhanced the contemporary value of Wyclif's theories about lay preaching by showing how women's past experiences could help to advance a Protestant agenda for reform and to establish the proper role for women in the reformed church of the future.[15]

Most of the women included in the *Acts and Monuments* represent such traditional feminine social roles as wives, mothers, and virgins. These women are accorded status as martyrs because of their willingness to attest to their faith in dangerous settings; yet they do so, according to Foxe, within the conventional institutions of marriage and family. Foxe's first example of a female martyr is Peter's wife, who died in Nero's persecution of Christians (64–68 C.E.):

> Eusebius, moreover, writing of the death not only of Peter, but also of his wife, affirmeth, that Peter, seeing his wife going to her martyrdom (belike as he was

> yet hanging upon the cross), was greatly joyous and glad thereof, who, crying
> unto her with a loud voice, and calling her by name, bade her "remember the
> Lord Jesus." Such was then (saith Eusebius) the blessed bond of marriage among
> the saints of God.[16]

In this story Foxe raises up the loyalty of Peter's wife both to her husband
and to Christ as an example for all women to follow. By citing Eusebius's
account of Peter's wife, Foxe establishes that women of strong character were
willing to die for the sake of Christ in the earliest days of the church. Because
Protestant reformers placed high value on the purity of the early church,
this example serves to authenticate the religious experience of women in
the reformed tradition, while reinforcing the notion that marriage is an appropriate institution through which women can express their faith.

Foxe also commends women as propagators of the faith through the education of their children. He notes the story of Anthia, "a godly woman, who
committed her son Eleutherius to Anicetus bishop of Rome, to be brought
up in the christian faith; who afterwards, being bishop of Illyricum, was
beheaded with his aforesaid mother Anthia."[17] Foxe also recounts the story
of "two virgins very fair and proper, with their mother also, who had studiously
brought them up, even from their infancy, in all godliness, being long sought
for, and at the last found, and strictly kept by their keepers; who, whilst they
made their excuse to do that which nature required, threw themselves down
headlong into a river."[18] These mothers achieve saintly status first by raising
their children in the Christian faith and then by sharing with them the persecution that followed their profession of that faith. In such examples, Foxe
stresses again the connection between family loyalty and religious commitment in the lives of female saints; but he also underscores the fact that martyrs are raised in faith by conscientious mothers who transmit the teachings
of the church to succeeding generations. Although this teaching takes place
within the relatively private sphere of the home, it becomes public when a
mother stands with her children to face persecution. Such stories imply that
women can find opportunities for public witness to the faith while consci-
entiously exercising their daily responsibility to teach the faith to their children. Their willingness to take risks for faith grows out of a common commitment to God and family. Thus the family provides a woman with powerful
avenues for proclaiming the Gospel through word and deed.[19]

To support the assertion that proclaiming the Gospel in this manner is
an appropriate activity for women, Foxe includes numerous stories of women
who stood bravely with their Christian brothers to face the most painful
torture rather than deny their faith. One of the most striking of these comes
again from the writings of Eusebius:

> Another person, a Libyan by birth, named Macar, . . . having resisted much
> importunity of the judge to deny Christ, was burnt alive. After these Epimachus

and Alexander, who had long sustained imprisonment and undergone infi-
nite tortures with razors and scourges, were burnt to death; and along with
them four women;—viz. Ammonarion, a holy virgin, who, though she was long
and grievously tormented by the judge, for having declared beforehand, that
she would not repeat the blasphemy which he dictated, yet was true to her
word, and was led off to execution. The other three, viz. the venerable matron
Mercuria—and Dionysia, a mother indeed of many children, but a mother who
did not love her children more than the Lord—and another Ammonarion,—
these were slain by the sword without being first exposed to torments: for the
judge was ashamed of torturing them to no purpose, and of being baffled by
women; which had been remarkably the case in his attempt to overcome the
first of the four, Ammonarion, who had undergone what might have been
esteemed sufficient torture for them all.[20]

The four women represent Foxe's conviction that the individual believer's
confession of faith is the most honorable of Christian acts, taking precedence
even over family obligations. Moreover, women and men are equally capable
of performing such an act. Women and men alike are called to baffle blasphemous judges and to love the Lord as much as they love their own children. The very fact that a woman might baffle a judge with her learning or
be killed for doing so is powerful testimony to successive generations of the
faithful. That a woman might deserve greater praise for her courage in the
face of persecution than for her attention to her children challenges restrictive conventional assumptions about women's religious experience and
firmly establishes Foxe's profound commitment to universal Christian witness.

Many of Foxe's female martyrs are compelling figures precisely because
they were forced out of their conventional roles within the family to be public witnesses to the faith of Christ. This intersection between private and public expression of faith allows Foxe to make an important observation about
women's voices in the church. Within the private sphere of the family, women
accomplish the vital but routine work of propagating the Gospel by supporting
their husbands and teaching their children. Their true integrity as Christians
is measured, however, by their willingness to carry their convictions into the
public sphere of the hostile tribunal. Foxe suggests that women engaged in
traditional activities can have a significant role in advancing reform in the
church because they can bear witness to the authority of their own individual lives of faith and teach that faith to their children. Their willingness to
move outside of this sphere, to proclaim the Gospel more publicly and at
greater personal risk, is an even more powerful model for Christian behavior,
both for the laity and for the clergy.

In addition to these fairly conventional roles for women, Foxe's *Acts and
Monuments* offers examples of women acting in more public spheres as queens,
deaconesses, prophets, and theologians. Although the incidence of women
in such roles is much less frequent than the incidence of men in comparable

roles, Foxe appears at least to acknowledge that women have had some influence on the history of the church. These powerful women do more than simply establish the authority of individual believers and teach indirectly through their actions. They also demonstrate that women can claim a measure of authority in the institutional structures that govern the church. Although they may lack the power and authority of kings, bishops, and priests, these women clearly represent the reformed laity by fully exercising the authority that has been accorded to them.[21] From Foxe's perspective as a reformer, therefore, women who effectively govern, prophesy, and teach prove that lay people have the right to assume positions of authority within the institutional church.[22]

Foxe's treatment of queens, for example, reflects his assumption that women can have considerable influence on the history of the church. His own persecution under Queen Mary I convinced him, however, that this influence might not always be positive. To illustrate a negative use of secular power in ecclesiastical affairs, Foxe cites the example of the eighth-century empress Irene:

> In the mean time, while this Edelburga was thus working her feats in England, Irene, empress of the Greeks, was as busy also for her part at Constantinople: who first, through means of pope Adrian, took up the body of Constantine V., emperor of Constantinople, her husband's own father; and when she had burned the same, she caused the ashes to be cast out into the sea, because he disannulled images. Afterwards, reigning with her son Constantine the Sixth, son to Leo the Fourth (whom also we declared before to be excommunicated for taking away images), being at dissension with him, she caused him to be taken and laid in prison; who afterward through power of friends being restored to his empire again, at last she caused the same her own son to be cast into prison, and his eyes to be put out so cruelly, that within a short space he died. After this the said Irene empress, with the counsel of Tarasius bishop of Constantinople, held a council at Nice[a], where it was decreed, that images should again be restored unto the church; which council was later repealed by another council holden at Francfort by Charlemagne.[23]

Foxe's main reason for including this account of Irene, of course, is to repudiate the use of images in worship, which was a common theme in Reformation theology.[24] Irene's ruthlessness and cruelty underscore the repugnance of her views, as does Foxe's account of her eventual fall from power.[25] Yet for all that, Foxe portrays Irene as a dynamic and skillful political figure, fully capable of establishing her own theological agenda.

As Foxe notes in his dedication of the *Acts and Monuments* to Queen Elizabeth, women can also attain the authority and skill required to promote a more positive theological agenda—that is, one that incorporates elements of Foxe's reformed theology:

> And though the story [*Acts and Monuments*], being written in the popular tongue, serveth not so greatly for your own peculiar reading, nor for such as be learned, yet I shall desire both you and them to consider in it the necessity of the igno-

rant flock of Christ committed to your government in this realm of England. . . . Furthermore, what inconvenience groweth of ignorance, where knowledge lacketh, both I considered, and experience daily teacheth. And therefore, hearing of such virtuous inclination of your majesty, what a provident zeal, full of solicitude, you have, minding (speedily I trust) to furnish all quarters and countries of this your realm with the voice of Christ's gospel and faithful preaching of his word, I thought it also not unprofitable to adjoin, unto these your godly proceedings and to the office of the ministry, the knowledge also of Ecclesiastical History.[26]

Foxe suggests that Elizabeth's obligation to provide adequate theological education for her subjects is based on her office, not on her gender. As a monarch, she has the responsibility to discern what her people need and the authority to grant it. This dedication reflects Foxe's Protestant perspective that civil leaders have the right to reform the church when ecclesiastical leaders are unable or unwilling to do so themselves. In according Elizabeth this power, Foxe acknowledges a woman's capacity to exercise authority in the church in a very public sphere indeed.

Foxe found it more difficult, naturally, to show women wielding power from within the ecclesiastical hierarchy. Queens such as Irene and Elizabeth can be seen as symbols of reform of the church from the outside: They represent the authority of the laity in general and the secular government in particular, which Protestant reformers wished to promote as a challenge to the excessive power of priests and bishops.[27] Because women could not be ordained as priests, they generally had fewer options than men for expressing their theological views in public. Even so, Foxe included in *Acts and Monuments* a few striking examples of women who exercised a kind of public authority within the church.

In his accounts of the early church, Foxe includes material that identifies women directly or indirectly as deaconesses and therefore authenticates this type of public service for women. Foxe cites Pliny's letter to the emperor Trajan, which states: "I judged it quite necessary to examine two young women, who were said to be deaconesses, by torture, in order to get at the real truth; but I found nothing except absurd raving and superstition."[28] Shortly thereafter, Foxe recounts the story of two young women who, though not called deacons, act quite publicly as deacons:

Praxedes, a blessed virgin, [was] the daughter of a citizen of Rome, who, in the time . . . Anicetus [was] there bishop, was so brought up in the doctrine of Christ, and so affected to his religion, that she, with her sister Patentiana, bestowed all her patrimony upon the relieving of poor Christians, giving all her time to fasting and prayer and to the burying of the bodies of the martyrs. And after she had made free all her family with her servants, after the death of her sister, she also departed, and was buried in peace.[29]

Praxedes appears to exercise a true vocation of diaconal service to the church:

she chooses this life after a considerable period of study and discernment; she gives up her personal wealth in order to help the poor; and she engages in a regular discipline of fasting and prayer. She lives, in fact, according to standards Wyclif wished to apply to all the priests of the church.[30] Although Foxe does not directly state that women were ordained as ministers in the early church, he suggests through his stories that women in the past have responded publicly to Christ's call to ministry, and that answering such a call remains an option for lay women and men in the reformed church as well.

Foxe also acknowledges a limited but significant public role for women as prophets and teachers in the church. One of the most interesting examples of a female prophet in the *Acts and Monuments* is the account of the twelfth-century nun Hildegard. According to Foxe, Hildegard received a vision from God in which the church appeared "in the shape of a woman, complaining that the priests had bewrayed her face with dust, and rent her coat, etc., and that they did not shine over her people, either in doctrine or in example of life; but rather the contrary, and that they have driven the innocent lamb from them. She said moreover, 'That all ecclesiastical order did, every day, become worse and worse, and that priests did not teach, but destroy the law of God; and for these horrible crimes and impieties, she threateneth and prophesieth unto them God's most heavy wrath and displeasure, and doleful punishments.'"[31]

Given his Protestant agenda, Foxe interprets this prophecy as a condemnation of "the whole rout of Romish prelates, and the fall of that church, as especially against the begging friars and other such unprofitable bellies of the church."[32] Moreover, argues Foxe, "whereas the priests and monks, that is the whole rabble and spirituality, do account Hildegard a true prophetess, they ought to consider that by her they are more severely accused, not as by a woman, but as by God himself."[33] Here, despite his clearly biased and selective interpretation of Hildegard's vision, Foxe recognizes a woman's capacity to speak for God in matters that affect the institutional structure and theological teachings of the church.[34] In fact, Hildegard's wide and public acclaim as a prophet is crucial to his argument that the "the whole rout of Romish prelates" were warned about the inevitability of reform. Although Hildegard's prophetic activity is not preaching, strictly speaking, it is public teaching from a theological perspective about particular problems facing the church. Admittedly, Foxe claims both her controversial statements and her established status as a prophet to advance his own agenda. By acknowledging that Hildegard could prophesy in this way and be respected for it, Foxe underscores his larger contention that all Christians, whether women or men, lay or ordained, have the authority to speak publicly about the issues that affect the church.

Like Margery Backster, Hildegard engages in a public theological discourse by the authority of her personal faith in God, informed by her study of Scripture and expressed in her own language. This kind of activity, according to Wyclif's theoretical construct, is preaching: It has both evangelical and theological content; it is rooted in the personal experiences of the speaker; it is based on biblical models of itinerant prophecy; and it captures the spirit of Christian witness that reaches back to the earliest days of the church. Through his selection of stories about women, Foxe encourages women to take their place in a reformed church in which the laity have the authority to study and proclaim the faith. Foxe assumes, perhaps, that women will exert their authority most often within the traditional roles of wife and mother; but he recognizes the precedents for women to move into wider spheres of authority. Indeed, Foxe commends most the women who choose to leave the relatively safe sphere of home and family to face courageously the enemies of Christianity in a hostile public setting.

Ultimately, for Foxe, the source of Christian authority cannot be located in any institution such as marriage or the family or the church; rather, authority is a revelation from God to the individual believer. Because all Christians in the reformed church are called to proclaim their faith, gender, wealth, or social status should not be barriers to Christian witness. Conventional roles and responsibilities merely provide starting points for evangelical activity. It is perfectly appropriate for women and men to step out of these conventional roles if they do so to promote the faith. Thus in the *Acts and Monuments* Foxe includes many defiant voices and offers many unconventional role models. His attentiveness to women's voices and his appreciation for their ability to preach the Gospel can be discerned in the words of Julitta, a fourth-century martyr, who said:

> Stick not, O sisters to labour and travail after true piety and godliness. Cease to accuse the fragility of feminine nature. What! are not we created of the same matter that men are? Yea, after God's image and similitude are we made as lively as they. Not flesh only did God use in the creation of the woman, in sign and token of her infirmity and weakness, but bone of bones is she, in token that she must be strong in the true and living God, all false gods forsaken; constant in faith, all infidelity renounced; patient in adversity, all worldly ease refused. Wax weary, my dear sisters, of your lives led in darkness, and be in love with my Christ, my God, my Redeemer, my Comforter, who is the true light of the world. Persuade yourselves, or rather the Spirit of the living God persuade you, that there is a world to come, wherein the worshippers of idols and devils shall be tormented perpetually; the servants of the high God shall be crowned eternally.[35]

Foxe's women make it clear that they are fully capable of meeting the intellectual, spiritual, and physical demands of proclaiming their faith in a hostile world. Although they usually perform this ministry within conventional spheres of home and family, these women are not afraid to accept verbal retribution or physical punishment when their consciences demand public expression of their beliefs. Through these examples of female martyrs, Foxe universalizes the experience of public religious testimony. He does not imply that women should always have the right to exceed the boundaries of conventional behavior. Only when the integrity of the community of faith is at stake are they empowered by God to confound their persecutors. Nevertheless, as baptized Christians, both women and men can exercise their calling to study, teach, and preach the Gospel in whatever settings they occupy. They ought to be commended all the more if they continue in this calling after they are exposed to the dangers of public persecution.

Foxe's *Acts and Monuments* offered sixteenth-century audiences dramatic illustrations of Protestant theological principles. By vividly describing the testimony and suffering of Christian martyrs, Foxe gave concrete expression to Wyclif's abstract notions about the centrality of individual Christian witness and the importance of lay vernacular preaching. Foxe's consistent emphasis on female martyrs underscored his conviction that service and witness were activities open to all Christians, lay or ordained, poor or wealthy, female or male. His favorable interpretation of martyrdom and his inclusion of women in his treatment of martyrdom helped to define a legitimate place for women's religious experience in the history of the church. Yet despite the continued popularity of the *Acts and Monuments,* women were consistently denied access to theological education, and their contributions to the church as teachers and preachers were marginalized.[36] Foxe's treatment of female martyrs demonstrated that women's voices had been heard often throughout the history of the church. That women were usually discouraged from using their voices in Foxe's reformed church is a testament to the difficulty of establishing divine principles of individual authority in a human institution fraught with competing claims for status and power.

NOTES

1. *The Acts and Monuments of John Foxe,* 8 vols., ed. George Townsend (New York: AMS Press, 1965). This massive edition of Foxe's writings includes a biography of Foxe, Foxe's prefaces to the original edition of the work, and numerous appendixes. According to Viggo Norskov Olsen, *John Foxe and the Elizabethan Church* (Berkeley: University of California Press, 1973), p. 1, "Book of Martyrs" is a common or unofficial name for *Acts and Monuments.* I have chosen in this chapter to refer to the edition cited above. For further information about Foxe, see Olsen, *John Foxe;* William Haller, *The Elect Nation: The Meaning and Relevance of Foxe's Book of Martyrs* (New York: Harper and Row, 1963); and Warren W. Wooden, *John Foxe* (Boston: Twayne, 1983).

2. *Acts and Monuments,* vol. 3, pp. 595–96.

3. Ibid., pp. 594–95.

4. For additional information on Wyclif, see Herbert Workman, *John Wyclif: A Study of the English Medieval Church* (Oxford: Clarendon Press, 1926); Kenneth B. McFarlane, *John Wycliffe and the Beginnings of English Nonconformity* (New York: Macmillan,

1953); Anthony Kenny, *Wyclif* (Oxford: Oxford University Press, 1985); John Stacey, *John Wyclif and Reform* (Philadelphia: Westminster Press, 1964); Louis Brewer Hall, *The Perilous Vision of John Wyclif* (Chicago: Nelson-Hall, 1983); Anthony Kenny, ed., *Wyclif in His Times* (Oxford: Clarendon Press, 1986); and *From Ockham to Wyclif, Studies in Church History* 5, ed. Anne Hudson and Michael Wilks (Oxford: Basil Blackwell, 1987).

5. *The Oxford Dictionary of the Christian Church*, ed. F. L. Cross and E. A. Livingstone (New York: Oxford University Press, 1990), p. 526.

6. *Acts and Monuments*, vol. 2, pp. 790–806; vol. 3, pp. 3–94.

7. For additional information about the Lollard movement, see John A. Thompson, *The Later Lollards, 1414–1520* (London: Oxford University Press, 1965); Margaret Deanesly, *The Lollard Bible and Other Medieval Biblical Versions* (New York: AMS Press, 1978); Margaret Aston, *Lollards and Reformers: Images of Literacy in Late Medieval Religion* (London: Hambledon Press, 1984); Anne Hudson, *Lollards and Their Books* (London: Hambledon Press, 1985); Anne Hudson, *The Premature Reformation: Wycliffite Texts and Lollard History* (Oxford: Clarendon Press, 1988); and Anne Hudson, *"Laicus litteratus:* The Paradox of Lollardy," in *Heresy and Literacy,* ed. Peter Biller and Anne Hudson (Cambridge: Cambridge University Press, 1994), pp. 222–36.

8. In addition to references cited in note 4, see A. K. McHardy, "The Dissemination of Wyclif's Ideas," in *From Ockham to Wyclif,* pp. 361–68; and Olsen, *John Foxe,* pp. 35–38.

9. See Edith Wilks Dolnikowski, "The Encouragement of Lay Preaching as an Ecclesiastical Critique in Wyclif's Latin Sermons," in *Models of Holiness in Medieval Sermons,* ed. Beverly Mayne Kienzle et al. (Louvain-la-Neuve: Fédération Internationale des Instituts d'Études Médiévales, 1996), pp. 192–210, in which these issues are explored in Wyclif's *Johannes Wyclif Sermones* (London: Wyclif Society, 1886–89) and *De veritate sacrae scripturae* (London: Wyclif Society, 1906).

10. Wyclif made this assertion on many occasions and in many contexts. See, for example, *De veritate,* pp. 242–43: "debet ergo proporcionaliter excellere in vite santitate, in sensu scripture et efficaci edificacione, et per consequens oportet, eum noscere ligwam populi, cui preest, quia aliter non perfeccius ipsum instrueret quam ydiota. ideo dicit apostolus primus Cor. quarto decimo et notat Archidiaconus super quadragesima tercia dist. 'Sit Rector' quod est differencia inter locucionem ligwa, que est oracio deo facta, et prophetacionem, quam dicit oportere esse factum hominibus ad edificacionem."

11. Ibid., p. 157: "dictum autem verbum predicatum est veritas et per consequens essencialiter deus ipse. ideo eius predicacio est opus dignissimum creature. item omnis cristianus debet pre omnibus operi precipuo sibi limitatio a deo diligenter intendere, sed illud est opus ewangelizandi iniunctum a domino sacerdoti, ut patet proximo capitulo, igitur sacerdos debet pre omnibus operi illi intendere."

12. Ibid., pp. 137–38: "sexto sequitur, quod omnes cristiani, et precipue sacerdotes atque episcopi tenentur cognoscere primo omnem legem scripture. . . . quod dominicus sermo debet audiri humiliter ac delectabiliter ab omnibus cristianis. patet ex hoc, quod in fide illius scripture necesse est, omnes salvandos salvari. . . . igitur hoc spectat ad spirituales patres et per consequens ad sacerdotes, in quantum huiusmodi. predicare, dico, in opere vel sermone primum debet est continuum. . . . illi enim debent duplici honore secundum quandam excellenciam honorari."

13. See Dolnikowski, "The Encouragement of Lay Preaching"; also Hudson, "*Laicus litteratus,*" pp. 228–34.

14. Many have noted Foxe's ability to enliven his theological arguments with references to particular saints and martyrs. For more information about Foxe's treatment of women, see Carole Levin, "Women in *The Book of Martyrs* as Models of Behavior in Tudor England," *International Journal of Women's Studies* 4 (February 1981): 196–207; and Fredrica Harris Thompsett, "Protestant Women as Victims and Subjects: Reformation Legacies from John Foxe's *Book of Martyrs,*" in *This Sacred History: Anglican Reflections for John Booty,* ed. Donald S. Armentrout (Cambridge, Mass.: Cowley, 1990), pp. 182–98.

15. See Catharine Randall Coats, "John Foxe's *Actes and Monuments:* The Body of the Book as Mediator," in *(Em)bodying the Word: Textual Resurrections in the Martyrological Narratives of Foxe, Crespin, de Bège and d'Aubigné* (New York: Peter Lang, 1992), pp. 37–56. According to Coats, "Foxe regards the Protestant church as actually reconstituting the body of the early Christian church, and reverses the Catholic status to make Rome appear the theological interloper" (p. 37). Thus he emphasizes scriptural references and employs a style typical of contemporary preaching practice in which powerful bodily imagery underscores the meaning of the word of God (pp. 37–38 and 50–51).

16. *Acts and Monuments,* vol. 1, p. 101.

17. Ibid., p. 119.

18. Ibid., p. 227.

19. For further analysis of the theme of female witness within traditional roles, see Levin, "Women in *The Book of Martyrs,*" pp. 204–5.

20. *Acts and Monuments,* vol. 1, pp. 178–79.

21. In *"Laicus litteratus,"* pp. 235–36, Hudson considers the implications of an educated laity: once a theologian such as Wyclif opened up the possibility that lay people could learn Scripture and church doctrine, it became increasingly difficult to prevent lay people from expressing their views publicly.

22. As Thompsett observes in "Protestant Women as Victims and Subjects," pp. 184–85, it is important to recognize Foxe's criteria for selecting the martyrs for his book. His frequent use of examples of poor women and men emphasizes the distinction between the simple virtue of the martyrs and the arrogance of the entrenched ecclesiastical hierarchy. Here Foxe echoes Wyclif's strong anticlerical bias.

23. *Acts and Monuments,* vol. 1, pp. 378–79.

24. For background on the iconoclastic controversy, see André Grabar, *L'iconoclasme byzantin: le dossier archéologique* (Paris: Flammarion, 1984); Paul Julius Alexander, *The Patriarch Nicephorus of Constantinople: Ecclesiastical Policy and Image Worship in the Byzantine Empire* (Oxford: Clarendon Press, 1958); and P. Brown, "A Dark-Age Crisis: Aspects of the Iconoclastic Controversy," *English Historical Review* 88 (1973): 1–34. For attitudes toward images in the English Reformation, see Horton Davies, *The Worship of English Puritans* (Philadelphia: Westminster Press, 1948); Gordon S. Wakefield, *Puritan Devotion: Its Place in the Development of Christian Piety* (London: Epworth Press, 1957); Patrick Collinson, *The Elizabethan Puritan Movement* (Berkeley: University of California Press, 1967); and John Phillips, *The Reformation of Images: Destruction of Art in England, 1535–1660* (Berkeley: University of California Press, 1973).

25. Foxe notes in *Acts and Monuments,* vol. 1, p. 379, that Irene eventually "was

deposed by Nicephorus (who reigned after), and was expulsed from the empire; who, after the example of Edelburga above-mentioned, condignly punished for her wickedness, ended likewise her life in much penury and misery."

26. Ibid., p. viii. In Townsend's edition, the prefaces are placed between the biography of John Foxe and the beginning of Foxe's text.

27. This is a particularly strong theme in Wyclif's theology, and it pervades virtually all of his writings. See, in particular, *De civili dominio* (London: Wyclif Society, 1885, 1900–1904); *De ecclesia* (London: Wyclif Society, 1886); and *De potestate pape* (London: Wyclif Society, 1907). For additional information on these texts, see Williell R. Thompson, *The Latin Writings of John Wyclyf* (Toronto: Pontifical Institute of Mediaeval Studies, 1983), pp. 48–55, 58–60, and 62–63.

28. *Acts and Monuments*, vol. 1, p. 116.

29. Ibid., p. 127.

30. Wyclif's criticism of the institutional church of his day included severe attacks on what he considered to be a negligent clergy obsessed with its own status and wealth. In texts such as *De symonia* (London: Wyclif Society, 1898), *De apostasia* (London: Wyclif Society, 1889), and *De blasphemia* (London: Wyclif Society, 1893), Wyclif argued that all clerical, monastic, and mendicant orders should be abolished and replaced by "poor priests," who preached and lived in apostolic fashion. As Christina von Nolken observes (in "Wyclif, Another Kind of Saint," *From Ockham to Wyclif*, pp. 441–43), Wyclif's notion of the "poor priest" had enormous influence on views of service in the reformed tradition. For additional information on Wyclif's texts cited above, see Thompson, *The Latin Writings*, pp. 63–67.

31. *Acts and Monuments*, vol. 2, pp. 353–54.

32. Ibid., p. 353.

33. Ibid., p. 354.

34. That Foxe's main interest in Hildegard was her supposed condemnation of the friars is confirmed by his repetition of her story in *Acts and Monuments*, vol. 3, pp. 86–88, where Wyclif's criticism of the friars is commended in an essay about John Huss's defense of Wyclif. For additional information about Hildegard and her influence in the history of the church, see Barbara Newman, *Sister of Wisdom: Hildegard's Theology of the Feminine* (Berkeley: University of California Press, 1987); Sabina Flanagan, *Hildegard of Bingen, 1098–1179: A Visionary Life* (New York: Routledge, 1989); Frances Beer, *Women and Mystical Experience in the Middle Ages* (Rochester, N.Y.: Boydell Press, 1992); and Carolyn Wörman Sur, *The Feminine Images of God in the Visions of Saint Hildegard of Bingen's "Scivias"* (Lewistown, N.Y.: Edwin Mellen Press, 1993).

35. *Acts and Monuments*, vol. 1, p. 275.

36. For additional information about women's experience during the Reformation, see Roland Bainton, *Women of the Reformation: In France and England* (Minneapolis: Augsburg Press, 1973); Lawrence Stone, *The Family, Sex and Marriage in England, 1500–1800* (New York: Harper and Row, 1977); Steven Ozment, *When Fathers Ruled: Family Life in Reformation Europe* (Cambridge, Mass.: Harvard University Press, 1983); Rhetha M. Warnicke, *Women of the English Renaissance and Reformation* (Westport, Conn.: Greenwood Press, 1983); and M. J. Boxer and J. H. Quataert, eds., *Connecting Spheres: Women in the Western World, 1500 to the Present* (Oxford: Oxford University Press, 1987).

ELEVEN

Preaching or Teaching?

Defining the Ursuline Mission in Seventeenth-Century France

Linda Lierheimer

In 1616 Mère Perrette de Bermond, one of the founding mothers of the French Ursulines, was sent by the Ursulines of Lyons to establish a congregation in Moulins. Although the Ursulines, one of the Catholic Reformation's new active congregations for women, were often viewed with distrust and hostility because of their uncloistered status and unorthodox activities, the townspeople of Moulins welcomed them with open arms and found in Perrette de Bermond a charismatic teacher. The Ursulines "began to sing Vespers in the Choir, to teach Christian Doctrine, and to perform all the functions of Ursulines with so much profit and ardor that everyone flocked to the Chapel on feast days and Sundays to hear the Catechism that Mère Perrette de Bermond gave there. The most respected people of the Town were always among the first to arrive, and with such a crowd that it was necessary to turn some away; and seats were taken as at a Sermon. This lasted until the year 1623 when the male Superiors (with good reason, for this was an unusual thing) forbade the Sisters to teach any longer in the Church."[1]

What was happening here? What gave Perrette de Bermond the authority to teach Christian doctrine publicly in church, and in what capacity was she speaking? Could her activities and those of other Ursulines be reconciled with traditional views of the roles assigned to women in the church? What did male clerics think of the Ursulines who, by teaching Christian doctrine publicly in their chapel, were performing a function that was indistinguishable—at least to the uneducated laity—from that of a priest? And, if the public teaching of the Ursulines was threatening to the male religious hierarchy, how were they able to continue their activities unchecked for seven years?

Just as important is Perrette's own understanding of her role. She and others like her—for this was not an isolated event—must have been aware of the implications of their actions and familiar with the prohibitions regarding women's teaching in church. Perrette seems to have been testing the waters, seeing how far she could stretch the limits of acceptable behavior for a female teacher and holy woman. But in so doing, she and other early Ursulines were forced to confront two basic problems: first, how to establish their authority as teachers and catechizers when women did not have access to clerical office; and second, how to legitimize their activities in a way that satisfied both their clerical superiors and public opinion.

These concerns often conflicted, which helps to explain the ambivalent tone of the passage quoted above. The Ursuline historian who recorded the event clearly admired Perrette de Bermond, but she also commended the authorities for putting an end to her "unusual" behavior. Ursulines like Perrette de Bermond and her biographer knew they had to challenge traditional conceptions of women's place in the church in order to play an active role in the religious reforms of the seventeenth century. But they also understood that their challenges had to be tempered with respect for the authorities who had the power to silence them.

Perrette and her fellow Ursulines in Moulins were part of an army of female teachers and catechizers who spread across Catholic Europe during the seventeenth century. The Catholic Reformation saw the development of a female apostolate with women devoting themselves to the care of souls through charity work, nursing, teaching, and missionary work. The entry of religious women into the public sphere caused tensions, and female teachers and missionaries had to defend their activities against opposition from clergy and laity alike. As it became increasingly common to find women teaching the faith to the French laity, questions about how to define the activities of these women arose. The distinction between women *teaching* and women *preaching* was unclear, and in order to legitimize the teaching mission of women, some differentiation between the two activities became necessary.

Although most Ursulines did not overtly lay claim to the role of preacher, in practice their activities often amounted to the same thing. In what follows, I explore some of the strategies used by Ursuline teachers and writers to create space for the female teacher of the Word of God. Throughout the seventeenth century, Ursulines both addressed and skirted the question of the public voice of women and its relationship to preaching and clerical authority. On the one hand, Ursuline teachers and catechizers, by imitating priests and preachers, evoked the close relationship between teaching and preaching to gain some measure of authority—though this could be a precarious position for a woman. On the other hand, Ursulines negotiated the tensions raised by female teaching by defining their teaching as a domestic activity. Despite the efforts of male clergy to sever the connection between teaching and preaching and Ursuline disclaimers that they were assuming clerical functions, the two activities remained closely linked.

URSULINE PUBLIC SPEAKING

The first French Ursuline congregation was founded in about 1592 by Françoise de Bermond, who persuaded twenty-four devout young women in Avignon to join her in devoting their lives to God while remaining in the world. They were supported by the Fathers of Christian Doctrine, who taught them their method of catechizing, and in 1594 the new congregation received permission from the pope to teach Christian doctrine publicly to girls.[2] Like the Italian Ursulines, founded in 1535 by Angela Merici, the Avignon Ursulines were not cloistered and did not take permanent vows.[3] The women in Avignon soon found imitators. By 1610, there were twenty-nine Ursuline congregations in southern France.[4]

The early *congrégées* met with a mixed reception. In Avignon, they were successful in attracting the women and girls of the town who preferred their catechisms to dances; however, many were shocked by their unusual lifestyle: "A way of life so unusual for girls . . . created varying opinions among the people, some praising that Institute [the Ursulines], and others criticizing it; so that several young ladies who felt a calling for [the Ursulines], did not dare to become associated with them; and their doubtful reputation sufficed to deter them."[5]

In a society where the only acceptable choices for a woman were marriage or the cloister, the ambiguous status and public visibility of the early Ursulines sometimes led to serious misunderstandings. As *congrégées*, they were denied the authority and status of nuns, and to many the lifestyle and activities of the Ursulines seemed scandalous. In Lyons, townspeople mistook Ursulines for repentant prostitutes, and in Avignon there were rumors of sexual misconduct between the Ursulines and their male adviser and patron, Père Romillon.[6]

In an effort to reach as many people as possible, Ursulines gave public catechisms in churches, barns, and poultry yards to large, often mixed audiences. Their goal was not only to instruct young girls and women, but to reform whole communities, and they directed their reforming zeal at the lay population as a whole—men and women, young and old—and even, occasionally, at the clergy itself. As historians have noted, seventeenth-century religious reformers had their work cut out for them.[7] The people of the French countryside often had little or no knowledge of the formal teachings of the church—at least as the reformers understood them—and attended church infrequently. Traveling missionaries wandered the countryside trying to remedy this state of affairs. But France was a country of dialects, and in order to reach the populace, preachers and missionaries had to communicate with them in Breton, Auvergnat, and Occitan.[8] The Council of Trent had ordered parish priests to explain "in the vernacular tongue" the "efficacy and use" of the sacraments to those about to receive them, and bishops were to provide catechisms "translated into the language of the people."[9]

The sorry state of pastoral care at the beginning of the seventeenth century helps to explain why many Ursulines felt justified in taking on public roles that were traditionally the preserve of men. Although the Council of Trent had set the reform of the clergy as one of its central goals, efforts in this area had little effect on parish life in France before the middle of the seventeenth century. Stories about members of the clergy who did not tend to their flocks—and of Ursulines instructing them about how to do so—are commonplace in Ursuline histories and biographies. In Dijon, Anne de Vefure visited nonreformed monks, exhorting them to reform and instructing them in prayer. She incited the priests in the towns she visited to teach the catechism to the children in their flock, "and as they gave the excuse that they did not know the proper order to follow; she freely and modestly showed them the method."[10] Because male clerics were not fulfilling their duties, Ursulines stepped in to fill the void.

Ursulines believed that unorthodox methods were necessary to "christianize" the French populace. As one Ursuline writer explained, the early Ursulines had to be flexible and move about freely "because devotion was at that time very little known; and ignorance reigned to such an extent that the majority of those who approached these devout girls, did not know the obligations of a Christian, nor even the commandments of God."[11] The public catechisms of Ursulines like Antoinette Micolon in Ambert helped to rectify this state of affairs. Her memoirs recount the transformation of the peasant women whom she instructed in Auvergnat, the local dialect, from "idiots" and "women without devotion" into devout women "well instructed in the truths of the faith and of salvation." These women, who had previously taken communion only twice a year, began to take it at least once a month.[12] Antoinette Micolon's public catechisms thus supported the broader goals of the Catholic Reformation, which explains why the religious authorities tolerated them.

In such an environment, the church was inclined to be flexible. Although the Council of Trent had taken a strong stance against semireligious congregations and declared that all religious women were to take solemn vows and submit to cloister, the church also recognized that women's activism and religious fervor were essential in the fight against Protestantism. Besides, the rules established at Trent could not be enforced effectively until the reorganization of the church hierarchy was complete. But as the Protestant threat moved into the background and the program of parish reform outlined at Trent was realized, the French church became less tolerant of what it considered stopgap measures. Women's teaching congregations were a matter of particular concern. Even supporters of the Ursulines believed it was dangerous to allow their activities to go unchecked and suggested measures to circumscribe them, forbidding public catechisms in church and, most important, advocating enclosure.

With the establishment of the first Ursuline convent in Paris in 1614, the freedom and flexibility of the early *congrégées* began to disappear. During the 1620s and 1630s, most existing congregations adopted *clausura*, and new houses were founded as enclosed monastic communities with members taking formal vows of religion. Some Ursulines welcomed this change as a move to a "more perfect state" and believed the respectability and spiritual authority that monastic status offered could provide a firmer basis for the Ursuline mission.[13] But many Ursulines, and some male clerics, objected to enclosure as a restriction of their teaching mission that would undermine the Ursulines' broad and flexible definition of teaching and limit their educational activities to the classroom.

Church authorities viewed enclosure as the solution to the problems raised by Ursuline teaching, but it did not completely resolve the tension between teaching and preaching. Some Ursulines simply defied attempts to limit their teaching activities. In Avignon, Marthe de la Visitation taught Christian doctrine publicly in the convent's church "for several years," and the public catechisms of Paule de la Mère de Dieu in Montélimar attracted such crowds that "their church was too small to contain the people who flocked there," including the Protestant governor of the town.[14]

In the long run, however, enclosure had a dampening effect on the public aspects of the Ursuline mission. Nonetheless, Ursuline nuns still found ways to address large audiences, albeit in more restricted ways. Some, like Louise de Saint Paul, taught "publicly" at the choir grill.[15] Suzanne Marie des Anges's Sunday catechism classes were filled to overflowing with women who "left everything to come listen to her: and the place of assembly with a capacity of about five hundred people was ordinarily full."[16] At the Ursuline convent in Paris, catechisms were sometimes given in front of audiences. Claude Anne de S. Benoît taught the catechism to young girls "in front of a great number of people of both sexes and all stations," including, from time to time, such illustrious figures as the dauphin and future King Louis XIII of France and the Papal Nuncio, later Pope Urban VIII.[17] Even within the convent walls, Ursuline teaching retained a public quality that associated it with preaching, and the need to define its boundaries more clearly remained.

CROSSING BOUNDARIES:
THE PREACHER AS MODEL FOR THE FEMALE APOSTLE

Ursulines embraced the connection between teaching and preaching as a way to establish their authority as teachers and catechizers and defined their apostolate in terms that linked their activities to those of priests and preachers. One writer defined the Ursuline mission in the following terms: "The Ursulines according to the spirit of their institute should be of one voice like John the Baptist to preach Jesus Christ . . . the purpose of their institute being to procure the glory of God by advancing one's neighbor in the Christian virtues."[18] Although in a formal sense "preaching" the Gospel of Jesus Christ, a central activity of male congregations like the Jesuits, was forbidden to women, Ursulines identified closely with male "apostles" and saw themselves as participants in the same reforming mission.

Like priests and preachers, Ursulines acted as ministers of Christ by teaching the Word of God. Because of its efforts to save souls, explained Mère de Pommereu, the Ursuline order "is associated with prelates, pastors and all others who act as spiritual guides."[19] In their capacity as teachers, Ursulines, who brought their students to Jesus Christ, were "the ministers of his blood, and of his word."[20] In accounts of Ursuline teaching and catechizing, these activities were often explicitly compared to preaching. The students of Michelle de Sainte Cecile claimed that "her speeches touched them more than sermons." The women who came to hear the catechisms given by Elizabeth des Nots in the parlor of the Paris convent "said that she was no different from good preachers"; the catechisms of Anne de Beaumont were compared to the "the preaching of Saint Paul."[21]

This identification with preachers was the inspiration behind the original vocation of many Ursulines. The autobiographical writings of two Ursulines show how important the model of the preacher was to their self-presentation and illustrate the apostolic proclivities that inspired them to join the order. As a young widow, Marie de l'Incarnation loved to attend sermons. Returning home, she felt compelled to communicate what she had heard to others: "I spoke out loud . . . to the people in our house with great zeal, telling them what the preacher had preached, adding my own thoughts which rendered me eloquent."[22] Like many other devout women, Marie saw it as her duty to act as the preacher's mouthpiece by reforming her own family, and the process of communicating what she had learned in sermons—which involved more than mere repetition—allowed her to develop her own skills at speaking and persuasion. These skills proved useful when Marie carried her imitation of preachers a step further to become one of the first female missionaries in Canada.

A similar episode occurred in the life of Antoinette Micolon. Returning home from a sermon on usury, Antoinette came upon her father settling accounts with a peasant and collecting interest on the money he had lent the man. Seeing this, Antoinette seized the moment: "An interior voice urged her to say to her father what she had remembered from the sermon. She thus began to speak and said: 'My father, do not lend money at interest, because the preacher said that all those who did so would be damned.'"[23] Her words were so effective that her father promised he would never lend money at interest again, though one must wonder if he remained true to his word. In any case, this event presaged Antoinette's later public speaking, which she consciously modeled after that of a preacher.

As an Ursuline *congrégée*, Antoinette Micolon took on the persona of a preacher and a priest when she taught publicly and used the ambiguity between teaching and preaching to establish her authority and give added power to her teaching. A description of her public catechisms suggests how Ursuline public speech might have been perceived by an audience:

> Her zeal for the glory of God and for the salvation of souls led her to assemble every Sunday in a large poultry yard fifty or sixty peasant women who came to the town to hear the holy mass of the parish, after which they came eagerly to hear the good instructions that she gave them. And in order to be better heard, she raised herself above them, and standing on a chair, she spoke to them in the local dialect. . . . It seemed that God put the words in her mouth, so appropriate and effective were they for the salvation of these poor peasant women.[24]

Antoinette's catechisms—pronounced in Auvergnat—were a complement to the mass, and the peasant women probably associated the two activities, despite the fact that the catechisms were held in a humble poultry yard. These women, who knew neither Latin nor French and had only a limited understanding of the mass, may have invested Antoinette with priestly authority.[25] She encouraged this by speaking from a raised position—standing on a chair—thus placing herself in a position that resembled a priest giving a sermon.

Antoinette seems to have enjoyed the authority and attention she commanded, though at the time she may not have fully understood the prohibitions against women speaking about religious matters in public. Looking back in later years on another occasion, when as mother superior of the Ursuline convent in Tulle she had given what amounted to a sermon, Antoinette adopted a self-critical tone: "Once, at the profession of a novice, I made . . . a long speech on the vows of religion, before I gave her the black veil. . . . This was in the presence of a numerous company of more than a hundred people who were in the chapel to attend the profession and who listened to me with unparalleled attention." Antoinette chastised herself for the "pride" and "vanity" that led her to indulge in such "follies."[26] In retrospect, she realized the dangerous ground she had been treading—perhaps reflecting the changed circumstances of Ursuline life as the order became better established and its activities more restricted. At the time, however, Antoinette closely modeled her behavior on that of a priest exhorting his flock.

Ursulines like Antoinette Micolon imitated preachers and used the connection between teaching and preaching (a connection not lost on their audience) to establish their authority over the laity. Those who attended Anne de Vefure's catechisms, which were held in a large barn, certainly understood this connection: "Once they rang the great bell of the parish, to assemble the people; and they would have continued this on other days, if she had not forbidden it."[27] The ringing of the parish bell announced Anne's catechisms as public community events and reminded the townspeople of the calling of the flock to mass. Anne herself saw the dangers of such an obvious link and put a stop to the bell ringing. But she continued to give public catechisms. Ursulines like Anne de Vefure invoked the association between teaching and preaching but at the same time were careful to limit public recognition of such a connection.

Because enclosure limited the scope of Ursuline public teaching, there was less danger of confusing it with preaching and fewer opportunities for Ursulines to "impersonate" preachers and priests as fully as Antoinette Micolon. But the preacher remained a powerful model for the Ursuline teacher and catechist and continued to influence Ursuline self-conceptions. "Preaching" became the dominant metaphor for all kinds of Ursuline speech, and we find it everywhere in the writings of Ursulines of the time. Mother superiors addressed the nuns in their care with the zeal of preachers. Conversations in the parlor and at the grill resembled "the most beautiful sermons"—though the Paris *Rules* warned that Ursulines should instruct visitors without *seeming* to preach.[28] Sick and dying Ursulines continued to "preach" from their beds: Dauphine Lanfreze transformed her sickbed into "a preacher's pulpit"; on her deathbed Françoise de Bourrily "spoke only of God and the salvation of souls, and preached eloquently, as if she had a great assembly to convert."[29]

The association of preaching with such a broad range of activities may have helped to allay concerns about the ambiguous relationship between preaching and teaching in the eyes of the authorities. An Ursuline "preaching" from her sickbed or in the convent parlor was much less threatening than an Ursuline "preaching" in church. By defining preaching in such a way as to deemphasize its official overtones, Ursulines could claim certain aspects of male clerical office without appearing subversive. And while Ursulines may have seen their activities as preaching, the language they used was ambiguous enough so that preaching could be read simply as a metaphor for their activities, not as a claim to male office.

DRAWING BOUNDARIES: MALE SUPPORTERS OF THE URSULINES

While Ursulines themselves exploited the fluid boundaries between teaching and preaching, their clerical supporters were much more likely to differentiate between the activities of male preachers and female catechists. These men believed that in order to justify the newfound apostolate of women it was necessary to draw clear boundaries between teaching and preaching. Their arguments in defense of women teachers and missionaries emphasized the limited nature of Ursuline activities, presented them as supporters of apostolic men, and denied the more public aspects of female teaching.

Claude Martin, son of the Ursuline mystic and Canadian missionary Marie de l'Incarnation, praised Ursuline teachers and missionaries by comparing them to preachers but was careful to make a clear distinction between the activities of apostolic men and women. As editor of his mother's autobiography, Martin wanted to legitimize her extraordinary career without diminishing the heroic nature of her activities. His strategy was to emphasize the role she played in supporting the efforts of male reformers.

In Marie's autobiography, Martin included an extended commentary on the distinction between teaching and preaching. He began by recognizing the principal objections to women's serving as preachers and missionaries: the association of "public" women with immodesty; the natural weakness and simplicity of women; the belief that public opinion could not accept women in positions of authority; and the fact that preaching was associated with the office of the priest, from which women were prohibited. For these reasons, the title of apostle was reserved for men. In Canada, Marie de l'Incarnation performed "evangelical duties as far as her sex and condition would permit: so that if one cannot give her the title of Apostle, one can at least give her that of Apostolic woman."[30] By differentiating between male "apostles" and "apostolic women" (*femmes apostoliques*)—a distinction not made by Ursulines themselves—Martin drew a clear line between the activities of male preachers and Ursuline teachers and emphasized the limits of women's apostolic activity.

Martin described apostolic women in much the same way that Saint Teresa of Avila had—as supporting male "apostles" through their prayers.[31] Although his mother was not free to imitate the preachers and missionaries whom she admired, her zeal for the salvation of souls led her to accompany them in spirit. She also encouraged apostolic men through her prayers and letters. Marie and the other Canadian Ursulines participated vicariously in the achievements of male apostles; they were "angels and guardian spirits . . . who entreated heaven to send them Apostles to convert [the Indians]."[32] Such a statement is ironic in view of the fact that Ursulines in Canada taught and catechized native girls and women and thus participated actively in the missionary efforts of the Catholic Church there. But this activity was not defined by Martin as the work of apostles. Martin's commentary domesticated Marie's activities, placing them within the confines of conventional, though heroic, female behavior. By downplaying the apostolic *actions* of Marie de l'Incarnation and highlighting her apostolic *spirit*, Martin could argue that she did not attempt to appropriate a role the church reserved for men.

Another strategy used by male supporters of apostolic women was to distinguish between *preaching* in public and *teaching* in private. Such an approach was common in male defenses of women's participation in a variety of spheres in early modern Europe. As Merry Wiesner has noted, "Men, whether humanists, reformers, or political thinkers, often argued that the activity concerned— such as writing, education, or inheriting an estate—was essentially private and thus should be open to women."[33] Pierre Fourier, founder and patron of the Congrégation de Notre-Dame, used such a distinction to defend the right of women to teach. Against those who argued that Saint Paul had forbidden women to teach, Fourier cited Saint John Chrysostom: "It is to preside over an assembly and to mount the pulpit that he [Saint Paul] forbids them, and not to teach. . . . How could it be that Priscilla instructed Apollo (Acts 18)? Thus it is not to put an end to a teaching of doctrine given in private [*donné en particulier*] that he says this, but to one that is given in public and in the middle of an assembly, and which is proper only for preachers."[34] Although women were barred from preaching publicly from the pulpit, they were permitted to teach the faith "in private," following the example of the women of the early church.

In Bordeaux the powerful reforming archbishop Cardinal de Sourdis, patron and founder of the local Ursuline congregation, adopted a similar strategy. In 1609 some townspeople brought a complaint against the Ursulines before the Parlement of Bordeaux. The Parlement declared that because the company had not yet been approved by the pope it should be disbanded, since the girls who joined the congregation could leave at any time and adopt another condition in life, without consulting their parents.[35] In response to these attacks, Sourdis issued a pastoral letter in which he chastised the people of Bordeaux for their ill-treatment of the *congrégées*. Sourdis praised the Ursulines for their virtue and utility—"These are virgins who consecrate themselves through virginity and their work to instruct and teach those of their sex"—and explained that their teaching was legitimate because they taught "not through public preaching, but through private instruction [*instructions particulières*] of Christian doctrine, and this, principally to those of their own sex."[36]

Sourdis was concerned lest Ursuline activities be misinterpreted as preaching, and he explained to the people of Bordeaux the difference between "private instruction" and "public preaching" in an effort to convince them that the Ursuline mission was legitimate. Whether this allayed the anxieties of the townspeople is unclear—the documents are silent about whether they were troubled by the similarity of Ursuline teaching to preaching—their major concern was the institutional status of the Ursulines.

The limits of female teaching were defined even more clearly in the *Constitutions* of the Bordeaux Ursulines, drawn up by the cardinal himself in 1609, which offered a method of teaching Christian doctrine designed to avoid any confusion between teaching and preaching. All members of the company were to adopt "a single method for teaching Christian doctrine to their students, conforming entirely to the Roman Church, taking care not to teach about lofty matters which they do not understand. This is why they will be content to teach simply what is contained in the catechism of the most reverend Cardinal Bellarmin, ordered by the holy and sacred Council of Trent."[37] Ursuline teachers were to adhere strictly to the catechism and were not to give detailed explanations or interpretations or aspire to teach things beyond their understanding—that is, theology. If Ursulines taught exactly the same things following exactly the same method, the issue of charismatic teaching and its resemblance to preaching would not arise.

Similar restrictions on female teaching appeared frequently in various Ursuline constitutions. The Paris *Constitutions*, used by many Ursulines throughout France, warned Ursuline teachers to follow the "text of the catechism, without adding any speeches or unnecessary questions."[38] The *Constitutions* of the Ursulines of Châlons declared that those teaching the articles of the faith should do so "according to the manner that they are contained in the catechism, and this will be done in the classrooms, if there is a grill, or in a parlor, but with so much discretion and moderation that one does not sin in any way against the Rules of the Apostle, which do not allow women to pontificate in the church."[39] Here female teaching was clearly distinguished from preaching through limits on content, style, and site. Unlike a preacher, an Ursuline must not depart from the official catechism; she must not "pontificate" but rather use a discreet and modest style when teaching matters of the faith. Finally, Ursuline teaching must be conducted in private spaces deemed appropriate for women—the classroom or convent parlor, not the church.

In the long run, men like Claude Martin and Archbishop de Sourdis successfully defined female teaching as "private" and an acceptable activity for women. By the mid-seventeenth century enclosure had become the reality for almost all Ursulines, and teaching outside the convent walls and to large crowds had ceased. In essence, enclosure was the putting into practice of the distinction between public preaching and private teaching—the enclosed space of the convent limited both the venues and the audience for Ursuline instruction. The definition of Ursuline teaching as private activity, in conjunction with the success of enclosure, situated Ursuline speech in an appropriate setting with clear boundaries and signaled its domestication.

These efforts to define Ursuline teaching as private rather than public support the observations of historians like Joan Kelly and Merry Wiesner about a "new division between public and private life" and "the contraction of women's public role" during the early modern period.[40] The restriction of lay women's activities to the domestic sphere was paralleled by the Catholic Church's increased preoccupation with enclosing religious women behind convent walls. Like those who opposed women teaching, male defenders of the Ursulines believed women did not belong in the public sphere, but differed in their definition of "public." While opponents focused on the *activity* of teaching—by teaching the Word of God, Ursulines were carrying out a public, institutional function—supporters of the Ursulines emphasized the *circumstances* in which this teaching took place. In contrast to public preaching, conducted in unrestricted spaces open to all, Ursuline teaching was restricted in both space and audience, and thus controllable.

However, Ursulines themselves did not accept the terms of this debate. While male clerics made clear distinctions between teaching and preaching, Ursulines played on the ambiguities between the two activities and thus challenged, however indirectly, the hard lines these men drew between public and private. Wiesner argues that early modern women "saw a continuum from the household to the world beyond rather than a sharp split between public and private."[41] Similarly, Ursulines saw a continuum from the *convent* to the world beyond and resisted the attempts of men to define their activities as strictly "private." This strategy left open the possibility for women to claim "public" authority.[42]

By emphasizing the limits of female teaching and defining it as private, male supporters of the Ursulines denied the revolutionary aspects of the Ursuline apostolate and were able to present it as "safe" and therefore legitimate. But what they failed—or refused—to recognize was that the novelty of the Ursuline apostolate required new strategies for establishing authority. The traditional basis of female spiritual authority, mysticism, was both individualistic and premised on a contemplative model of religious life and thus not generally applicable to an order of apostolic women. Understandably, Ursulines turned to the most obvious models—priests and preachers—to define their authority.

The active participation of women in religious reform during the sixteenth and seventeenth centuries raised new questions about the spiritual authority of women. Women on both sides of the confessional divide entered the public sphere as preachers, teachers, and missionaries. In Catholic areas, women's "public" speech was institutionalized and became associated with whole communities of religious women. This change did not take place without a fight. Faced with opposition from both clergy and laity, female teachers and missionaries in the Catholic Church had to defend and define their newfound apostolate. Some female teaching congregations failed. The English Ladies of Mary Ward were suppressed in 1631 largely because they refused to accept enclosure. In contrast, Ursulines adapted to enclosure and used the institutional stability it offered to expand their apostolate—as an uncloistered *congrégée*, Marie de l'Incarnation would have faced insurmountable obstacles to setting up an Ursuline mission in Canada. By recognizing the dangerous ground they were traversing and by purposefully blurring the boundaries between teaching and preaching, Ursulines succeeded in creating a space in the Catholic Church for the female teacher of the Word of God.

NOTES

1. Marie-Augustine de Pommereu, *Les chroniques de l'ordre des Ursulines recueillies pour l'usage des Religieuses du mesme Ordre*, vol. 1 (Paris, 1673), part 2, p. 173, henceforth cited as M.D.P.U. (Mere de Pommereu, Ursuline); this usage is standard in stud-

ies of the Ursulines. See also Linda Lierheimer, "Female Eloquence and Maternal Ministry: The Apostolate of Ursuline Nuns in Seventeenth-Century France" (Ph.D. diss., Princeton University, 1994). This essay is a revised version of chapter 4 of the dissertation. All translations are mine, unless otherwise indicated.

2. On the Fathers of Christian Doctrine, see Jean de Viguerie, *Une oeuvre d'éducation sous l'ancien régime: Les Pères de la Doctrine Chrétienne en France et en Italie, 1592–1792* (Paris: Editions de la Nouvelle Aurore, 1976); also Henri Brémond, *Histoire littéraire du sentiment religieux en France*, vol. 2 (Paris: Bloud et Gay, 1920–33), pp. 10–31.

3. On Angela Merici and the Italian Ursulines, see Thérèse Ledóchowska, *Angèle Merici et la Compagnie de Ste-Ursule*, 2 vols. (Rome: Ancora, 1967).

4. Elizabeth Rapley, *The Dévotes: Women and Church in Seventeenth-Century France* (Montreal: McGill–Queen's University Press, 1990), p. 52. The most thorough study of the French Ursulines remains Marie de Chantal Gueudré's *Histoire de l'ordre des Ursulines en France*, 3 vols. (Paris: Editions St-Paul, 1957).

5. M.D.P.U., *Chroniques*, vol. 1, part 1, p. 97.

6. Claude Bourguignon, *La vie du Père Romillon, prestre de l'Oratoire de Jésus et fondateur de la congrégation des Ursulines en France* (Marseille, 1649), pp. 219–20, 298.

7. Jean Delumeau, *Catholicism between Luther and Voltaire* (London: Burns and Oates, 1977), esp. pp. 159–79. Although I do not agree with Delumeau's assertion that the popular Christianity confronted by the reformers was "pagan," there was a gap between popular practices and Catholic doctrine as defined at Trent.

8. Christian Anatole, "La réforme tridentine et l'emploi de l'occitan dans la pastorale," *Revue des langues romanes* (1967): 1–29.

9. H. J. Schroeder, *Canons and Decrees of the Council of Trent* (St. Louis, Mo.: B. Herder Book Co., 1941), p. 197.

10. M.D.P.U., *Chroniques*, vol. 1, part 1, pp. 72, 80; and Jeanne Cambounet de la Mothe, *Journal des Illustres Religieuses de l'Ordre de Sainte Ursule*, vol. 2 (Bourg-en-Bresse, 1684–1690), p. 180. Most historians view efforts to reform the clergy as part of an institutional movement from above unconnected to the grassroots activities of women. If, as Jean Delumeau claims, one of the great accomplishments of the Catholic Reformation was to create a new model of the parish priest, the efforts of women like Anne de Vefure in bringing about this transformation have yet to be recognized. See Delumeau, *Catholicism between Luther and Voltaire*, pp. 179–89.

11. M.D.P.U., *Chroniques*, vol. 1, part 1, p. 79.

12. Henri Pourrat, ed., *Mémoires de la Mère Micolon* (Clermont-Ferrand, 1981), pp. 98–99.

13. M.D.P.U., *Chroniques*, vol. 1, part 2, p. 275. It is tempting to conclude that enclosure was a step backward, but it is important to remember that many Ursulines supported this development and that the impetus behind establishing an Ursuline convent in Paris was a woman, Madame de Sainte-Beuve. See Marie-Andrée Jégou, *Les Ursulines du Faubourg St-Jacques à Paris 1607–1662* (Paris: Presses Universitaires de France, 1981). As Jodi Bilinkoff has argued for the Spanish Carmelites, voluntary enclosure could be liberating and provide spiritual autonomy; see *The Avila of Saint Teresa: Religious Reform in a Sixteenth-Century City* (Ithaca, N.Y.: Cornell University Press, 1989), pp. 132–33.

14. Cambounet de la Mothe, *Journal*, vol. 3, pp. 445, 78.

15. *Circulaire mortuaire* of Louise de S. Paul (Chambéry, 1684), Bibliothèque de l'Arsenal, ms. 4990, 124r.

16. M.D.P.U., *Chroniques*, vol. 2, part 3, "Congrégation de Bordeaux," p. 504; and Cambounet de la Mothe, *Journal*, vol. 1, pp. 289–90.

17. Cambounet de la Mothe, *Journal*, vol. 4, p. 309.

18. Cambounet de la Mothe, *Journal*, vol. 3, p. 256.

19. Marie-Augustine de Pommereu, *Annales des Ursulines du premier monastère de la Congrégation de Paris rue St. Jacques*, vol. 1, pp. 103–4. This manuscript history of the first fifty years of the Paris convent was compiled in the 1650s and 1660s and is currently in the archives of the Ursulines de Saint-Alyre in Clermont-Ferrand.

20. Cambounet de la Mothe, *Journal*, vol. 2, p. a4 (verso).

21. *Circulaire mortuaire* of Michelle de Sainte Cecile (Dijon, 1682), Sorbonne, ms. 769, 134r; M.D.P.U., *Chroniques*, vol. 1, part 3, p. 63; and vol. 2, part 3, "Congrégation d'Arles," p. 413.

22. Marie de l'Incarnation, *La vie de la vénérable Mère Marie de l'Incarnation, première supérieure des Ursulines de la nouvelle France* (Paris, 1677), pp. 17–18. This version of Marie's "spiritual relation" was edited, and in some cases altered, by her son, Claude Martin. For a detailed account of the manuscript and publishing history of her spiritual relation, see Natalie Zemon Davis, *Women on the Margins: Three Seventeenth-Century Lives* (Cambridge, Mass.: Harvard University Press, 1995), p. 259n.

23. Pourrat, *Mémoires de la Mère Micolon*, p. 54.

24. Ibid., p. 98.

25. The women may have had their own distinctive understanding of the mass that was not based on a literal comprehension of the words spoken by the priest; but their understanding of the mass probably would not have been an "orthodox" one in the eyes of church authorities.

26. Pourrat, *Mémoires de la Mère Micolon*, p. 182.

27. M.D.P.U., *Chroniques*, vol. 1, part 1, p. 78; Cambounet de la Mothe, *Journal*, vol. 2, p.179.

28. Cambounet de la Mothe, *Journal*, vol. 4, p. 388; *Reglemens des Religieuses Ursulines de la Congrégation de Paris*, vol. 1 (Paris, 1705), book 2, p. 95.

29. M.D.P.U., *Chroniques*, vol. 1, part 1, pp. 66, 53.

30. Marie de l'Incarnation, *Vie*, pp. 303–4.

31. On Teresa's "apostolate of prayer" see Bilinkoff, *The Avila of Saint Teresa*, p. 134; and Emmanuel Renault, *L'idéal apostolique des Carmélites selon sainte Thérèse d'Avila* (Desclée de Brouwer, 1981).

32. Marie de l'Incarnation, *Vie*, pp. 438, 443.

33. Merry Wiesner, "Women's Defense of Their Public Role," in *Women in the Middle Ages and the Renaissance: Literary and Historical Perspectives*, ed. Mary Beth Rose (Syracuse, N.Y.: Syracuse University Press, 1986), p. 5.

34. Hélène Derréal, ed., *Pierre Fourier: Sa Correspondance, 1598–1640*, vol. 2 (Nancy: Presses Universitaires de Nancy, 1987), p. 35.

35. Chanoine Jean Bertheau, "Actes de l'Archevêché de Bordeaux sous le Cardinal François de Sourdis," *Archives historiques du département de la Gironde* 50 (1915): 300–301. The absence of solemn vows in uncloistered congregations raised legal issues that concerned the parents of potential students and postulants. Without solemn vows,

nuns could still contract valid marriages and claim inheritance rights (see Rapley, *The Dévotes,* pp. 38–39, 55).

36. "Lettre Pastoral de très illustre et très révérend père en Dieu, Mgr le Cardinal de Sourdis, archevesque de Bordeaux . . . , à tous ceux de son diocèse de Bordeaux" (1609), in Bertheau, "Actes de l'Archevêché de Bordeaux," p. 399.

37. Cardinal François de Sourdis, "Reigles et constitutions de l'institut et compagnie des religieuses de Sainte-Ursule" (1609), in ibid., p. 347.

38. *Les Constitutions des religieuses de Sainte Ursule, de la Congrégation de Paris* (Paris, 1640), part 1, p. 34.

39. *Constitutions des Filles de la Vierge, religieuses de Sainte-Ursule, établies au diocèse de Chaalons* (Chaalons, 1695), p. 138.

40. Wiesner, "Women's Defense," pp. 3, 21; and Joan Kelly, "Did Women Have a Renaissance?" in *Women, History and Theory: The Essays of Joan Kelly* (Chicago: University of Chicago Press, 1985), p. 47.

41. Wiesner, "Women's Defense," p. 21.

42. For a similar argument about another of the Catholic Reformation's new active congregations for women, see Colin Jones, "Sisters of Charity and the Ailing Poor," *Social History of Medicine* 2 (1989): 347.

TWELVE

A Voice for Themselves

Women as Participants in Congregational Discourse in the Eighteenth-Century Moravian Movement

Peter Vogt

That women should be allowed to preach was nearly unthinkable in seventeenth- and eighteenth-century German Protestantism. The long subordination of women's voices and experiences, insofar as it was caused by the scriptural injunction that women should keep silence in the church (1 Cor. 14:34), became even more pronounced through the Reformation emphasis on preaching. With the sermon emerging as the focal point of Lutheran and Reformed worship, women were in effect further removed from the center of organized religious life. Their role was that of the mute, passive listener. All the more important, then, are the few instances in which this order was subverted and women appeared as religious speakers and leaders. The advent of the Pietist movement, a powerful reaction against the status quo of the established institutional churches, opened up the possibility of defining the religious role of women in new and unconventional terms. Among the various branches of Pietism, such a shift occurred at first in radical Pietism (ca.1680–1720) and then, from 1722 on, also in the *Brüdergemeine* or Moravian movement under the leadership of Count Zinzendorf (1700–1760). Women began to enjoy an exceptional measure of equality, assumed leadership roles, and voiced their insights and experiences in written and oral testimonies. In some cases women even engaged in preaching and received ordination to various ministerial offices.

This essay describes the practice of female speaking, preaching, and teaching in the Moravian movement. I begin with a historical overview of the movement, focusing particularly on the role of women and the importance of communication, then present direct evidence for various forms of female speaking, and finally discuss how the Moravians dealt with biblical passages prohibiting the speaking of women.

THE MORAVIAN MOVEMENT

The story of the eighteenth-century Moravian movement, origin of the present worldwide Moravian Church, began in 1722 with the arrival of Protestant exiles from Moravia—spiritual descendants of the persecuted Unity of Bohemian Brethren—at the estate of Nikolaus Ludwig von Zinzendorf and the subsequent establishment of a small village called Herrnhut—The Lord's Watch.[1] Zinzendorf, an imperial count of Lutheran faith with Pietist leanings, had high aspirations for a life devoted to Christ and regarded the appearance of the Moravian settlers as the opportunity to gather together a true Christian community of regenerate souls. During the following years the flow of Moravian immigrants and other spiritual-minded people from all over Germany to the germinating Pietist colony continued. In 1727 a spiritual revival unified the residents of Herrnhut as a *Gemeine* ("congregation" or "fellowship") determined to pattern itself after the ancient apostolic church.[2] The local community rapidly evolved into a larger movement with contacts and establishments throughout Europe and numerous mission stations overseas, particular liturgical customs, and a distinct Christocentric spirituality.

Although the Moravians reinstated parts of the church discipline of the Bohemian Brethren, Zinzendorf, their charismatic and at times even autocratic leader, did not intend to establish the Moravian *Gemeine* as a separate church. Nor did he regard it as the only true Christian community. His intention was simply that its external organization should serve as a "roof" under which earnest Christians from all confessions could convene in fellowship and work together for the expansion of Christ's reign. This fellowship, as it developed in Herrnhut and then also in other Moravian settlement congregations, represented a visible image of the true, invisible Church Universal—Christ's bride—and prepared her glorious restitution in the millennium. At the time of Zinzendorf's death, the Moravian movement counted about two dozen settlements in Europe and North America, enclaves of an intense religious life specific to the Moravians and substantially different from that of the established Protestant churches.

The fact that from its beginning the Herrnhut settlement and the movement that subsequently grew out of it strove to form an exemplary Christian community had a significant bearing on the role and status of women.[3] Conventional "worldly" norms and concepts about womanhood were questioned and modified according to the communal spiritual ethos, which was to some degree egalitarian. At the same time, the situation of Moravian women was also shaped by the movement's steadily evolving needs and experiences, especially the emphasis on communicative interaction as a decisive element of communal and spiritual life. The conjunction of both aspects, the egalitarian tendency and the importance of communication, resulted in an involvement of women as leaders and speakers that was uniquely Moravian and that, in its own way, reversed the traditional interpretation of 1 Corinthians 14:34, "let the women keep silence in the churches."

EGALITARIAN TENDENCIES

Emphasizing the ideal of fraternal love between true believers, the theology and social order of the Moravian movement tended toward egalitarianism with regard to class, possession, and gender.[4] People's differences were not completely abrogated, but it was agreed that ultimately faith was the essential criterion for membership in the community and that through faith in Christ all should be one. Consequently, the Moravians referred to the male members of the community as "brothers" and to the female members as "sisters," terminology reminiscent of the New Testament. It signified at once a particular ethical ideal and an organizational vision. For Moravian women the designation "sister" denoted a sense of equality and autonomy insofar as their social status was not defined exclusively in terms of a subordinating relationship to a man such as wife or daughter.

Theologically, the status of women in relation to men was worked out through a differentiated argumentation. With Galatians 3:28 in mind, Zinzendorf stated in 1747 that men and women were essentially equal in their faith in Christ and that, in turn, Christ's love for believers was impartial: "With Him, none comes up short, and He also does not prefer one person to another. He loves with an inexpressible and inimitable egality."[5] Although Zinzendorf shared the common belief that women had caused the "fall," he argued that their full worth and dignity had been restored by the fact that Christ was born of a woman:

> Because the old regulation from the fall that the female sex can have nothing to do with priestly matters had already been ignored in case of one or another important woman, e.g., the old matron in the temple, but now, since the Creator [i.e., Christ] is born of a woman, it is abolished, and [because] now the sisters belong to the class of those whom the Saviour has declared to his heavenly Father as priests just as much as the men: hence there is no question that the whole band, the whole company, the whole choir of his maidens and brides, are priestesses, and not only priestesses but also priestly women.[6]

Thus, Zinzendorf believed that women did not lack anything that would prevent them from being fully qualified to serve Christ in various ministries within the church.

At the same time, however, Zinzendorf and the Moravians were reluctant to ignore those New Testament passages that speak about the submission of women. Despite their spiritual equality, women, especially wives, were still to be subordinate to men in temporal matters. Here, Zinzendorf and the Moravians emphasized particularly the analogy of the church's subordination to Christ as his bride (Eph. 5:22–24), a prominent notion in Moravian theology and spirituality during the 1740s and 1750s. This imagery effectively inhibited the complete emancipation of Moravian sisters, yet in implying that *all* human souls are feminine it also prevented the depreciation of women.

The organizational structure of the Moravian congregations, known as the choir system, corresponded to the theological view about the equality and difference of men and women.[7] The choirs were smaller units within the whole community, consisting of people of the same gender and similar life circumstances. In many instances, members of a particular choir, especially the choirs of the single brothers, single sisters, widowers, and widows, lived together communally, thereby attaining a high degree of autonomy, social support, and economic security.[8] The rationale for the choir system was the insight that people in different circumstances had different spiritual needs and experiences. In particular, the separation of the sexes, although at first implemented in order to avoid any reason for suspicion or slander, reflected the acknowledgment that each gender had specific strengths and weaknesses, gifts and needs, and that it therefore was best if only people of the same gender ministered to one another. Accordingly, the responsibility for pastoral care of the sisters rested almost exclusively in the hands of the sisters.[9]

Altogether, the organizational structure of the choir system was one of symmetry between the sexes, a symmetry especially apparent in the architecture of Moravian settlement congregations and in their pastoral and administrative hierarchy. The typical design of an eighteenth-century Moravian settlement is a square around which the meetinghouse, the houses of the choirs, and the other buildings of the congregation are arranged symmetrically.[10] The axis through the center of the meetinghouse divides the settlement into the "Sisters' Side" and the "Brothers' Side." Thus, the Sisters' House, the Widows' House, the school for the girls, and so on are located on the "Sisters' Side" of the square, and the corresponding buildings for the brothers stand opposite on the "Brothers' Side." The meetinghouse, likewise, has a "Sisters' Side" and a "Brothers' Side," each with separate seating and entrances. On either side of the central "liturgist's table" (in place of pulpit or altar) are the so-called *Arbeiterbänke*, benches facing the congregation reserved for the male and female *Arbeiter* ("laborers"), the pastoral and administrative leaders of the congregation.

Following Romans 12:6–8, the Moravians had early on begun to establish a wide variety of offices for the spiritual and temporal welfare of their community. The list originally included the seven apostolic offices (prophecy, ministry, teaching, exhortation, giving, leading, and caring) and was later modified according to the changing needs and resources of the movement.[11] From the beginning, however, the offices were assigned doubly to men and women, providing the sisters with their own set of offices and leadership positions.

Thus, women served as eldresses, teachers, and overseers, headed the female choirs, and nourished the expressions of piety particular to the sisters.[12] With their male counterparts the female leaders served on the committees that governed the congregations, and some sisters even took part in the leadership of the Moravian movement as a whole.[13] It lay within the inherent logic of this symmetrical system of ministry and leadership that, like the brothers, the sisters should be consecrated and ordained to their particular ministerial offices. Although consecrations of some kind had probably been practiced since the 1720s, the ordination of Moravian women to ministerial offices began in 1745. By that time the Moravians acknowledged the threefold ministerial order of the Bohemian Brethren (deacon, presbyter, bishop) and the consecration as acolyte, a spiritual dedication for ministry on a more general level. Except for the episcopal office, women were consecrated and ordained to all ranks, altogether 420 *Akoluthae*, 202 *Diaconissae*, and 14 *Priesterinnen* ("priestesses," i.e., female presbyters) until 1760.[14] These offices were mainly related to the pastoral work among the sisters but also included instances of ministry to the sisters during congregational worship such as foot washing, blessing, praying, distributing the elements, and laying on of hands.

In what way did Moravian sisters, being in so many ways equal to the brothers, have a voice within their community? Did they preach? Did they speak? Did they "have a say"? In order to answer these questions adequately, we will take a glance at the significance of "preaching" and "speaking," or, in more general terms, of communication and dialogue, in the communal life of the Moravian *Gemeine*.

CONGREGATIONAL DISCOURSE

For spiritual and practical reasons, communication played a very important role within the Moravian movement. In 1754 Zinzendorf stated that it was necessary for a "living congregation" to unite itself each day through communal "thinking, speaking, praying, and singing."[15] This remark reflected directly on the Moravian practice of assembling for daily worship and expressed a fundamental theological insight: Without continuous communication, a Christian community cannot exist. Hence, in Moravian piety the aspects of worship and communication were closely interrelated. Aspiring to grow ever closer as a community and to live "liturgically" (that is, in worshipful devotion) at all times, the Moravian *Gemeine* accentuated and developed both the communicative aspects of worship and the spiritual aspects of communication.

Like other pietistic groups, the Moravians placed great stock in spiritual experience, both that of the individual and that of the community. Faith, in their view, was not so much a matter of the external, given teachings of the church as of the internal, experienced religious perceptions and emotions of the individual, whose personal agency thereby gained enormously in significance: Each believer had to give testimony of his or her faith individually by him- or herself. Accordingly, the religious life of the Moravian community was fundamentally oriented toward the active involvement and participation of all, and it depended largely on the continuous articulation of and conversation about religious experience. The natural place for such a conversation was first the personal pastoral interview and the devotional gathering of like-minded believers in small groups in the tradition of the *Collegia Pietatis*. Both forms of interaction were provided through circles and gatherings within each choir and through the arrangement of voluntary associations of three to eight persons called *Banden*, where people could talk freely about their religious and personal concerns.[16]

A different setting for the communication of religious experience was worship, oriented, of course, more toward the spiritual mood of the whole community.[17] The Moravians believed that genuine worship required the expression of their shared faith and piety. Thus, they shifted the focus of worship from preaching as doctrinal education and moral exhortation to the elevation and articulation of the communal spiritual experience through liturgy, speech, song, and prayer. The settings and forms of worship became quite diverse, involving daily meetings of the congregation and several short services during the day within the choirs. The Moravians developed their own ceremony for Holy Communion and created new forms of worship such as the Litany, the Singing Hour, the Love Feast, and the *Pedilavium* (foot washing), each of which provided specific avenues for the communication of the communal religious experience.

Another area of significance for communication was in organization and administration. As an evolving movement, the Moravians had a particular need for effective communication. From the earliest community gatherings dealing with the establishment of Herrnhut to the "constitutional synod" of 1764 striving to consolidate the worldwide Unity after Zinzendorf's death, the members of the Moravian movement faced the challenge to solve problems, make decisions, and mediate conflicts through seemingly unending deliberations. With the geographical expansion of the community, a steady increase in membership, and the dynamic development of its spirituality, efficient communication proved crucial for the survival and prosperity of the movement. Numerous meetings and conferences occurred on all levels, and a dense web of mutual visitations and correspondence connected its individual members. Although this ongoing administrative communication dealt mostly with temporal matters, it was nevertheless regarded by the Moravians as a spiritual task.

In sum, communication formed an integral part of the all-embracing Moravian spiritual life. The multifaceted dialogue within the community, partly religious and partly organizational in character, was carried out with great intensity and had a significant spiritual function. It linked all members of the movement together, thereby forming the pulsing, life-sustaining circulation of the whole organism. For lack of a better term, the entirety of this ongoing cycle of communication could be described as "congregational discourse."

Five forms of oral communication played a prominent role in congregational discourse. First, preaching continued to be a part of Moravian worship, although it changed along the lines indicated above and served primarily the purpose of edification. Unpretentious in character, sermons were called *Gemeinrede* (community speech) if addressed to the whole local congregation and *Chorhomilie* (choir homily) if addressed to the members of a particular choir. Their goal, as characterized by Zinzendorf in 1758, was "that there be a communication of the spirits, that one may understand one another and affect one another, that a person may enter into the other's soul and thus into the view and the emotion of the one who speaks."[18]

Second, "teaching," while largely synonymous with preaching in eighteenth-century German Protestantism, denoted in Moravian usage the instruction about questions of faith for members of the congregation. Unlike preaching, it generally occurred in gatherings separate from worship.[19] Third, discussion and deliberation were forms of discourse in synods and conferences, where either the whole congregation or a particular committee dealt with matters of business and community life. Fourth, conversation was a more intimate form of discourse, taking place in small groups in the choirs and in the *Banden* and focusing mainly on personal and spiritual issues. Fifth, the pastoral interview sought to facilitate the spiritual development of the individual member, and, including aspects of counseling, exhortation, and hearing confessions, it formed an important part of life within the choirs.

The written forms of congregational discourse comprised both personal and official writings. Personal writings, which articulated and testified to one's experiences, included poetry, private diaries and letters, and a kind of autobiographical memoir, called *Lebenslauf*, which was to be read at one's funeral service. Official writings, reflecting the communal experience, included the *Diarium* (journal) of the congregation and of the individual choirs, and correspondence, reports, and memoirs.

In sum, Moravian congregational discourse bridged the spiritual and temporal dimensions of communal life. To varying degrees it occurred in public, ranging from the confidential conversation with one other person, to small groups and the choirs, to the whole congregation, to the whole movement, and beyond it to the outside. It was in this complex world that Moravian women lived and in which they by no means kept silence.

MORAVIAN WOMEN AS SPEAKERS, PREACHERS, AND WRITERS

Most of the female participation in congregational discourse was related to the offices and ministries of women within the Moravian *Gemeine*. There are indications that sisters sometimes contributed to the discussion at synods and conferences, although they seem to have been more restrained than the brothers. The sisters also had their own meetings and conferences, occurring mostly on the congregational level, and three "Sisters' synods" were held in 1755, 1756, and 1760.[20] Less public, yet of great significance for the spiritual life within the church, were the conversations among the sisters in the choirs and *Banden*. Here, women had a place for sociable conversation where they could articulate their experiences and speak freely about religious and personal concerns. Altogether, the symmetrical organization of pastoral ministry in the Moravian movement provided women with opportunities and responsibilities for speaking within their religious community that were unprecedented in the German Protestant state churches. However, did women also preach?

That women were allowed to preach was a charge repeatedly leveled against Zinzendorf and the Moravians in the controversial literature of their opponents. According to them, female preaching was one of the many instances in which the Moravians falsified doctrine, disobeyed Scripture, and corrupted the order of the church. Thus Johann Georg Walch (1693–1775), a Lutheran professor of theology at the University of Jena, wrote in 1747:

> The sect of the Herrnhuters is dangerous to the profession of preaching [*Lehrstand*], as the authority to speak in public is given without differentiation of gender, age, and scholarship, and as it is sufficiently known that in this sect educated and uneducated, men and women, young men and maidens can teach and preach, become ordained, go to the heathen, and seek to make them Herrnhuter Brethren.[21]

Noting that women, like young or uneducated men, lacked the capability to comprehend "the wholesome teaching of the ground and order of our salvation" and were unable "to present it clearly and orderly," Walch pointed out disapprovingly that among the Moravians the "public teaching office" (that is, preaching) was entrusted to them and that "not only uneducated males, but also females are installed as teachers" and even sent out on apostolic excursions.[22] Other pamphlets against the Moravians contained similar accusations of permitting female preaching and teaching.[23]

In their own publications, Zinzendorf and the Moravians rejected these charges and asserted that women neither preached in public nor violated the biblical commandment to keep silence.[24] Thus, in printed sources we do not find much evidence of female preaching, although some passages indicate its possibility. A declaration of the Herrnhut congregation from 1730, for example, states that the pulpits in the churches should be left to the preachers but that "no child of God" should be hindered "to bear witness to his faithful Saviour, secretly and publicly, and to proclaim the virtue of the one who has called us from darkness to his mysterious light."[25] Eight years later, Zinzendorf pointed out that the teaching office in the Moravian *Gemeine* was generally administered by two kinds of people: by ordained preachers and by other witnesses "endowed by God," who "speak the word, as often as the Lord prompts them."[26] Presumably, the group of God's children and divinely appointed witnesses entitled to proclaim their faith and to "speak the word" could have included women. Yet the texts, careful not to foster any rumors about female preaching among the Moravians, do not elaborate on this point.

Sources not addressed to the general public paint a different picture. According to the journal of the Herrnhut congregation, at least during the early years sisters spoke at communal services when women were confirmed and received as new members of the congregation. A mentoring sister gave an address testifying to the spiritual life of the candidate and admonishing her to remain faithful. Then the eldress of the sisters offered up a prayer of dedication.[27] Similarly, women in leading positions prayed publicly at the installation of sisters into ministerial offices, performed the ordination of sisters, and pronounced blessings on the birth of a girl or the death of a sister.[28] Thus, although the sisters evidently did not preach, they did speak occasionally in communal worship.[29]

There are some indications that occasionally a sister gave testimony of her faith in a gathering of men and women outside of worship. Anna Dober, for example, wrote in her diary of talking to brothers and sisters about the Saviour. On February 22, 1737, she writes: "I spoke with my sisters about the blessedness of those who have put on the coat of Christ's righteousness." Then in December she mentions that the occasional coming of people had provided her with some opportunities for "witnessing of our Saviour." In May 1738, she notes: "On the tenth in the evening, I spoke in a group of people, who had come to visit us, of the blessed fellowship we can have in Christ Jesus and with one another."[30]

Apparently Anna Dober was not timid about conversing on religious matters even in the presence of men, and other Moravian sisters probably felt and acted likewise. Genuine preaching by sisters, however, seems to have occurred only when women were among themselves in the choirs. About this practice, Zinzendorf remarked in 1755:

> In a living congregation it is required for a sound discourse, which one could call a choir homily, that foremost one would hear some brethren speaking to their choir who speak out of their own experience. This is the reason why I persistently advocated, as long as it was even possible, that in all choirs members of the same kind should hold the choir addresses. This [rule] I have extended so far that in some congregations I have let no one else deliver addresses to the single sisters except some of them themselves. Not so much

that this [practice] was proper, but also that the aim was reached and not merely pious talks were given but conversations to the heart and soul of the members which were coming out of an inner experience.[31]

This passage suggests that the delivery of the choir homily by a sister was an occasional practice, fully in line with the Moravian idea that people of the same gender and social group who shared similar experiences should minister to each other. Yet, the Moravians were not fully consistent in this regard. More often than not, trustworthy brothers presided over worship in the female choirs, delivering addresses and holding liturgies.[32] In turn, numerous entries in the journals of the congregations and sisters' choirs suggest that the heads of the female choirs, especially of the Single Sisters' Choir, preached and spoke repeatedly within their choirs.[33] A report of the festival day of the single sisters at Herrnhut from 1755, for example, mentions the speaking of Anna Nitschmann (1715–60), the most prominent leader of the Moravian sisters, who was affectionately called "Mother" by many: "At 7 o'clock our choir gathered in our prayer hall for a morning meditation. Our dear Mother spoke devoutly and emphatically of the virgins' covenant, which she, together with seventeen others of her companions, had made twenty-five years ago, and for which the Saviour since then had used such a large number, and also us."[34]

Four years later, Anna Nitschmann spoke at the Single Sisters' festival day at Zeist in the Netherlands. Her address was recorded in indirect speech. Reflecting on the twenty-ninth anniversary of the formation of the Single Sisters' covenant, she addressed the apparently difficult situation of the Single Sisters' Choir at Zeist:

> The Bridegroom has thoughts of peace about us. He cannot, however, rejoice over us as much as He would like. We are still a good portion removed from the whole and so far behind that we must therefore bow and feel ashamed. Yet this day should really be a day of joy, and we also have, if we think about how much He has done for us, more reason to rejoice than to grieve. All the more it makes us ashamed and humble that we are still not yet whole, both in tenderness toward Him and in the grace of the choir. Thus, each could be much more attached to His person, much more accustomed to the odor of His blood and in love with His martyred figure, and also the blessedness of the choir could be more enjoyed.[35]

Sometimes a sister, rather than preaching herself, read a sermon written by Zinzendorf or another leading brother.[36] In sum, it seems that female preaching occurred, yet as the exception rather than the rule.

This account of the sisters' participation in the congregational discourse of the Moravian movement would be incomplete without reference to their writings, which often recorded personal experiences and were sometimes read publicly at community gatherings, thus functioning in many ways like preaching. Both men and women were encouraged to write hymns for use in worship and for special occasions. In the 1740s, so-called *Poeten-Liebesmahle* ("poets' love feasts") took place; they were sociable competitions in which the participants, brothers and sisters alike, individually composed hymns to a common theme, which were afterward sung and discussed.[37] Much of the sisters' poetry, created at these and other occasions, was incorporated into the hymnody of the Moravian movement. The *Herrnhuter Gesangbuch* of 1735 with its twelve appendixes (1735–47) contains the hymns of thirty-five female authors (about 11 percent of the total of 312 authors), of whom twenty-three belonged to the Moravian movement.[38] The sisters also wrote the official journals of the sisters' choirs, sometimes kept personal diaries, and occasionally were in charge of recording communal events.[39] Finally, beginning in the 1750s Moravian women and men took up the custom of writing the autobiographical *Lebenslauf*, whose purpose was to record, as it were, the continuation of the Acts of the Apostles in the life of each believer; after his or her death it was read aloud at the public funeral service as a final testimony and "fare well."[40] Thus, in writing her *Lebenslauf* a Moravian sister would contribute in anticipatory fashion to the congregational discourse and would, if only indirectly, make her voice heard in the community one final time.[41]

THE QUESTION OF SCRIPTURAL INTERPRETATION

This survey of female participation in Moravian congregational discourse reveals the variety of ways in which women appeared as religious leaders and speakers, and it also sheds light on some of the inconsistencies in the status of women within the Moravian movement. Despite the egalitarian ethos of the Moravians, reflected in the symmetrical organization of the congregations, the sisters did not preach in the communal services as the brothers did. However, the sisters did speak and preach in their own choirs, even though the New Testament, the basis of Moravian communal order, contained passages explicitly prohibiting the speaking of women in the church. It appears that the Moravians were caught between two conflicting tendencies: one affirming and one opposing the voice of women within the community. For Zinzendorf and the Moravians, the task of defining and defending their own position in the midst of this tension involved a great deal of reflection about Scripture and its proper interpretation.

The inclusion of women in congregational discourse challenged the Moravian community to justify female speaking against Paul's order that women should keep silence within the churches. How could the Scripture-based communal order of the Moravian community accommodate the voices of the sisters in light of these passages? And how could it be shown to adversaries that there was no violation of Scripture in light of the sisters' activities as speakers and leaders? Although the spiritual authority of the Bible was beyond all doubt for the Moravians, they ventured to reinterpret Scripture on the basis of their own theological presuppositions and with close attention to the original languages and historical context. The resulting reading and synthesizing of scriptural passages concerning the speaking of women was not without wit and sophistication.

The earliest pertinent comments date from 1734, when Zinzendorf and some scholarly assistants produced an annotated translation of several New Testament books, including 1 Corinthians and 1 Timothy.[42] Here, 1 Timothy 2:12 is explained with reference to Titus 2:3. Although women are generally prohibited from teaching in the midst of the congregation by rising up and expressing their opinions, they are capable of teaching and "may teach themselves amongst each other."[43] For 1 Corinthians 14:34, "let your women keep silence in the churches," the comment reads:

> From this it cannot be inferred that women could not be used in the congregation, for previously that has been explicitly stated in 11:5. The passage here deals only with the regular and general teaching when the whole congregation is together. And yet there might occur circumstances in which even in this setting a woman could and had to serve the congregation with her gifts.[44]

With these notes, Zinzendorf and his colleagues upheld the validity of Paul's injunction in general terms, conceding, however, that there could be exceptions. They recognized that women had teaching abilities and were needed with their gifts in the congregation, and they admitted the possibility for women to teach each other and, in certain circumstances, also to teach the assembled congregation. Unfortunately, we are not told what those circumstances were.

Further reflection on the subject was prompted when Zinzendorf and the Moravians came to know the practice of female preaching in Quaker meetings. According to his diary, Zinzendorf met a female Quaker preacher in Amsterdam in 1736, and he also might have encountered preaching Quaker women during his first trip to England in the following year.[45] Thus, when during a discussion of Quakerism at a Moravian synod in 1740 it was mentioned that the Quakers believe "that women may preach if the Saviour directs them to," Zinzendorf replied:

> Oh Yes! If the Saviour commands them, I have nothing against it. The Bible only says that the matrons should not teach, thus the maidens may well do it. To the matrons the teaching is forbidden for the very reason that the husbands do not become jealous if they are ignorant. The Apostle also adds a reason, namely that the women have naturally not the soundness of the men, even if

it would appear so, and that it therefore would be good if they kept silence in the congregation. Yet, he would be in the wrong, if he had forbidden it to all. Peter says: I will pour out my Spirit over all flesh, sons and daughters, manservants and maidservants, and the maidens shall have visions. If the women should not teach, this surely would not have come true.[46]

Although this statement does not refer directly to the speaking of Moravian women, its positive evaluation of the practice of female preaching among the Quakers seems to indicate a growing willingness on the part of Zinzendorf and the Moravians to acknowledge the possibility of female preaching in principle, if not in practice. To be sure, Zinzendorf remained critical of female Quaker preaching, regarding the predominance of women preachers as an "excess" and suspecting that some unmarried women felt compelled to become preachers only in order to make a good match.[47] Yet, it can be assumed that the Quaker connection between speaking and inner experience, as well as the resulting notion that all are equally entitled to bear witness when moved by the spirit, resonated well with the spirituality of the Moravian movement. Possibly, the example of the Quakers prompted Zinzendorf and the Moravians to look at female preaching more positively and to think more critically about the scriptural prohibitions of women's speaking. At any rate, it appears that from the time of the encounter with the Quakers the evolving Moravian exegesis of 1 Corinthians 14:34 and 1 Timothy 2:12 was less bound to the traditional interpretation and more accommodating toward the practice of female speaking within the community.

A case in point is the *Manual of Doctrine* of 1742, a booklet consisting of about 1,700 doctrinal questions answered by citations from the Bible.[48] Compiled by Zinzendorf as a tentative synopsis of Moravian theology, it includes a section on the preaching of women, beginning with question 1226: "What did the Apostles [in] some way subjoin, when they spoke of Particulars which were not for all?" The answer reads, "Your Church, You, &c.," and it is illustrated first with the singularity of the Philippian church (Phil. 4:15, 2 Cor. 11:8) and then with Paul's well-known command to the Corinthians to let their women keep silence. The examples of Priscilla (Acts 18:26), Phoebe (Rom. 16:1), and Tryphaena, Tryphosa, and Persis (Rom. 16:12) establish that Paul's prohibition of female speaking is indeed specific, rather than universal. The text then continues:

[Question 1229:] Have we also an Instance of Women's speaking in publick?
[Answer:] As the Women also at Jerusalem were filled with the Holy Ghost, and spake with new Tongues, Peter said: This is that which was spoken by Joel, On my Handmaidens I will pour out my Spirit, and they shall prophesy. Acts i, 14. ch. ii. 4, 17, 18
[Question 1230:] Did even the Corinthian Women prophesy?

> *[Answer:]* Paul saith: It is a Shame for a Woman, when she prophesieth with her Head uncovered. I Cor. xi.5.[49]

With this argument, the exclusive validity of 1 Corinthians 14:34 is overtly called into question. In comparison with the traditional interpretation, the message intimated by questions 1126–30 seems almost subversive.

Although the *Manual of Doctrine* represented merely a preliminary proposition without official authority, it may have signaled to the Moravians the possibility of greater openness toward female speaking. To their opponents, however, it showed the increasing danger of the Moravian movement to the ecclesiastical institution.[50] In Bern, Switzerland, where the Moravians had begun to gather supporters in 1738, an ambitious professor of theology, Johann Georg Altmann (1695–1758), immediately responded to the German edition of the *Manual of Doctrine* with the publication of a scholarly rebuke entitled *Disquisitio Philologico-Critica, Ad illustranda Loca I. Cor. XIV. 34, I. Tim. II. 12, Actor. XVIII. 26, Rom. XVI. 1. et 12.*[51] Charging that the Moravian exegesis of the passages in question was guided by inappropriate motives, namely, their interest in justifying female teaching rather than searching for the unbiased truth, Altmann proceeded to assert that the mandate of 1 Corinthians 14:34 and 2 Timothy 2:12 was a general one and that the alleged scriptural proofs of female teaching (Rom. 14:1.12, Acts 2:17, 1 Cor. 11:4) were erroneous. In conclusion he pointed out that the Moravian doctrine of female teaching amounted to nothing less than Montanism.[52] Zinzendorf was quick to reject Altmann's attack. In a letter to Altmann's superior he denied that the Moravians were instituting the practice of female preaching in their congregations, while insisting that his scriptural interpretation in support of female preaching was sound.[53]

Manuscript sources from the years after the controversy with Altmann indicate that Zinzendorf increasingly questioned the validity of 1 Corinthians 14:34 and 1 Timothy 2:12. With creative ingenuity, he found again and again new arguments against the universal authority of Paul's prohibition of female speaking in the church. Besides the above-mentioned notions that women may teach women and that 1 Corinthians 14:34 applied only to the Corinthian women, Zinzendorf used three other lines of reasoning.

First, Zinzendorf suspects that Paul's injunction refers only to married women—since they are advised to ask their husbands at home (1 Cor. 14:35)—not to single women and widows.[54] Second, Zinzendorf argues that Paul's injunction can be superseded by a divine command, especially in the case of prophecy. In 1745 he points out that Paul himself presupposes that women are not excluded from prophesying since he says "a woman who prophesies shall cover her head" (1 Cor. 11:5). "Teaching" and "prophesying" are different in that women "may witness as much as the Saviour gives them grace to it, but they should not dogmatize."[55] Furthermore, Zinzendorf repeatedly emphasizes that, according to Acts 2:17–18, in the "last days," when the Holy Spirit is poured out, "daughters" and "handmaidens" shall prophesy. In 1747, he recalls specifically that it was not only the twelve apostles who received the Holy Spirit, but the whole group of 120 believers "who sat among the apostles and the mother of the Lord" (see Acts 1:15), and that therefore at Pentecost "an equality with regard to the teaching office between these sisters and brothers" was established and both male and female believers alike were spiritually consecrated for "their future apostolic office."[56] This linking of female preaching and prophecy with eschatology and pneumatology corresponded to the overall orientation of Moravian spirituality. Slightly millennialistic, the Moravians, not unlike other pietistic groups, were likely to admit the prophesying of women as a sign of the "last days." The appropriateness of spirit-filled female speaking was further supported by the image of the Holy Spirit as "Mother," which had come into use around 1742 and denoted the comforting and instructing role of the Holy Spirit within the Trinity, conceived of as "the Divine Family."[57] Thus conceptualized, the Spirit provided both impetus for and sanction of female speaking and perhaps even represented a divine role model for the sisters in their ministry.

Finally, Zinzendorf argues against Paul's injunction on the basis that Jesus himself had instituted the equality of men and women. Addressing the issue of the apparent subordination of women by the apostles, he says in 1756: The apostles "knew what reasons they had for their conduct: they were called out of the Jews. We poor gentiles have the basic plan, that we act precisely like the Saviour, who chose us. After him, we work toward the equality of brothers and sisters."[58]

Aware of the subordination of women in ancient Judaism, Zinzendorf believes that through the incarnation, ministry, and teaching of Jesus the equality of women has been restored. Noting the absence of female priests and Levites in the Old Testament and stating that there "a woman who spoke with God" is always something extraordinary, he points out: "The dear Saviour has intervened in this rule [and] has disclosed himself to a good number of sisters, even more than before to the brothers; yes, he has used them as evangelists to the brothers, particularly after his resurrection."[59]

Although the apostles themselves have not entirely overcome the "accustomed *praejudicium*," as is evident in Paul's prohibition of female speaking, Zinzendorf is certain that the fundamental vision of Christ and the Gospel is one of equality:

> The proof is clear enough in Paul's words: in Christ there is neither male nor female. There, the difference of the sexes as regards the privilege to spiritual

things is completely abolished; before Him they appear as the same. Because of this principle, the sisters can also teach in the congregation, and it is quite probable that they have taught in the earliest church, since Paul made an order for it and said how they should be dressed in doing so.[60]

Thus, Zinzendorf's ability to discern opposing tendencies in Scripture enabled him to put Paul's prohibition of women's speaking into a larger perspective, thereby relativizing its authority.

Zinzendorf's continuing endeavor to reinterpret 1 Corinthians 14:34 and 1 Timothy 2:12 shows how seriously he took the issue of female preaching. Although his exegesis always maintained Scripture as its basis, it changed considerably over the years, diverging increasingly from the official Protestant teachings and becoming more and more favorable to female speaking. His later statements affirm repeatedly that women should teach women and that their speaking within the whole congregation might be possible in special cases. We can safely assume that this position corresponded to the symmetrical structure and the inclusion of women in congregational discourse in the Moravian movement. In 1757, three years before his death, Zinzendorf explicitly acknowledged the relevance of the exegesis of 1 Corinthians 14:34 to the practice of female speaking in the Moravian community and showed regret that for reasons of caution the gift of the sisters' voice had not fully been welcomed. Pointing out that the injunction for women to keep silent in the church had been applied in most churches in the general sense, he said:

> In order to avoid strife with others, we have followed the other denominations and have thrown out the baby with the bath water. The phrase, however, is wrong and against the Holy Scriptures. It has been a disorder that the motherly office of the Holy Spirit has been disclosed to the sisters not through a sister but through me. . . . Since the sisters ceased to speak in the place where they are supposed to, a jewel has been lost and the female affairs among us do not stand anymore under the blessing as before. It is odd, when the Holy Spirit says: your daughters shall prophesy, that we say: they shall not prophesy.[61]

CONCLUSION

The preceding discussion has provided an overview of the extent and the limitations of women's participation in congregational discourse in the Moravian movement between 1722 and 1760. According to the available evidence, the sisters spoke at community gatherings and preached or taught occasionally within their own choirs. They did not, however, preach to the whole community. These findings may appear modest in the eyes of a contemporary beholder. Yet, in the context of eighteenth-century Protestantism, the Moravian practice, embedded in a distinct spirituality and communal organization, was radical and virtually unique. Even though Moravian sisters did not speak and preach in the same way that the brothers did, their voices were heard and valued within the community, and the traditional code of keeping silence was broken.

The emergence of women as active participants in congregational discourse coincided with significant changes in the understanding of "preaching" and "church." The Moravians, seeing themselves as a congregation (*Gemeine*) of committed believers rather than as a church in the territorial and institutional sense, widened the traditional notion of preaching as doctrinal teaching and moral exhortation to include a variety of forms of religious speaking. There was, in other words, a shift from the one-directional churchly preaching of the ordained clergy person to the dialogical congregational discourse of the whole community. The privilege of religious speaking was extended to all members, decisively affecting the life of each individual and the organization as a whole.

When we consider what it means to speak or to keep silence within a community, we must note that speaking signifies, first of all, power and agency. Only those with a voice can actively participate in the communal interplay of power and decision making. In addition, speaking is a means of self-expression. The ability to articulate one's experience within a community signifies the recognition and validation of one's experience, and hence of oneself, through the community. In the Moravian movement, the inclusion of the sisters in congregational discourse, even if it seldom involved preaching in the traditional sense, meant that women held some power in the community, especially with regard to the affairs of the female choirs, and that their experiences were recognized. That power, however limited, and the possibility to make their voices heard lend significance to the Moravian practice of women's speaking in the history of female preaching.

It was not an Enlightenment understanding of human equality but a deeply religious, biblical vision of human community and a particular receptiveness to spiritual experience that opened up the possibility for women to speak, to preach, and to teach within the Moravian *Gemeine,* and it seems ironic that the driving force behind this development was a male aristocrat, Count Zinzendorf. After his death in 1760, the trend toward female equality reversed. The Unity synods of 1764 and 1769 restricted the participation of women in congregational leadership and instituted male administrators for the female choirs. Soon it again became unthinkable that a woman would not keep silence in communal worship. The original impulse toward the speaking of women, however, was not entirely lost. The sisters maintained their traditional roles in the choirs and continued the tradition of writing the *Lebenslauf;* and possibly their example left its imprint on Friedrich Schleiermacher, reared in Moravian boarding schools from 1783 to 1787, who acknowledged in his early writings, notably in *Die Weihnachtsfeier* (1806), that women indeed had a voice for themselves.[62]

NOTES

1. For a history of the Moravian movement, see Kenneth G. Hamilton and J. Taylor Hamilton, *History of the Moravian Church: The Renewed Unitas Fratrum 1722–1957* (Bethlehem, Penn.: Moravian Church in America, 1967); and Hans-Christoph Hahn and Hellmut Reichel, eds., *Zinzendorf und die Herrnhuter Brüder: Quellen zur Geschichte der Brüder-Unität von 1722 bis 1760* (Hamburg: Wittig, 1977). The standard bibliographical aide for Zinzendorf and the Moravians is Dietrich Meyer, ed., *Bibliographisches Handbuch zur Zinzendorf-Forschung* (Düsseldorf: Blech, 1987), hereafter abbreviated *BHZF*. Many of Zinzendorf's writings are available in a reprint edition: Erich Beyreuther and Gerhard Meyer, eds., *Nikolaus Ludwig von Zinzendorf: Hauptschriften in sechs Bänden*, 6 vols. (Hildesheim: Olms, 1962–63); and *Nikolaus Ludwig von Zinzendorf: Ergänzungsbände zu den Hauptschriften*, 16 vols. (Hildesheim: Olms, 1966–78), hereafter abbreviated *HS* and *EB*, respectively. This study would have been impossible without the friendly assistance of the staff at the Unity Archives at Herrnhut, Germany, and at the Moravian Archives in Bethlehem, Pennsylvania, whose help I gratefully acknowledge. I also would like to thank my wife, Jill, as well as Heinz Burkhardt, Colin Podmore, Katherine Faull, Paul Peucker, Edward Roslof, and Beverly Smaby for their help and advice. Unless stated otherwise, all of the translations of foreign-language passages are mine.

2. See Hans Joachim Wollstadt, *Geordnetes Dienen in der Christlichen Gemeinde: dargestellt an den Lebensformen der Herrnhuter Brüdergemeine in ihren Anfängen* (Göttingen: Vandenhoek and Ruprecht, 1966), pp. 41–47.

3. On the history of women in the eighteenth-century Moravian movement, see Otto Uttendörfer, *Zinzendorf und die Frauen: Kirchliche Frauenrechte vor 200 Jahren* (Herrnhut: Missionsbuchhandlung, 1919); and Hahn and Reichel, *Zinzendorf*, pp. 292–95.

4. See Hahn and Reichel, *Zinzendorf*, pp. 312–19; Peter Zimmerling, *Gott in Gemeinschaft: Zinzendorfs Trinitätslehre* (Gießen: Brunnen, 1991), pp. 228–35.

5. *Gemeinreden* (1748, *BHZF* A 181) in *HS*, vol. 4, part 2, p. 311.

6. Ibid., part 1, pp. 88–89.

7. On the choir system, see Wollstadt, *Geordnetes Dienen*, pp. 104–13; and Hahn and Reichel, *Zinzendorf*, pp. 250–58.

8. See Beverly Smaby, "Forming the Single Sisters' Choir in Bethlehem," *Transactions of the Moravian Historical Society* 28 (1994): 1–14.

9. See Wollstadt, *Geordnetes Dienen*, pp. 209–22; Kay Ward, "The Pastoral Role of Women in the Bethlehem Settlement," *The Moravian Historian: Newsletter of the Moravian Historical Society* 3 (1987).

10. See Peter Vogt, "The Shakers and the Moravians: A Comparison of the Structure and the Architecture of their Settlements," *Shaker Quarterly* 21 (1993): 79–97.

11. See Wollstadt, *Geordnetes Dienen*, pp. 130–33.

12. See Bevery P. Smaby, "Female Piety among Eighteenth-Century Moravians" (unpublished paper, Clarion University, 1995).

13. See Uttendörfer, *Frauen*, pp. 28–35.

14. See Wollstadt, *Geordnetes Dienen*, pp. 346–48; Uttendörfer, *Frauen*, p. 29; and Vernon H. Nelson, "Ordination in the Moravian Church in America, 1736–1790" (unpublished paper, Moravian Archives, Bethlehem, Penn., 1996).

15. Hahn and Reichel, *Zinzendorf*, p. 218.

16. Ibid., pp. 68–92.

17. About Moravian worship, see Otto Uttendörfer, *Zinzendorfs Gedanken über den Gottesdienst* (Herrnhut: Winter, 1931).

18. Ibid., p.25.

19. See Wollstadt, *Geordnetes Dienen*, pp. 173–79.

20. See Uttendörfer, *Frauen*, pp. 31, 33.

21. *Theologisches Bedencken*, 2d ed. (1749, *BHZF* B 220.2); reprinted in *Antizinzendorfiana*, ed. Erich Beyreuther, Gerhard Meyer, and Amadeo Molnar, 5 vols. (Hildesheim: Olms, 1976–82), vol. 3, p. 130.

22. Ibid., pp.130–32.

23. See Carl Regent, *Unparteyische Nachricht* (1729, *BHZF* B 3), in *Antizinzendorfiana*, vol. 1, pp. 96–97; Ernst Salomon Cyprian, "Letztes Votum" (1748), in *Antizinzendorfiana*, vol. 2, p. 280; Joachim Lange, "Väterliche Warnung" (1744, *BHZF* B 160), in *Antizinzendorfiana*, vol. 3, pp. 502–3; Johann Gottlob Carpzov, *Religionsuntersuchung* (1742, *BHZF* B 116), pp. 588–89; Georg Jacob Sutor, "Licht und Wahrheit," in Johann Philipp Fresenius, *Bewährte Nachrichten* (1746–51, *BHZF* B 201), vol. 1, p. 681; Johann Georg Schützen, *Herrnhutianismus in Nuce* (1750, *BHZF* B 300), pp. 594–95.

24. See *Freywillige Nachlese* (1735–40, *BHZF* A 123), in *EB*, vol. 11, p. 765; *Büdingische Sammlung*, vol. 1 (1740–42, *BHZF* A 146), in *EB*, vol. 7, pp. 775–80; August Gottlieb Spangenberg, *Apologetische Schluß-Schrifft* (1752, *BHZF* B 350), in *EB*, vol. 3, p. 211.

25. *Büdingische Sammlung*, vol. 1 (*EB*, vol. 7), p. 49.

26. *Theologische Bedencken* (1742, *BHZF* A 120.3), in *EB*, vol. 4, p. 171.

27. See Uttendörfer, *Frauen*, pp. 22, 30–31; Wollstadt, *Geordnetes Dienen*, p. 215.

28. See Uttendörfer, *Frauen*, pp. 30–31; Wollstadt, *Geordnetes Dienen*, p. 346; Smaby, "Female Piety," p. 8.

29. Uttendörfer cites one instance of public preaching by a Moravian sister, Catharina Freymann, who addressed large crowds in Norway in the 1730s (Uttendörfer, *Frauen*, p. 27; see also Hahn and Reichel, *Zinzendorf*, p. 295). Recently, however, it was shown that Freymann's preaching took place before she joined the Moravians; see Katharina Rühe, "Catharina Maria Freymann: Eine Schwester der Brüdergemeine im 18. Jahrhundert" (thesis, Unity Archives, Herrnhut, 1989).

30. "Etwas aus dem Diarium der Anna Dober, geb. Schindler," *Der Brüder-Bote* 11 (1883): 273–76.

31. *Jüngerhausdiarium* (Moravian Archives at Königsfeld, Germany), July 17, 1755; cf. Uttendörfer, *Frauen*, p. 55.

32. See Uttendörfer, *Frauen*, pp. 14, 56; Hahn and Reichel, *Zinzendorf*, p. 295.

33. See Otto Uttendörfer, *Altherrnhut: Wirtschaftsgeschichte und Religionssoziologie Herrnhuts während seiner ersten zwanzig Jahre (1722–42)* (Herrnhut: Winter, 1925), pp. 250, 256–57; *Frauen*, p. 31; Smaby, "Female Piety," p. 8.

34. *Jüngerhausdiarium* (Moravian Unity Archives at Herrnhut, Germany), June 6, 1755.

35. Ibid., May 4, 1759.

36. See Smaby, "Female Piety," p. 8.

37. See Hans-Walter Erbe, *Herrnhaag: Eine religiöse Kommunität im 18. Jahrhundert* (Hamburg: Wittig, 1988), pp. 84–87.

38. *BHZF* A 505 (reprint, Hildesheim: Olms, 1981). The third volume of the reprint edition contains a helpful index of authors compiled by Gudrun Meyer.

39. For a fine example of such a journal, see Aaron S. Fogleman, "Women on the Trail in Colonial America: A Travel Journal of German Moravians Migrating from Pennsylvania to North Carolina in 1766," *Pennsylvania History* 61, no. 2 (1994): 206–34; published in German in *Pietismus und Neuzeit* 19 (1993): 98–116.

40. See Hellmut Reichel, "Ein Spiegel der Frömmigkeit und des geistlichen Lebens: Zur Geschichte des brüderischen Lebenslaufes," *Brüderbote*, no. 464 (March 1988): 4–7; Katherine Faull, "The American *Lebenslauf*: Women's Autobiography in Eighteenth Century Moravian Bethlehem," *Yearbook of German American Studies* 27 (1992): 23–48.

41. For examples of such memoirs, see Katharine M. Faull, *Moravian Women's Memoirs: Their Related Lives, 1750–1820* (Syracuse, N.Y.: Syracuse University Press, 1997).

42. See August Gottlieb Spangenberg, *Leben des Herrn Nicolaus Ludwig Grafen und Herrn von Zinzendorf und Pottendorf* (Barby: 1773–75; reprint, Hildesheim: Olms, 1971), pp. 873–75.

43. *Freywillige Nachlese* (*EB*, vol. 11), p. 37.

44. *Büdingische Sammlung*, vol. 1 (*EB*, vol. 7), p. 550.

45. Paul M. Peucker, "Das Diarium von Nikolaus Ludwig Graf von Zinzendorf, geschrieben während seiner Reise durch die Niederlande," *Nederlands Archief voor Kerksgeschiedenis* 74 (1994): 104–5. See also Spangenberg, *Leben Zinzendorfs*, pp. 1042–44. In 1742 Zinzendorf witnessed the preaching of a Quaker woman at an interdenominational gathering in Pennsylvania; see *Pennsylvanische Nachrichten* (1742, *BHZF* A 159), in *HS*, vol. 2, p. 108.

46. Document R2a.43b, II (26) at Unity Archives, Herrnhut; cf. Uttendörfer, *Frauen*, p. 49.

47. Uttendörfer, *Frauen*, pp. 49, 53.

48. *Manual of Doctrine* (London: James Hutton, 1742); *BHZF* A 140.E. This is the translation of *Andere Probe [eines Lehrbüchelchens]* (1742, *BHZF* A 140.2).

49. *Manual of Doctrine*, pp. 194–95.

50. See Christian Moritz Kromayer, *Genaue Untersuchung* (1742, *BHZF* B 110), pp. 221–25; and Johann Gottlob Carpzov, *Religionsuntersuchungen* (1742, *BHZF* B 116), pp. 588–89.

51. *BHZF* B 72; reprinted in the journal *Tempe Helvetica* 5 (1741–42): 430–59. I am indebted to Mrs. Mary Tipton at the Library of the University of Wisconsin for making this rare publication available to me.

52. See Rudolf Dellsperger, "Frauenemanzipation im Pietismus," in *Zwischen Macht und Dienst: Beiträge zur Geschichte und Gegenwart von Frauen im kirchlichen Leben der Schweiz,* ed. Sophia Bietenhard et al. (Bern: Stämpfli, 1991), pp. 131–52.

53. See *EB*, vol. 7, pp. 775–80; Spangenberg, *Leben Zinzendorfs*, p. 1330.

54. See Zinzendorf's statement on female Quaker preachers in the text at note 46 and Uttendörfer, *Frauen*, p. 57.

55. Uttendörfer, *Frauen*, pp. 51–52.

56. *Gemeinreden* (*HS*, vol. 4), part 2, p. 70. See also notes 46, 49, and 61.

57. See Matthias Meyer, "Das 'Mutter-Amt' des Heiligen Geistes in der Theologie Zinzendorfs," *Evangelische Theologie* 43 (1983): 415–29; Gary Kinkel, *Our Dear Mother the Spirit: An Investigation of Count Zinzendorf's Theology and Praxis* (Lanham, Md.: University Press of America, 1990); Craig D. Atwood, "The Mother of All Souls: Zinzendorf's Doctrine of the Holy Spirit," *Koinonia* 4 (1992): 106–36.

58. Uttendörfer, *Frauen*, p. 45.

59. Ibid., pp. 44–45.

60. Ibid., pp. 56–57.

61. Ibid., pp. 58–59; see also Hahn and Reichel, *Zinzendorf*, p. 293.

62. See Ruth Richardson, *The Role of Women in the Life and Thought of the Early Schleiermacher (1768–1806): An Historical Overview* (Lewiston, N.Y.: Edwin Mellen Press, 1991), pp. 36–42, 105–9, 149–64.

THIRTEEN

In a Female Voice

Preaching and Politics
in Eighteenth-Century British Quakerism

Phyllis Mack

A small garden well cultivated, produces abundance. The earth, like the human mind, generally pays well for proper cultivation.
                    HANNAH BARNARD[1]

During his visit to England in 1726–29, Voltaire made the acquaintance of a retired Quaker merchant who received and entertained him in his simple country house.

> The Quaker was a hale and hearty old man who had never been ill because he had never known passions or intemperance; never in my life have I seen a more dignified or more charming manner than his. . . . He kept his hat on while receiving me and moved toward me without even the slightest bow, but there was more politeness in the frank, kindly expression on his face than there is in the custom of placing one leg behind the other and holding in one's hand what is meant for covering one's head.[2]

Voltaire admired the man's estate (comfortable but not luxurious), his contempt for the superstitions of Catholics and Jews, and his pacifism, which, in Voltaire's rendition, was expressed with the naive wit of a character in *Candide:* "Our god . . . undoubtedly does not wish us to cross the sea to go and slaughter our brothers just because some murderers dressed in red . . . enroll citizens by making a noise with two little sticks on tightly stretched ass's skin."[3] So the Quaker took his place alongside the Incas, Tahitians, and other exotics who provided the philosophes with a mouthpiece for debunking their own corrupt society.

Voltaire was clearly impressed by the Quakers, but he was also bemused by the coexistence of rational piety and good common sense with certain curious and irrational customs, particularly their mode of worship:

> Eventually one of them rose, doffed his hat, and after making a few faces and fetching a few sighs he recited, half through his mouth and half through his nose, a rigmarole taken from the Gospels, or so he believed, of which neither

he nor anyone else understood a word. . . . "We even let women speak [he said].
Two or three of our devout women often become inspired at the same time,
and then there is a fine old rumpus in the House of the Lord."[4]

Eighteenth-century Quakers (or Friends, as they called themselves) were
indeed a peculiar people. As social reformers and innovators in science, education, medicine, and mental health, they seemed to be breathing the clear
air of the Enlightenment. Dr. John Fothergill, for one, was an experimental
gardener, member of the Royal Society, humanitarian, and friend of Ben-
jamin Franklin.[5] Yet these same Quakers were also quietists striving for self-
transcendence, mystical insight, and radical pacifism, all of which isolated
them from the social and political worlds of their contemporaries. From the
middle years of the century onward, Quakers also subjected themselves to a
system of discipline that seemed to give them no air to breathe at all. "How
safe is diffidence," wrote John Fothergill's brother Samuel, an eminent minister, "even if obtained through chastisement for error!"[6]

Eighteenth-century Quaker women present us with a similar enigma. On
the one hand they lost power. Women prophets no longer chastised magistrates and monarchs in the public arena, and "mothers in Israel" no longer
had the right to attend important business meetings or hold their own Yearly
Meeting.[7] Constantly mindful of the need for respectability and virtue, women
ministers seem to have been launched on a familiar trajectory from political activist to domestic parasite. Certainly they had no conception of the transformative sexual practices or celebration of cosmic motherhood invoked by
working-class messiahs like Ann Lee or Joanna Southcott.[8]

Yet if we look for the origins of modern social reform movements—women's
suffrage, abolition of slavery, peace activism—we find Quaker preachers speaking out on matters of economics, slavery, the rights of women, and pacifism,
and they did so not only as instruments of divine authority but also as women.
Thus the new strictures on women's authority and women's own changing
self-definition worked both to limit their conception of appropriate public
behavior and to enhance their capacity for public speech in their own voices.

This said, it is not at all clear how Quaker values affected either women's
spirituality or their political thinking. Ann Braude, the historian of American spiritualism, argues that nineteenth-century feminists were *disaffected*
Quakers.[9] The most free-thinking woman preacher, Hannah Barnard, was
condemned by Friends in 1801 and consorted with Unitarians. London male
Friends refused to let women have their own Yearly Meeting for nearly the
whole eighteenth century, and they refused to let women attend the London meeting for Sufferings until the late nineteenth century. How, then, did
Quakerism help, and hinder, women's spiritual authority and public activism?
And what was the specific gendered identity of those Friends who wrote and
spoke about public issues in a female voice?

QUIETISTS AND CAPITALISTS

Seventeenth-century Friends were farmers, artisans, shopowners, housewives, and servants, mainly from the remote northern counties of Yorkshire and Lancashire. Generated in part by the conflicts of the civil war period, including the suspension of censorship, Quakerism was an egalitarian movement whose adherents affirmed the existence of an inner, divine light in every human being, regardless of class, status, or gender. Quakers harangued their listeners in churches, fields, and marketplaces. Some transformed themselves into visual signs of the corruption of church and state by preaching naked or in sackcloth. In meetings for worship, they quaked (hence the name Quaker); they wept, stared, became catatonic, and were even said to defecate. In personal letters men called themselves brides or babies, sucking the milk of the Word from God's womanly breasts; and in public, women spoke with the voices of male Old Testament prophets.[10]

In contrast, eighteenth-century Quakers, living in an atmosphere of relative religious tolerance, were a remarkably prosperous, industrious, and respectable people, engaging in the textile and clothing trades, iron foundries, and the production of domestic ironware, mining, and banking.[11] Alongside this expansion of energy toward trade and manufacture went a spiritual transformation from evangelical prophecy to quietism. Self-transcendence and enlightenment were no longer achieved through the traumatic physical and emotional violence of the early ecstatic, quaking Friends. Instead, eighteenth-century Friends described a more subtle process of introspection or sinking down—a slow erasure of the self—which gradually evolved into a condition of balance and detachment, a sense that the unworthy personality had been permeated by a silent, overwhelming infusion of divine love. Quietism was anti-intellectual but not irrational; indeed soul and mind, spirituality and reason, were defined as allied if not identical concepts, "so far connected in religion, that the Spirit of God can only act upon a reasonable being."[12] Thus Friends adopted and helped shape a discourse of benevolent human action and rational piety, as they became involved in and helped shape new and complicated social and economic relationships.

As a virtuous wife, businesswoman, or preacher, the persona of the ideal female Quaker was a weighty complement to Voltaire's genial host. Their authority, wrote one observer, "produces in them thought, and foresight, and judgment. . . . It elevates their ideas. It raises in them a sense of their own dignity and importance as human beings. . . . Fond as they are of the animal-creation, you do not see them lavishing their caresses on lap-dogs. . . . You never see them driving from shop to shop. . . . [T]heir pursuits are rational, useful, and dignified."[13]

Rational, yet sensitive; chaste (even glacial), yet maternal; competent, yet delicate; these were the stock features of the virtuous Quaker woman found in contemporary plays and magazines. "I think," observed a writer in the *Monthly Magazine*, "that the distinguishing attribute of the sect—equanimity—is . . . discoverable in that undisturbed regularity of features, particularly among the females—the placidity of countenance, . . . an infelt serenity of soul—a deeply charactered composure."[14]

The Quaker woman was symbolic of Quaker values in their undiluted state because the values of quietism itself were feminine values. Modesty, compassion, privacy, domestic order, passivity, "gentle, peaceable wisdom"—long before the advent of the Victorian "angel in the house", these social virtues evolved in the early eighteenth century as attributes not only of women but also of the saintly Quaker man. Thus the busy trader and capitalist was elevated to a higher spiritual plane when he became privatized, retired into his family, transcended class differences by treating his workers and servants as his children, and divested his mind of all aggression and greed.

The problem, of course, was that men's private, "feminine" virtues could not be balanced by a corresponding movement of women into the public sphere, for eighteenth-century Friends were striving for a synthesis of masculine and feminine values in a world where "masculine" and "feminine" were coming to denote two increasingly rigid categories of biology and behavior. Whatever actual work women did as shopkeepers, traders, or farmers, however many miles they traveled as itinerant preachers, their reputation for virtue and honesty required that they deport themselves—both in public and at home—as gracious, sensible wives and daughters. The image of their placid faces and simple Quaker clothes, unsoiled by the grime of politics or industry, was essential to the larger image of Quakerism as both high-minded and of high reputation (and, one suspects, to their husbands' own peace of mind).

The addition of the Victorian pedestal to the Quaker woman's persona did not imply any diminution of respect for women as ministers, moral arbiters, or helpmeets. Hundreds of women received certificates to preach, which entitled them to financial support from their home meetings as well as support for the families they left behind; many other hundreds of women were elders, overseeing the pastoral care of their home meetings; and every woman who married participated in a ceremony that was more egalitarian than any other comparable Christian rite.[15] What the pedestal did imply was the loss of any right to engage in overtly political behavior, whether the politics of the nation or that of the meeting. Unlike the ecstatic political prophets of the seventeenth century, a woman could not act like a man in the public spaces reserved for men alone.

Not surprisingly, male praise of women in public often held a note of anxiety, not about the flamboyant physical gesturing that characterized seventeenth-century female prophets, but about personal and political ambition. For at least one male observer who watched her preach to the students at Oxford, the young Catherine Payton fully embodied the ideal of Quaker womanhood:

> Free, solemn, and distinct her Doctrine flow'd
> Charm'd every Ear, and every Bosom glow'd
> No empty Period, all was sterling sense
> Tinctured with love and pure Benevolence

Still, the minister Samuel Fothergill felt the need to caution his young friend about feminine ministerial decorum: "And, dear Kitty, bear thy testimony . . . by a humble, watchful conduct: be not led . . . out of the leadings of truth, in the appointment of large meetings in *court houses, etc.,* for in this respect, I am sensible there is some danger, unless, really, the very burden of the word be upon thee . . . if [a companion] fall to thy share, let her . . . not . . . hinder thee by any disagreeable demeanour."[16]

Payton became a minister and missionary of some eminence, but her forceful manner—what one male Friend called "a thirst for meddlement"—made the men cower before a bossy woman and criticize her behind her back as a tyrant. James Jenkins wrote in his diary: "I recollect that Catherine [Payton] Phillips like a great Autocratrix, sometimes governed . . . this assembly—to an austerity of conduct that had much the appearance of domination, she added a sourness of temper, that disgraced the woman. . . . She publicly enquired of William Cowles . . . why Thomas Rutter had not also attended that meeting? The answer was, 'he was prevented, by an unexpected pressure of business.' 'Don't tell me (she rejoined) about his being hindered by business, it is not a sufficient excuse—he *ought* to have been here'; William Cowles was intimidated, and made no reply."[17]

Elsewhere, Jenkins criticized Payton for giving advice on a Friend's proposed marriage "from a prudential point of view" rather than one based on "her *feelings* on the subject." According to Jenkins: "In consulting, his appeal was to the high priestess, supposed to possess oracular powers, and therefore frequently under the influence of prophecy, and inspiration. But, she only answered him as a woman, exerciz[ing] her judgment on the expedience, and policy of such a union."[18]

After her death, Jenkins grudgingly acknowledged Payton's eminence in the ministry, describing her for posterity as "rather tall of stature, a wide mouth, with masculine features, and mien, upon the whole, the reverse of that feminine softness, which to our sex is so generally attractive."[19]

WOMEN AND QUIETISM

As Quaker women learned to breathe in a new social and spiritual atmosphere, they also struggled to understand themselves and their mission in an entirely new language; or rather, they struggled to graft a new vocabulary of reason and sensibility onto their original language of Old Testament imagery and bodily signs, to infuse their preaching with a conviction of self-transcendence and divine inspiration while presenting an image of self-control and ladylike restraint. As an adolescent, Catherine Payton described her heart, "which, by reason of its passions and inclinations, might well be compared to an uncultivated wilderness; through which I must travel, and wherein I must receive the law for the ordering of my outward conduct."[20] In her twenties, traveling hundreds of miles on horseback, sleeping near wild animals in the American wilderness in order to preach to isolated Friends, she still worried that revelation and ecstatic prophecy might be merely self-serving. By age thirty, a minister for eight years, she was finally able to envision her own heart as a walled garden: "I believe there is such a state of rectitude and strength to be attained as that we shall not be greatly moved either by outward or inward trials."[21]

Not surprisingly, women's diaries and private letters reveal a degree of anxiety and overt depression that was absent or repressed in the writings of seventeenth-century preachers. From the outside, Mary Peisley appeared as both fanatic and heroic, as her husband remembered after her death: "She stood in great singleness, no relationship either of affinity or consanguinity bribed or stop'd her giving her judgment impartially; neither did the favors or frowns, the riches or exalted stations of any professing membership with her, cramp or obstruct a steady compliance with what she believed to be her duty."[22]

From the inside, however, Peisley experienced an almost unbearable weight of loneliness and self-doubt. "I . . . find myself so exceeding poor that I hardly know what to say to you," she wrote to a girlhood friend. "I feel the stream of communications so dried up towards you, that I can not, I dare not enlarge. . . . [I am] thy poor sincere friend who stands in need of the benefit of the prayers of her friends."[23]

Quaker women's public writing also showed the fissures and inconsistencies that resulted from the effort to recast themselves as both competent and feminine, rational and prophetic. "I hate, I despise your feast-days," wrote Sophia Hume in her Address to Magistrates against the celebration of holidays. "I will not smell your solemn assemblies; your new moons, and your appointed feasts, my soul hateth: your solemn meetings are iniquity." A few pages later her prophetic voice abruptly became rational and deferential: "I hope no reasonable person will take any offence at this plainness of speech to my superiors . . . though it drop from a female pen . . . and were people to lay aside all religious considerations, and only view these evils in a political light, they would see the great disadvantages arising from the observations of *Days* and *Times*." In a single paragraph she argued like an Enlightenment philosophe ("as reasonable, social and benevolent creatures, there is a reciprocal service and joint assistance necessary among men, without which societies or bodies of people could not subsist") and a quietist ("mere men, . . . [their] faculty of reason unenlighten'd and unassisted by a divine power . . . are ignorant and weak").[24] Elsewhere, she strongly asserted the incompatibility of femininity and intellect: "What has our sex to do with mathematics . . . what business have we with the study of the globes, what have we to do with geometry; what with natural or experimental philosophy; what business have women with physics and metaphysics; what business have we with language . . . but to gratify pride, and a vain mind."[25] Yet she described the bliss of salvation to her "fellow citizens" as a "rational pleasure."[26]

We should be wary of dismissing the unevenness of Sophia Hume's discourse as mere muddled thinking, for the Quakers' suspicion of enthusiasm encouraged women to express their convictions calmly and rationally, which in turn threatened to undermine their mandate to speak or write publicly only when immediately commanded by God. When Catherine Payton visited Philadelphia in 1755, the Quakers who were still members of the Pennsylvania Assembly were attempting to reach a compromise whereby they might raise needed funds for the French and Indian Wars and still retain their seats. The ministers of the Philadelphia Yearly Meeting took the position that Friends should resign from government rather than be involved in raising war taxes. Payton proposed that influential Friends arrange an opportunity for her to preach to Assembly members; she was invited to attend and duly testified against war.[27] This was certainly a political act, but it may not have been a visionary or oracular one, done spontaneously under immediate divine commandment. No wonder Payton was defensive about her behavior: "This was no more than consistent with my office as a minister, and my commission to that country, which was to preach Truth and Righteousness, and strengthen the hands of my brethren, against their opposers. Both myself and companion were so clear of improperly intermeddling with the affairs of government, that we . . . but seldom so much as read their newspapers."[28]

IN A FEMALE VOICE

Clearly, the self-perception of these eminent women ministers was far more complex, and far more conflicted, than the seamless feminine icon their audiences admired. Yet by the middle years of the century, women had also begun to articulate a distinctively female voice: one that stressed the importance of feminine virtue and modesty, to be sure, but one that also urged the cultivation of the mind, the unity of all humanity based on universal reason, and the special solidarity of women as both caregivers and victims of male prejudice. The event that galvanized these female voices, giving them a collective and explicitly political dimension, was the campaign for women's meetings that grew out of the movement to reform Quaker discipline in England and America during the 1750s and 1760s.[29] Since the seventeenth century, Quaker women had met alone in small "preparatory meetings" near their homes, in larger Quarterly Meetings, and—in Ireland and America—in an autonomous Yearly Meeting. There they prayed, found apprenticeships for poor Quaker children, collected and dispensed charity, visited the sick, set down their testimonies against the payment of tithes (an act of civil disobedience), and composed epistles to sustain their sisters in England, Ireland, and America.

The reformation of English Quakerism was an effort to revitalize Quaker discipline by regularizing the meeting system. It also aimed to increase family visits to monitor Friends' morality and behavior, require stricter adherence to strictures against marrying outside of the Quaker community, and improve Quaker education. These efforts have always been perceived, by both Friends and outsiders, as a period of decline in the Society of Friends, a substitution of rule for spirit.[30] From the perspective of the eminent Quaker men who dominated the meetings of London and Bristol, this was at least partly true. For these prosperous and sophisticated citizens, disciplinary reform had as much to do with worldly values as with spiritual striving. Their reputation for integrity as Friends was inextricably linked to their reputation for fairness and dependability in business, which in turn was linked to their impeccable (and conventional) social behavior. They thus understood the campaign for greater discipline as a further separation and stratification of men's and women's powers, which they rationalized as a more just and efficient system of jurisdiction.

If men's understanding of the new discipline was a strengthening of Quaker order in harmony with the social order, women's understanding was radically different. They saw a need for autonomous women's meetings at the highest level, in order to disseminate epistles from America and London to the meanest Quaker communities, to galvanize and pass judgment on their lazy or delinquent sisters, and to act as moral helpmeets to the men, even advising them on their own marriages. When the men requested that the women in one meeting sit together with them in worship, the women responded that they wanted to meet separately to increase their opportunity "of giving reasonable advice to those of our own sex on whom depends [a] great part of the education of the youth; and sometimes perhaps straiten our brethren."[31] In Bristol, men wanted women to encourage each other in the ministry and to collect and dispense charity. The women wanted more: to interview couples to determine their fitness for marriage (a practice that existed in the seventeenth century but was not reinstituted until 1783), to interview prospective female members, and to be authorized to visit transgressing females. These women accepted the principle of the difference between the sexes, but they saw that difference not in terms of a hierarchy that privileged public men over private women, but as a balance of authority in which men and women acted in parallel if not entirely equal roles. This was more than a return to the practice of a hundred years earlier, for, like Catherine Payton, eighteenth-century women wanted to speak both as mothers in Israel—as prophets, sufferers, or givers of charity—and "prudentially."

The women who led the movement for a female discipline were of two kinds. Many belonged to poorer and more rural northern meetings in Lancashire and Yorkshire, where women's meetings and activism had always been strong, and where there was a long tradition of civil disobedience in the matter of paying tithes and refusing to swear oaths. Others, like Catherine Payton and Sophia Hume, were part of the more sophisticated and sexist world of London and Bristol Friends, who had also traveled in Ireland and America and observed a more egalitarian order. Their campaign for a women's Yearly Meeting began in 1746 and lasted for more than thirty years. Six women ministers from different counties submitted a paper on the value of a women's national meeting to halt the decline of Quakerism and set an example to youth, assuring the men that they would seek no further authority and might meet only every other year. The proposal was tabled. Then a group of American male ministers proposed a Yearly Meeting to the York women's meeting, and a delegation (including, among others, Catherine Payton, Sophia Hume, and two American women) was eventually empowered to carry the minute to London in 1753. It was tabled. (Samuel Fothergill was reported to have agonized, "I see it, but not now; I behold it, but not nigh!")[32] Thirty years later, again with the encouragement of American male Friends, the women of the Lancaster meeting sent a minute to London requesting that epistles from America be sent to all women's meetings. In London, a number of American women urged on the Englishwomen, and the men's meeting finally approved a meeting to distribute epistles, but not to make rules or present queries without approval of the men. A male Friend commented, "The women Friends held long meetings and appear very willing to be invested with greater power, but it was somewhat limited by the prudence of the men." A woman Friend commented, "Painful is the jealousy of men Friends."[33]

In 1798 Hannah Barnard, a Quaker minister born in Nantucket and married to a carter, went to England and Ireland to preach.[34] There, in an unprecedented action, she led a delegation of women in an appeal to the London meeting to allow ministers of other societies to use Quaker meetinghouses, persisting in that request until the meeting for discipline ordered her to withdraw. She then joined a group of Irish Friends who questioned the veracity of biblical passages that urged the Hebrews to wage war, thereby aligning herself with those who upheld the original, undogmatic theology of a universal inner light, as against those who were beginning to insist on a biblical, Christ-centered religion. "I do not look up," she wrote, "to any visible gathered church, or to any book, or books in the world, as being absolutely endowed with divine infallibility; but, as a moral agent, I endeavour to exercise that freedom of enquiry, and right of judging, which I believe to be the indisputable privilege, and indispensable duty, of all mankind . . . having no desire . . . to command the implicit faith and blind obedience of any, not even my own children."[35]

James Jenkins was not impressed by Barnard's integrity, accusing her of preaching peace (with the aid of quotations from Alexander Pope) but privately expressing sympathy for the ideals of the French Revolution. In Ireland, "at her public meetings, she frequently disturbed the arrangements made by friends . . . by calling to the upper end of the meeting, and there mingling up, rich, and poor, clean, and dirty promiscuously together, and in . . . refusing to visit such as objected to sit with their own servants, during the time of such visit." Nevertheless, Jenkins observed after meeting her that "this is an extraordinary woman." (His companion answered, "Yes . . . indeed she is—she is a clever, *very clever fellow.*")[36]

Hannah Barnard was censured and then expelled by the elite leadership of the London meeting for being too rationalistic (this was done over the objections of women Friends, who claimed the right to judge her behavior for themselves). She made prolonged and futile appeals and petitions, insisting throughout on her right and duty to stand by her own convictions against "*assumed* power."[37] Finally she returned to America, was expelled from her home meeting, and continued to attend both Quaker and Unitarian services.[38]

Twenty years after her expulsion, at age sixty-six, Barnard used her own savings to publish *Dialogues on Domestic and Rural Economy* (with an appendix on the treatment of burns).[39] The *Dialogues* tell the story of one Jenny Prinks, a thoughtless young woman from a profligate family who is trained in housewifery by Lady Homespun, a paragon of enlightened womanhood. "I don't despair of soon making you a rational creature," says Lady Homespun, "and in a few years, an intelligent, respectable young woman. . . . And when you have learnt to cook, wash, spin, weave, knit and sew . . . and read . . . geography, history, useful biography . . . and understand writing, arithmetic as well, I think it is very probable you will yet be . . . well married."[40] The characters proceed to discuss the perils of addiction to luxury and the evils of religious fanaticism: "You and I have great cause to be thankful, for the general diffusion of that light and knowledge, which has drawn that infernal monster's fangs, disarmed him of his power to imprison, torture and roast. And in most countries in Christendom, reduced him to the merited mortification of being laughed at and despised."[41]

The profligate wife learns the skills of butter-making and reasonable economy, to the great delight of her husband, and feels herself "very happy in again becoming a plain farmer's plain economical wife. And I now look forward with the pleasing prospect of future content, competence, and rural happiness." By cultivating their reason, and their gardens, women may attain not only a state of salvation but a state of economic and social utility in the wider world. "I have long labored," Barnard wrote, "for that expansion of thought, which would enable me to estimate what would most likely tend to promote in the best manner, *the good of the whole.*"[42]

CONCLUSION: SELF-TRANSCENDENCE AND THE PUBLIC LIFE

In one of her many epistles to backsliding Friends, Mary Peisley wrote, "I am not afraid to say and give it under my hand that . . . people in future ages should make an improvement on [early Friends'] labor and carry on the reformation even farther than they did. . . . [W]hat if I say . . . that God has designed to carry some of this generation in these parts of the world, higher and farther in righteousness than their forefathers were carried."[43]

Nineteenth-century Quaker activism—the movements for women's suffrage, abolition of slavery, and antimilitarism—did take Friends higher and farther as crusaders for social and political justice. The cradle of those reform movements was the writing and activism of those complex eighteenth-century women who were groping toward a language with which to negotiate the private and public worlds of home and meetinghouse. By the end of the century, some of them had begun to articulate a new relationship among the issues of pacifism, slavery, and gender. Mary Birkett, an Irish Friend writing in the 1790s, moved the discourse on abolition to a new stage by speaking to women as mothers and political actors, urging them collectively to boycott slave-produced consumer goods. Linking slavery with women's own oppression, she implored her fellow Irish-women, "whose bosoms feel pity's soft glow" to abjure sugar, and to influence

> . . . your brothers, husbands, sons, or friends,
> Whose precepts or whose laws you erst obey'd,
> And reverence due concomitantly paid.[44]

But it took an American, a republican, and a delinquent Friend to bring together the disparate elements of English Quaker women's mentality. Hannah Barnard's portrait of the ideal housewife and citizen offered a synthesis of high-minded morality and the concerns of domestic and material life; she taught her readers how to improve the world and to make good butter. Her work also fused the values of domesticity, simplicity, rationality, and a collective spirit in a way that was both familiar and totally creative. In a sense, she was at least fifty years behind the times, for women's conduct books of the late eighteenth century were already beginning to feature nonproductive, housebound women whose attention was focused exclusively on their families—harbingers of the Victorian angel in the house.[45] By contrast, Barnard's Lady Homespun might have been a character in an Enlightenment fantasy. Indeed, she might easily have starred in a sequel to *Candide*, spelling out, as Voltaire did not, the practical and moral particulars of a constructive private life—cultivating one's own garden for one's own family—and its implications for life as a citizen. This was not a feminist vision by any means; neither she nor any British Quaker had a concept of women's individual or collective political rights. But in her own assertive person, and in her religious and social preoccupations, she both harked back to the original women prophets of the 1650s and anticipated the English and American women activists of the nineteenth century. Given the power with which she articulated her vision of Quaker theology and womanhood, it is ironic but not surprising that male Friends thought of her as manly.

What does the story of eighteenth-century Quaker women teach us about the relation between religion and women's political consciousness? First, it would be simplistic to assume that women's growing political and social activism was part of a larger trajectory from a religious to a secular worldview. It might be argued that Quakers in general were becoming more secular; certainly Friends believed themselves to be in a state of crisis over just this issue. But if we ask about the relationship between religion and social action among individuals, we find that those Friends who were most creative in affirming their authority and urging social reform were also those who struggled hardest to unite the Enlightenment doctrine of universal reason with the Quaker doctrine of the universal inner light. It was the concept of truth as both rational and mystical, not indifference to the Christian tradition, that moved Hannah Barnard and some Irish Friends to assert the relativity of biblical texts. It was the desire to purify tradition, not to dilute it, that moved Catherine Payton and other English Friends to assert the importance of autonomous and powerful women's meetings.

It would also be simplistic to set the concept of women's agency against that of religious self-transcendence, as though female visionaries were, by definition, unconscious of or indifferent to their own goals and interests. Christianity had the potential to promote women's public role because it privileged the soul, a part of the individual that existed apart from social position or gender. But the Christian understanding of the word "soul" changed over time, and it was crucial for women that "soul" came to be allied with "mind" in eighteenth-century Quakerism. It meant that the experience of self-transcendence changed from a cataclysmic visionary experience or loss

of mundane consciousness to a feeling of calm and stability, a powerful awareness of divine purpose expressed through the individual's activities as a par-
ent, a merchant, or a minister. Eighteenth-century women lost the capacity
to feel and express their religious insights with their bodies; they gained the
capacity to perceive and articulate those insights with their intelligence.
Catherine Payton, Hannah Barnard, and other eighteenth-century women
may not answer to a modern description of subjectivity or autonomy, but they
were indisputably awake.

Finally, it would be simplistic to assert that religion in general, even Quakerism in general, had a positive influence on women's political evolution.
Women of all types—the class-bound, thoroughly elitist Catherine Payton and
the countrywoman Hannah Barnard—were active social campaigners, but
the initiative for concerted action on behalf of women appears to have come
not from worldly and prosperous London and Bristol Friends but from Quakers on the geographic and social margins: Rachel Wilson in Lancashire, Mary
Peisley and Mary Birkett in Ireland, Hannah Barnard and Rebecca Jones in
America. Indeed, Barnard's defection and that of Irish Friends—for so their
behavior was portrayed by the London meeting—inaugurated a much wider
and more devastating struggle. On one side were those quietists whose concept of the inner light made them reject parts of the Bible as both immoral
and unreasonable; on the other were the more prosperous evangelical
Friends who taught a Bible-centered Christianity and elevated the authority
of tradition. The struggle led to an open schism in 1827 (two years after Hannah Barnard's death), which was not resolved until the triumph of liberal theology among late Victorian Quakers.[46] Within that struggle, the group that
generated the most support for abolition of slavery and for women's rights
were the poorer, more rural, and less evangelical Friends called Hicksites.[47]
Thus women stood to benefit most—in spiritual and political, if not material
terms—from a theology that privileged universal grace over written tradition,
and a social identity that was relatively independent of the demands of wealth
and property. For Quakers, the gender revolution and the bourgeois revolution appear to have been generated at different, though closely related sites.

Self-transcendence was, and is, at the core of the Quaker religious experience. It might be constructive to ask whether the idea of all public life presupposes an ideal of self-transcendence or going beyond oneself; "an enlarge-
ment toward fellow beings," as the women of one London meeting put it.
Certainly, the study of Quakerism helps us to keep our eyes fixed on that point
where religion, rationality, and public action meet, for Quakerism challenged
eighteenth-century women to synthesize three very different things: a discourse
based on reason and the fundamental sanctity of human nature, a prophetic
tradition of heroic action, and a concept of womanhood as the basis for collective activism. Feminists today still struggle to sustain the heroism of the
early leaders of our movement, to reconcile our womanhood with our uni-

versal humanity, and to attain some kind of self-transcendence, an enlarge-
ment toward fellow beings.

NOTES

1. Hannah Barnard, *Dialogues on Domestic and Rural Economy, and the Fashionable Follies of the World* (Hudson: Printed for author, 1820), p. 41.

2. Voltaire, *Letters on England,* tr. Leonard Tancock (London: Penguin, 1980,) Letter No. 1, "On the Quakers," p. 23.

3. Ibid., p. 26.

4. Ibid., Letter No. 2, p. 27.

5. Arthur Raistrick, *Quakers in Science and Industry: Being an Account of the Quaker Contributions to Science and Industry during the 17th and 18th Centuries* (London: Bannisdale Press, 1950); Frederick B. Tolles, *Meeting House and Counting House: The Quaker Merchants of Colonial Philadelphia 1682–1763* (Chapel Hill: University of North Carolina Press, 1948).

6. Samuel Fothergill to his sister, Warrington, October 18, 1766, *Memoirs of the Life and Gospel Labours of Samuel Fothergill* (London: W. and F. G. Cash, 1857), p. 463. On quietism, Rufus Jones, *The Later Periods of Quakerism,* 2 vols. (London: 1921); and William C. Braithwaite, *The Second Period of Quakerism* (1919; reprint, York: William Sessions, 1979). For a trenchant discussion of the latter works, see Nicholas Morgan, *Lancashire Quakers and the Establishment, 1760–1830* (Krumlin, Halifax: Ryburn Academic Publishing, 1993), pp. 244–53.

7. Morgan, *Lancashire Quakers,* pp. 70–71.

8. Barbara Taylor, *Eve and the New Jerusalem: Socialism and Feminism in the Nineteenth Century* (London: Virago, 1983), p. 166; J. F. C. Harrison, *The Second Coming: Popular Millenarianism 1780–1850* (London: Routledge and Kegan Paul, 1979), pp. 31–38.

9. Ann Braude, *Radical Spirits: Spiritualism and Women's Rights in Nineteenth-Century America* (Boston: Beacon Press, 1989), pp. 12–15, 57–59.

10. Phyllis Mack, *Visionary Women: Ecstatic Prophecy in Seventeenth-Century England* (Berkeley: University of California Press, 1992), chaps. 4 and 5.

11. Raistrick, *Quakers in Science and Industry,* pp. 77–79, 102–60; Morgan, *Lancashire Quakers,* pp. 179–80.

12. Thomas Clarkson, *Portraiture of Quakerism,* vol. 2, p. 124, quoted in Patricia Howell Michaelson, "Religious Bases of Eighteenth-Century Feminism: Mary Wollstonecraft and the Quakers," *Women's Studies* 22 (1993): 239.

13. Clarkson, *Portraiture,* vol. 3, pp. 295–96, quoted in Michaelson, "Wollstonecraft," p. 286.

14. *Monthly Magazine* 12 (1804): 14, quoted in Michaelson, "Wollstonecraft," p. 285.

15. From 1700 to 1800, seventy-four women crossed the Atlantic, thirty-one British and forty-three American, one-third of all ministers to travel abroad (Margaret Hope Bacon, "An International Sisterhood: Eighteenth Century Quaker Women in Overseas Ministry," *Friends Quarterly Examiner* 28, no. 5 [January 1995]: 193–206). By the early nineteenth century, there were many more women ministers than men (Elizabeth Isichei, *Victorian Quakers* [Oxford: Oxford University Press, 1970], p. 95).

16. Samuel Fothergill to Catherine Payton, *Memoirs,* p. 124.

17. James Jenkins, *The Records and Recollections of James Jenkins*, ed. J. William Frost, *Texts and Studies in Religion*, vol. 18 (Lewiston, N.Y.: Edwin Mellen Press, 1984), pp. 423, 118, 119.

18. Ibid., pp. 120–21, 461–62.

19. Ibid., p. 262.

20. *Memoirs of the Life of Catherine Phillips: To which are added some of her Epistles* (Philadelphia: Robert Johnson, 1798), p. 10.

21. Ibid., p. 15; Payton to Samuel Fothergill, 1756, *Memoirs*, p. 274.

22. "A Testimony concerning my dearly beloved & deceased Wife Mary Neal who departed this life ye 20th of 3 mo. 1757," Letters Dreams Visions, Mss. S.78, p. 247, Friends Historical Library, London.

23. Mary Peisley to Elizabeth Shackleton, November 16, 1754, Mss. 859, Haverford Quaker Collection, Haverford College, Haverford, Penn.

24. Sophia Hume, *A Caution to such as observe Days and Times: To which is added, An Address to Magistrates, Parents, Masters of Families, etc.,* 5th ed. (London: J. Ridley, G. Kearsly, and L. Urquhart, 1766), pp. 5, 15, 23.

25. Sophia Hume to a young woman, Catchpool Mss. I No. 156, pp. 292, 294, Friends Historical Library, London.

26. Hume, *A Caution*, p. 12.

27. Payton, *Memoirs*, pp. 133, 141 ff.

28. Ibid., p. 142.

29. My discussion of the women's Yearly Meeting draws on Margaret Hope Bacon, "The Establishment of London Women's Yearly Meeting: A Transatlantic Connection," *Journal of the Friends Historical Society* 57, no.2 (1995): 151–65. I am grateful for her generosity in allowing me to read it before publication.

30. For a discussion of the historiography of the campaign for greater discipline, see Morgan, *Lancashire Quakers*, chaps. 4 and 7.

31. Mss. of the London Box Meeting, 1759, Friends Historical Library.

32. Bacon, "London Women's Yearly Meeting."

33. Joseph Woods to William Matthews, 1787, quoted in ibid.

34. David W. Maxey, "New Light on Hannah Barnard, A Quaker 'Heretic,'" *Quaker History: The Bulletin of Friends Historical Association* 76, no. 1 (Spring 1987): 60–86.

35. *Some Tracts relating to the Controversy between Hannah Barnard and the Society of Friends, wherein the Primitive Christian Principles of the said Society are presented to the Public* (London: Darton and Harvey, 1802), p. 17; Jones, *Later Periods of Quakerism*, vol 1, pp. 293–98, 299–307.

36. Jenkins, *Memoirs*, pp. 340–41.

37. Ibid., p. 358.

38. On the elitism of the London meeting, see ibid., p. 347.

39. Barnard, *Dialogues on Domestic and Rural Economy*.

40. Ibid., p. 6.

41. Ibid., p. 11.

42. Ibid., pp. 17, 44–45.

43. Mary Peisley to F. P[arvins], n.d., U.T. Mss. vol. 348, #428 (London: Friends Historical Library).

44. Mary Birkett, "A Poem on the African Slave Trade," pp. 10–16, quoted in Moira

Ferguson, *Subject to Others: British Women Writers and Colonial Slavery, 1670–1834* (New York: Routledge, 1992), pp. 178–81.

45. Nancy Armstrong, *Desire and Domestic Fiction: A Political History of the Novel* (New York: Oxford University Press, 1987), chap. 2, "The Rise of the Domestic Woman."

46. Isichei, *Victorian Quakers*, pp. 32–44.

47. Margaret Hope Bacon, *Mothers of Feminism: The Story of Quaker Women in America* (San Francisco: Harper and Row, 1986), pp. 92 ff.

PART FOUR

Nineteenth and Twentieth Centuries

FOURTEEN

Spirituality and/as Ideology in Black Women's Literature

The Preaching of Maria W. Stewart and Baby Suggs, Holy

Judylyn S. Ryan

PREAMBLE

Although much recent scholarship has convincingly demonstrated the theoretical and sociopolitical significance of Black women's fiction, this scholarship has not attained its full interpretive potential because of insufficient attention to explicit and implicit aspects of spirituality in this literary corpus. Of the diverse range of critical methodologies used in the explication of Black women's literature, few admit serious consideration of elements of spirituality. Indeed, with the notable exception of womanist scholarship, the acknowledgment of spirituality in Black literature has generally been restricted to a discussion of Black church life, as prototypically depicted in James Baldwin's novels. Womanist scholars have spearheaded the interpretation and celebration of the many ways in which African American religious traditions and ethics are represented in Black women's literature. Drawing on their personal and professional grounding in the Black church, Katie Cannon, Delores Williams, Cheryl Townsend Gilkes, Emilie Townes, and others have provided compelling analyses of the role of spirituality in Black women's texts, focusing largely on that sector of the African American religious continuum that is Christocentric.[1] In underscoring the need for critical attention to the influence of African religious traditions in Black women's literature, however, literary critic Barbara Christian has sought to expand the mapping of the African American religious continuum. "The perspective I am proposing," Christian notes, "is one that acknowledges the existence of an African cosmology, how that cosmology has been consistently denigrated in the West, and its appropriateness for texts that are clearly derived from it."[2]

To what extent and in what ways do Black women's texts "derive" from an African cosmology? And why have African American women artists, whose cultural community is most frequently associated with Christianity (one thinks of "the Black community" and "the Black church" almost synonymously) chosen to utilize an African spirituality in the articulation of their artistic and political visions? This essay probes these related questions by highlighting the elements of African cosmology that attend the Christocentric orientations of the Black church and help to define Afro-Christianity;[3] by positing a spiritual continuum characterized by an ethos of interconnectedness common to Afro-Christianity, other New World African religions— santería, voodun, hoodoo, candomblé, and the like, which are not Christological and traditional African religions; and by demonstrating how the African cosmology that engenders this ethos of interconnectedness shapes an enabling vision of Black women's spiritual and sociopolitical leadership, which is exemplified in the preaching of two nineteenth-century Black women, Maria W. Stewart and Toni Morrison's fictional character Baby Suggs, holy.

SPIRITUALITY AND/AS EPISTEMOLOGY

In "Rootedness" Nobel laureate Toni Morrison writes:

> I don't regard Black literature as simply books written *by* Black people, or simply as literature *about* Black people, or simply as literature that uses a certain mode of language in which you just sort of drop g's. There is something very special and very identifiable about it and it is my struggle to *find* that elusive but identifiable style in the books. . . . I got there in several places when I knew it was exactly right. Most of the time in *Song of Solomon*, because of the construction of the book and the tone in which I could blend the acceptance of the supernatural and a profound rootedness in the real world at the same time with neither taking precedence over the other. It is indicative of the cosmology, the way in which Black people looked at the world. We are very practical people, very down-to-earth, even shrewd people. But within that practicality we also accepted what I suppose could be called superstition and magic, which is another way of knowing things. But to blend those two worlds together at the same time was enhancing, not limiting. And some of those things were "discredited knowledge" that Black people had; discredited only because Black people were discredited therefore what they *knew* was "discredited." . . . That kind of knowledge has a very strong place in my work.[4]

She attributes the successful expression of an identifiably Black style to the depiction and re-creation of an African cosmology in the text, *not* to biology or defective orthography.[5] Morrison's discussion has several important implications, not the least of which is the fact that she identifies aspects of African spirituality—"what I suppose could be called superstition and magic"

—as an epistemology or "another way of knowing things." This spirituality-cum-epistemology is central to the depiction of an African cosmology and, in Black women's literature, enables the protagonists to withstand ideological assaults and develop their own sustaining ideologies.[6]

Here, spirituality refers to a combination of consciousness/ethos, lifestyle, and discourse that privileges spirit—life force—as a primary aspect of self, and that defines and determines health and well-being, broadly conceived to include spiritual, psychological and emotional, physical, and material well-being. Spirituality, as depicted in Morrison's works and other literature by Black women, is recognizably African/Black, but rarely conforms to any single traditional African religion. Instead, its contours are shaped by the informing blueprint around which several heterogeneous traditions cohere within the African cultural domain.[7] These Black women artists depict this Africa-centered spirituality in varying configurations along a syncretistic range.[8] Although elements of several religious traditions are depicted in these works, they are not equally effective in the world of the text. Indeed, the elements that derive from traditional African religion have important sustaining functions.

As described in E. B. Idowu's *African Traditional Religion*, the major components of traditional African religion include belief in God, belief in divinities and other spirits, belief in the sustaining presence of ancestors, and the practice of magic—that is, the "attempt on the part of man to tap and control the supernatural resources of the universe for his own benefit," situated within a nonlinear concept of time.[9] This diffused monotheism—in which divinities are derived from and are ministers of a single Deity—also features a notable acceptance of the interconnectedness of male and female aspects of Deity. These elements map a cosmology in which being and kinship encompass the dead, the living, and the unborn; in which kinship and communication between the living and ancestors is neither ruptured nor interrupted by death; in which every aspect of human activity involves spirituality; and in which the primary ontological goal is to preserve or restore an equilibrium of interdependent relationships among animate and inanimate beings. Within this cosmology, the expression of spirituality is not restricted to religious praxis, which perhaps explains why theology, as an institution or discourse, is neither dominant nor centralized. For contemporary Black women literary artists, this Africa-centered spirituality provides access and attests to the specificity of a Black woman's epistemology—an epistemology that designates and validates culturally specific ways of knowing, and of confirming and transmitting knowledge. It determines what knowledge is valuable, for what purposes, what responsibilities this knowledge confers, and what functions these have within and outside the community.

SPIRITUALITY AND/AS IDEOLOGY

You had this canny ability to shape an untenable reality, mold it, sing it, reduce it to its manageable, transforming essence, which is a knowing so deep it's like a secret. In your silence, enforced or chosen, lay not only eloquence but discourse so devastating that "civilization" could not risk engaging in it lest it lose the ground it stomped.

TONI MORRISON[10]

Although Black women's writings incorporate various syncretistic configurations of religious praxis, the prominence given to elements of New World African religions has several distinct implications for theological discourse.

As defined within Western tradition, theology is discourse on the existence and nature of the divine in a universe that is theocentric. Given the thesis that all human life is, to *varying* degrees, created in the likeness of the divine image, Western theology seeks to identify the rights and responsibilities of the human person through an assessment of God, the prototype of righteousness. As an extension of this theological praxis, racial and physical variations within the human family have been construed as degrees to which specific groups "resemble" the invisible God. The resulting hierarchy of "godlikeness" has both ideological and sociological functions in determining the global distribution of rights and resources.

In the context of traditional African religions that posit an anthropocentric universe, however, the nature or power of the divine is diffused and does not occupy a static and monolithic center. In this cosmology, power is the salient characteristic of Deity, and it is directed toward attaining and maintaining a righteous equilibrium of interdependent relationships among animate and inanimate beings. Mamphela Ramphele defines power in ways that reveal the democratic diffusion of the divine nature throughout the universe. According to Ramphele, power connotes "the use of resources of whatever kind to secure outcomes, power then becomes an element of action, and refers to a range of interventions of which an agent is capable."[11] From an African cultural/spiritual and theological perspective, righteous agency need not be the exclusive province of Deity. Since every aspect of human activity involves spirituality, one need not focus on overtly religious phenomena in order to depict or detect expressions of spirituality. Because the primary goal within an African cosmology is to attain and preserve an equilibrium of interdependent relationships, to the extent that these artists privilege this cosmology, the ethos within Black women's literature *necessarily* constitutes a discourse on interconnectedness. Black women's discursive focus on an ethos and ideology of interconnectedness reveals distinct ways of being human, with attendant responsibilities.

To understand the full significance of this ethos of interconnectedness and the specific ways in which it disrupts a hegemonic agency that Morrison dubs "civilization," one has to return to the site of Slavery. More important, one has to examine the traditional African cosmology in which these structures of interconnectedness were developed and which were partially eroded by Slavery.

Within traditional African cosmology, cultural nationality—one's participation in a particular "ethnic" heritage or tradition—and spiritual identity are coterminous. For example, being Ibo is a description of cultural and spiritual identity and membership. The presence of ancestors is the crucial link that fuses cultural and spiritual identity. As Idowu explains, "The ancestors are regarded still as heads and parts of the families or communities to which they belonged while they were living human beings: for what happened in consequence of the phenomenon called death was only that the family life of this earth has been extended into the after-life or super sensible world. The ancestors remain, therefore, spiritual superintendents of family affairs and continue to bear their titles of relationship like 'father' or 'mother.'"[12]

An agenda to colonize, skillfully disguised by a putative mission to convert, presented the first threat to cultural/spiritual connectedness. For fifteenth-century Africans, conversion—as an act and process of relinquishing prior beliefs, customs, and practices in order to adopt new, different, and "better" ones—was unthinkable, if not ontologically impossible. Among other things, such a conversion would have involved a radical and untenable disconnection from one's kin, living and dead, a removal from one's own self. Nonetheless, the relocation and renaming of African peoples via the Atlantic slave trade prioritized and promoted the imposition of a "new" cultural/spiritual subjectivity. More than the force with which this "superior" cultural/spiritual cosmology was imposed, the ubiquitous practice of unnaming and renaming jeopardized the spiritual/cultural kinship among African peoples, as it was designed to render them strangers to and alienated from themselves.

Africans in the "New World" faced a loss of identity from Christendom, an agency that gained both its authority and an ideological "immunity from prosecution" from the institution whose surface features it appropriated—Christianity. Although the terms *Christendom* and *Christianity* are frequently used synonymously, this analysis seeks to identify radical differences between the two.[13] The distinction between the two that this analysis posits is absolutely essential for any accurate analysis of the history of contestation involving Black people's identity. Equally important, acknowledging this distinction enables one to understand why, during and after Slavery, Africans were able to use Christianity as a vehicle for their own empowerment.

Christendom, as used in sixteenth-century Europe, refers to the conglomerate of nation-states for whom racial or cultural identity—as determined by Whiteness, region, or territory—Western Europeanness, and theological subscription were alchemized. Christendom denotes both a regional *constituency* and a state-sponsored *agency* responsible for unleashing a veritable holocaust on several non-White, non-European cultures.

As an agency, Christendom refers to the branch of the European imperialist apparatus disguised under religious rhetoric that espoused the goals of territorial expansion, colonization, and the accumulation of wealth through the exploitation of human labor and natural resources. Like any hegemonic agency, Christendom needed to erase and elide the identities of the peoples it sought to dominate, in order to more effectively "govern." Christendom operates on the presupposition of an entrenched cultural and racial hierarchy that coincides with, and is masked by, a theological hierarchy of believers and unbelievers. One of the most obvious signs of this operation is in the expansion of the biblical categories of Jews, Gentiles, and church to include, in most translations, a fourth category: "Heathens." In the expanded system, "Gentiles" denotes non-Jews who are White, while "Heathens" denotes non-Jews who are non-White. And while Jews and Gentiles can become part of "the church," even "Heathen" converts remain outside this new definition and privileged relationship to God. As a further expropriation, the term *Christian* is used to refer to Europeans as a racial or cultural group, a departure from New Testament usage where it designates a covenant relationship that is not racially exclusive. As Winthrop Jordan notes, "From the first, then, vis-à-vis the Negro the concept embedded in the term Christian seems to have conveyed much of the idea and feeling of *we* as against *they:* to be Christian was to be civilized rather than barbarous, English rather than African, white rather than black."[14] Although the practices within Christendom—including missionary-style colonization, assigning "Christian" or European names, and Slavery itself—did not have biblical sanction, they were essential to the advancement of European imperialism.

Christianity refers to a body of teachings that have been given very diverse theological interpretations and applications in the two millennia since Jesus and his disciples first articulated them. The New Testament term used to refer to the global aggregate of those who accept Jesus as the Christ and who commit to following his teachings is "the church." Christianity *proposes* a new identity. For those who accept the invitation to be "in Christ," prior identities are sublimated. This transformation stems from a new disposition toward God and God's creatures (beginning with the self), which, as a sustained commitment, engenders a reformed character and revised identity. As Paul summarizes it, "So if anyone is in Christ, there is a new creation: everything old has passed away; see, everything has become new!"[15] Elsewhere, Paul explains this transformation as a voluntary sublimation of various dimensions of personal identity.[16]

Because of somewhat parallel mechanisms of sublimation, the ideological demands of Christendom could be and were superimposed on the ontological demands of Christianity. As a result, African peoples—converts and nonconverts alike, during and after Slavery—were required to disguise, disinherit, and divest themselves of important aspects of their cultural and spiritual identity and assimilate to a European cultural paradigm, beginning with the exchange of African names for "Christian" European names. Despite the relentless enforcement of this cultural and theological standard, Africans in the diaspora maintained key aspects of their cultural and spiritual identity. Describing the development of diverse New World African religions, Albert Raboteau notes that "new as well as old gods have come to be worshipped by Afro-Americans, but the new, like the old, have been perceived in traditionally African ways."[17] Looking specifically at the development of Afro-Christianity among the Gullah, historian Margaret Washington Creel notes that they "converted Christianity to their African world view, using the new religion to justify combating objective forces, to collectively perpetuate community-culture, and as an ideology of freedom. Thus it was less a case of Christianity instilling a sense of resignation because of beliefs in future rewards than of an African philosophical tradition being asserted in the slave quarters."[18] Ethicist Peter Paris concludes, "The preservation of their spirituality under the conditions of slavery was an astounding accomplishment, due principally to their creative genius in making the Euro-American cultural forms and practices serve as vehicles for the transmission of African cultural elements."[19] Consequently, when Zora Neale Hurston states that "the Negro is not really a Christian," she is not, as some scholars have charged, accusing Black people of religious insincerity. Hurston's extensive knowledge of the cultural and spiritual life of Africans in several "New World" communities, the subject of much of her fiction, warrants a more complex interpretation. Given her awareness of the concurrence of cultural and spiritual identity, Hurston is perhaps simply acknowledging the fact that Christendom could not have eliminated an African cultural/spiritual belonging. After all, Hurston's observation comes in the midst of her discussion of "those elements which were brought over from Africa" and subsequently unnamed.[20] Morrison's discussion attests to the fact that this Africa-centered spirituality-cum-epistemology has been actively unnamed. Until recently, the only term available for designating this "other way of knowing things" was "what I suppose could be called superstition and magic." African religious traditions were preponderantly viewed as *an absence* of religion. The dearth of names, labels, and terminology for describing this and other key aspects of Black people's lives in the diaspora, as on the continent, is intimately connected to the fact that the African cultural domain has been designated as the *absence of culture,* so that one need not assign any further definitions. As Katherine Bassard notes, "the lack of an appropriate collective nomenclature for descendants of Africans enslaved in the Americas" creates what Bill Lawson calls a "functional lexical gap."[21] Hurston, therefore, makes a critical interpretive intervention in *naming* the necessary point of departure for contemporary Black women literary artists: "The Negro is still an African."

As ancestor and "theorizing" foremother, Hurston underscores the historical context of, and necessity for, a renaming and revalidation when Janie observes, in *Their Eyes Were Watching God,* that "Nanny's head and face looked like the standing roots of some old tree that had been torn away by storm. Foundation of ancient power that no longer mattered."[22] Hurston's statement, with its careful omission of a subject, prompts several questions: In whose judgment does this foundation "no longer matter"? From whose or what perspective might this foundation still be relevant? And what, after all, is this "ancient power"? And while Hurston acknowledges the assault to which this cultural/spiritual tradition has been subjected, her phrasing does not deny the reality of that "ancient power." The conscious resistance to a disempowered position in this sentence typifies the stance of Black women artists in revisiting Slavery. Paradoxically, returning to that temporal site facilitates an enabling encounter because it simultaneously allows a recognition of, and reaccess to, the spiritual resources needed to withstand a continuing assault.

Significantly, Black women literary artists have been among the first to engage these questions.[23] They extensively interrogate assumptions of fragmentation and debilitation and respond with the common vision of (inter-)connectedness, with a primary emphasis on kinship matrices. Black women writers provide another view of Black peoples' histories, another set of things to be known, another way of knowing those histories. These writers underscore the connection between the subversion of cultural/spiritual identity and the history of Slavery, as well as the need to revise, reclaim, and rename ancient identities, kinships, and responsibilities. They view the survival of African peoples throughout the globe as part of a deliberate and comprehensive agenda, one in which an Africa-centered spirituality—unrestricted to religious praxis—was and remains a central component, one in which women fulfill important spiritual and social leadership roles.

BLACK WOMEN'S SPIRITUAL LEADERSHIP:
MARIA W. STEWART AND BABY SUGGS, HOLY

If such women as are here described have once existed, be no longer astonished then, my brethren and friends, that God at this eventful period should raise up your own females to strive, by their example both in public and private, to assist those who are endeavoring to stop the strong current of prejudice that flows so profusely against us at present.

MARIA W. STEWART[24]

Maria W. Stewart (1803–79), the first American-born woman political speaker, and Baby Suggs, holy (1795?–1865), the spiritual center of Morrison's novel *Beloved,* exercised a degree of spiritual leadership that gives critical insights into Black women's spiritual authority and autonomy. Their careers demonstrate that, in the context of Black women's lives, authority is based not on the assertion of "rights" but on the embrace of responsibility—responsibility to meet the spiritual, psychological, and material needs of the cultural community. Indeed, Nellie McKay notes that nineteenth-century Black women's spiritual autobiographies "focus on their religious convictions, on their willingness to respond to a calling that demanded they overcome formidable personal and societal hindrances in the process, and on a consciousness of the authority that came to them in the service they carried out."[25] In attempting to embrace their responsibilities, these "imagined contemporaries" displayed a remarkable degree of autonomy, amid a social and political context that severely curtailed Black women's freedom. In referring to Maria W. Stewart and Baby Suggs, holy, as "imagined contemporaries," I want to direct attention to the fact that while only Black women who were situated like Stewart—in the North and as "free" persons—could write and leave textual record of their preaching, Stewart, Jarena Lee, Zilpha Elaw, Julia Foote, and Amanda Berry Smith were not alone in their preaching. Even more numerous were the (formerly) enslaved southern Black women like Baby Suggs, holy, who, without benefit of denominational affiliation or literacy, spoke to the spiritual and psychological needs of the majority enslaved Black population. While the textual record gives a unidimensional location to the early-nineteenth-century Black woman preacher, the juxtaposition of these two figures provides a more comprehensive description of the diverse locations from which Black women preachers spoke.

The fictional ministry of Baby Suggs, holy, and the historical ministry of Maria Stewart exemplify the ways in which aspects of African religion/cosmology inform Black people's engagement with Christianity—Afro-Christianity—and engender a transformative spiritual and social vision. The primary indications of the influence of an African cosmology appear in the unsanctioned belief in their own capacity for creative or righteous agency, and in the fact that their vision of the role and responsibility of preacher is informed by and expresses an ethos of interconnectedness.

Although scholars have paid little attention to the interconnectedness of male and female aspects of Deity in African cosmology, this feature may well account for Black women's clear conviction of their own entitlement to and capacity for spiritual leadership. More than the fact of access to spiritual leadership through the office of the priestess, the acceptance of the female aspects of Deity—whether in the recognition of the male-female nature of Deity, as in Mawu-Lisa, or in the existence of female archdivinity, as in Ala—sanctioned Black women's spiritual power, leadership, and responsibilities. According to Paris, "it is difficult to get a precise estimate of the extent of female imagery pertaining to the supreme Deity in Africa because many African languages do not have gender-specific pronouns."[26] "Nevertheless," Paris notes, "various subdivinities are male, female, or androgynous. Female imagery with respect to the supreme deity and the reality of female subdivinities and their priestesses enhances the status of women in the sphere of religion. . . . Thus African cosmological thought not only demonstrates the limits of male authority but also provides considerable resources for the exercise of female authority."[27] Indeed, in her analysis of the goddess Osun, Diedre L. Bádéjò notes that "power and femininity coexist in Osun's orature" and that "mythical images and myriad roles of Osun and countless other African deities . . . traversed the Atlantic."[28] The existence of this cultural model meant that although enslaved Black women met few examples of women's spiritual leadership in the sociocultural environment of Euro-America, they nevertheless brought to their early engagement with Christianity and the formation of Afro-Christianity an indomitable sense of entitlement to and preparedness for such roles.

Historical records give no indication of gender restrictions on Black women's participation in the spiritual life and leadership of the enslaved Black community in the early plantation era. Were gender restrictions already established in the spiritual/religious life among Blacks on the plantation, there would have been no experiential basis from which Black women could envision and embrace their spiritual/cultural responsibilities. Without such a tradition, the leadership, authority, and effectiveness of women like Baby Suggs, holy, Sojourner Truth, and Harriet Tubman would have been unimaginable.

The move away from the plantation and the development of denominational theologies brought an orthodoxy—borrowed from Euro-American theologies—that opposed Black women's spiritual leadership. Early-nineteenth-century Black women preachers resisted this trend. Most Black (male) church administrations responded to their resistance by adopting a policy that allowed a semantic and symbolic difference between men's preaching and women's preaching. In deciding that women could give exhortations—but not preach—Black churches effectively barred women from the symbolic sphere of spiritual authority: the pulpit. For Stewart, Baby Suggs, holy, and other nineteenth-century Black women preachers the question was not simply one of rights but of responsibility—responsibility conferred by both cultural tradition and the exigencies of life in Slavery-era America.

In *Righteous Discontent*, historian Evelyn Brooks Higginbotham demonstrates "that women were crucial to broadening the public arm of the church and making it the most powerful institution of racial self-help in the African American community." Higginbotham explains that "in the closed society of Jim Crow, the church afforded African Americans an interstitial space in which to critique and contest white America's racial domination. In addition, the church offered black women a forum through which to articulate a public discourse critical of women's subordination." Higginbotham also notes Stewart's early leadership in articulating a vision of Black women as social activists and institution builders, which would later be crucial to Black women of the club movement era: "It is conceivable that all were influenced by Stewart's speeches, since she lived to publish her collected works in 1879."[29] In her published essays and speeches, Maria W. Stewart envisions, exemplifies, and inspires the Black woman preacher/priestess as social activist.

Born in Connecticut and raised in Boston, Maria Stewart began her public speaking ministry at the age of twenty-seven, shortly after the death of her husband and a conversion experience. Describing her new spiritual commitment, in 1831 Stewart wrote, "[I] now possess that spirit of independence that, were I called upon, I would willingly sacrifice my life for the cause of God and my brethren." Confirming the political dimension of her spiritual commitment, Stewart noted, "Many will suffer for pleading the cause of oppressed Africa, and I shall glory in being one of her martyrs."[30] Her consciousness of a spiritual and cultural connectedness to African peoples is one of the striking aspects of Stewart's preaching; and this pronounced sense of kinship gives a distinct thematic configuration to Stewart's spiritual leadership. Stewart's preaching develops around three related themes: economic self-reliance, promises of divine assistance to oppressed Africans, and women's participatory and leadership rights. She provides a deconstructive theological and political analysis of the marginalization of African peoples and culture, and a program for transformation.

Although Stewart is generally regarded as simply a public speaker, not a preacher, the content and form of her addresses justify the designation of preacher. Stewart's written and oral addresses take the form of religious exhortations petitioning Black people to a Christocentric standard of moral behavior and to a degree of political, social, and economic analysis and self-reliance inextricably bound to the former. In her comprehensive introductory essay, editor Marilyn Richardson offers confirmation: "Not only did she master the Afro-American idiom of thundering exhortation uniting spiritual and secular concerns, she was able early on to exercise that skill with equal success on the printed page and at the podium." Richardson also notes Stewart's "command of such sophisticated techniques as the implied call-and-response cadence set in motion by sequential rhetorical questions; of anaphora, parataxis, and the shaping of imperative and periodic sentences; along with the powerful and affecting rhythms of her discourse."[31] In an early essay titled "Religion and the Pure Principles of Morality, the Sure Foundation on Which We Must Build," Stewart asked: "Shall it any longer be said of the daughters of Africa, they have no ambition, they have no force? By no means. Let every female heart become united, and let us raise a fund ourselves; and at the end of one year and a half, we might be able to lay the corner stone for the building of a High School, that the higher branches of knowledge might be enjoyed by us; and God would raise us up, and enough to aid us in our laudable designs."[32] Here and elsewhere, sociopolitical commentaries are expertly sutured into Stewart's religious appeals and her exhortations to self-reliance. In the context of nineteenth-century Black women's spiritual texts, Maria Stewart's articulation of her passionate commitment to her cultural community is unusual. While preaching women like Jarena Lee, Amanda Berry Smith, and Zilpha Elaw were clearly opposed to oppressive practices in all forms, their writings display a curious and steadfast silence on the political status of African Americans, and about the political and cultural environment within the United States.[33] But because "God . . . has inspired my heart to feel for Afric's woes," Maria Stewart's preaching and writing provide extensive critiques of the political and social conditions in which African Americans lived. Unmasking the ostensible benevolence of the Colonization Society, whose goal was to repatriate free Blacks to West Africa, Stewart notes that "if the colonizationists are the real friends to Africa, let them expend the money which they collect in erecting a college to educate her injured sons in this land of gospel, light, and liberty." She offers her own penetrating critique of the racial discrepancy in U.S. government foreign policy, noting that while the "mighty men of America" rejoiced in the liberation struggles of the Poles, the Greeks, and Catholics, they "have acknowledged all the nations of the earth, except Hayti." And in her "defence of African rights and liberty," Stewart delivers an astute analysis of the ways in which the historical distribution of privilege has benefited Euro-Americans: "Had we as a people received one-half the early advantages the whites have received, I would defy the government of these United States to deprive us any longer of our rights." Stewart's preaching is not restricted to theological/religious issues but instead exemplifies how an ethos of connectedness generates a multithematic preaching.[34]

During the early nineteenth century, there were few precedents for Stewart's multithematic preaching. Indeed, Stewart's mentor, David Walker, provides the single example of a free Black preacher whose preaching did not simply condemn Slavery but who passionately entreated Black people to self-reliance, to exercise their capacity for righteous agency, and to take immediate steps to redress political, social, and economic oppression. Walker's *Appeal* incurred the wrath of both Whites and Blacks, and there is much to suggest that he was assassinated because of the analyses and recommendations put forward in that text. Stewart, a woman, inspired an even greater hostility among members of the Black community, and, it appears, was run out of town because of the perception that her unladylike public speaking and the strident tone of her exhortations jeopardized the carefully cultivated image free Blacks wanted to preserve. In "Mrs. Stewart's Farewell Address to Her Friends in the City of Boston," she observed:

> Yet, notwithstanding your prospects are thus fair and bright, I am about to leave you, perhaps never more to return. For I find it is no use for me as an

individual to try to make myself useful among my color in this city. It was contempt for my moral and religious opinions in private that drove me thus before a public. Had experience more plainly shown me that it was the nature of man to crush his fellow, I should not have thought it so hard. Wherefore, my respected friends, let us no longer talk of prejudice, till prejudice becomes extinct at home. Let us no longer talk of opposition, till we cease to oppose our own.[35]

In this farewell address, Stewart offers a lengthy defense of the right of women to exercise spiritual and political leadership, citing both historical and biblical precedents. Insightfully gauging the responsibility involved in women's spiritual leadership, Stewart tells her audience, "If such women as are here described have once existed, be no longer astonished then, my brethren and friends, that God at this eventful period should raise up your own females to strive, by their example both in public and private, to assist those who are endeavoring to stop the strong current of prejudice that flows so profusely against us at present."[36] The fact that this defense forms the larger part of her farewell address indicates Stewart's awareness that the opposition to her preaching was gender-based. Stewart's compelling defense of women's spiritual leadership is rearticulated in later texts by nineteenth-century Black women preachers, most prominently Jarena Lee.[37] And while Black women in the post-Slavery era would indeed unite to implement her vision of Black women as institution builders, Stewart did not have the communal support necessary to fulfill her vision of Black women exercising righteous and creative agency.[38] Faced with the impenetrable closed-mindedness of her peers, Stewart, like other visionaries before and after, redirected her energies toward transmitting her vision to the next generation. As a teacher in New York, Philadelphia, Baltimore, and Washington, D.C., Stewart had ample opportunity to teach and preach a message of economic self-reliance and women's participatory and leadership roles to scores of children, many of whom would undoubtedly become active participants in the Black women's club movement at the turn of the century.

Like Stewart's, the public ministry of Baby Suggs, holy, begins after a conversion experience of sorts. Arriving in Cincinnati after a lifetime of enslavement in Carolina and Kentucky, Baby Suggs "decided that, because slave life had 'busted her legs, back, head, eyes, hands, kidneys, womb and tongue,' she had nothing left to make a living with but her heart—which she put to work at once."[39]

> Accepting no title of honor before her name, but allowing a small caress after it, she became an unchurched preacher, one who visited pulpits and opened her great heart to those who could use it. In winter and fall she carried it to AME's and Baptists, Holinesses and Sanctifieds, the Church of the Redeemer and the Redeemed. Uncalled, unrobed, unanointed, she let her great heart beat in their presence.[40]

In navigating these denominational boundaries, Baby Suggs, holy, reveals the primary goal of her preaching: the recollecting of a cultural and spiritual community distributed among various theological sites, and whose connectedness has been jeopardized by Slavery.

Like most Slavery-era Black preachers, Baby Suggs, holy, could neither read nor write. As Albert Raboteau notes, however, "Illiteracy proved less of an obstacle to knowledge of the Bible than might be thought, for biblical stories became part of the oral tradition of the slaves."[41] In claiming the right and responsibility of spiritual leader and preacher, Baby Suggs's sole qualification is the vision of grace that came with the recognition that her heart was always already beating. Despite a lifetime of enslavement by Whites, *her* humanity was intact.

Morrison's characterization of Baby Suggs, holy, displays several elements that suggest a Christocentric context. The allusion to Christ, the Rock, in the description of Baby Suggs, holy, "situating herself on a huge flat-sided rock" is indisputable. Her invitation to first "Let the children come!" again resounds Jesus' statement, "Suffer little children to come unto me, and forbid them not." Like his, her body has been broken; like him, she takes her message to "her own"—the Black people dispersed among various denominational sites. Her appearance in the novel is clearly liberating.

Baby Suggs's spiritual leadership encompasses three distinct phases: her role as preacher, in the Clearing; her quest for a liberating theodicy, in the keeping room; and her role as ancestor, after 1865. Looking at the first of these roles, Morrison emphasizes the many ways in which the preaching of Baby Suggs, holy, exemplifies a chosen and self-conscious agency that is contiguous with the parameters of an African cosmology. While the Christian preacher usually receives a "call" to the ministry, Baby Suggs "decided" to put her heart to work. In an incremental counterpoint to that of the Christian preacher, her message rejects the assumption that Black people have "sinned" on the one hand, or that they are destined for some future glory on the other hand. Her implicit rejection of the view of Black people's oppression as either retributive or salvific indicates Baby Suggs's refusal to posit a rational or theological "cause" for that condition. Instead, her message details an enabling vision of survival and reveals aspects of divinity— capacity for creative/righteous agency—within the self, which promote healing, survival, growth.

> "Here," she said, "in this here place, we flesh; flesh that weeps, laughs; flesh that dances on bare feet in grass. Love it. Love it hard. Yonder they do not love your flesh. They despise it. They don't love your eyes; they'd just as soon pick em out. No more do they love the skin on your back. Yonder they flay it. And O my people they do not love your hands. Those they only use, tie, bind, chop off and leave empty. Love your hands! Love them. . . . and the beat and beating heart, love that too. More than eyes or feet. More than lungs that have yet

to draw free air. More than your life-holding womb and your life-giving private parts, hear me now, love your heart. For this is the prize."[42]

This sermon conveys a clear analysis of the ways in which oppression generates self-hatred and social and spiritual death. In assisting her people in loving, collecting, and connecting the dismembered/unremembered parts of themselves, Baby Suggs, holy, enacts a literal remembering of the dismembered African body.

Baby Suggs's ministry centers on the enactment of ritualized healing performances epitomized in the sermon in the Clearing. Several features of an African spiritual cosmology appear in these rituals. Among other things, Baby Suggs's instruction to "Cry . . . For the living and the dead" attests to the unbroken kinship between the living and the dead. The ethos of connectedness is also discernible in the reconfiguration of a multidimensional subjectivity with which the healing ritual ends.

> *It started that way: laughing children, dancing men, crying women and then it got mixed up. Women stopped crying and danced; men sat down and cried; children danced, women laughed, children cried until, exhausted and riven, all and each lay about the Clearing damp and gasping for breath.* In the silence that followed, Baby Suggs, holy, offered up to them her great big heart.[43]

The pivotal event in this ritual is the rotation of roles—participatory *and* observational—that enables women, children, and men to become whole through experiencing and loving others and themselves. Since this experience of their multiple human capacities facilitates a healing regeneration, the participants are—like the newborn—"damp and gasping for breath."

Baby Suggs's spiritual leadership in the role of healer is abruptly terminated by the need to fulfill another responsibility. The attempt of Sethe's former enslaver to reenslave her and the four grandchildren culminates a lifetime of abuses by Whites and overshadows the creative agency she has tried to enact to such an extent that Baby Suggs, holy, is forced to confront the ubiquitous manifestation of evil—reaching to her very door—despite the existence of God, despite her own attempts at righteous intervention. Thus begins her quest for a liberating theodicy.

While Baby Suggs, holy, may or may not have known of the lengthy duration or extensive geography of Slavery, by 1855 she has personally witnessed a barrage of violations committed by Whites. The cumulative weight of those violations is so heavy that, after this last event, "Baby Suggs, holy, believed she had lied. There was no grace—imaginary or real—and no sunlit dance in a Clearing could change that. Her faith, her love, her imagination and her great big old heart began to collapse twenty-eight days after her daughter-in-law arrived. . . . The whitefolks had tired her out at last."[44]

The magnitude of the abuses she has witnessed forces Baby Suggs, holy, to withdraw to the keeping room "to consider what in the world was harmless." In the context of a social environment characterized by a system of violence predicated on a color or racial hierarchy, Baby Suggs's extended meditation on color—"the only thing in the universe that was harmless"—is ironic. The question that motivates her search for a liberating theodicy is not: Why must I suffer? Instead, Baby Suggs questions the potency and extensiveness of evil, given its apparent ability to defeat her attempts at creative agency. The theodicy that this meditation enables her to formulate is both subversive and liberating.

> Except for an occasional request for color she said practically nothing—until the afternoon of the last day of her life when she got out of bed, skipped slowly to the door of the keeping room and announced to Sethe and Denver the lesson she had learned from her sixty years a slave and ten years free: that there was no bad luck in the world but white people. "They don't know when to stop," she said, and returned to her bed, pulled up the quilt and left them to hold that thought forever.[45]

Among its many critical insights, Baby Suggs's theodicy rejects and dismantles color/race as an intrinsic category that denotes good or evil. Although color/race has been used to construct a hierarchy of dominance, Baby Suggs, holy, concludes that color itself, and itself alone in the universe, is "harmless." This view rejects the equation of Whiteness with goodness and the right to dominate, and the equation of "Blackness" with evil and a predestination to be oppressed. And while it may appear that this theodicy simply reverses the poles of an untenable hierarchy, it is important to note that Baby Suggs does not equate Whiteness with evil but attributes agency to White people for the unrelenting violence directed toward herself and other Black people. While theodicy is generally understood as a vindication of Deity or righteous agency, in view of the existence of a metaphysical evil— that is, oppressive agency—Baby Suggs's theodicy regards evil as the manifestation of a *human* capacity for, and tendency toward, excess or a lack of (self-)moderation. Early in the novel, the narrator informs us that "Baby Suggs, holy, didn't approve of extra. 'Everything depends on knowing how much,' she said, and 'Good is knowing when to stop.'"[46] For Baby Suggs, holy, both good and evil are defined in epistemological terms: knowing, and not knowing, when to stop. In regarding this historical pattern of White people's excessive abuses as "bad luck," the assumption is that this can be negotiated, if not contained. If Whites cannot—because of a deep-rooted socialization—determine when to stop, then someone else must embrace that responsibility. Coming at the end of an extended meditation on color, Baby Suggs's theodicy frees and enables her to resume her spiritual leadership, in the realm of the ancestors. Understanding racist violence and violations as "bad luck" means that one need not withdraw or retreat, but that one can continue to negotiate one's way toward a righteous equilibrium of interdependent relationships, armed with that knowledge. So, after warning her granddaughter, Denver, of this manifest tendency toward excess, she tells her, "Know it, and go on out the yard."[47] Significantly, this counsel is communicated in the final phase of her spiritual leadership, in her ancestor role. And it is this ancestor role that propels the recuperative direction of the plot.

Although Baby Suggs, holy, has no embodied role for most of the novel, her presence is central to the lives of the Black people in the novel, and to the novel's development as a whole. At the start of the novel, we learn that her capacity for creative agency is not reduced, but in fact increases, with death. When, for example, the baby ghost fails to appear at Sethe and Denver's bidding, Denver concludes that "Grandma Baby must be stopping it."[48] And in her ancestor role she outfits Beloved with shoes needed for the journey of intercession to free Sethe, Paul D, and the entire Cincinnati Black community from the stagnation in which they are trapped because of their failure to utilize their own transformative and righteous agency, beginning with the community's failure to protect Sethe from Schoolteacher. Beloved's new shoes are the authenticating symbol of her connection to the ancestor, Baby Suggs, holy, and this connectedness enables the reader to recognize the ways in which her catalytic presence facilitates a recovery and release that emanates from Baby Suggs's theodicy. The primary aspect of this theodicy is its emphasis on knowing as an intervention that undermines and transforms "evil." For Denver, Janie, Ella, and each of the agents involved in the novel's multifaceted resolution, *knowing* that it is time to end their various acts of omission prompts specific interventions that release them from pain, regret, and longing.

CONCLUSION

As illustrated in the discussion above, the preacher through the text (Stewart) and the preacher in the text (Baby Suggs, holy) shared an ethos of (inter)connectedness derived from an African cosmology. This ethos of (inter-)connectedness engendered a connectedness and commitment to cultural/spiritual kin and a vision of women's responsibility and capacity for creative agency. It informed and inspired their spiritual and sociopolitical visions and fueled the determination with which these Black women preachers contested gender and, to a lesser degree, class-based restrictions on the exercise of creative or righteous agency. For Stewart, the confinement of institutional discourses was surmounted by taking her message to the podium. For Baby Suggs, holy, similar discursive restrictions were negotiated through itinerancy and a self-directed redefinition of the form of her creative agency: "she didn't deliver sermons or preach—insisting she was too ignorant for that—she *called* and the hearing heard."[49]

NOTES

This essay is excerpted from the introductory chapter to a book-length manuscript, *Foundation of Ancient Power: Spirituality and/as Ideology in Black Women's Fiction and Film,* begun during my postdoctoral fellowship year in the Women's Studies in Religion Program at Harvard Divinity School. I would like to thank Constance Buchanan, then the director, and my colleagues Denise Ackermann, Caroline Ford, Karen King, and B. Sree Padma for their comments on earlier drafts of this essay. I would also like to thank Gerard Aching, Katherine Clay Bassard, C Dale Gadsden, Anthonia C. Kalu, Kelechi Kalu, Estella Conwill Májozo, and Nellie Y. McKay for their constant support and encouragement, and for challenging and sharpening my vision. A special thanks to Emilie Townes for taking the time to read the essay and for making helpful suggestions.

1. See, for example, Katie Cannon, *Black Womanist Ethics* (Atlanta: Scholars Press, 1988); Delores Williams, *Sisters in the Wilderness: The Challenge of Womanist God-Talk* (New York: Orbis, 1993); Jacquelyn Grant, *White Women's Christ and Black Women's Jesus: Feminist Christology and Womanist Response* (Atlanta: Scholars Press, 1989); and Emilie Townes, *In a Blaze of Glory: Womanist Spirituality as Social Witness* (Nashville, Tenn.: Abingdon Press, 1995).

2. Barbara Christian, "Fixing Methodologies: *Beloved,*" *Cultural Critique* (Spring 1993): 7. See also literary critic Karla Holloway's discussion of African cosmology in Black women's literature in *Moorings and Metaphors: Figures of Culture and Gender in Black Women's Literature* (New Brunswick, N.J.: Rutgers University Press, 1992).

3. Although used in the singular, "Afro-Christianity" does not refer to a discrete or single location. Rather, it refers to the total range of diverse Christological positions and denominational traditions developed by African Americans and discernibly informed by key aspects of African cosmology. It is, therefore, a plural signifier. The "Black church" refers to people and institutions; "Afro-Christianity" refers to a *discursive* range.

4. Toni Morrison, "Rootedness: The Ancestor as Foundation," in *Black Women Writers (1950–1980): A Critical Evaluation,* ed. Mari Evans (New York: Anchor/Doubleday, 1984), p. 342.

5. Throughout this discussion the word *African* is used interchangeably with *Black* to denote cultural identity and praxis, in contradistinction from its usage to denote a collective geopolitical nationality. The term *continental African* is used to indicate the latter.

6. As used in this essay, *ideology* refers to a way of thinking or system of ideas developed by and in the interest of a specific group or constituency. Ideologies, therefore, are never neutral and are *not* always or necessarily hegemonic.

7. In the modern world, territorial and national boundaries no longer coincide with or contain single cultural identities and linguistic traditions. Consequently, the term *cultural domain* acknowledges the continuing connectedness among globally distributed communities that claim a particular cultural identity and heritage. So, in addition to the African cultural domain, one can identify the Asian cultural domain, the European cultural domain, and so on.

8. Throughout this analysis, *Africa-centered* is used to mean literally and meta-

physically centered on Africa, a specific cultural domain. This usage is not to be confused with the term *Afrocentric*, which has acquired many pejorative meanings, apart from its own intrinsic debilitation. Barbara Christian aptly summarizes these shortcomings: "In effect the use of the term *centrism* betrays the fact that Afrocentrism is generated from narrow nationalist Western thinking, that it is akin to Eurocentrism, to which it is apparently opposed but which it mimics. Thus many contemporary forms of Afrocentrism undercut the very concept they were intended to propose, that there are different interpretations of history, different narratives, depending on where one is positioned, in terms of power relations as well as distinctive cultures and that there are, given the various cultures of our world, multiple philosophical approaches to understanding life." See also Cheryl Townsend Gilkes, "We Have a Beautiful Mother: Womanist Musings on the Afrocentric Idea," in *Living the Intersection: Womanism and Afrocentrism in Theology*, ed. Cheryl J. Sanders (Minneapolis: Fortress Press, 1995). According to Townsend Gilkes, Afrocentrism "signifies a commitment to standing in the middle of the black experience, either in the United States or in Africa or worldwide, and starting one's thinking there" (p. 26).

9. E. B. Idowu, *African Traditional Religion: A Definition* (London: SCM Press, 1973), p. 190.

10. Toni Morrison, "A Knowing So Deep," *Essence*, May 1985, p. 230.

11. Mamphela Ramphele, "Are Women Not Part of the Problem Perpetuating Sexism?—A Bird's Eye View from South Africa," *Africa Today* 37 (Spring): 12.

12. Idowu, *African Traditional Religion*, p. 184.

13. A central thesis of this analysis is the integrity and indeed the inevitability of culturally informed and nuanced engagements with Christianity. It is therefore important to note the existence and integrity of Euro-Christianity, a theological range comparable to Afro-Christianity but distinguishable from what is here defined as Christendom.

14. Winthrop Jordan, *White over Black: American Attitudes toward the Negro, 1550–1812* (Chapel Hill: University of North Carolina Press, 1968), p. 94.

15. 2 Cor. 5:17 NRSV.

16. "As many of you as were baptized into Christ have clothed yourselves with Christ. There is no longer Jew or Greek, there is no longer slave or free, there is no longer male and female; for all of you are one in Christ Jesus" (Gal. 3:27–28 NRSV).

17. Albert J. Raboteau, *Slave Religion: The "Invisible Institution" in the Antebellum South* (New York: Oxford University Press, 1978), p. 16.

18. Margaret Washington Creel, "Gullah Attitudes toward Life and Death," in *Africanisms in American Culture*, ed. Joseph E. Holloway (Bloomington: Indiana University Press, 1990), p. 74.

19. Peter J. Paris, *The Spirituality of African Peoples* (Minneapolis: Fortress Press, 1995), p. 35.

20. Zora Neale Hurston, *The Sanctified Church: The Folklore Writings of Zora Neale Hurston* (Berkeley, Calif.: Turtle Island Foundation, 1981), pp. 56, 105.

21. Katherine Bassard, "Diaspora Subjectivity and Trans-Atlantic Crossings: Phillis Wheatley's Poetics of Recovery," forthcoming in *American Literary History;* Bill E. Lawson, "Moral Discourse and Slavery," in *Between Slavery and Freedom: Philosophy and Amer-*

ican Slavery, ed. Howard McGary and Bill E. Lawson (Bloomington: Indiana University Press, 1992), p. 78.

22. Zora Neale Hurston, *Their Eyes Were Watching God* (1937; reprint, New York: Harper, 1990), p. 15.

23. See, for example, Ama Ata Aidoo, *Anowa,* in *The Dilemma of a Ghost and Anowa* (London: Longman, 1987); Grace Nichols, *i is a long memoried woman;* Ntozake Shange, *Sassafras, Cypress, and Indigo* (New York: St. Martin's, 1983); Paule Marshall, *Praisesong for the Widow* (New York: Dutton, 1983); Tess Onwueme, *Go Tell It to Women* (Detroit: African Heritage Press, 1992); Sherley Anne Williams, *Dessa Rose* (New York: William Morrow, 1986); Erna Brodber, *Myal* (London: New Beacon Books, 1988); and Estella Conwill Májozo, *Libation: A Literary Pilgrimage through the African-American Soul* (New York: Harlem River Press, 1995).

24. Marilyn Richardson, ed., *Maria W. Stewart, America's First Black Woman Political Speaker* (Bloomington: Indiana University Press, 1987), p. 69.

25. Nellie Y. McKay, "Nineteenth-Century Black Women's Spiritual Autobiographies: Religious Faith and Self-Empowerment," in *Interpreting Women's Lives: Feminist Theory and Personal Narratives,* ed. Personal Narratives Group (Bloomington: Indiana University Press, 1989), p. 142.

26. Paris, *Spirituality,* pp. 32–33.

27. Ibid., p. 33.

28. Diedre L. Bádéjò, "The Goddess Osun as a Paradigm for African Feminist Criticism," *Sage: A Scholarly Journal on Black Women* 6, no.1 (1989), p. 27.

29. Evelyn Brooks Higginbotham, *Righteous Discontent: The Women's Movement in the Black Baptist Church, 1880–1920* (Cambridge, Mass.: Harvard University Press, 1993), pp. 1, 10, 124.

30. Richardson, *Maria W. Stewart,* pp. 29, 30.

31. Ibid., p.14.

32. Ibid., p. 37. In light of the oratorical and rhetorical features of Stewart's essays and speeches, Richardson identifies her as "predecessor to Sojourner Truth, Frederick Douglass, Henry Highland Garnet, Frances Harper, and other black nineteenth-century masters of language deployed to change society."

33. I am indebted to Emilie Townes for pointing out that, in keeping with the vision of the second Great Awakening, these evangelical preachers were more concerned with the salvation of souls, which they saw as the means of promoting a just social order.

34. Richardson, *Maria W. Stewart,* pp. 61, 39.

35. Ibid., p. 70.

36. Ibid., p. 69.

37. In *The Life and Religious Experience of Jarena Lee, A Coloured Lady* (1836), Lee asked, "If a man may preach, because the Saviour died for him, why not the woman? seeing he died for her also. . . . Did not Mary *first* preach the risen Saviour, and is not the doctrine of the resurrection the very climax of Christianity—hangs not all our hope on this, as argued by St. Paul?" See William L. Andrews, ed., *Sisters of the Spirit: Three Black Women's Autobiographies of the Nineteenth Century* (Bloomington: Indiana University Press, 1986), p. 36.

38. By contrast, Beloved's presence acts as a catalyst in galvanizing the Cincin-

nati Black community to act in concert. Since the crisis afflicting the community—unresolved pain and emotional paralysis—predates Beloved's appearance, Morrison shows that without collective involvement righteous agency cannot be fully exercised.

39. Morrison, *Beloved* (New York: Knopf, 1987), p. 87.

40. Ibid.

41. Raboteau, *Slave Religion*, p. 241.

42. Morrison, *Beloved*, pp. 87–88.

43. Ibid. (emphasis added).

44. Ibid., pp. 89, 140.

45. Ibid., p.104.

46. Ibid., p. 87.

47. Ibid., p. 244.

48. Ibid., p. 4.

49. Ibid., p. 177.

FIFTEEN

A Chaste and Fervid Eloquence

Catherine Booth and the Ministry of Women in the Salvation Army

Pamela J. Walker

The Salvation Army invaded the streets of East London in 1865, bombarding these working-class neighborhoods with brass bands and flamboyant preachers. The Hallelujah Lasses, as the Army's women preachers were known, excited the most controversy. Salvationist women preached and assumed positions of leadership and authority at a time when few Protestant denominations or other working-class organizations allowed women to perform any such work. Salvationist women drew large crowds and helped transform the Salvation Army from a small London mission into a recognized national and international denomination with a strong social-service wing. The distinctive role of women had its origin in the work of Catherine Mumford Booth, who founded the Salvation Army with her husband, William Booth. She fervently argued for women's right to preach the gospel and was a respected independent evangelist. Her interpretation of female ministry drew upon Methodism and American holiness teachings, as well as her own class position and family life. Under her aegis, the Salvation Army institutionalized women's preaching and provided an extraordinary range of possibilities for women. The Hallelujah Lasses followed Catherine Booth's example, but they also seized the opportunity to build on her work and to transform the practice of female ministry.

Catherine Mumford was born in 1829 and brought up in Brixton, South London. Her father, John Mumford, was a coach builder, a skilled artisanal trade. He and his wife, Sarah Milward Mumford, were members of a Wesleyan Methodist chapel, and as a young man John served as a lay preacher. As a child, Catherine was intensely attached to her mother and to her religion, and these two were intertwined. When she was away from home, Catherine wrote in her diary, "I have felt much cast down at the thought of being from home when I so much need its comforts and away from my Dear

Mother. . . . [W]e shall soon meet again and after all our meetings are past on earth we shall meet to part no more in Glory."[1] These religious convictions were not shared by John Mumford, who took to drink and lost his faith in the 1840s. Subsequently, he was unable to support the family and often did not live with his wife. Catherine and her mother struggled to make ends meet, practicing every economy. They took in lodgers and Catherine considered going out as a domestic servant. Catherine and her mother worried, moreover, about the state of John Mumford's soul. In January 1848, Catherine wrote in her diary, "My dear father is a great trial to us."[2] Catherine mentioned her only brother, John, very rarely in her correspondence. But her infrequent comments make it clear she counted him among the unsaved. Catherine's ardent belief in the faithfulness and righteousness of women, which she expressed so frequently in her later writings, was first apprehended in her own family.

If piety and righteousness were female virtues in the Mumford family, the family religion, Methodism, offered women an unusual opportunity to exercise these virtues in institutional ways. The Methodists embraced popular religion, and the laboring people who joined created a distinctive religious language and practice that included female preaching and a lay piety that infused all aspects of the believer's life. All Methodists joined classes in which members prayed aloud, spoke of their spiritual experiences, and testified to God's work in their lives. This duty provided a powerful inducement for Methodist women to reconsider the meaning of Paul's injunction that women remain silent. Some Methodist women preached to female and mixed audiences with great effect during the later eighteenth and the earlier nineteenth centuries. They were known for direct, unadorned vernacular speech, emotional fervor, and an independence that was hardly an example of feminine decorum and submission. This religious culture provided Catherine with an important foundation for her own work and left a legacy that she strived to revitalize throughout her life.[3]

In 1855, Catherine married William Booth and began the evangelical partnership that lasted the rest of her life. William Booth, also born in 1829, was beginning his career as a Methodist preacher. He ardently wished to be a revivalist in the tradition of Americans James Caughey and Charles Finney. Both men had toured Britain in the 1850s, and William had been deeply impressed by their enthusiastic, dramatic preaching and their ability to effect conversions. In 1854, William joined the Methodist New Connexion. This body permitted him to work as a circuit preacher while also organizing revivals in different towns, where he preached to large, enthusiastic congregations.[4] Catherine traveled to revivals with William whenever she could, but after the birth of Bramwell in 1857, Ballington in 1858, Catherine in 1859, and Emma in 1860, Catherine was increasingly occupied with domestic concerns.

Nevertheless, during those years Catherine began to reconsider the position of women in the church. In particular, she questioned the prohibitions against women's preaching. Methodists had allowed women preachers some limited opportunities, but the denomination was changing, and so too were the restrictions placed on women. Despite her evident skill and knowledge, Catherine, like her husband, had little formal education. The heavy demands of her household always precluded any sustained, formal study. Although Methodist leaders of an earlier generation often educated themselves, this practice was increasingly devalued as Methodism grew and new standards for the ministry were established. This particularly excluded women who could not attend the institutions where such credentials were granted.[5] Moreover, by mid-century few Methodist women preached, despite John Wesley's cautious endorsement of women's preaching for those who had received a distinct call and the history of many prominent and influential Methodist women preachers. Indeed, many Methodists accepted that Scripture forbade women's preaching. Catherine's own views in the 1850s reflected the ambivalence shared by many Methodists. She firmly believed women must answer the call of the Holy Spirit but not defy the commandment to remain in feminine submission. This view is exemplified in a letter to William, in which she asked, "Who shall dare thrust women out of the Church's operation or presume to put *my* candle which *God* has lighted under a bushel?" Yet she wrote in that same letter, "Perhaps sometime with thy permission (for I am going to promise to *obey* thee before I have any intention of entering such work) I may write something more extensive" on women's role in the church.[6]

The American holiness movement offered a theological approach to women's place in the church that was to have a profound influence on Catherine's thought. The holiness and revivalist movements were intertwined, drawing on similar theological sources; both opened up new possibilities for women. Moreover, this evangelical culture was transatlantic. British and American evangelists read each other's literature, adopted each other's music, and borrowed preaching techniques, thus influencing the direction of theology and practice in Britain and America. The Booths' place in this transatlantic evangelical culture engaged them with ideas and practices that were outside the mainstream of British Nonconformity at mid-century, opening up a whole range of possibilities.

The mid-century American holiness theologians taught that it was the duty and the privilege of all Christians to achieve entire sanctification. All believers were to renounce sin, and when infused with the Holy Spirit their hearts, minds, and wills would become the very likeness of God. This theology allowed for a reconsideration of long-standing injunctions against women's authority in the church because it did not regard original sin as the permanent state of humanity and thereby lessened the burden of Eve's sin. It also relied heavily on the Acts of the Apostles, in which women figured prominently. Third, holiness theologians justified deviating from a literal reading of the Bible when a greater good was served. Last, it emphasized Jesus' active ministry and the prophetic call of the Holy Spirit over a text-based religiosity. Women took up these opportunities in a number of ways, and these innovative women were important to Catherine's growing conviction that the restrictions placed on women were not based in Scripture and damaged women and the church. Most important, Catherine avidly followed the progress of Mrs. Phoebe Palmer, the author of a number of influential holiness books and a noted preacher, who visited England in 1859.[7]

Not everyone shared Catherine's enthusiasm. Shortly after Mrs. Palmer's arrival in England, several pamphlets condemned her ministry. The Reverend Arthur Augustus Rees was one who denounced her. In his pamphlet *Reasons for Not Co-operating in the Alleged "Sunderland Revivals,"* Rees argued that Paul specifically and unequivocally forbade women to speak in church, that Eve's sin placed women "under a denser cloud of suffering and humiliation," and that they must remain in subjection to men.[8] Catherine, enraged, wrote to her mother, "I am determined that fellow shall not go unthrashed," and she thereupon carried out her earlier ambition of writing something more extensive on the position of women in the church.[9] Her pamphlet *Female Teaching: or the Rev. A. A. Rees versus Mrs. Palmer, Being a Reply to a Pamphlet by the Above Named Gentleman on the Sunderland Revival,* was published in December 1859, just a few days before the birth of Emma, her fourth child.[10] Catherine wrote her parents, "it is pretty well-known that a *Lady* has tackled him [Rees] and there is much speculation and curiosity abroad it seems. . . . I should like to have given him more *pepper* but being a Lady I felt I must preserve a becoming dignity! I suppose his pamphlet is deemed unanswerable by some. Bah! I could answer a dozen *such* in my way."[11]

Catherine's defense of women's preaching rested on two lines of argument. First, she considered Christian women's place in the order of things, and second, she closely examined specific scriptural texts that addressed women's prophecy. She began with a consideration of creation. She cited the first creation story, Genesis 1:27–31, in which God created male and female together and gave them dominion over the earth. The subordination of woman occurred later, as a punishment for her transgressions. Thus women's subjection was neither natural nor eternal. "If woman had been in a state of subjection from her creation, in consequence of natural inferiority, where is the force of the words, 'he shall rule over thee,' as a part of her curse?"[12]

Like Rees, Catherine believed women's nature was different from men's, but she maintained that such differences especially fitted women for preaching.

> Making allowance for the novelty of the thing, we cannot discover anything either unnatural or immodest in a Christian woman, becomingly attired, appearing on a platform or a pulpit. By *nature* she seems fitted to grace either. God has given to women a graceful form and attitude, winning manners, persua-

sive speech, and, above all, a finely-tuned emotional nature, all of which appear to us eminent *natural* qualifications for public speaking.[13]

Women, Catherine recognized, were also bound by a social order put in place after the Fall. God had decreed distinct spheres of labor for men and women and had placed women in subjection to their husbands. But, Catherine maintained, these injunctions did not preclude female ministry.

Catherine attested, furthermore, that the curse did not place women in subjection to men as beings, but only to their husbands. Neither an unmarried woman nor a widow "is subject to man in any sense in which one man is not subject to another; both the law of God and man recognize her as an independent being."[14] Even a wife's subjection was mitigated by Christ. Although woman and man shared in the Fall, woman had brought Christ into the world with the aid of no man. Furthermore, the resurrected Christ first appeared to Mary Magdalene and charged her to spread the news. This public duty was given to her because her faith was so much greater than that of the men. The Resurrection did not remove the curse but rather redeemed women "in a moral sense" and ought to have dispelled any belief in the spiritual superiority of men.[15]

Catherine devoted the body of her pamphlet to examining the biblical passages that Rees and others used to justify excluding women from the pulpit. For Catherine, this was undoubtedly the core of the debate. For if female preaching were forbidden in Scripture, she could offer no possible justification for the practice. Catherine used what she termed a "common sense" interpretation of Scripture. She considered the key passages in Corinthians and Timothy in the larger context of the Bible as well as the particular historical context of each passage. She concluded that these passages did not enjoin women to silence but merely forbade disorderly speech and the usurpation of authority from men. She supported her position by citing the prophecy of Joel, "I will pour out my spirit upon all flesh, and your sons and your daughters will prophesy" (Joel 2:28), which was echoed in Acts 2:17, as well as the examples of biblical women prophets and preachers whose work must have been in harmony with divine injunction.

Catherine's pamphlet was not hermeneutically original.[16] Yet it was exceptional, and her argument had significant consequences for the position of women. The most innovative and ultimately significant aspect of Catherine's thinking was her assertion that women could possess spiritual authority as women and could preach as Christian women in their own voices as a part of the natural order. Women in various Protestant traditions had justified their public preaching by limiting the kinds of authority women could acquire through their activities. Mrs. Palmer, in particular, whose ministry Catherine so fervently defended, published *The Promise of the Father; or a Neglected Spirituality of the Last Days* in 1859 to defend her own work. She put forth a very different justification of her own activities. Her book began, "Do not be startled, dear reader. We do not intend to discuss the question of 'Women's Rights' or of 'Women's Preaching,' technically so called. . . . We believe woman has her legitimate sphere of action, which differs in most cases materially from that of man; and in this legitimate sphere she is both happy and useful."[17]

In her interpretation, women did not possess any particular right to preach but could only prophesy at the prompting of the Holy Spirit. Clearly women could hold no authority as women, and therefore preaching would not threaten women's subjugation in any way. Mrs. Palmer's argument was by no means unique; similar arguments had been used by many women since the Reformation.

Catherine agreed that the Holy Spirit must call women to preach. However, this requirement was not, in her view, any different from the requirement for a man. A Christian was one who was filled with the Holy Spirit and acted in accordance with God's will. But Catherine clearly stated that any qualified woman had *the right* to preach "independent of any man-made restrictions." The only legitimate exception was silence imposed by her own husband; but then what Christian husband would withstand God's call to his wife?[18]

Catherine also refused to justify women's preaching by claiming that women were the weak, the foolish, or the low who would confound the wise, as many Methodist women before her had done. She rejected the disorderly, loud style of some sectarian Methodists because she believed it did not depend on clear theological reasoning and an appropriate feminine demeanor. These distinctions were critical to her justification of women's preaching. She always insisted that Christian women possessed the right to preach and that this right was based on their natural capacities and qualities. Therefore, she did not justify her claim by placing herself outside of social convention and order but rather proclaimed her right to preach as a part of the contract between God and humanity. Similarly, she never employed the prophetic language of Revelation like many nineteenth-century women, including Joanna Southcott, visionary and prophet, and Mother Ann Lee, founder of the Shakers. She did not regard herself as a singular prophetic figure but rather as a dutiful Christian wife and mother. For Catherine, women's preaching was not extraordinary, and it could be sustained within the conventional social order.

In summary, Catherine's insistence on women's right to preach the gospel had several sources. Catherine's own family life demonstrated the constancy and depth of women's faith. She owed much to the Methodist tradition, which offered women a wide range of opportunities to speak of God's work in their lives and to guide others. It is not surprising that Catherine Booth built on this tradition. The holiness movement provided Catherine with an important theological frame to reconsider the scriptural and practical aspects of women's preaching as well as examples of women's ministry. The intersection of these influences shaped Catherine's interpretation of women's preaching and provided the ground for her claim for women's right to preach.

Nevertheless, when Catherine wrote her pamphlet proclaiming women's right to preach the gospel, she had not yet preached herself. Her first attempts at public speaking were occasioned by the mundane struggles of life. In 1857 she reported to her mother that she had lectured on temperance to a female audience. She was anxious for success for four reasons: "*first* to do good, 2ly to gain something towards meeting the extra expenses my delicate health occasions to my husband 3ly to be able to do something towards educating my children and 4ly tho' not least to be able to make some little return for all your kindness past and present, are these not worthy motives?"[19]

These financial considerations were part of the daily reality of Catherine's life. Like other women of her class, Catherine was brought up in a household where women's labor was essential to survival. Hence, the financial struggles that led to her preaching career were part of the ordinary course of life for a woman of the artisanal class. In contrast, a middle-class woman of her generation could not have engaged in waged labor without the loss of her gendered class status. It was therefore possible for Catherine to regard preaching as an eminently suitable course of action from a practical as well as theological standpoint in ways that a middle-class woman like Mrs. Palmer could not. Catherine regarded her ministry as a fully justified and unexceptionable course of action for a Christian woman. And she relished her work, writing to her mother, "I felt quite at home on the *platform*—far more than I do in the *kitchen*."[20]

Catherine's career began in earnest in 1860 when William fell ill and she took his place in the pulpit.[21] She needed to succeed for financial reasons. The demands on her time were exceedingly trying. She summed up her situation when she wrote to William, "I must try to possess my soul in patience and do *all* in the kitchen as well as in the Pulpit to the glory of God—the Lord help me. I will attend to the Jacksons' accn't as soon as I get some money."[22]

The Booths' remarkable arrangement met with little resistance. Catherine's preaching style was decidedly restrained and no doubt reassured some who feared the disruptive consequences of women's ministry. The *Wesleyan Times* described how a congregation "sat with evident interest listening to her chaste and fervid eloquence."[23] Still, Catherine's situation was trying, and the chapel did not always recognize her particular difficulties. She wrote William, "But I cannot give my time to preparation unless I can afford to put my sewing out. It never seems to occur to anybody that I cannot do two things at once, or that I want means to relieve me of the one while I do the other! What I do, I do to the Lord. Still I am conscious they are the partakers of the benefit, and could wish that they would remember our temporalities a little more than they do!"[24]

After William's return, Catherine continued to preach on occasional Sundays with William as well as to speak by invitation. The Booths, however, were deeply dissatisfied with the Methodist New Connexion. They firmly believed that William's talents were squandered in a regular circuit, and they repeatedly asked the connexion to allow William to devote himself fully to evangelistic labor. The connexion refused. In 1862, with the fervent conviction of their singular commitment to God's service, the Booths left the Methodist New Connexion and never again worked under any human authority except their own.

In the autumn of 1865, the Booths decided to settle in London when several evangelical friends supplied the necessary funds and support to establish a home mission. This arrangement allowed them the independence they required and the stability necessary for a growing family with an uncertain income. William began work in the heart of the East End, a neighborhood that exemplified the new urban landscape. Its working-class populace, densely packed housing, pubs, and music halls seemed to make it especially ripe for Christian evangelization. Soon a small number of men and women, attracted to Booth's theology and his revivalist preaching, began to assist him in the work.[25]

London also provided Catherine with her own sphere of work. She responded to invitations to preach in London's West End, resort towns, and provincial cities, often to largely middle-class audiences. She not only supported her family but also raised significant sums for the Mission with her preaching. Many wealthy Christians heard her preach and became regular supporters of the Mission in its early years.[26] Catherine also sat on various Mission committees and preached at the Mission; she never held an official position or rank but was known as the Army Mother. Thus Catherine and William settled in London and established their careers as independent revivalists and the leaders of a growing religious organization.

One of the most unusual features of the Christian Mission, later renamed the Salvation Army, was the authority granted to women. At its first annual conference in 1870, it was decided, "As it is manifest from the Scriptures of the Old and especially the New Testament that God has sanctioned the labors of Godly women in His Church; godly women possessing the necessary gifts and qualifications shall be employed as preachers itinerant or otherwise and class leaders and as such shall have appointments given to them on the preachers plan; and they shall be eligible for any office, and to speak and vote at all official meetings."[27]

Joining the Salvation Army entailed learning to preach indoors and out, to give out a hymn, to guide penitents, and to administer the daily business of renting halls, paying for gas, and keeping the accounts. Such work was an enormous change for the working-class women who joined the movement. Pamela Shepard, for example, was born in Wales in the 1830s. When her husband went to prison, she was left to support their three children with her work as a rag sorter. She later worked as a hall keeper and cook to the Christian Mission while taking in laundry to make ends meet. In 1878 she was sent to "open fire" on Aberdare, Wales, with her two daughters and Sarah Sayers. Sayers, a forty-year-old widow and mother of two, had earned her living as a charwoman while working as an exhorter for the Mission.[28] The women set off with £ 5 to cover their expenses. Upon arrival, they rented the Temperance Hall, which held 1,500 people. The women preached in the streets to whomever would listen and announced the forthcoming meeting at the hall. After the first meeting, they telegraphed Headquarters, "Lots in a pickle and three in the fountain."[29]

Catherine Booth was an inspiration to Salvationist women as well as an important influence on the Army's doctrine and practice. Many women recalled being drawn into the Army by her example, and her work and writing inspired many other women as well. But for all that they were inspired by Catherine Booth's writing and preaching, the Hallelujah Lasses, as Salvationist women were known, did not simply act on her example but transformed the practice of female ministry. The Hallelujah Lasses worked within an organizational structure that permitted them greater license than Catherine's career as an individual, independent evangelist had allowed. The Army endorsed their work and provided women with a place in an established structure; but at the same time it imposed strict regulations and order. The Salvation Army was a tightly disciplined, hierarchical organization that demanded obedience from all its members. Officers, for example, were frequently moved with no choice about when or where they were placed. Moreover, women's authority had its limits. The Lasses created their ministry in a context that still offered few models of female authority. Women's religious authority was strongly associated with sexual abandon and chaos. The Salvation Army also restrained women by insisting that wives must obey their husbands while at the same time endorsing women's public religious authority. Hence, the Hallelujah Lasses worked within complicated constraints and opportunities.

The Salvation Army invariably began work in the streets, where the very presence of the Lasses was striking. Working-class women used the streets to carry out their domestic responsibilities as well as their waged work.[30] Salvationist women, however, stood in the streets, claiming spiritual authority and agency for themselves, calling upon others to repent. But they were not simply preaching in the streets as other evangelicals had done; their activities were extraordinary. Salvationist women borrowed their inventive preaching style from the urban commercial culture that surrounded them. This clearly distinguished them from Catherine Booth and their other predecessors. The music halls and working-class theaters were simply not part of the provincial, Nonconformist communities where Catherine began her career.[31] The Hallelujah Lasses used the broad gestures and dramatic effects of popular commercial entertainment to dramatize their spiritual vision. In 1880, Eliza Haynes paraded the streets of Marylebone with her hair loose and flowing and a sign around her neck that read, "I am Happy Eliza." She played the fiddle and handed out announcements of an upcoming meeting where she would preach. To "the immense sensation of the whole population," two women in Hackney put on their nightgowns and paraded the streets to announce a meeting.[32] No Victorian woman went out without a hat, and a woman would never be seen with loose hair because these things showed an utter disregard for propriety, decency, and respectability. Wearing a nightgown in the street was simply breathtaking in its transgression of proper conduct and appearance.

Like the celebrated women of the music hall, Salvationist women used costume, song, and gesture to capture their audience. Many women played musical instruments, composed songs, or wrote new words to popular music hall tunes. These young women were well aware of the enormous appeal of commercial entertainment, and they eagerly capitalized on it. As soon as a woman succeeded with a new technique, others picked it up and often added their own innovations. Crowds gathered for Army meetings, and everyone realized the Lasses were an important draw. When Salvationists were unable to fill a hall in Coventry, the Chief of Staff concluded, "If there is no other plan of working the place, we had better send lasses."[33]

The Lasses horrified many observers. Crowds pelted them with rotting vegetables and told them to go home, and they were subjected to a particularly sexualized form of abuse and ridicule. Salvationist women reported that "the language used by the men . . . has been of the vilest character. . . . You have only to be known as a Salvationist in Eastbourne to have the filthiest language used to you."[34] While the vicar's wife or a Biblewoman would be met with great respect even if her message were ignored, Salvationist women were regarded as utterly disreputable.[35]

This view of Salvationist women was remarkably widespread. The bishops of Oxford and Hereford asserted in 1883 that Army meetings encouraged immorality and resulted in many illegitimate births among Salvationist women.[36] The music halls put forth a similar view, albeit in a very different way. One song, "Sister 'Ria," performed by Miss Lizzie Fletcher, told of a woman who sang and danced in the street for the Army until "some wicked individual had tempted her you know, to leave the mighty Army and become a real live 'pro.'"[37] In another song the singer related that he joined the Army because he fell in love with two girls.

> They call one Happy Eliza, and one Converted Jane
> They've been most wicked in their time, but will ne'er do so again;
> They said pray come and join us and I was just in the mood
> They're Hallelujah Sisters and they're bound to do me good.[38]

This song testifies to Happy Eliza's fame and comically reduces her performance on the streets of London to little more than an effort to attract men.

But the Hallelujah Lasses were not using spectacle and theater just to draw attention to their cause. Their activities were made meaningful by the context of their religious vision. Salvationists practiced a distinctly bodily form of religious expression. Like most Christians, they affirmed their faith through words and deeds, but they also expressed their faith through the body. They trembled and shook, shouted, rocked to and fro, clapped their hands, fell into trances, and spoke of their bodies levitating. Women's public spectacles occurred in this larger context, where religious experience was emotional, spiritual, and physical. Using their bodies to express their convictions invited ridicule and abuse, but as Christians they accepted persecution. It allowed women to test their faith and to display their zeal to any who doubted them.[39]

Moreover, the Hallelujah Lasses' manipulation of images of disorderly women and sexual license built on images of prostitution, which was one of the most pressing social questions of the day, particularly for working-class women, who were the majority of prostitutes and the most frequent objects of reform efforts. Prostitutes were associated with disease, putrefaction, and death. They were the "seminal drains" through which all Victorian society's excretions were washed away, ensuring the purity of the whole. These images were particularly salient in the new, densely populated cities where the Army was active.[40] The Hallelujah Lasses took these images and reversed them. They would "net the gutters" and "sweep the social sewers" and reclaim all those rushing to death and destruction.[41] When the "perishing masses" came to the Hallelujah Lasses, they were purified. Like prostitutes, they went where other women would not go and acted as vessels through which society's ruin and disease could pass. But the Lasses were agents of cleanliness and sanctification. If prostitutes saved society by siphoning off its waste, the Hallelujah Lasses could do even better by purifying the pestilence and banishing death. Using representations of sexual license and disorder allowed the Hallelujah Lasses to dramatically express the purity and power of their mission.

When Catherine Booth died in 1890, thirty thousand people lined the streets of East London to watch her funeral procession. She was called the "most famous and influential Christian woman of the generation."[42] Her own preaching and writing persuaded many Christians of the value of women's ministry. When she founded the Salvation Army, she institutionalized women's right to preach the gospel and provided a unique opportunity for thousands of women to preach without having an extraordinary call or inhabiting a world turned upside down. She claimed for women both the prophetic call of the Holy Spirit and a place within the ongoing life of the church based on the scriptural text. Women's authority was both inspirational and institutional. She created a new lexicon of Christian activity.

The Hallelujah Lasses seized the opportunity. They drew upon the urban, working-class culture that surrounded them to create an evangelizing style that expressed their religious convictions. The significance of their activities can best be appreciated when compared with other Protestant denominations, which offered women no such authority. Similarly, other working-class organizations such as trade unions lamented the impossibility of organizing working-class women, and few working-class women took leadership positions in any such organizations. Catherine's vision persisted in the Army even as the movement underwent significant changes in the early twentieth century. Her legacy also inspired women in more surprising ways. The American Pentecostal preacher Aimee Semple McPherson borrowed heavily from Catherine's theology as well as the spectacular style of the Hallelujah Lasses. She was the daughter of a Hallelujah Lass, and her mother firmly believed Aimee was the reincarnation of Catherine Booth, destined to be a great evangelist.[43]

Salvationist women claimed a moral subjectivity that flew in the face of injunctions to passivity, the subjugation expected of Christian women, and the deference required of working-class men and women within the established denominations. Salvationist women were part of a long tradition of Nonconformist radicalism that challenged both the church and the state. They built on that tradition, creating a prophetic alternative to the dominant models of female religiosity.

NOTES

Many thanks to Major J. Fairbank and the staff at the Salvation Army Heritage Centre, London, for making my research so pleasant and productive. I am grateful for the perceptive questions raised when I presented earlier versions of this essay at Harvard Divinity School, the Institute of Biblical Exegesis at the University of Copenhagen, and the Institute for Historical Research at the University of London. I am especially grateful to Constance Buchanan, now at the Ford Foundation, and the Women's Studies in Religion Program at Harvard Divinity School for providing such a stimulating environment for thinking about the themes raised in this essay. Thanks also to Michael A. Budd, Scott Cook, Paul Dervis, C Dale Gadsden, Gretchen Galbraith, Laura C. Mitchell, Judith R. Walkowitz, and Susan Whitney for invaluable comments.

1. Catherine Mumford, Manuscript Diary, May 13, 1847, British Library (hereafter BL), Add. Mss. 64806, f. 153.

2. Ibid., February 6, 1848, f. 183.

3. Membership in a class was compulsory for Methodists. The class ticket was evidence that an individual was a member in good standing and could partake of communion and the other benefits of membership in the chapel. F. de L. Booth-Tucker, *The Life of Catherine Booth: Mother of the Salvation Army* (London: Fleming Revell, 1891), vol. 1, pp. 53–63, 72–88. On the significance of speech for evangelical women, see Christine L. Krueger, *The Reader's Repentance: Women Preachers, Women Writers, and Nine-*

teenth Century Social Discourse (Chicago: University of Chicago Press, 1992), esp. part 1. On her experience speaking in class, see Mumford, May 30, 1847; and Booth-Tucker, *Life of Catherine Booth,* vol. 1, pp. 49–50.

4. St. John Ervine, *God's Soldier: General William Booth,* 2 vols. (London: Heinemann, 1934).

5. Dale Johnson, "The Methodist Quest for an Educated Ministry," *Church History* 51, no. 3 (September 1982): 304–20.

6. Catherine Mumford to William Booth, letter, April 9, 1855, BL, Add. Mss. 64802, f. 88.

7. Richard Carwardine, *Transatlantic Revivalism: Popular Evangelicalism in Britain and America, 1790–1865* (London: Greenwood Press, 1978); Cheryl Townsend Gilkes, "'Together and in Harness': Women's Traditions in the Sanctified Church," *Signs* 10, no. 41 (1985): 678–99; Cheryl Townsend Gilkes, "The Politics of 'Silence': Dual-Sex Political Systems and Women's Traditions of Conflict in African-American Religion," in *African-American Christianity,* ed. Paul E. Johnson (Berkeley: University of California Press, 1994); Nancy Hardesty, *Women Called to Witness: Evangelical Feminism in the Nineteenth Century* (Nashville, Tenn.: Abingdon Press, 1984), pp. 63–76; Jean Humez, "'My Spirit Eye': Some Functions of Visionary Experience in the Lives of Five Black Women Preachers, 1810–1880," in *Women and the Structure of Society,* ed. Barbara Harris and JoAnn McNamara (Durham, N.C.: Duke University Press, 1984); John Kent, *Holding the Fort: Studies in Victorian Revivalism* (London: Epworth Press, 1978); and Charles Edward White, *The Beauty of Holiness: Phoebe Palmer as Theologian, Revivalist, Feminist and Humanitarian* (Grand Rapids, Mich.: Francis Asbury Press, 1986). For Booth's response to these women, see Catherine Mumford, letter to William Booth, April 9, 1855, BL, Add. Mss. 64802.

8. A. A. Rees, *Reasons for Not Co-Operating in the Alleged "Sunderland Revivals"* (Sunderland: Wm. Henry Hills, 1859). See also the Reverend Dr. Jarbo, *A Letter to Mrs. Palmer in Reference to Women Speaking in Public* (Northshields: Philipson and Hare, 1859).

9. Catherine Mumford Booth, letter to her mother, 25 December 1859, BL, Add. Mss. 64805, f. 48.

10. The first edition of the pamphlet was published locally, but I do not know the precise publication details. No known copy of that pamphlet has survived. The second edition, published in London by G. J. Stevenson, was published the next year, and my analysis is based on the second edition. The pamphlet was probably only slightly different from the first edition, judging from her correspondence with her mother. It is, however, significantly different from the edition published in 1870 entitled *Female Ministry, or Women's Right to Preach the Gospel* (London: Morgan and Chase, 1870). I am grateful to Dr. Dorothy Thompson, Dr. Hugh McLeod, and the librarians of the Methodist Central Archive, Manchester, for helping me to find the elusive 1860 pamphlet. Roger J. Green's *Catherine Booth: A Biography of the Co-founder of the Salvation Army* (Grand Rapids, Mich.: Baker Books, 1996) also discusses these pamphlets at length. His argument draws very extensively on my 1992 Ph.D. dissertation.

11. Catherine Mumford Booth, letter to her parents, December 25, 1859, BL, Add. Mss. 64805, f. 48.

12. Catherine Booth, *Female Teaching: or, the Rev. A. A. Rees versus Mrs. Palmer, Being a Reply to a Pamphlet by the Above Named Gentleman on the Sunderland Revival* (London: G. J. Stevenson, 1861), p. 6.

13. Ibid., p. 3.

14. Ibid., p. 22.

15. Ibid.

16. Other writers had previously made similar arguments. See, for example, Hugh Bourne, "Remarks on the Ministry of Women" (1808), in John Walford, *The Life and Labors of Hugh Bourne* (London: T. King, 1855); Antoinette Brown, "Exegesis of I Corinthians XIV, 34, 35 and 1 Timothy II, 11, 12," *Oberlin Quarterly Review,* January 1849; Luther Lee, *Women's Right to Preach the Gospel* (Syracuse, N.Y.: By the Author, 1853); Phoebe Palmer, *The Promise of the Father* (New York: Garland, 1985); J. H. Robinson, "Female Preaching," *Methodist New Connexion Magazine,* March 1848, pp. 138–42; Z. Taft, *The Scripture Doctrine of Women's Preaching: Stated and Examined* (New York: Printed for the Author, 1859); the Reverend Robert Young, *North of England Revivals: Prophesying of Women* (Newcastle on Tyne, 1859).

17. Phoebe Palmer, *Promise of the Father; or a Neglected Spirituality of the Last Days* (Boston: Henry V. Deglen, 1859), p. 1.

18. Booth, *Female Teaching,* p. 30.

19. Catherine Mumford Booth, letter to her parents, December 23, 1857, BL, Add. Mss. 64804, f. 63.

20. Ibid.

21. Booth-Tucker, *Life of Catherine Booth,* vol. 1, p. 376.

22. Catherine Mumford Booth, letter to William Booth, undated [mid-1860], BL, Add. Mss. 64802, f. 145.

23. *Wesleyan Times,* August 20, 1860, p. 541. The Bethesda Chapel Leaders' Meeting minutes recorded "its cordial thanks to Mrs. Booth for the addresses delivered in the chapel Sunday last which it has no doubt will be productive to good and earnestly hopes that she may continue in the course thus begun in which we unitedly pray that the blessing of God may attend her and crown her labors with success." Bethesda Methodist New Connexion Chapel, Leaders' Committee Meeting Minutes, May 30, 1860, Newcastle-on-Tyne, Tyne and Wear Archives.

24. Catherine Mumford Booth, letter to her mother, December 31, 1860, BL, Add. Mss. 64805, f. 93.

25. Ervine, *God's Soldier,* vol. 1, pp. 280–87; and Robert Sandall, *The History of the Salvation Army,* vol. 1 (1947; reprint, New York: Salvation Army, 1979), chaps. 6 and 7.

26. Catherine Bramwell Booth, *Catherine Booth: The Story of Her Loves* (London: Hodder and Stoughton, 1970), pp. 234–42; and Booth-Tucker, *Life of Catherine Booth,* vol. 1, pp. 588–605.

27. Minutes of the First Conference, the Christian Mission, 1870. On the 1870 Circuit Plan for Whitechapel, five of the thirteen preachers were women, and nine of the sixteen exhorters and prayer leaders were women. By August 1880, women were in charge of 46 of the 118 corps. See *The War Cry,* August 7, 1880, p. 4.

28. The biographical material on Shepard is drawn from Charles Preece, *Woman of the Valleys: The Story of Mother Shepard* (West Glamorgan, Wales: New Life Press, 1988). For Sarah Sayers, see Census of 1871, RG 10 413, f. 24; and the Christian Mission, Whitechapel Circuit Plan, 1870 and 1872.

29. Robert Sandall, *The History of the Salvation Army,* vol. 2 (London: Salvation Army, 1950), p. 112. This is a reference to the hymn lyrics, "there is a fountain filled with

blood, drawn from Emmanuel's veins, where sinners come and wash away all their guilty stains."

30. Andrew Davies, *Leisure, Gender and Poverty: Working-Class Culture in Salford and Manchester, 1900–1939* (Buckingham: Open University Press, 1992); Deborah Nord, *Walking the Victorian Streets* (Ithaca, N.Y.: Cornell University Press, 1995); Ellen Ross, *Love and Toil: Motherhood in Outcast London, 1870–1915* (New York: Oxford University Press, 1993); and James Winter, *London's Teeming Streets, 1830–1914* (London: Routledge, 1993).

31. Peter Bailey, ed., *Music Hall: The Business of Pleasure* (Milton Keynes: Open University Press, 1986); J. S. Bratton, ed., *Music Hall: Performance and Style* (Milton Keynes: Open University Press, 1986).

32. *Borough of Marylebone Mercury,* June 26, 1880, p. 3; *The Indicator,* May 29 1880, p. 3, and July 3, 1880, p. 2; and Metropolitan Police Special Division Report, April 13, 1880, PRO MEPO 2/168. Bramwell Booth, letter to William Booth, March 10, 1893, William Booth file, Salvation Army Heritage Centre, London.

33. Bramwell Booth, letter to Elijah Cadman, December 10, 1879, Cadman file, Salvation Army Heritage Centre, London.

34. *Eastbourne Gazette,* March 16, 1892.

35. See, for example, issues of *The Missing Link Magazine: or the Biblewomen at Home and Abroad.*

36. *Saturday Review,* August 19, 1882, p. 243; *The Times,* April 11, 1883, p. 5; *Daily Telegraph,* April 23, 1883, p. 3; and *The Guardian,* 1882 and 1883. See also Sandall, *History of the Salvation Army,* vol. 2, p. 199; and Stewart Mews, "The General and the Bishops: Alternative Responses to DeChristianization," in *Later Victorian Britain,* ed. T. R. Gourvish and Alan O'Day (London: Macmilian Education, 1988). Mews incorrectly identifies the bishops as from Oxford and Gloucester. See also E. M. Benson Papers, vol. 7, ff. 98–147, Lambeth Palace Library, London.

37. "Sister 'Ria," words by A. J. Mills and music by Arthur Lennard. I am grateful to Mr. Max Tyler for providing me with a copy of this song and for generously allowing me to look through his extensive collection of music hall material.

38. "Happy Eliza and Converted Jane," written and composed by Will Oliver. A copy of this song was kindly provided by the staff of the Raymond Mander and Joe Mitchenson Theatre Collection.

39. Ann Taves, "Knowing through the Body: Dissociative Religious Experience in the African- and British-American Methodist Traditions," *Journal of Religion* 73, no. 2 (April 1993): 200–222.

40. Alain Corbain, "Commercial Sexuality in Nineteenth-Century France: A System of Images and Representations," in *The Making of the Modern Body,* ed. Catherine Gallagher and Thomas Laqueur (Berkeley: University of California Press, 1987); and Judith R. Walkowitz, *Prostitution and Victorian Society: Women, Class, and the State* (Cambridge: Cambridge University Press, 1980).

41. *Daily News,* June 17, 1879, p. 5.

42. *Bible Christian Magazine* 69 (November 1890): 710.

43. Daniel Mark Epstein, *Sister Aimee: The Life of Aimee Semple McPherson* (London: Harcourt Brace Jovanovich, 1993).

SIXTEEN

Prophetess of the Spirits

Mother Leaf Anderson and the Black Spiritual Churches of New Orleans

Yvonne Chireau

Mother Leaf Anderson, a thirty-two-year-old missionary, preacher, and prophetess, went to New Orleans, Louisiana, in 1919 to establish a church that would reflect her distinctive vision of sacred reality. In 1927, when she died, she left a legacy of women's leadership and spiritual innovation that had transformed the religious landscape of the city for both blacks and whites. Anderson, a woman of African and Native American ancestry, founded a religion that would carry her signature into the present day. Leaf Anderson's role in the formation of the New Orleans black Spiritual churches reveals the unusual and complex cultural configurations that she embodied in both her life and her ministry. The ways that she redefined gender and religious empowerment for women in the Spiritual tradition influenced all who came after her.

This essay considers gender and race as intersecting categories in its analysis of the churches established by Anderson, a network of congregations that synthesized elements of Protestantism, Catholicism, nineteenth-century American spiritualism, and neo-African religions. My focus on African American women serves as a counterbalance to interpretations of religious history that fail to account for race, class, and gender as determinants of female subjectivity. The contrasting social and cultural realities for black and white women underscore the differences in the religious options that both groups have historically sought and chosen. The black Spiritual movement is one product of those differences.

The New Orleans Spiritual churches were paradigms of female religious empowerment. The churches expanded public roles for women, who were able to benefit from the economic advantages that attended their ministries. Furthermore, the emergence of the Spiritual churches as a loosely organized movement precluded many of the structural constraints to female leadership that have existed historically within denominational systems. Through the creation of informally associated networks and autonomous local congregations, and the maintenance of female-centered traditions, the unique pattern of women's leadership in the black Spiritual churches has endured.

Unlike their mainstream ecclesiastical counterparts, Spiritual churches were organized around women's leadership from the start. Although black denominations in the United States were initially established as sites of resistance against racial oppression, within many of these churches women have experienced discrimination on account of their sex. While not excluded from leadership roles, women in black Christian denominations have for the most part been denied the status and prestige of the pastorate and clerical ordination. Even in the present day, African American women's visibility as public leaders in black denominations remains, by and large, extremely limited, their activities varying from ceremonial functions to the exercise of "influence" and "surrogate leadership" in congregations.[1]

By contrast, female authority in both official and ceremonial capacities is conspicuous within the Spiritual churches, a movement whose evolution occurred apart from that of the mainstream black denominational bodies.[2] At their inception, the Spiritual churches created standards of leadership that were legitimated by women. The founders of many of the early Spiritual churches in New Orleans were female, their honorary status indicated by such titles as Mother, Reverend Mother, Prophetess, and Queen. Women were represented in Spiritual church hierarchies as pastors, bishops, and archbishops, and in lay capacities many became religious advisers. As with white American and British nineteenth-century spiritualist women who asserted latent feminist claims to social equality, black women in the early-twentieth-century Spiritual churches linked their religious empowerment to alternative visions of divinity, to the establishment of authoritative roles, and to strategies by which they challenged conventional perspectives of race and gender. Members of the Spiritual churches drew from collective cultural resources that incorporated diverse strands from African and American traditions. Woven together, these sources gave New Orleans Spiritualism its eclectic flavor.[3]

Throughout history, women whose aspirations for leadership have been thwarted by mainstream religions have found appealing alternatives in sects, intentional communities, and so-called marginal traditions. Women-led religious movements have epitomized female dissatisfaction with aspects of male-dominated religion, such as patriarchal language and conceptions of God, and conservative expectations of women's social roles.[4] In many sectarian traditions, female congregants have accounted for a sizable proportion of church membership, and where the sect's founder was a woman such groups generally accept women as leaders and persons of authority.[5] While numerically dominating membership in nearly all African American religious groups, black women have also been instrumental within sectarian traditions in the United States. Sometimes described derogatorily as "cults," black sects tend to be offshoot movements, typically smaller than mainstream African American denominations, usually centered on a charismatic figure and often distinguished by uncommon ritual styles. The female-centered character of the black sects has been noted by numerous scholars of religion.[6] Like their sectarian counterparts in the early twentieth century, the Spiritual churches in New Orleans were noteworthy for the emphasis they placed on female clergy and church leadership.

The beginnings of the Spiritual movement coincide with the rise of African American religions in northern cities shortly after the turn of the nineteenth century. One of the earliest Spiritual churches, the Eternal Life Spiritualist Church, was established in Chicago by Mother Leaf Anderson in 1913. Chicago, the archetypal "black metropolis," was a veritable mecca for thousands of blacks who departed the South between 1914 and 1918 and between 1939 and 1945, during what was known as the Great Migration. Fleeing poverty, labor exploitation, a devastated agricultural economy, and political and social repression, masses of black southerners poured into the cities to fill a demand for cheap labor by northern industries, seeking promising futures and economic opportunity. Concurrent with the rising tide of migration, an increasingly pluralistic religious situation developed in Chicago's African American neighborhoods.[7]

In Chicago, blacks founded and joined Baptist and Methodist denominations, storefront holiness congregations, Muslim temples, Afro-Judaic sects, and numerous missionary organizations. Within this religiously diverse and rapidly growing population, the first black Spiritual churches appeared.[8] In the same decade as the founding of Leaf Anderson's church, several Spiritual congregations emerged in other parts of the country. Scholars have noted the presence of Spiritual storefronts in several metropolitan areas in the United States early in the 1900s, but it is not clear whether these churches were related to one another.[9] In New Orleans, however, the Spiritual churches developed an independent and culturally distinct character, spreading via a chain of congregations through that city's black and poor ethnic communities.

Leaf Anderson moved to New Orleans before the third decade of the twentieth century, possibly in 1919.[10] Before her arrival, it is believed that she had organized churches in St. Louis, New Jersey, and Indiana. The establishment of those mission churches was essential to the early growth of the movement. Eleven congregations grew out of Anderson's original Eternal Life Spiritualist Church, including churches in Chicago, Memphis, Little Rock, and Pensacola. Yet of all the cities where black Spiritualism flourished, New Orleans became the integral center for the movement, with at least 175 churches established there over the fifty years following Anderson's initial appearance.[11]

It is possible to create only a sketchy portrait of Leaf Anderson's life before 1918. According to some reports, Anderson was born in Balboa, Wisconsin, in 1887.[12] Other sources say that she had been married once and divorced, and that she had traveled to numerous locations before settling on New Orleans as the site of her Spiritual headquarters. She is listed in Chicago's city directories for 1914, 1916, and 1917 as residing in the southside ward, where she operated a lunch counter. Only a few other historical facts have been uncovered regarding Anderson's background before arriving in New Orleans, when she began to attract a following among black and white residents of the city.[13]

Shortly after establishing her first church in New Orleans, Anderson started a class to instruct others in the doctrines and practices of spiritualism. Anderson taught students how to prophesy, heal, pray, see spirits, and interpret selections from the Bible. Alumnae of these classes were considered qualified to start their own Spiritual ministries. According to one of her students, Anderson influenced a great number of those who would follow her as ministers: "there was eighty-five to a hundred of us in her first class and she charged a dollar a lesson. She taught healing and prophesying and calling up spirits. Of course most of them didn't ever finish, because everybody ain't got the power, but most of the Mothers in New Orleans now learned what they know from Mother Anderson."[14]

From the beginning, the advancement of female authority was an integral feature of the Spiritual movement. Leaf Anderson's class system functioned as a training center for novices to acquire valuable skills. As a teacher, she helped proficient students to develop their own nascent ministries; many second-generation Spiritual churches in New Orleans began through the work of women who had attended her classes. Early churches grew out of the accumulation of clients of Spiritual ministers, as well as others who had been instructed by Anderson. As the client bases expanded, many eventually coalesced into congregational bodies. Thus, by supporting their church-building initiatives, Leaf Anderson conferred a ministerial status upon students who had once been under her tutelage.[15]

The black Spiritual churches provided institutional support for women in their pursuit of meaningful careers as preachers and pastors and in private settings as "readers" and "spirit advisers." Spiritual ministers offered services such as healing, counseling, and guidance on secular and religious matters for church members and non-church members alike. These extra-ecclesiastical businesses were an important means of economic self-determination for black women. Severely hampered by segregation, sexual and racial discrimination, and threats to their personal security, black women could not travel as freely as their white counterparts in American spiritualism, who had constituted the majority of itinerant mediums in the nineteenth century. An effective alternative was the establishment of Spiritual ministries in homes, storefronts, and other settings, where ministers offered advice and counseling on matters of health, employment, relationships, and other personal concerns. Unlike many of the mainstream denominations, in which the women engaged in lay ministries were only infrequently compensated for their duties, Spiritual women were free to establish profitable ventures that ensured their economic security. Because the average black female in 1920s and 1930s New Orleans was likely to be employed in a low-wage, unskilled job, spiritual advising offered some women the means for redefining their status as professionals and exercising some financial autonomy.[16]

Black Spiritual women preachers were distinctive for the ways they combined religious authority and community activism. An ardent concern for social justice appears to have characterized the work of female missionaries in the black Spiritual tradition. In its early days, Spiritual church founders were among those actively involved in grassroots charitable endeavors in the city of New Orleans. Mother Catherine Seals, founder of one of the largest Spiritual churches after Leaf Anderson's, established a sanctuary in her church, the Temple of the Innocent Blood, for unwed mothers. Seals was unyielding in her opposition to the practices of local abortionists and the "shedding of innocent blood" and provided facilities for the care of women and their babies until her death in 1930. Other Spiritual ministers were active in the climate of social and economic distress of the 1920s and 1930s. Mother Kate Frances, an early student of Anderson's, led a barefoot procession of congregants through the city streets in protest during the Great Depression. Another Mother, Maud Shannon, pastor of St. Anthony's Helping Hand Divine Spiritual Chapel, founded her church in the heart of one of New Orleans's poorest neighborhoods, distributing food, gifts, and money to destitute families.[17]

An emphasis on religious self-empowerment functioned for black women in the New Orleans churches in much the same way that it did for white women in a previous movement, the nineteenth-century American Spiritualists. Visionary experience and revelation were primary sources of authority for women in the Spiritual churches. One of Leaf Anderson's assumed responsibilities was to identify for her students who their particular spirit mediators were, thereby reinforcing each woman's acknowledgment of her own guiding forces in the spirit realm. The practice of "calling up spirits," which Anderson taught, was central to black Spiritual theology. In Spiritual belief, unseen beings called "saints," "spirit guides," and "forces" communicated directly with individuals through inner voices, dreams, or visions. Every person, taught Anderson, possessed a spirit guide, an entity who might live on the earthly plane or exist in the realm of the dead. Another central conviction in the black Spiritual tradition was belief in the Divine Spirit, identified with the Holy Ghost of revivalistic Christianity, who spontaneously "possessed" believers during worship ceremonies. The Divine Spirit, understood by Spiritualists as a composite of the third person of the Christian Trinity and other unseen beings, prompted those spiritually possessed to perform healings, speak in tongues, and deliver prophetic messages.[18]

Healing was a dominant concern for practitioners in the black Spiritual churches. Catherine Seals, one of the early Mothers in New Orleans, helped expand the traditional roles of domestic caregivers by institutionalizing public healing ministries. Seals was a missionary organizer who had worked with Leaf Anderson in the 1920s. Spiritual lore alleges that Seals was "called" after being miraculously cured of a paralytic stroke, but other sources suggest that she and Anderson might have parted after disputes over personal differences in leadership style.[19] In 1930 Seals founded a settlement on the outskirts of the city that housed her church, her home, and a small hospital. Pilgrimages were made to her church by a predominantly female following who sought cures through the power of an elixir Seals prepared with castor oil and salt. On the strength of her reputation as a healer, Mother Catherine Seals became one of the most famous charismatic ministers in New Orleans. She passed on her knowledge of healing and spiritual principles in much the same way that Leaf Anderson had, by training selected followers who became her apprentices before starting out on their own. After her death in 1930, several new congregations were formed in connection with Seals's Temple of the Innocent Blood. In this manner vital traditions were continued by those who came after Seals and other successful female leaders. According to folklore, both Catherine Seals and Leaf Anderson (who died in 1927) appear periodically in spirit form with instruction for the women who carry on their work.[20]

The establishment of female-centered traditions contributed profoundly to women's authority in the black Spiritual churches. An emphasis on feminine imagery, including birth and motherhood, characterized the religious perspectives of both Leaf Anderson and Catherine Seals. For example, when anthropologist Zora Neale Hurston visited the Temple of the Innocent Blood in the 1920s, she observed that Seals was "strongly matriarchal." According to Hurston, Seals considered herself an equal with Christ. In their adaptations of sacred myths and stories, both Seals and Anderson focused on birth imagery and feminine metaphors that were appropriated in conjunction with the traditional biblical accounts. From one sermon, Hurston recounted Seals's re-rendering of the creation story: "It is right that a woman should lead. A womb was what God made in the beginning, and out of that womb was born time, and that fills up space. So says the beautiful spirit."[21]

Seals's female-centered interpretations corresponded with the beliefs of Leaf Anderson, who was strongly opposed to the concept of a male supreme divinity. Anderson's disciples were not even permitted to use the name of Jesus in prayer or for healing because, according to one of her students, "Jesus as a man was not important—he was merely the earthly body of a 'spirit' by which name the deity is always addressed." Accordingly, in church hymnody

Spiritualists replaced "Jesus" in the song "Jesus Is the Light of the World" with the word "Spirit," at Anderson's request.[22]

Historians have noted that the earlier spiritualist movement in the United States, American spiritualism, articulated theological conceptions that attracted many white, middle-class women, who made up a majority of the professional mediums in the nineteenth century. It has been argued that the spiritualist notion of divinity, a radically transcendent, nonpatriarchal being, represented an ideal for female radicals who had repudiated Christianity's emphasis on the incarnation of the deity as a male, or the androcentric *imago dei*.[23] In direct contrast to the impersonal god of the white spiritualists, black Spiritual practitioners emphasized multiple aspects of divinity. Leaf Anderson taught her mediums to "manifest" or incarnate a variety of gendered beings, for in the black Spiritual tradition, spiritual possession by male and female spirits was equally significant, as was the operation of the Holy Ghost, a nongendered spirit, within the experience of the believer.

The social distance between black and white women's lives reflected the disparate motivations behind female interest in the two spiritualist movements. According to historians, members of the earlier spiritualist movement consisted primarily of women who unselfconsciously exalted traditional ideals of piety, passivity, purity, and Victorian notions of femininity. Accordingly, nineteenth-century spiritualist mediumship became identified with gender values that equated true womanhood with domesticity and virtue.[24] By this same ideology, however, African American women could not aspire to the ranks of true women. Prevailing racist and sexist stereotypes devalued black womanhood and designated most African American females as morally depraved, sexually corrupt persons. Conventional definitions of femininity, including conceptions of chastity, purity, and beauty, were rarely applied to black women.[25]

These normative conceptions of gender were subverted in African American Spiritual traditions. Leaf Anderson appears to have treated gender as a fluid concept, adopting both "male" and "female" characteristics in her role as preacher and prophet in equally powerful ways. For example, Anderson's spirit guides included two male personalities, Black Hawk and Father Jones, and on occasion she wore an Indian chieftain's mantle or a man's dress suit during services in which these spirits would manifest themselves. The alliance of ecstatic religion and cross-dressing, a combination signifying liminality and the blurring of categories, illustrates the manner in which Anderson simultaneously engaged sexuality and spirituality as dual sources of authority. By dressing "as a man" while possessed by a male spirit, Anderson symbolically enacted masculine privilege within the domain of her church. These transgressive gender strategies contrasted with Anderson's public behavior outside the Spiritual churches, where her "womanly" street attire, including elegant jewelry and lavish, expensive wardrobe, served to contest derogative representations of African American feminine beauty in the public sphere.[26]

Equally important to the gender representations of black women in the Spiritual tradition were the figures that Leaf Anderson exhibited as medium. Powerful women such as Queen Esther, the heroic matron of the Old Testament, figured prominently in Anderson's repertoire of spirit forces. The biblical Queen Esther, a virtuous female character, was an important source of authority for black women. Queen Esther has historically functioned as a prominent symbol for African Americans, especially within black Freemasonry, where in the women's counterpart of the men's fraternity, the Order of the Eastern Star, Esther presides over the third degree of initiation, symbolizing fidelity and courage. The presence of Queen Esther in the pantheon of spirit guides evoked conceptions of black female dignity, poise, and leadership. A dominant spirit, Esther was identified with feminine aspects of the gendered identities that Anderson explored in ritual contexts.[27]

The black Spiritual churches adopted an eclectic blend of beliefs and practices that drew from a variety of cultural sources. New Orleans Spiritualists instituted numerous innovations that derive from spiritualism, Protestantism, occultism, Afro-Caribbean *vodou*, and Italian American folk religion. Another possible source was Anderson's alleged Native American ancestry, which might have influenced her Spiritual beliefs early on.[28] Native American culture, it is certain, inspired the design of the ceremonial garb that Anderson wore. In addition, the great spirit Black Hawk, one of Anderson's favorite spirit guides, emerged as the preeminent saint of the Spiritual churches in the South, and his statues are found even today in church sanctuaries, along with other Native American symbols. Yet even with the identifiable presence of Native American accoutrements in the Spiritual churches, it is uncertain that these originated with Anderson. Spirit guides such as Raging Bull, Red Cloud, and White Eagle were popular characters who made frequent appearances at public readings and seances within Spiritualist circles in the nineteenth century. Ironically, the tradition of Native American spirit guides in the New Orleans Spiritual churches is more likely to have been drawn from the nineteenth-century American spiritualists, whose movement and membership was predominantly white.[29]

Significant parallels between practices of the earlier white spiritualists and the African American churches in New Orleans indicate that the members of the two movements may have had some contact with each other. In particular, Leaf Anderson's activities in the early 1920s, which included the patronage of a number of white spiritualists' functions and events, suggest more than a passing acquaintance with their practices and beliefs. Even considering these shared associations, it is difficult to ascertain the precise nature of the relationship between Anderson and the other American spiritualists.[30] Mutual practices of spirit mediumship and possession, which link the two movements, evolved in different forms in the New Orleans churches. In both traditions, communication through psychics and mediums (called prophets, divine healers, and advisers) was established by deceased persons, spirits, and other entities who had "passed on." Although Leaf Anderson instituted the custom of calling up spirits through trance and meditation, possession by the Holy Spirit appears to have been a hallmark of black Spiritual worship and points to the strong influence of revivalist Christianity.

Leaf Anderson was said to have brought her favorite saints and spirit guides with her to New Orleans from Chicago. These included the aforementioned Black Hawk, Father Jones, and Queen Esther, as well as other beings who were invoked to bring messages or deliver prophecies from the other world.[31] A possible link exists with the sensational practices of "manifesting" established figures that occurred within white Spiritualist circles during public readings and seances in the latter part of the nineteenth century.[32] However, in the African American Spiritual churches of New Orleans the prominence of Black Hawk demands an alternative explanation, since he eclipsed many of the other spirits and was celebrated with an honorary place in a "cult of saints" that included Roman Catholic figures as well.

Spiritual traditions that revere a cult of saints appear to have been the consequence of cross-cultural exchanges between ethnic groups in New Orleans during the early twentieth century. Interactions between blacks, Italians, and immigrant groups in New Orleans had significant consequences for the formation of the black Spiritual religion. Catholicism, in particular, played a vital role in the cultural development of the New Orleans churches. With patterns that have persisted to the present day, Spiritual churches are distinguished by their Catholic-style iconographic representations, including church sanctuaries that are decorated with statues of the Virgin Mary, Saint Anthony, Saint Jude, and two favorites particular to the New Orleans churches, Saint Raymond and Saint Rita, patroness of women's ailments.[33] Spiritual altars adorned with crucifixes, votive candles, and other decorations provide a visual link with Catholicism, and the robes and vestments of Spiritual ministers resemble the elaborate finery of priests and clerics.

It is difficult to determine whether these innovations were the product of the Catholic confluences in *vodou*, an Afro-Caribbean religion that fused African and Christian elements, or traditions inherited directly from the folk practices of ethnic Italians in New Orleans. The latter possibility is not implausible, considering that in its early history Anderson's church had a representative Italian American membership and that interracial unions between immigrant Italians and blacks were not uncommon within these two communities, which shared much in terms of their social and class status. Affinities between the folk beliefs of Italian Catholics and the traditions of the Spiritualists indicate a reasonable possibility of syncretism. Similarities with regard to occult worldviews, beliefs in supernatural forces, miraculous cures and faith healing, and the efficacy of magical formulations indicate some degree of overlap. Other practices possibly derived from popular Catholic traditions include prayers to the Blessed Mother and the Trinity, the use of Holy Oil, and the celebration of saints' feast days, especially the feast of Saint Joseph, a shared holiday that remains popular in New Orleans among black Spiritualists and Italian American women today. Nevertheless, although many practices appear to have been linked, and some black Spiritualists refer to themselves as "sanctified Catholics," the religious content and significance of their traditions hold vastly different meanings for the two groups.[34]

Similarly, the practices of the New Orleans Spiritual churches and those of vodou practitioners suggest possible cultural and religious interrelationships but no definite connections. Some scholars have speculated that most of what appear to be Catholic ritual influences were actually derived from vodou when it was widely practiced in New Orleans during the nineteenth century. Influences from vodou in the Spiritual churches can be discerned from similarities in organization; for example, the strong commitment to female leadership and spiritual mediumship is a conspicuous feature of the Afro-Caribbean religion.[35] Other early practices provide clues of an informal relationship between belief systems in which saints and spirits were freely exchanged. Black Hawk, Leaf Anderson's personal spirit guide, was believed to have been adopted by vodou and voodoo practitioners in the city during the era of his appearance in the 1920s. Distant kin to the African-derived religion from Haiti, voodoo was a popular system of magic and supernaturalism that was embedded in New Orleans spiritual consciousness from its earliest days. Among black practitioners, voodoo and vodou were entwined in unusual and innovative ways. Robert Tallant noted that two of the early Mothers from Anderson's school set up temples to Expédite, a popular spirit from Louisiana's nineteenth-century voodoo cult.[36] Kaslow and Jacobs report that Catherine Seals and several of the early Mothers wore blue cords or ropes around the waist of their robes in the tradition of early voodoo saints. Numerous Spiritual practitioners and Mothers proudly trace their spiritual lineage back to Marie Laveau, the great nineteenth-century voodoo priestess of New Orleans who was shrouded in legend and mystery. Sources also mention the contemporary custom of placing sacred stones and glasses of water on altars in black Spiritual churches, a custom that is identical to that of some New World African religions.[37]

Black American folk traditions explain some of the elements that exist in the Spiritual churches. While it is possible that early African-derived religions such as vodou were the foundation of many Spiritual beliefs, another possible connection can be assumed from the tradition of hoodoo, the complex of southern magical arts. Hoodoo is an uninstitutionalized system of healing, charms, and other occult practices that developed from the merging of African and European beliefs among blacks during slavery. However, widespread negative associations among hoodoo, witchcraft, and conjuring have caused wary black Spiritualists to publicly repudiate such traditions in connection with their own beliefs. Nevertheless it is possible to speculate on the possible connections between them. For example, ritual items commonly used by black Spiritualists, including candles, incense, and sacred oils, were and continue to be easily obtained in occult shops and drugstores frequented by hoodoo practitioners. Practices traditionally favored by African American conjurers, including the use of "roots," countermagical spells, and supernatural healing techniques, have been documented by observers in the early black Spiritual churches. In a detailed article on black folk religion written in the early twentieth century, Zora Neale Hurston noted that eleven of the early Spiritual congregations were "stolen" by hoodoo doctors, and she found "a strong aroma of hoodoo" hovering about the churches she visited in the 1930s.[38]

Despite evidence of shared traditions, black Spiritual practitioners in New Orleans deny that a formal historical relationship exists between themselves and the American Spiritualists, vodou devotees, or practitioners of black folk magic. By the 1940s many of their congregations officially became known as Spiritual churches rather than Spiritualists, ostensibly to disassociate themselves from members of the American spiritualist movement, who were perceived by many in the African American community to be "ungodly."[39] Despite the practice of mediumship, spiritual readings, and advising among ministers and churchgoers, black Spiritualists today emphasize liturgical styles that corroborate their genealogy as part of the African American Protestant tradition.

Living in a patriarchal and racially oppressive society, African American women have historically turned to their religious faith as a source of validation, strength, and healing. In so doing, they have also restructured their religious roles and asserted their own claims to sacred authority within their church institutions. Defying sexual discrimination and racism, women in the New Orleans Spiritual churches exercised power in ways often denied them by the larger society. The Spiritual movement provided women who aspired to religious leadership with the opportunity to lead based upon their own charisma and initiative. Spiritual churches thus created a haven for black women who sought public religious roles. Through their promotion of local missionary work and professional ministries, they also provided ecclesial structures within which women could assume some control of their social and economic circumstances.

As prophet and preacher, Leaf Anderson embodied the values of the Spiritual tradition. Appropriating her model of leadership, African American women in New Orleans became ministers and church founders, creating alternative communities in which conventional gender constructions were transformed. Their continued prominence as religious authorities was validated by the emphasis that black Spiritualists placed on "carrying forth" the customs instituted by Anderson as the first Mother and exemplar of the church. In providing African American women with alternative possibilities for spiritual, economic, and social development, the Spiritual religion, as conceived by Leaf Anderson, instituted a black sectarian women's church in which female-centered traditions were established and perpetuated.

NOTES

1. C. Eric Lincoln and Lawrence Mamiya, *The Black Church in the African American Experience* (Durham, N.C.: Duke University Press, 1990), pp. 274–308. On women's ordination, see Jacqueline Grant, "Black Women and the Church," in . . . *But Some of Us Are Brave,* ed. Gloria Hull et al. (Old Westbury, N.Y.: Feminist Press, 1982), pp. 142–44. See also Evelyn Brooks Higginbotham, *Righteous Discontent: The Women's Movement in the Black Baptist Church, 1880–1920* (Cambridge, Mass.: Harvard University Press, 1993); Cheryl Gilkes, "Together and in Harness: Women's Traditions in the Sanctified Church," *Signs* 10, no. 4 (Summer 1985): 678–99; Jualynne Dodson, "19th-Century AME Preaching Women," in *Women in New Worlds,* ed. Hilah Thomas and Rosemary Skinner Keller (Nashville, Tenn.: Abingdon Press, 1981).

2. The Spiritual churches of New Orleans have been examined by scholars of anthropology and sociology, but none have taken an explicitly historical approach. See Andrew Kaslow and Claude Jacobs, *The Spiritual Churches of New Orleans: Origins, Beliefs and Rituals of an African American Religion* (Knoxville: University of Tennessee Press, 1991). Hans Baer devotes a section to a discussion of the New Orleans churches in *The Black Spiritual Movement: A Religious Response to Racism* (Knoxville: University of Tennesee Press, 1984), as does Zora Neale Hurston in her monograph "Hoodoo in America," *Journal of American Folklore* 44 (1931): 317–417. Michael Smith documents contemporary Spiritual churches in his photo essay *Spirit World* (New Orleans: New Orleans Urban Folklore Society, 1984). Authors with more literary interests include Robert Tallant, *Voodoo in New Orleans* (New York: Collier Books, 1946); and recently, David Estes, "Ritual Validations of Clergywomen's Authority in the African American Spiritual Churches of New Orleans," in *Women's Leadership in Marginal Religions: Explorations Outside the Mainstream,* ed. Catherine Wessinger (Urbana: University of Illinois Press, 1993), pp. 149–71; and Jason Berry, *The Spirit of Black Hawk: A Mystery of Africans and Indians* (Jackson: University Press of Mississippi, 1995).

3. See Hans Baer, "The Limited Empowerment of Women in Black Spiritual Churches: An Alternative Vehicle to Religious Leadership," in *Gender and Religion,* ed. William Swatos (New Brunswick, N.J.: Transaction Publishers, 1994); see also Estes, "Ritual Validations of Clergywomen's Authority."

4. Mary Farrell Bednarowski, "Outside the Mainstream: Women's Religion and Women Religious Leaders in Nineteenth-Century America," *Journal of the American Academy of Religion* 48 (June 1980): 207–31.

5. Ibid. See also Barbara Brown Zikmund, "The Feminist Thrust of Sectarian Chris-

tianity," in *Women of Spirit,* ed. Rosemary Radford Ruether (New York: Simon and Schuster, 1979).

6. Miles Mark Fisher, "Organized Religion and the Cults," *Crisis* (January 1937): 28. See also Ira D. Reid, "Let Us Prey!" *Opportunity* 4 (1926): 168–70; E. Franklin Frazier, *The Negro Church in America* (New York: Schocken Books, 1974), p. 60; Joseph Washington, *Black Sects and Cults* (New York: Doubleday, 1973), pp. 2–18; Arthur H. Fauset, *Black Gods of the Metropolis* (Philadelphia: University of Pennsylvania Press, 1971).

7. St. Clair Drake and Horace Cayton, *Black Metropolis* (New York: Harcourt, Brace, 1945), pp. 58–64.

8. A sociological study of Chicago's Bronzeville District noted that in 1928 there were seventeen Spiritual churches on the south side. By 1938 that figure had grown to fifty-one. This count did not include the vast number of unaffiliated Spiritualists who operated house altars and served as advisers, whose number was said to be more than a hundred in the district on the eve of World War I. See Drake and Cayton, *Black Metropolis,* p. 642.

9. Edith White, *The Spiritualist Sect in Nashville* (New York: Vantage Press, 1970), p. 27; Alan Spear, *Black Chicago: The Making of a Negro Ghetto, 1890–1920* (Chicago: University of Chicago Press, 1967), p. 177.

10. Hurston, "Hoodoo in America," p. 319; cf. Tallant, *Voodoo in New Orleans,* p. 173.

11. Baer, *The Black Spiritual Movement,* p. 19; Federal Writers Project, *New Orleans City Guide* (Boston: Houghton Mifflin, 1938).

12. *Louisiana Weekly,* December 17, 1927; other sources list her birthplace as Norfolk, Virginia. For a general background of Anderson's early life, see Berry, *The Spirit of Black Hawk,* p. 57–78.

13. Biographical information on Leaf Anderson is gathered from the following sources: Robert Tallant Collection and Papers, New Orleans Public Library; Works Progress Administration, Federal Writers Project files, New Orleans Public Library; *Louisiana Weekly,* 1926–30. I am grateful to David Estes and Claude Jacobs for providing residence information on Anderson from the Chicago city directories located in the Newberry Library, Chicago.

14. Mother Dora Tyson, "Mother Letha or Leaf Anderson," Robert Tallant Papers, reel 8, n.d., n.p. See also Tallant, *Voodoo in New Orleans,* p. 169; and Michael Smith, *Spirit World* (New Orleans: New Orleans Urban Folklore Society, 1984), p. 46.

15. As David Estes has pointed out, the Spiritual emphasis upon a hierarchically organized clergy challenges Mary Farrell Bednarowski's model of marginal, women-headed religions that deny the need for a traditionally ordained clergy. Although rejection of the male-dominated structures of churches seems to have motivated some women to join the African American Spiritual movement, many of its members embraced the densely stratified clergy structure that evolved, an episcopacy governed by pastors, bishops, and archbishops. See Estes, "Ritual Validations of Clergywomen's Authority," p. 150.

16. Kaslow and Jacobs, *Spiritual Churches of New Orleans,* p. 153; Baer, *The Black Spiritual Movement,* p. 80.

17. Kaslow and Jacobs, *Spiritual Churches of New Orleans;* "When the Thunder Is

Over Mother Kate Francis Will March Right through Hebbin's Door," November 1939, and "Dora Tyson Interview," Robert Tallant Papers, reels 7 and 9.

18. Ibid.

19. Louisiana Writers Project, *Gumbo Ya-Ya* (Boston: Johnson Reprint Company, 1945), p. 399; cf. Smith, *Spirit World*, p. 46.

20. Tallant, *Voodoo in New Orleans,* p. 169; Hurston, "Hoodoo in America," p. 319; Baer, *The Black Spiritual Movement*, p. 20. On Mother Catherine Seals, see Louisiana Writers Project, *Gumbo Ya-Ya*, p. 399; Smith, *Spirit World*, p. 46; Federal Writers Project, *New Orleans City Guide*, p. 199; Edward Laroque Tinker, "Mother Catherine's Castor Oil," *North American Review* 230 (1930): 148–54; and Zora Neale Hurston, *The Sanctified Church* (Berkeley, Calif.: Turtle Island Press, 1981), pp. 23–29.

21. Hurston, *The Sanctified Church,* p. 26.

22. Hurston, "Hoodoo in America," p. 319; Kaslow and Jacobs, *Spiritual Churches of New Orleans,* p. 52.

23. Bednarowski, "Outside the Mainstream," p. 214.

24. See Ann Braude, *Radical Spirits: Spiritualism and Women's Rights in Nineteenth-Century America* (Boston: Beacon Press, 1989), and Braude, "Spirits Defend the Rights of Women: Spiritualism and Changing Sex Roles in Nineteenth-Century America," in *Women, Religion and Social Change,* ed. Yvonne Haddad and Ellison Findley (Binghamton: State University of New York Press, 1985); Alex Owen, *The Darkened Room: Women, Power and Spiritualism in Late Victorian England* (Philadelphia: University of Pennsylvania Press, 1990); Bednarowski, "Outside the Mainstream"; and Mary Farrell Bednarowski, "Women in Occult America," in *The Occult in America: New Historical Perspectives,* ed. Howard Kerr and Charles Crow (Urbana: University of Illinois Press, 1983).

25. See Higginbotham, *Righteous Discontent;* see also Hazel Carby, *Reconstructing Womanhood: The Emergence of the Afro-American Woman Novelist* (New York: Oxford University Press, 1987); Linda M. Perkins, "Black Women and Racial Uplift prior to Emancipation," in *The Black Woman Cross-Culturally,* ed. Filomena Steady (Cambridge, Mass.: Schenkman Publishing Company, 1981); Linda M. Perkins, "The Impact of the Cult of True Womanhood on the Education of Black Women," *Journal of Social Issues* 39 (1983); see also Deborah White, *Ar'n't I a Woman?* (New York: Norton, 1985), pp. 27–61.

26. Anderson's ritual transvestism also led to numerous rumors of lesbianism and public accusations that she was "really a man" in disguise, according to one of the early Spiritual Mothers. See "Mother Letha or Leaf Anderson," interview with Mother Dora Tyson, reel 9, Robert Tallant Papers.

27. Claude Jacobs, "Spirit Guides and Possession in the New Orleans Black Spiritual Churches," *Journal of American Folklore* 102 (1989): 45–67; see esp. p. 50.

28. One researcher has suggested a geographic link between the Wisconsin-born Anderson and the historical Black Hawk, leader of the Sauk Nation in Illinois in the late nineteenth century. See Berry, *The Spirit of Black Hawk*, pp. 68–69. See also Smith, *Spirit World,* p. 81.

29. Ruth Brandon speculates that the Native American component may have first been adopted by Indian-influenced Shakers in upstate New York, many of whom were active Spiritualists. See Ruth Brandon, *The Spiritualists: The Passion for the Occult in the Nineteenth and Twentieth Centuries* (New York: Knopf, 1983), p. 37; and Geoffrey Nelson,

Spiritualism and Society (New York: Schocken, 1969), pp. 162, 201. For a discussion of African-Indian relations in the context of the world of Leaf Anderson in early New Orleans, see Berry, *The Spirit of Black Hawk*, pp. 80–86.

30. Lily Dale was the name of the Cassadaga Free Lake Association, one of the most famous camp-meeting sites for Spiritualists after the Civil War. See Laurence Moore, *In Search of White Crows* (New York: Oxford University Press, 1977), p. 67. The event spoken of occurred in 1927 when Leaf Anderson invited a white minister from Lily Dale to speak at her church in New Orleans. *New Orleans Weekly*, January 22, 1927, p. 8. Estes, "Ritual Validations of Clergywomen's Authority," p. 170.

31. Claude Jacobs, "Spirit Guides and Possession," p. 49. Tallant, *Voodoo in New Orleans*, p. 168. See also Smith, *Spirit World*, pp. 81ff.; Berry, *The Spirit of Black Hawk*, pp. 69–72; "Saint Black Hawk—Indian Worshipped by Spiritualists," Robert Tallant Papers, reel 9.

32. See Ruth Brandon, *The Spiritualists*, p. 37; see also Nelson, *Spiritualism and Society*, pp. 162, 201; Kaslow and Jacobs, *Spiritual Churches of New Orleans*, p. 129.

33. See Lyle Saxon, *Fabulous New Orleans* (New York: Century Company, 1928), pp. 306–7; Baer, "Black Spiritual Churches," p. 218; Jacobs, "Spirit Guides and Possession," p. 48.

34. See David Estes, "Across Ethnic Boundaries: Saint Joseph's Day in a New Orleans Afro-American Spiritual Church," *Mississippi Folklore Register* 21 (1987):11–12; Louisiana Writers Project, *Gumbo Ya-Ya*, p. 105. On Italian American occult worldviews, see Robert Orsi, *The Madonna of 115th Street* (New Haven: Yale University Press, 1985), pp. xiv, 6; Rudolph Vecoli, "Cult and Occult in Italian-American Culture," in *Immigrants and Religion in Urban America*. ed. Randall Miller and Thomas Marzik (Philadelphia: Temple University Press), p. 29.

35. See especially Karen McCarthy Brown, "Women's Leadership in Haitian Vodou," in *Weaving the Visions: New Patterns in Feminist Spirituality*, ed. Judith Plaskow and Carol Christ (San Francisco: Harper, 1989), pp. 226–34.

36. Tallant, *Voodoo in New Orleans*, p. 201; Louisiana Writers Project, *Gumbo Ya-Ya*, p. 210.

37. Kaslow and Jacobs, *Spritual Churches of New Orleans*, p. 28.

38. "Saint Black Hawk," Robert Tallant Papers, reel 9; Hurston, "Hoodoo in America," p. 319.

39. Baer, *The Black Spiritual Movement*, pp. 51, 115.

SEVENTEEN

Transforming the Pulpit

Preaching and Prophecy
in the British Women's Suffrage Movement

Jacqueline R. deVries

In 1923 the famous British suffragette Christabel Pankhurst published a work of prophetic social criticism titled *The Lord Cometh*. A year later she produced *Pressing Problems of the Closing Age*, which featured a foreword by the well-known evangelist Rev. F. B. Meyer and claimed to address "some modern problems in the light of Biblical prophecy."[1] Pankhurst combined the publication of these books with an extensive speaking tour of the United States and Canada, where, from the pulpits of numerous churches and chapels, she proclaimed God's impending judgment on modern-day humanity.[2] What had happened to the committed advocate of women's interests and courageous leader of the spectacular Women's Social and Political Union (WSPU)?

Other suffragists and suffragettes joined Christabel Pankhurst in the pursuit of preaching careers after women over the age of thirty won the vote in 1918. A. Maude Royden, former editor of the suffrage monthly *Common Cause*, established a wide reputation in the 1920s as the minister of London's Nonconformist City Temple.[3] Edith Picton-Turbervill, who had belonged to the National Union of Women's Suffrage Societies (NUWSS), regularly preached in the pulpits of both Anglican and Nonconformist churches before she became a Labour member of Parliament in 1929.[4] And Emmeline Pethick-Lawrence, former treasurer of the WSPU, preached at the all-woman Church of the New Ideal.[5] Other suffrage campaigners wrote streams of pamphlets and books in the 1920s advocating women's right to preach. Of these, Edith Picton-Turbervill was especially prolific.[6] Even a few Catholics like Alice Abadam, who had been a member of the Catholic Women's Suffrage Society (CWSS) and Women's Freedom League (WFL), argued that women should be allowed into the Catholic priesthood.[7] In addition, a number of former suffrage leaders lent their organizational skills to the campaign for women's ordination. Millicent Garrett Fawcett, leader of the NUWSS, served on a women's ordination advisory committee for the League of the Church Militant (LCM), the bold new name adopted by the (Anglican) Church League for Women's Suffrage (CLWS) in 1919, when it voted to make women's ordination to the Anglican ministry a central goal. Was it just coincidence that so many suffragists and suffragettes went on to champion women's leadership in religious contexts? Did this apparent "turn toward religion" constitute a repudiation of their feminism?

At first glance, suffrage workers' departure from campaign platforms and their entrance into church pulpits may appear to be a dramatic about-face. Indeed, several historians have interpreted it as such. David Mitchell depicts Christabel Pankhurst's postsuffrage preaching career as a rejection of the radical feminist vision she advanced at the height of the suffrage movement. He also scathingly dismisses other suffragettes who "got religion" after the war.[8] Similarly, Martin Pugh condemns Christabel's evangelizing as a product of "the shallowness of Pankhurst politics and their ceaseless search for self-promotion."[9] Yet to interpret Christabel's or any other suffrage workers' preaching as a repudiation of the principles of the militant suffrage movement is misleading, particularly in light of the close links that existed in the nineteenth century between women's preaching and feminist activism.[10] Such an interpretation assumes that in the twentieth century women's activism within religious contexts, which engages religious ideas and employs religious languages, is a less potent form of radicalism than the demand for secular legal and political change. As I shall argue here, this assertion does not hold up under close scrutiny.

The decision of some suffragists to pursue preaching careers and champion other forms of activism in religious contexts was not a repudiation of the radical vision of prewar suffrage militancy but rather its direct extension and even its advancement.[11] At its height between 1903 and 1914, the suffrage movement aimed to open opportunities for women to exercise their moral and spiritual influence in public.[12] Suffragists and suffragettes broadcast this message in the streets of London; from the platform of Royal Albert Hall; in the pages of their monthly newspapers; through their bloody confrontations with police and male hecklers; and in their own phrasing, through words as well as deeds. They envisioned the vote not as an end in itself but as the means to a purer, stronger, and more godly nation. Suffrage workers deliberately fashioned their activities to appear as a kind of secular evangelism, in which they preached the "good news" of women's political emancipation. From this position, the step many of them made in the 1920s toward more formalized preaching careers was a short one, and constituted a continuation of the drive both to achieve gender equality and to reform the public sphere.

The move toward activism in religious contexts, however, did begin to change—but hardly to repudiate—the prewar feminist vision. More often than not, suffragists had advanced their claim for the vote on the basis of their essential difference from and spiritual superiority to men. They had argued, "Give women the vote on equal terms to men and we will accomplish, by virtue of our difference, what men cannot." In contrast, women who chose to preach the gospel of Christ (rather than that of suffrage) tended to move away from a belief in women's essential moral superiority and intrinsic ability to solve all public evils toward a more constructivist understanding of gender roles. They recognized that women's entrance into national politics alone would bring neither the moral uplift nor the social cleansing they hoped for. Nor would mere political reform secure lasting gender equality. As Christabel Pankhurst reflected in *Pressing Problems of the Closing Age* in 1924:

> The shallow optimism of yesterday had vanished. . . . Various reasons forbid us to expect that, when other means are failing to save the world-situation, the votes of women will succeed. Some of us hoped more from woman suffrage than is ever going to be accomplished. My own large anticipations were based partly upon ignorance (which the late war dispelled) of the magnitude of the task which we women reformers so confidently wished to undertake when the vote should be ours.[13]

Instead of collapsing in the face of the "magnitude of the task," these women reformers pursued new strategies to enlarge women's influence and reform the public sphere. They recognized that to preach from a pulpit in a Christian church, rather than from a soapbox in Hyde Park or Nelson's plinth in Trafalgar Square, was to achieve a position of acknowledged authority. They also realized that preaching would allow them the opportunity not only to promote social and political reform but also to critique and combat the deeply rooted cultural sources of women's subordination.

"THE SWORD AND THE SPIRIT": MILITANT SUFFRAGISM AND SUFFRAGE REVIVALISM

A number of British women began their preaching careers within the context of the movement for women's suffrage. Extant since 1867, the movement had received a boost of energy from the Women's Social and Political Union, founded in 1903. Led by Emmeline Pankhurst and her daughters, Christabel and Sylvia, the WSPU adopted "militant" tactics and moved the campaign from quiet, middle-class parlors into the nation's streets and squares. By 1914 the WSPU had attracted thousands of members in nearly every area of England and maintained an annual budget of nearly £40,000. Its energy and publicity inspired thousands more to join other suffrage societies like the National Union of Women's Suffrage Societies, the Actresses' Suffrage League, the Artists' Suffrage League, the Church League for Women's Suffrage, and the Catholic Women's Suffrage Society.

Much of the WSPU's success at attracting publicity can be attributed to the fact that its members regularly spoke in public and confronted their opponents both verbally and physically. The WSPU borrowed many of its methods directly from late-nineteenth-century revivalist movements. WSPU leaders and members have left a thin but clearly identifiable trail of evidence that a main inspiration was the Salvation Army. In her memoir, *My Own Story*, Emmeline Pankhurst directly attributes the WSPU's revivalist methods to the Salvation Army.[14] Teresa Billington-Greig commented that the militant suffrage movement had "become as effective in its methods of revivalism, advertisement, and management as the Salvation Army, to which it bears more than a superficial resemblance."[15] Christabel Pankhurst instructed local WSPU organizers to adopt the Salvation Army's strategies of holding open-air meetings, staging giant processions, and selling newspapers and pamphlets door-to-door.[16] Several former Salvation Army officers brought their ideas and expertise to the WSPU. Jennie Baines, for example, was known for the extraordinary preaching abilities she had developed while serving as a Salvation Army captain. Her preaching skills "stood her in good stead in suffrage work. She had a magnificent voice, which no opposition could drown."[17] The Salvation Army also provided an inspiring example of a courageous and egalitarian organization aimed at social reform. With strict observance of sex equality among its members, as well as a commitment to the ideals of Christian socialism, the Salvation Army caught the imagination of a generation of socially conscious middle-class women who had come of age during the 1870s and 1880s.[18]

The WSPU borrowed the Salvation Army's evangelical methods and put them to use in their efforts, not to save souls but to save the nation through the votes of women. Suffragettes flooded the streets with parades, pamphlets, billboards, and soapbox speakers. They held thousands of meetings and sent numerous deputations to Parliament. At opportune moments, they staged huge rallies, patterned after evangelical revivals, to reenergize and galvanize suffrage supporters. One popular setting for WSPU rallies was the Royal Albert Hall, which at least one observer regarded as the "cathedral" of the women's movement.[19] Annie Kenney once remarked, "only those who attended those meetings [at Albert Hall] can ever realize the burning enthusiasm that prevailed. They represented the soul of the Movement."[20] Resembling a massive, Nonconformist house of worship, Albert Hall's expansive interior featured a central platform, a Willis organ, rows of velvet-covered seating, and a huge dome soaring overhead. With every movement carefully choreographed, a typical WSPU rally began with a solemn procession through the West London streets, with rows upon rows of women carrying brightly colored banners featuring tributes to queens, scientists, artists, saints, and suffrage pioneers.[21] Upon arrival at Albert Hall, crowds of up to 15,000 crammed into the galleries designed to hold two-thirds that number. The curious and eager participants sang suffrage songs, listened attentively to their colleagues speak, and then generously showed their approval by opening their purses and donating vast sums to the cause.

The "preachers" of militant suffragism promoted not only a thrilling revivalist atmosphere but also an entirely new paradigm—a new life inspired by feminist ideals. As Sandra Stanley Holton has observed, militant suffragism "must be understood primarily in terms of a cast of mind, a moral philosophy, a way of looking at the world."[22] Whether sudden and dramatic or gradual and unspectacular, almost every woman's decision to join the suffrage movement required a deliberate choice, born out of new perspective on herself and her society. Suffragettes frequently described their socialization into the WSPU's radical cosmology in terms of a quasi-religious conversion process.[23] To persuade potential recruits to make the first step, suffragettes openly spoke and wrote about their conversions. In her autobiography, Annie Kenney recalls her own transformation, which came shortly after her first imprisonment in 1905, when she and Christabel had refused to pay a fine for speaking publicly at a parliamentary candidate's campaign rally: "I knew *the* change had come into my life. The old life had gone, a new life had come. Had I found on my return that I had taken on a new body, I should not have been in the least surprised. I felt absolutely changed. The past seemed blotted out. I had started a new cycle."[24]

Other suffragettes echoed this language. In her popular book *Prisons and Prisoners,* ostensibly an exposé of England's decrepit prison system, Lady Constance Lytton offers a moving account of her conversion to militancy, which occurred while she was on holiday in Littlehampton, serendipitously staying at the same hostel as WSPU leaders Emmeline Pethick-Lawrence and Annie Kenney. Lytton was immediately taken with their otherworldly bearing: "Their remarkable individual powers seemed illumined and enhanced by a light that was apart from them as are the colours and patterns of a stained-glass window by the sun shining through it. I had never before come across this kind of spirituality. I have since found it characteristic of all the leaders in the militant section of the woman's movement, and many of the rank and file."[25]

Conversion testimonies such as Kenney's and Lytton's guided new and potential recruits along the narrow path toward militant suffragism, endowing it with a purpose and meaning extending well beyond the campaign for political rights. New converts were urged to "leave everything that stands in the way of your giving all your spare time, all the energy that you possess, all the money that can give to the WSPU."[26] They were also told that their participation would contribute not just to the emancipation of women but also to the salvation of society.

Thus, it is perhaps not surprising that some suffrage campaigners referred to their suffrage work as *religious* activity. These suffragists equated militancy with a spiritual quest and a holy war, aimed at securing justice for women and protecting the nation from the forces of vice. Some militants who espoused confrontational and even violent tactics argued pointedly that their cause and methods were those of Christ himself. Their confidence in the Christian nature of the movement's aims and methods led them to confront the nation's highest religious authorities. WSPU member Ethel Smythe wrote an impassioned letter to Archbishop of Canterbury Randall Davidson in which she boldly pronounced, "Let me remind you . . . Christ was a lawbreaker— a moral revolutionary and was crucified as a felon. There is no blame unctuously pronounced by the Church and State against us that could not have been pronounced against Him."[27] Similarly, suffragette Dorothy Davis boldly declared to Archbishop Davidson, an opponent of militant suffragism, that God was on their side: "We believe He is on our side because we are working for justice and in the cause of charity. It is the conviction that men by themselves will never put a stop to the sweating of women homeworkers. . . . We are certain that God is blessing this movement, but, if He is, will not the church take part with us in the Crusade against injustice and immorality?"[28] While such appeals had little effect on Davidson, suffragists were undaunted in their claims to a spiritual authority. Indeed, as we shall see, the resistance they encountered in some clergy compelled a number of women to assert that the nation's established religious leaders were incapable—because of male gender bias—of accurately interpreting God's teaching and will.

The suffragists' adoption of religious languages and motifs to advance their political goals was not unique for this time and, in fact, was noticeably similar to that of Britain's labor movement, of which the WSPU was itself a product.[29] British socialists also co-opted various religious forms, which scholars have argued can be seen as an expression of their radical democratic ethos and belief in the innate integrity of each individual, regardless of birth or profession. The socialists' claim to a working-class spiritual authority constituted a potent challenge to the dominant class hierarchies and an assertion of a new basis and ethic of political power.[30] Similarly, suffragists' assertion of spiritual authority was an expression of their democratic vision, although they aimed at confronting the hierarchy of gender. Thus, while systematically challenging Victorian notions of women's social and intellectual inferiority, these women left intact the idea of women's spiritual authority, using it to their own advantage. Their claim was only strengthened by the prevailing belief in the innate moral goodness of middle-class Victorian women.

The suffrage movement's revivalist style, combined with the assertion of women's spiritual nature, proved to be a potent mix. It enabled suffragists to cast their opponents not simply as antisuffragists but as pharisees, crucifiers, and even Antichrists. Some women went so far as to declare that their efforts would bring about a second reformation and fulfillment of God's divine plan. Acting on their spiritual convictions, suffragists challenged the nation's political (and spiritual) leaders not just verbally but physically as well.[31] After landing in jail for their arson and window-breaking campaigns, the militant campaigners went on hunger strikes and withstood repeated forced feedings; liquid was forced through tubes inserted into their nostrils, causing severe vomiting and leaving sores in their mouths, nasal passages, and stomachs. Through their moral courage and physical suffering, these women envisioned themselves as "recreating the spirit of the early Christians."[32] Following in the path of the early Christians, a few women even chose martyrdom.

Emily Wilding Davison is the suffrage movement's best-known martyr and a poignant example of suffragists' aspirations to be spiritual teachers and guides to a nation they perceived as morally bankrupt. An early convert to the WSPU, Davison had earned a first-class degree in English language and literature at Oxford and was an aspiring writer. In 1912, during her second imprisonment at Holloway, Davison penned the essay "The Price of Liberty," in which she explores, with language rich in biblical allusions, the idea that individuality came not only from one's rational capabilities but from one's spiritual integrity.[33] "The true Suffragette," she wrote, "is an epitome of the determination of women to possess their own souls. . . . Ever since history peeps out of the mists of time the male of the race has . . . withheld from her that which is above all temporal things, namely, the possession of a soul, the manifestation of the godhead."[34]

To "possess" their souls, suffragettes were willing to sacrifice friends, family, reputation, and honor—"the Pearls of Great Price." Some suffragettes, she divined, might even choose to surrender life itself and "reenact the tragedy of Calvary for generations yet unborn."[35] Davison equated the suffragettes' physical struggles with Christ's on the eve of his death: with him, they cried, "'Cannot this cup of anguish be spared me?' 'No' was Davison's firm reply: 'Better to be Anathema Maranatha for the sake of Progress than to sit lapped in ignoble ease in the house of good Fame!'"[36] Written while alone in prison, Davison's essay is the expression of a desperate woman trying to comprehend her surroundings and choices. Cut off from friends and family, surrounded by ugliness and squalor, Davison sought solace in her spiritual convictions. Just a few months later, however, Davison's private expressions of her spiritual convictions were transformed into public testimony, when on Derby Day in June 1913 she deliberately stepped onto the Epsom racetrack in front of the oncoming pack. Trampled by the king's horse, Davison never regained consciousness and died five days later. Her death was greeted with a sense of awe and sparked a fury of letters and editorials debating the virtues of martyrdom.[37] Her essays were published posthumously in the WSPU's journal, *Suffragette.*

Perhaps in death even more than in life, Davison served as a sublime representative of the suffragettes' intense spiritual convictions. Her funeral cortege offered a public symbol of women's sacrifices for national morality and progress. Crowds lined the streets to witness the procession from Victoria Station to St. George's Church in Bloomsbury. At the head of the procession walked the tall, fair Charlotte Marsh, clothed in white and bearing a gold martyr's cross. She was (incorrectly) identified by at least one newspaper account as Joan of Arc, giving testimony to the public's close associations between suffragettes and saintly martyrdom.[38] Behind Marsh came a group of young girls carrying a purple banner inscribed with the words of Joan of Arc: "Fight On, and God will Give the Victory." Then, a military band played the music of Chopin, Handel, and Beethoven, "written in acknowledgment of the majesty of death." Groups of women followed, some in the black robes of mourning, graduates in their scarlet and blue robes, London suffragists in white (for purity), others in prison garb, and still more in the colors of their own suffrage organizations.[39] Behind the coffin were the male sympathizers—members of the men's suffrage associations, clergy, and representatives of various labor unions. Five thousand marchers walked the route from Victoria Station to Hyde Park Corner and on to Piccadilly Circus, "through the heart of London's pleasure district . . . [where] painted women, sisters of the world's sorrow and vice . . . stood on tiptoe to see the coffin of one of their sex who died for them."[40] The procession finally halted in Bloomsbury, where mourners crammed into St. George's Church for a memorial service conducted by three clergymen who were members of the Church League for Women's Suffrage. Mourners listened to the words of Isaiah: "God is our hope and strength: a very present help in trouble. Therefore will we not fear." They sang the hymns "Nearer My God to Thee," "Onward Christian Soldiers," and "Fight the Good Fight." And they carried away a memorial card inscribed with the words "Greater Love hath no man than this, that he lay down his life for his Friend."[41] This massive, choreographed event conveyed through actions and symbols the message that Davison was a fearless and godly visionary, following in the very footsteps of Christ.

The message did not fall on deaf ears. Writer and suffrage advocate Laurence Housman later remembered how the news of Davison's death had spontaneously sparked a wave of open public sympathy. In some strange way, he suggested, her sacrifice had "caught the public imagination."[42] Many who might otherwise have been critical of Davison's martyrdom withheld their comments. A few onlookers displayed minor disapproval during the procession, but in general they were silent and respectful. As one observer suggested, they "might have been saluting the corpse of some great conqueror, instead of the dead body of a rebel heroine who had laid down her life as a protest at the insane cruelty of the present order of things."[43] Emboldened by Davison's sacrifice and the public sympathy it inspired, suffragettes intensified their efforts to persuade the nation's religious leaders to sanction women's right to exercise spiritual authority in public ways.

Early in 1913 suffragettes began an effort to rouse Britain's churches from what they perceived as apathy toward women's spiritual leadership in the nation. The WSPU's annual report for 1913 made official this "War against the Church," stating that the WSPU "indicts the Church with having aided and abetted the State in robbing women of the vote. The Church is thus held guilty of the subjection of women and all the vice, suffering, and social degradation that result from the subjection."[44] Suffragettes accused the Church of England of having formed an "Unholy Alliance" with the government, instead of fulfilling its responsibilities to the weak, powerless, and suffering. The report also asserted, "it is the duty of the Church to insist upon the political enfranchisement of women—not only as a political reform, but as a moral and even a religious reform."[45] Until the Church was willing to do this, suffragettes would remind Church leaders of their God-given duties.

Suffragettes pursued a variety of strategies in their efforts to galvanize the church into action. Some chose to boycott their local churches until their parish ministers personally declared support for women's suffrage. Others decided to attend worship services but to walk out immediately before the sermon, or, even more dramatically, to interrupt the sermon with shouts of "votes for women." A few launched an all-out war, planting bombs in church sanctuaries or setting fires in church vestries. Between April 1913 and July 1914, more than fifty churches, as well as a few chapels and synagogues, became the targets of suffragette arson.[46] Far more than just angry outbursts, these disruptions and arson attacks constituted a challenge to both established religious authority and the gender roles it had traditionally prescribed. These women co-opted the strategies of radical nonconformists and set themselves up as the true representatives of Christian ideals, interpreting those ideals to include the political and spiritual equality of the sexes.

While some suffragettes, in the name of new and purer Christianity, launched a war on the churches, other suffrage campaigners frowned on such aggressive actions and chose instead to influence religious leaders through more official channels. More than 5,700 Anglican women and men joined the Church League for Women's Suffrage, founded in 1909 by a group of Anglican members of the militant Women's Freedom League. The main aim of the CLWS was to persuade both clergy and laity that a suffrage victory would benefit both the Anglican Church and the nation as a whole.[47] Those who joined the CLWS tended to be middle-class individuals influenced by late nineteenth-century Christian Socialist ideals, which fostered a strong belief in the potential of combining progressive social action with Christian faith, as well as the conviction that the Anglican Church was to be the main force in the regeneration of British society.[48] Such a focus helped to attract more than five hundred clergy to become CLWS members. Many who joined the CLWS saw it as a means not only to further the campaign for the national franchise but also to achieve more general reform within the Church of England. One central goal was to secure greater representation for women on the Church of England's representative lay councils, which CLWS members hoped would lead the Church to be more responsive to women's interests.[49] A significant number of CLWS members also threw their support behind their colleague Ursula Roberts when, in 1913, she initiated a public discussion on women's right to preach in official capacities by distributing a questionnaire to selected Anglican lay people and clergy to elicit their views on the ordination of women to the priesthood. Spurred on by the enthusiastic response, Roberts began planning a conference on the topic for September 1914, which never took place because of the outbreak of World War I.[50] By 1916, however, the issue of women's preaching in the Anglican Church had become a topic of national discussion.

FROM NATIONAL CRISIS TO NATIONAL MISSION IN THE GREAT WAR

World War I dramatically changed the context for women's claims to moral and spiritual leadership. Initially, the outbreak of hostilities in August 1914 threw Britain's suffrage organizations into crisis. Within days, Emmeline Pankhurst had called off all suffragette militancy and pledged the WSPU's support for Britain's war effort, and virtually all the other suffrage organizations followed her lead. The cessation of militancy, however, did not end suffragists' attempts to make their voices heard.[51]

World War I also ushered in a period of spiritual crisis for the British nation. The war years revealed more than ever before the alienation of many parishioners from the life and practice of the Church of England.[52] Historians have argued that the distance people felt was most often a product of the established political character of Anglicanism and was not necessarily a sign of general lack of belief. Indeed, as J. M. Winters has argued, the war sparked greater interest in spiritual affairs and a search for less orthodox (and more feminine) forms of religious experience, such as spiritualism.[53] Within this changing context, suffragists found widening opportunities for preaching and greater interest in their spiritual insight and authority.

As early as August 1914, Christabel Pankhurst seemed to anticipate some of the shifts that were to come. She was hiding from British police in France when news reached her of Britain's decision to enter the war, and immediately she sent an article to London for publication in the *Suffragette*. Its rhetoric displayed her sharpening apocalyptic vision:

> A dreadful war-cloud seems about to burst and deluge the peoples of Europe with fire, slaughter, ruin—this then is the World as men have made it, life as men have ordered it. A man-made civilization, hideous and cruel enough in

time of peace, is to be destroyed. . . . This great war . . . is Nature's vengeance—
is God's vengeance upon the people who held women in subjection, and by
doing that have destroyed the perfect human balance. . . . Only by the help of
women as citizens can the World be saved.[54]

Christabel was by no means the only observer to view the war in quasi-mil-
lennialist terms. Numerous Christian leaders in 1914 found a transcenden-
tal significance in the hostilities and interpreted them as a clear-cut conflict
between good and evil.[55] But by 1916, after witnessing two years of devasta-
tion, Britain's political and spiritual leaders began to adopt a more reflec-
tive attitude and to consider a host of institutional reforms. As the Reverend
William Temple argued: "Men's minds are open now to large ideas. The world
has to be rebuilt."[56] Within this context, Britain's official leaders were more
inclined than ever before to consider suffragists' arguments about women's
redemptive powers and to sanction women's moral and spiritual leadership.

Because of the upheaval of war, the Church of England came extremely
close to allowing women's preaching and teaching in official, though temporary, capacities. Discussion of the issue first arose in the summer of 1916
when, in an attempt to reclaim its waning influence in the everyday lives of
the British people, the archbishop of Canterbury launched the National Mission of Repentance and Hope. Designed as an unprecedented churchwide
attempt to minister directly to the spiritual needs of the war-torn nation, the
National Mission laid plans for revival-style retreats and conferences "through
all the cities and towns and villages of the land."[57] Interestingly, the archbishop called on several suffrage campaigners to help with the preparations.
Most notably, he appointed to the council of the National Mission A. Maude
Royden, the editor of the suffrage monthly *Common Cause*, member of the
NUWSS and CLWS, and open advocate of women's right to preach in the
Church of England.

The council first began to consider the possibility of using women to lead
local prayer and instructional meetings in response to the severe shortage
of clergy, many of whom were serving in the army as chaplains. News of these
deliberations leaked out and provoked a wide public discussion of the propriety of female Anglican priests.[58] Critics asserted a "slippery-slope" argument that the temporary use of women speakers would inevitably begin a
movement for the ordination of women to the priesthood. In the face of such
opposition, two council members withdrew their original support for women
speakers and allowed the proposition to die.[59] But the council's final decision was reached in such a bumbling fashion that many Anglican parishioners
were left uncertain about the Church's official position toward women's speaking and teaching in church.[60]

Within this atmosphere of confusion, advocates of women's ordination
saw their opportunity. The CLWS in particular quickly mobilized into action.
By the time the vote was granted to women over the age of thirty in Febru-

ary 1918, the CLWS had reshaped its goals to include not just equal political rights but also equal "spiritual rights." In a symbolic gesture, members voted in January 1919 to rename the organization the League of the Church Militant (LCM) to protest that the Church was "not half militant enough" (an interesting choice of words in light of the recently ended war).[61] In May 1919 the general council of the LCM voted to make women's ordination to the priesthood a central goal: "We repudiate 'subordination' just as earnestly as we repudiate 'inferiority'; we deny that upon man there is conferred according to the divine intention a permanent and essential headship."[62]

As the LCM attempted to chart a course into the male-dominated territory of the ministry, it at first adopted an equivocal tone. It included both negative opinions (some claimed too many) and positive opinions on women's ordination in its monthly publication, the *Church Militant*. The LCM executive explained: "Though we are indignant we are not disloyal . . . and though indignant we are not unreasonable."[63] They did not, for example, urge bishops to ordain women on their own responsibility, nor did they put pressure on Parliament to vote on Anglican polity. Instead, the LCM preferred to appeal directly to Church members in the hope that "the truth will prevail." But after mid-1919, when Anglican women were granted the right to equal representation on each of the Church's newly reorganized lay councils, the LCM grew bolder in its campaign for women's ordination. LCM members led study groups and public debates, and they initiated an educational campaign in schools, colleges, and training colleges to appeal to the "young, well-educated, and thinking class of women" about the position of women in the church.[64]

As the war-torn nation struggled to rebuild, the issue of women's ordination drew significant public interest. Some members departed in protest, but the LCM attracted more support than it lost. Subscriptions to the *Church Militant* in 1920 drew revenues nearly three times greater than in 1918 and four times greater than in 1914. Donations between 1918 and 1920 increased more than sixfold, although they were less than half of the 1914 total; many were interested in the issue of women's ordination, but fewer were willing to give it their wholehearted support.[65] The LCM also attracted the support of prominent suffragists, including Millicent Garrett Fawcett and Emmeline Pethick-Lawrence, who served on a women's ordination advisory committee.

Substantial interest in expanding women's leadership roles in the Church of England also came from official quarters. In February 1920 the lower house of the Canterbury Convocation defeated by a single vote a provision that would have allowed women to preach at nonliturgical services, an action that received resounding condemnation from several church newspapers.[66] The issue of women's ordination came to a head at the Lambeth Conference of Bishops in July 1920, where Church leaders continued to appear equivocal in their opposition to women's ordination. After some discussion, the conference avoided an explicit statement condemning women preachers and instead reaffirmed the office of deaconess as the sole order of ministry for women "with apostolic approval." But the bishops also indicated that women could on occasion be allowed to speak and lead prayer in unofficial capacities. With this small encouragement, the LCM continued to campaign for women's ordination with great energy and conviction.[67] Many women, of course, did not wait for the Church's official sanction of women preachers (which finally came in 1992) and instead began to preach in less orthodox traditions. But whether preaching from the pulpit of London's City Temple or campaigning for the right to preach in Westminster Abbey, these women continued the efforts of suffragists to speak with authority in public and to provide spiritual leadership to the British nation.

NOTES

1. Christabel Pankhurst, *The Lord Cometh* (London: Marshall, Morgan and Scott, 1923); Christabel Pankhurst, *Pressing Problems of the Closing Age* (London: Marshall, Morgan and Scott, 1924). These were followed by two additional prophetic works: Christabel Pankhurst, *The World's Unrest, or Visions of the Dawn* (London: Marshall, Morgan and Scott, 1926); and Christabel Pankhurst, *Seeing the Future* (New York: Harper and Bros., 1929).

2. Barbara Castle, *Sylvia and Christabel Pankhurst* (Middlesex, England: Penguin, 1987), pp. 143–44; David Mitchell, *Queen Christabel* (London: Macdonald and Jane's, 1977), pp. 286–305.

3. Sheila Fletcher, *A. Maude Royden: A Life* (Oxford: Basil Blackwell, 1989).

4. Edith Picton-Turbervill, *Life Is Good: An Autobiography* (London: Frederick Muller, 1939).

5. The Church of the New Ideal was a highly unconventional group of women that apparently functioned much like a suffrage society, with a president and an honorary secretary at its helm, but firmly identified itself as a "church organized by women." Begun in 1916 in a suburb of Manchester, the Church of the New Ideal filled its pulpit with Nonconformist ministers and veterans of the suffrage movement. Although the group had disappeared by the early 1920s, it apparently helped to spawn the esoteric monthly magazine *Urania*, dedicated to the promotion of gnostic principles. The few references I have been able to find to this interesting group are in the (as yet uncataloged) papers of M. A. R. Tuker, a Roman Catholic scholar and suffragette, which are housed at the Fawcett Library, London.

6. Edith Picton-Turbervill, *Musings of a Lay Woman on the Life of the Churches* (London: John Murray, 1919); Edith Picton-Turbervill, *Christ and Woman's Power* (London: Morgan and Scott, 1919); Edith Picton-Turbervill, *Should Women Be Priests and Ministers?* (London: Society for the Equal Ministry of Men and Women in the Church, n.d.).

7. A. A. [Alice Abadam], *Women Priests* (Lichfield, England: F. H. Bull and E. Wiseman, 1921).

8. Mitchell, *Queen Christabel*, pp. 287, 365 n. 22.

9. Martin Pugh, *Women and the Women's Movement in Britain, 1914–1959* (London: Macmillan, 1992), pp. 46–47.

10. See, for example, Jane Rendall, *The Origins of Modern Feminism: Women in Britain, France and the United States, 1780–1860* (Chicago: Lyceum, 1985), chap. 3; Olive Anderson provides an alternative view in "Women Preachers in Mid-Victorian Britain: Some Reflexions on Feminism, Popular Religion and Social Change," *Historical Journal* 12, no. 3 (1969): 467–84.

11. In typical usage, the term *suffragist* refers to suffrage campaigners who advocated nonmilitant methods such as education; *suffragette* denotes those who used militant methods, such as direct confrontations, window-breaking, and arson. The distinctions between the two groups were often blurred by women's memberships in multiple suffrage societies. In this essay I use *suffragist* to refer to both militants and nonmilitants when I believe no distinction is necessary for my argument; I reserve *suffragette* for those occasions when I wish to highlight their militant methods.

12. The best account of the militant women's suffrage campaign is Andrew Rosen's *Rise Up, Women! The Militant Campaign of the Women's Social and Political Union, 1903–1914* (London: Routledge and Kegan Paul, 1974); for other groups, see Roger Fulford, *Votes for Women: The Story of a Struggle* (London: Faber and Faber, 1952); and Constance Rover, *Women's Suffrage and Party Politics in Britain, 1866–1914* (London: Routledge and Kegan Paul, 1967). Two more recent studies are Sandra Holton's *Feminism and Democracy: Women's Suffrage and Reform Politics* (Cambridge: Cambridge University Press, 1987); and Susan Kingsley Kent, *Sex and Suffrage in Britain, 1860–1914* (Princeton, N.J.: Princeton University Press, 1987).

13. Pankhurst, *Pressing Problems*, pp. 1, 38.

14. Emmeline Pankhurst, *My Own Story* (1914; reprint, New York: Kraus, 1971), p. 62. See also Jane Marcus, introduction to Elizabeth Robins, *The Convert* (1907; reprint, London, 1980), p. x.

15. Teresa Billington-Greig, *The Militant Suffrage Movement*, reprinted in *The Non-Violent Militant*, ed. Carol McPhee and Ann Fitzgerald (London, 1987), p. 142.

16. Christabel Pankhurst to Mrs. Badley, April 3, 1911, Fawcett Autograph Collection, London.

17. Hannah Mitchell, *Hard Way Up* (London: Virago, 1977), p. 135.

18. See Pamela J. Walker's essay on the Salvation Army in this volume.

19. It was Israel Zangwill's term; see his speech "The Hithertos," Fawcett Library, London.

20. Annie Kenney, *Memories of a Militant* (London: Edward Arnold, 1924), p. 139.

21. See the brilliant description of these suffrage parades in Lisa Tickner, *A Spectacle of Women: Imagery of the Suffrage Campaign, 1907–1914* (Chicago: University of Chicago Press, 1988), esp. pp. 73–104.

22. Sandra Stanley Holton, "In Sorrowful Wrath: Suffrage Militancy and the Romantic Feminism of Emmeline Pankhurst," in *British Feminism in the Twentieth Century*, ed. Harold L. Smith (Amherst: University of Massachusetts Press, 1990), p. 10.

23. For a telling example, see Elizabeth Robins's novel *The Convert* (1907; reprint, London: Woman's Press, 1980). In his analysis of a similar phenomenon among British socialists, Stephen Yeo points out that conversion was only quasi-religious "if 'religious' is a label reserved for particular orthodoxies." Yeo, "A New Life: The Religion of Socialism in Britain, 1883–1896," *History Workshop Journal* 4 (Autumn 1977): 10.

24. Kenney, *Memories of a Militant*, p. 26.

25. Constance Lytton, *Prisons and Prisoners* (London: Heinemann, 1914), p. 9.

26. *Suffragette,* July 18, 1914, p. 281.

27. Ethel Smythe to Randall T. Davidson, February 11, 1914, Papers of Randall T. Davidson, Lambeth Palace, London.

28. Dorothy Davis to Randall T. Davidson, May 4, 1908, Papers of Randall T. Davidson.

29. Jill Liddington and Jill Norris, *One Hand Tied behind Us: The Rise of the Women's Suffrage Movement* (London: Virago, 1978).

30. Logie Barrow, *Independent Spirits: Spiritualism and English Plebians, 1850–1910* (London: Routledge and Kegan Paul, 1986), pp. 148–49. Barrow builds on the groundbreaking work of Stephen Yeo in "A New Life."

31. For an excellent study of suffragettes' physical suffering for the sake of spiritual growth, see Martha Vicinus, "Male Space and Women's Bodies: The Suffragette Movement," in *Independent Women: Work and Community for Single Women, 1850–1920* (Chicago: University of Chicago Press, 1985).

32. See, for example, articles in *Suffragette* by Annie Kenney (April 24, 1914); Alma White (May 8, 1914); and Emily Wilding Davison, "The Price of Liberty," *Suffragette,* June 5, 1914.

33. Emily Wilding Davison Papers, Fawcett Library, London. She also left behind unpublished essays titled "The Real Christianity" and "A Militant on May-Day."

34. Davison, "The Price of Liberty," p. 1.

35. Ibid., pp. 6–7.

36. Ibid., p. 5.

37. See, for example, Laurence Housman's letter to Mrs. Arncliffe-Sennett (June 7, 1913): "If one man a day, or a week, would immolate himself as Miss Davison has done, it might get at the public conscience. But as I haven't the courage and devotion to be one, I ought not to blame others for not employing the sequence"; see also Ethel Smythe to Archbishop of Canterbury (Arncliffe-Sennett Collection, vol. 23); George Bernard Shaw, letter to the *Times,* June 23, 1913; Rev. F. B. Meyer, letter to the *Times,* June 27, 1913.

38. Tickner, *Spectacle of Women,* p. 138.

39. The best description can be found in the *Daily Herald,* June 16, 1913.

40. Ibid.

41. The program of the memorial service can be found in the papers of Emily Wilding Davison, Fawcett Library, London.

42. Laurence Housman, *The Unexpected Years* (London: Jonathan Cape, 1937), p. 247.

43. *Daily Herald,* June 16, 1913.

44. Annual Report of the Women's Social and Political Union for 1913, Fawcett Library, London.

45. Ibid.

46. See, for example, the Suffragist Churchwoman's Protest Committee flyer, Arncliffe-Sennett Collection, vol. 21, British Library. Reports of suffrage arson attacks can be found scattered through the pages of the *Suffragette* as well as the national press.

47. Little has been written about the CLWS. The most comprehensive published account can be found in Brian Heeney, *The Women's Movement in the Church of England, 1850–1930* (Oxford: Clarendon Press, 1988).

48. For more on the Christian Socialists, see Edward Norman, *The Victorian Christian Socialists* (Cambridge: Cambridge University Press, 1987).

49. From its inception in 1903, women were denied the right to sit on the Representative Church Council, the Church of England's body of lay representatives. Women's sole means of influencing Church policy was through attendance at the annual Church congresses. These bodies, however, were nonauthoritative—no votes were taken or decisions made on any ecclesiastical issues. See Heeney, *The Women's Movement*, pp. 94 ff.

50. See the responses to Roberts's questionnaire in "Women in the Church," Fawcett Autograph Collection, Fawcett Library, London.

51. One organization that continued to campaign for the vote was the United Suffragists, an offshoot of the WSPU formed in early 1914.

52. Alan Wilkinson, *The Church of England and the First World War* (London: Society for Promoting Christian Knowledge, 1978); Alan Marrin, *The Last Crusade: The Church of England and the First World War* (Durham, N.C.: Duke University Press, 1974).

53. J. M. Winters, "Spiritualism and the First World War," in *Religion and Irreligion in Victorian Society*, ed. R. W. Davis and R. J. Helmstadter (London: Routledge, 1992), pp. 185–200.

54. *Suffragette*, August 7, 1914, p. 301.

55. John Wolffe, *God and Greater Britain: Religion and National Life in Britain and Ireland, 1843–1945* (London: Routledge, 1994), pp. 233 ff.

56. As quoted in G. I. T. Machin, *Politics and the Churches in Great Britain, 1869–1921* (Oxford: Clarendon Press, 1987), p. 319.

57. The best account of the National Mission can be found in Wilkinson, *The Church of England*, pp. 70 ff.

58. See, for example, the pamphlet by Athelstan Riley, "Women and the Priesthood" (July 1916, n.p.); Darwell Stone, "Ministrations of Women in the Church," *Guardian,* July 27, 1916; Henry Wace, "Questions of the Day: The Mission and a Single Eye," *Record,* July 27, 1916.

59. They were the bishops of London and Chelmsford.

60. For one account of the haphazard decision-making process, see Fletcher, *Maude Royden*, pp. 145–51.

61. "Title and Objects," *Church Militant*, February 1919, p. 12.

62. "Women and the Priesthood," *Church Militant*, May 1919, p. 36.

63. Ibid.

64. "Educational Campaign," *Church Militant*, December 1919, p. 91.

65. "Annual Reports of the Executive Committee," published in the March 1915 report of the Church League for Women's Suffrage and the February 1919 and January 1921 reports of the League of the Church Militant.

66. Including the *Guardian*, the *Church Family Newspaper,* and the *Challenge.* The *Church Times* withheld comment, which might be interpreted as a silent protest.

67. In 1928 the LCM dissolved itself, leaving advocacy of women's ordination to the Anglican Group for Bringing the Subject of the Admission of Women to the Priesthood before the Next Lambeth Conference (which occurred in 1930).

Voices of the Spirit

Exercising Power, Embracing Responsibility

Karen L. King

In reading the essays collected in this volume, what struck me most power-fully was the persistence of women's voices in enriching, shaping, and sustaining Christianity throughout its history. Women have persisted despite the fact that in every century the validity of women's public speech and leadership has been contested by those wishing to limit the extent and authority of women's religious participation in Christian life. Yet the overwhelming conclusion is still that, from the first century to the twentieth, women have made significant contributions to Christian thought and practice through their prophesying, preaching, and teaching.

Although there have been times and places where women were prominent and their participation is well documented, often the recovery of women's stories is difficult. Considerable effort is required to uncover these contributions. Because patriarchal historiography is so selective,[1] it is often necessary to look beyond the elite literary sources that are the most usual bases for the reconstruction of Christian history. The contributors to this volume, for example, point to evidence of women's religious activities in visual representations, in song and testimony, in visits to family and friends, in mothers' instruction to their children, and even in the polemic written against them. Karen Torjesen finds visual confirmation of women's public roles in the figure of the praying woman *orans*. Carolyn Muessig shows us theological creativity and spiritual edification in the songs of medieval women. Nicole Bériou perceives the pastoral activity of spiritual formation in child rearing. Roberto Rusconi supplies Italian examples of women pictured preaching and writing sermons in the late Middle Ages. And so on. Uncovering women's contributions entails not only examining new sources, like the *Gospel of Mary*, but also reinterpreting well-known materials, paying attention to polemical and rhetorical constructions, plumbing the margins, and pioneering new approaches.

The essays also surfaced strategies that have supported and enabled women's public speech, as well as those that have been used to limit, suppress, and delegitimate it. In the case of the opposition to women's speech, there seems to have been a rather limited and fixed set of strategies in place. They included attacking women's moral character, charging them with sexual license and heresy, and using institutional and legal sanctions. Women's opponents selectively appealed to Scripture, tradition, and patriarchal social norms (often represented as the "natural" order). These strategies have a long history, one that begins with one of the earliest examples of Christian literature, Paul's first letter to the Corinthians. This letter provides a vivid portrait of women's public prophecy and prayer within the Corinthian community. Although Paul assumes the legitimacy of women's public participation, he incongruously insists that women's subordinate status should be symboled through the wearing of veils (1 Cor. 11:2–16). To support his point, Paul appeals to tradition, scripture (Gen. 1–3), social convention, the practice of other churches, and even "nature." The appeal to "nature" is particularly interesting because it is so obviously a disguised appeal to social convention: "Does not nature itself teach you that for a man to wear long hair is degrading to him, but if a women has long hair, it is her pride?" Nature of course teaches us no such thing; only the habits of social practice would make it appear otherwise. That such an argument was at all persuasive illustrates how deeply entrenched the body can be in a culture's symbol system. At 1 Corinthians 14:33b–35, a later author or scribe interpolated a direct denunciation of women's speech into Paul's text, appealing to the law as well.

The statements in Corinthians were later granted canonical status and eventually became an authoritative basis for the refutation of women's exercise of spiritual freedom in and of themselves. So one of the very earliest glimpses into church life at once shows women teaching, preaching, and praying with their fellow male Christians, along with attempts to control, restrict, or silence women's public speech.[2] Whether these attempts were those of Paul or some later interpolator, the letter is clearly reacting to the pervasiveness of women's prophecy and teaching within the Corinthian community. The important point about Paul's letter is not only that it gives us information about women's participation in shaping early Christian community, but also that the strategic appeals of these passages became paradigmatic for later attempts to subordinate women and limit their participation.

In the following centuries, the three key texts from Scripture to which appeal was regularly made to silence women's voices are 1 Corinthians 14:33b–35; 1 Timothy 2:11–15; and Genesis 1–3 (especially 3:16). These passages are supplemented by appeal to the patriarchal household codes (Ephesians 5:22–24; Colossians 3:18; 1 Peter 3:1–6). Appeal is also made to examples of evil women whose counsel is said to have ruined their husbands, such as Eve, Job's wife (Job 2:9–10), and Pilate's wife (Matthew 27:19). Christian women preaching are compared to Jezebel (Kings and Revelations 2:20); indeed it was suggested that women preaching was one sign that the end of the world was at hand! Jesus' admonition to Mary Magdalene not to touch him is interpreted as an absolute injunction against all women teaching or administering the sacraments. Women are assumed to be particularly gullible and thus vulnerable to the heresies of false teachers (2 Timothy 3:6–7). The silence of Mary, along with her virginity, is held up as an exemplar for female behavior (Luke 2:19).

On the other hand, Scripture also was cited to support women's legitimacy to preach and prophesy. In particular, appeals were made to the risen Lord's command to Mary Magdalene (John 20:17–18), the declaration that the Spirit would be poured out on women (Acts 2:17–18; Joel 2:28–32), Paul's assumption that women were prophesying (1 Corinthians 11:5), and Titus's injunction for women to teach (2:3). Appeal was made as well to the many women preachers and prophets in the Bible in addition to Mary Magdalene, such as Deborah (Judges 4–6), Esther (Esther), Anna (Luke 2:36–38), Priscilla (Acts of the Apostles 18:26), Phoebe (Romans 16:1), Tryphaena (Romans 16:12), and Philip's four daughters (Acts 21:9). It was often noted that the Holy Spirit is conferred on all who are baptized (Acts 1:14; 2:4), and that after baptism there is no longer male or female; all are one in Christ Jesus (Galatians 3:28). In addition, many standard patriarchal interpretations of Scripture have been contested. For example, the view that all Christian women bear the burden and shame of Eve's sin no longer makes sense in light of Mary's overcoming that sin by bringing Christ into the world; now baptized women stand in Mary's priestly heritage. Women as well as men were made in the image and likeness of God (Genesis 1:27); they were not made only of flesh but of strong bone (Genesis 2:22). There is therefore no inherent or natural weakness in women as such. The injunctions in 1 Corinthians 14:35 and 1 Timothy 2:15 seem to apply only to married women and mothers, not to virgins, maidens, widows, or older women. These passages, therefore, do not have universal authority. Indeed, it was argued, the Spirit can at any time override such injunctions when it gives a woman a call to preach or prophesy, as Christ did to Mary Magdalene.

Examples of such "Scripture wars" for and against women's preaching abound in our essays. Beverly Kienzle shows that, in arguing against their accusers, the Waldensians firmly based their practices of women's speaking publicly on Scripture, appealing to Mary Magdalene (John 20:17–18), Anna (Luke 2:36–38), and Titus's injunction for women to teach (2:3). Peter Vogt gives some of the spirited response of Count Zinzendorf to attempts to silence Moravian women. Referring to Acts 2:17–18 (Joel 2:28–32), Zinzendorf wrote: "It is odd, when the Holy Spirit says: your daughters shall prophesy, that we say: they shall not prophesy." Pamela Walker shows that the Salvation Army's view of the church was based on the portrait of early Christianity in Acts, where women are prominent as Spirit-filled preachers and prophets. Catherine Booth directly challenged views claiming that women's nature was unsuited for public speech by noting that a woman had brought Christ into the world without the aid of any man, and that a woman was the first person to be charged to spread the good news of the resurrection.

As these examples illustrate, often the strategies used to support women's public speech were framed in reaction to the strategies of their opponents. So supporters might praise a woman's character, advocate the orthodoxy of women's teaching and behavior, and work to accommodate or change institutional strictures. Arguments in favor of the legitimacy of women's public speech also often appealed selectively to Scripture and tradition. At the same time, they challenged the "naturalness" of gender categories and roles.

Another strategy lay in the defense of women's moral character, insofar as charges that women's public speaking was shameful were used to delegitimize their contributions to church life. Sometimes, however, women used their good reputations to gain legitimacy for their teaching. Those who praised a woman preacher or prophet often emphasized her female characteristics, such as modesty, chastity, and being a good wife and mother. Nuns especially, whose exemplary renunciation of the worldly life has always placed them in special circumstances, were at times able to appeal to their purity to reinforce their independence. Such strategies could be effective, but they were limited insofar as they necessarily had to accept the reigning social standards for defining women's roles and character.

The defense of women's character in the face of moral slander was thus fraught with ambiguity because judgments about moral character were often based on conformity to patriarchal gender roles. Charges were routinely made that the speech of women in public was disruptive, sexually licentious, and unnatural—charges against the breathtakingly transgressive Hallelujah Lasses, "the unladylike behavior and strident tone" of Maria W. Stewart, and the "bossy and meddlesome" Quaker Catherine Payton. In some cases, responding to the charges launched against them led to direct refutation (in Catherine Booth's case, for example), but most often the women devised a variety of strategies that at least partially accommodated their opponents in order to avoid direct confrontation. Linda Lierheimer discusses how the Ursulines "exploited the fluid boundaries between teaching and preaching" in order not to appear subversive but to take full advantage of the situation. They changed the location of their preaching and deemphasized its official aspects, rejecting even the attempts of their supporters to define public and private space more precisely. Edith Dolnikowski emphasizes how Foxe presented his female martyrs as models but kept them otherwise within the conventional institutions of family and marriage. Pamela Walker tells us that

Catherine Booth did not consider women's public preaching to be a challenge to convention at all. Others developed new language to disguise what they were doing: Elaine Lawless tells us that her Pentecostal women "testify" rather than "preach"; Carolyn Muessig's sisters don't "preach," they "sing." Such strategies operated to give women power within limits already set by those who insisted that women had no right to preach officially, from the pulpit, in public, or before men.

In understanding their strategies, we also need to see the costs that were borne by women preaching in public under such criticism. In the *Gospel of Mary*, Mary Magdalene bursts into tears at Peter's charges against her. Phyllis Mack talks about the self-doubt, anxiety, and even depression those courageous Quaker women suffered. Today we see the need to oppose the injustice of such limits on women's full participation in the Christian life, but understanding those women's strategies in context also allows us to appreciate the magnitude of their accomplishments.

As the editors point out in the preface, the category of preaching is very fluid and flexible. How preaching is defined is not simply a matter of lexical determination but of rhetorical analysis. Whether women's activity is called "preaching" or given some other name can determine whether women will be included or excluded, as well as provide for compromise, negotiation, and accommodation.

Another strategy used by both supporters and opponents of women's authority is the appeal to tradition. When used to oppose women's authority, this appeal bases much of its legitimacy on a particular reconstruction of church history that largely marginalizes or excludes women. If women are prominently portrayed, they are often represented in ways that are meant to support patriarchal roles and ideas, such as the virgin Mother. Often, as with Paul's appeal to "the practice in all the churches," tradition is simply an appeal to the status quo.

The preservation of stories about women meant to inculcate patriarchal values can, however, still be useful to women's history. Moreover, it is not necessary to continue to give the same meaning to these women's activities. Darleen Pryds, for example, offers the story of Rose of Viterbo as an example of a woman's public preaching. Though her hagiographers did not intend her to be an argument for the general validity of women's preaching, in the context of this volume her story can potentially be empowering to contemporary women and men.

Another aspect of the "tradition" strategy is the appeal to early Christian origins as the authoritative model for all later Christian belief and practice. Supporters of women's authority have appealed to the examples of early Christian women prophets and preachers, as well as women followers of Jesus, for legitimacy for their ministries. But as several of the authors in this volume have pointed out, opponents simply counter that these women were *excep-*

tions. Katherine Jansen gives us a fascinating portrait of Mary Magdalene's widespread portrayal as a preacher throughout thirteenth- and fourteenth-century France; yet many clerics of the time assumed she was an exception, that her mandate from the Holy Spirit had exempted her from the Pauline ban. Darleen Pryds points out that even Rose of Viterbo, whose preaching defended the pope against the heretics, was praised and held up as a model to be admired but not imitated.

It is my own opinion, however, that appeals to origins are not only ambiguous but potentially dangerous. The logic of appeal to origins depends upon contrasting the purity, power, and goodness of the pristine originary moment with a corrupt, deviant, or wicked foil. Whether such a contrast is explicit or not, it is potentially available for exploitation. And too often it has been used, for example, to praise Jesus' egalitarianism at the expense of denigrating Jewish women, or to uphold pristine Protestant origins in the face of Catholic corruption. Even when anti-Judaism and anti-Catholicism are clearly eschewed as unacceptable appeals in the struggle for justice for women, the contrastive logic of origins remains in place, waiting for a new exploitation.

As powerful as the appeals to Scripture, moral purity, tradition, and origins are, such reactionary or oppositional strategies can at best take the argument only so far. One of the most important contributions of this volume is that the essays go beyond such strategies. They recall and construct for us, on historically sound grounds, the lives and models of Christian women who preached and prophesied: Mary Magdalene, Catherine of Alexandria, Guillelma Faure, Marie of Oignies, Perrette de Bermond, Margery Backster, Rose of Viterbo, Hannah Barnard, Catherine Booth, Maria W. Stewart, Mother Leaf Anderson, Christabel Pankhurst, and many, many other women preachers, teachers, and prophets. These women are their own argument for the legitimate authority of women's public speech and activity. They have sustained and nurtured their communities, while enriching their own spiritual lives.

These women understood their authority to be based upon a number of foundations: baptism, prophetic inspiration, the call of the Spirit, the requirements of the faith for public testimony and witness (including martyrdom), and institutional legitimation. Many times they simply stepped in to fill a need. Linda Lierheimer locates the impetus for the Ursuline missions to educate people in the basic catechism in a condition of general ignorance. Pamela Walker lets us see how Catherine Booth addressed a class of women and men largely ignored in the developing urban centers of Britain. Yvonne Chireau tells how Mother Leaf Anderson addressed the spiritual, economic, and practical needs of her congregations, providing healing, leadership education, and organizational structures. In the process, she "transformed the religious landscape of [New Orleans] for both blacks and whites." Women are not taking up the exercise of power only out of a sense of their rights, but out of their perception of the needs of their communities. To exercise power is, as Judylyn Ryan puts it, to embrace responsibility. The authority to act is based upon the need to do so.

The question is therefore less what the basis is for women's authority than what conditions or religious ideas have supported women's taking up public roles. Here there is no clear uniformity. One factor that surfaces repeatedly in the essays is a focus on the interior life. This interior life is not to be confused with a modern individualist ethic. These women do not understand the individual over, against, or in isolation from the community. The cultivation of the interior life finds the resources for women's empowerment within a vision of spiritual community. The question is only what kind of community life is envisioned. Anne Brenon provides one strong portrayal of a spiritual Christian community that recognized the legitimacy of women's leadership; the Cathar Christians rejected those aspects of the institution that they believed impeded the development of true Christianity, especially the doctrines of the atonement, original sin, and separate ordination for the priesthood. Baptism alone was recognized as sufficient to convey the ability to preach and baptize others. They also contested the view that "male" and "female" are essential characteristics of the soul, as the *Gospel of Mary* had done long before them. Like the *Gospel of Mary*, they stressed the inherent connection of the spiritual self with God, and they affirmed the inherent goodness and equality of souls with one another. Although the women preachers in this volume often did not directly challenge their institutional doctrines as the Cathars did, they did develop alternatives that resemble the views of the Cathars in many respects. Almost all of our women preachers in one way or another bent or contested the validity of the gender definitions of their day. They interpreted Genesis in such a way as *not* to place the entire blame for the fall of humanity and the crucifixion of Jesus on Eve and all women; and they tended to create communities in which participation was based on the quality of one's internal experience rather than on external structures. This was true to some extent for the *Gospel of Mary*, the Waldensians, the Cathars, Matthew Fox, the Moravians, the Inner Life Quakers, Catherine Booth, Mother Leaf Anderson, and the suffragettes. It was less so for Rose of Viterbo, Maria W. Stewart, and others. And even the examples I have cited show a wide range of theological beliefs. Also, several essays in this volume consciously and purposefully challenge the traditional confines of "Christianity" by including "heresy" and African cosmology within its compass.

There is even less uniformity in institutional structures than in theological perspectives. Women have exercised legitimate public authority in a variety of institutional contexts: Mary Magdalene in early missionary Gentile Christianity, Rose of Viterbo as a public defender of the Catholic faith, women deacons and presbyters within the gender-divided Moravian choirs, sisters with certificates to preach in the egalitarian Quaker meeting, officers within the hierarchical structures of the Salvation Army, the founder and ministers of the autonomous Spiritual churches of New Orleans, and ordained priests in an Episcopalian institution.

That legitimate public leadership is sanctioned by and for women in such a broad range of institutional structures should give us pause. Although it may be true that the opportunities for women's leadership are greater when structures of authority are relatively informal or during periods of crisis or disruption, these are by no means the only circumstances in which women have exercised and continue to exercise legitimate public authority. The need to embrace responsibility, and the accompanying authority to act, can give rise to women's public preaching in a variety of institutional and social contexts. Indeed the essays in this volume seem to suggest that women's exercise of public speech has a history of transgressing social and institutional boundaries, however variously they are defined at any particular time.

Moreover, by identifying spiritual need beyond the immediate confines of religious community structures, women are able to extend their authority and root its legitimacy in a larger sphere. Phyllis Mack, Judylyn Ryan, and Jacqueline deVries all suggest that women's spirituality, public preaching, and political consciousness are closely linked. In each of the examples they provide, when concerns about war and pacifism, slavery, suffrage, racism, and injustice led women into the public political sphere, often as preachers, their claims to exercise public leadership on these issues were rooted in their religious beliefs and practices. Black women's spiritual and sociopolitical leadership as preachers, for example, is based on "critiques of the social and political conditions in which African Americans live" and "is informed by and expresses an ethos of interconnectedness" common to Afro-Christianity. Similarly, deVries argues that the turn of many suffragettes toward preaching careers was not a repudiation of their radical vision. The vote was always considered only one means of achieving the larger goal of allowing women to exert their moral and spiritual influence publicly. The interconnections of religious belief with issues of human suffering, poverty, class, and race, as well as gender, have been strong motivating forces for women's political activism. Through their words and actions, women have conveyed a strong vision of Christian community, in which the full membership of all persons and the full personhood of all members are affirmed.

The essays in this volume are themselves an important contribution to the story of women preaching. But because they are limited to examples drawn from particular moments in European and North American history, they are only one element of the larger story of women's contributions to Christianity. The global character of Christianity requires that a full description of women's contributions to Christianity include women's voices from every age, every sexual orientation, every race, every continent, and every human situation. Only then will the "Voices of the Spirit" swell and be heard in full chorus.

NOTES

1. See the treatment of this question by Elisabeth Schüssler Fiorenza, *In Memory of Her: A Feminist Theological Reconstruction of Christian Origins* (New York: Crossroad, 1985), pp. 41–67.

2. See especially Antoinette Clark Wire, *The Corinthian Women Prophets: A Reconstruction through Paul's Rhetoric* (Minneapolis: Fortress Press, 1990).

CONTRIBUTORS

Nicole Bériou is Professor, Université Lumière—Lyon II. She is the author of more than forty books and articles on preaching and intellectual and religious life during the Middle Ages, including *La prédication de Ranulphe de la Houblonnière: Sermons aux clercs et aux simples gens à Paris au XIIIe siècle;* with Francois-Olivier Toutai, *Voluntate Dei leprosus: Les lepreaux entre conversion et exclusion aux XIIe et XIIIe siècles* (1991); with Jacques Berlioz and Jean Longère, *Prier au Moyen Age: Pratiques et expériences (XIIIe–XVe siècles)* (1991); and with David d'Avray, *Modern Questions about Medieval Sermons: Essays on Marriage, Death, History and Sanctity* (1994).

Anne Brenon is Conservateur du Patrimoine de France in charge of the Centre d'Études cathares. She is the author of many articles and books, including *Le vrai visage du Catharisme* (1988), *Les femmes cathares* (1992), *Montségur, Memoire d'hérétique* (1994), *Petit précis de catharisme* (1996), and *Les cathares, vie et mort d'une église chrétienne* (1996). She is an editor of the journal *Heresis.*

Yvonne Chireau is Assistant Professor of Religion at Swarthmore College. She is working on a book on African American religion and magic in the nineteenth century.

Jacqueline R. deVries is Assistant Professor of Modern European History and Women's Studies at Augsburg College. She has published several articles on British feminism before and after World War I and is completing a book entitled *A New Heaven and a New Earth: Feminism, Religion, and the Politics of Identity in Great Britain, 1890–1930.*

Edith Wilks Dolnikowski specializes in the study of late-medieval theology and preaching. Her publications include *Thomas Bradwardine: A View of Time and a Vision of Eternity in Fourteenth Century Thought* (1995) and "The Encouragement of Lay Preaching as an Ecclesiastical Critique in Wyclif's Latin Sermons," in *Models of Holiness in Medieval Sermons,* edited by Beverly Mayne Kienzle et al. (1996). She was ordained to the priesthood in the Episcopal Church in 1996 and currently serves at the Church of Our Saviour in Brookline, Massachusetts.

Katherine Ludwig Jansen teaches history at the Catholic University of America. Her book *Mary Magdalen and the Mendicants* will be published by Princeton University Press.

Beverly Mayne Kienzle is Professor of the Practice in Latin and Romance Languages at Harvard Divinity School and president of the International Medieval Sermon Studies Society. She is the author of many articles on medieval sermons; coeditor of *Models of Holiness in Medieval Sermons* (1996) and *De Ore Domini: Preacher and Word in the Middle Ages* (1989); and translator of *Bernard of Clairvaux: Sermons for the Summer Season* (1991). She has several works on medieval preaching forthcoming, including: *The Sermon, Typologie des sources du moyen âge;* a bilingual edition of Hildegard of Bingen's Expositiones evangeliorum; and a study of Cistercian preaching in the twelfth century.

Karen L. King is Professor of New Testament Studies and the History of Ancient Christianity at Harvard Divinity School. Her fields include early Christianity, Gnosticism, and women's studies in antiquity. She is the editor of *Images of the Feminine in Gnosticism* and *Women and Goddess Traditions.* Her most recent book is an edition of the Gnostic text "Allogenes" titled *Revelation of the Unknowable God.* She is writing a book on the *Gospel of Mary Magdalene.*

Elaine J. Lawless is Professor of English/Folklore and Women's Studies at the University of Missouri. She is the author of numerous articles on women and religion and also of four books, *God's Peculiar People: Women's Voice and Folk Tradition in a Pentecostal Church* (1988), *Handmaidens of the Lord: Pentecostal Women Preachers and Traditional Religion* (1988), *Holy Women/Wholly Women: Sharing Ministries through Life Stories and Reciprocal Ethnography* (1993), and *Women Preaching Revolution: Call for Connection in a Disconnected Time* (1996).

Linda Lierheimer is Assistant Professor of History and Director of the Program in Gender and Women's Studies at the College of Saint Benedict and Saint John's University in Minnesota. She is completing a book entitled *Women of Eloquence: The Apostolate of Ursuline Nuns in Seventeenth-Century France.*

Phyllis Mack is Professor of History at Rutgers University. She is also the project director of the Rutgers Center for Historical Research, directing the project "Varieties of Religious Experience." Her book *Visionary Women: Ecstatic Prophecy in Seventeenth Century England* won the Berkshire Prize in 1993 for the best book by a woman historian. Her recent work focuses on religious dissent and the origins of feminism.

Carolyn Muessig is Newman Research Fellow of Medieval Theology in the Department of Theology and Religious Studies at the University of Bristol. She researches thirteenth-century popular preaching, especially the sermons of Jacques of Vitry. Recent and forthcoming publications include editions of the sermons of Jacques of Vitry, and articles on his writings, which discuss chastity practiced by the Beguines and Cathar doctrine. She is also assistant editor of *Medieval Sermon Studies* and a councillor of the International Medieval Sermon Studies Society.

Darleen Pryds is Assistant Professor of Humanities in the Center for Interdisciplinary Studies at Virginia Polytechnic Institute and State University. Her research interests are lay preaching in late medieval Europe. In a forthcoming book she explores the political impact of the preaching of King Robert of Naples (1309–43).

Roberto Rusconi is Professor of the History of Christianity at the University of L'Aquila. He has published books and essays on the Italian religious at the end of the Middle Ages and Renaissance. He is the editor, with Daniel Bornstein, of *Women and Religion in Medieval and Renaissance Italy* (1996), and his critical edition of Christopher Columbus's *Libro de las profecas* will be published by the University of California Press.

Judylyn S. Ryan teaches African diaspora literatures at Rutgers University and has published several articles on African American women writers. She is currently at work on a book-length study, *Foundation of Ancient Power: Spirituality and/as Ideology in Black Women's Fiction and Film.*

Karen Jo Torjesen has taught at the Georg August Universitaet at Göttingen and Mary Washington College. She is currently the Margo L. Goldsmith Professor of Women's Studies in Religion at the Claremont Graduate School. Her work on gender and sexuality in early Christianity includes *When Women Were Priests: Women's Leadership in the Early Church and the Scandal of Their Subordination in the Rise of Christianity.*

Peter Vogt is a native of Germany and is completing a doctorate in theology at the Boston University School of Theology. His publications include "The Shakers and the Moravians: A Comparison of the Structure and Architecture of Their Settlements" (1993) and "Zinzendorf und die Pennsylvanischen Synoden 1742" (1994).

Pamela J. Walker is Assistant Professor of History at Carleton University. She was a visiting lecturer and research associate in Women's Studies in Religion Program at Harvard Divinity School in 1993–94. Her book *Pulling the Devil's Kingdom Down: The Salvation Army in Victorian England* will be published by the University of California Press.

INDEX

Abadam, Alice, 318
Abelard, Peter, 61, 64, 83n. 23, 85–86n. 41
Abels, Richard, 120, 122, 132n. 24
abolition, Quakers and, 258. *See also* slavery
abortion, 307
activism: political, xx, 248–261, 318–333, 342; social, 306–307
Actresses' Suffrage League, 320
Acts and Monuments (Foxe), xix, 199–211
Acts of the Apostles, 290; authority of baptism in (1:14, 24), 116, 118, 337; authority of Priscilla in (18:24, 26), 33n. 1, 221, 239, 337; Diana of Ephesus in (19:23–40), 94n. 95; gift of Spirit in (1:14; 2:4, 17–18), 77, 239, 240, 241, 242, 291, 337, 338; on obedience to God (5:29), 99; Philip's daughters in (21:9), 21, 29, 337
Ad abolendam (Lucius III and Barbarossa), 100, 108n. 5
Adam (of Bible), 105
Address to Magistrates (Hume), 253–254
Adémar de Chabannes, 131n. 8
Adrian I, 204
Adversus Waldensium sectam liber (Bernard of Fontcaude), 100–101, 103–105, 106, 108n. 7, 110–112nn. 25–38
Africa: divinities of, 275–276; languages of, 275; and Spiritual movement, 303, 305; widows in, 49
African Americans, xix, xx, 267–287, 303–317, 340

African Traditional Religion (Idowu), 269
Afro-Christianity, definition of, 271n. 4
Alain of Lille, 105, 108–109n. 7, 152, 161, 168n. 16
Alberto of Padua, 71
Alexander (martyr), 203
Alexander III (pope), 99
Alexander IV (pope), 162, 165
Alexander VI (pope), 179
Alexander of Hales, 144n. 23
Alexis (saint), 99
Altmann, Johann Georg, 240
Ambrose of Milan, 58, 59, 67, 68, 70, 71, 81n. 6, 154n. 2, 179
Ammia of Philadelphia, 21
Ammonarion (2) (martyrs), 203
Amsterdam, Quakers in, 230
Anderson, (Mother) Leaf, xx, 303, 317, 340
Andreas Paleologus, 179
Andrew (apostle), in *Gospel of Mary*, 21
Angelico, Fra (Guido di Pietro), 174, 183
"angel in the house" (Victorian ideal), 251, 259
angels, 119, 149
Anglican church. *See* Church of England
Anicetus, 202
Anna (of Bible), 104, 106, 111n. 33, 337
Anne de Beaumont, 217
Anne de Vefure, 215, 219, 224n. 10
Anonymous of Passau, 105
Anselm of Alessandria, 105
Anselm of Canterbury, 136

Compositor: Integrated Composition Systems
Text: 10/12 Baskerville
Display: Baskerville
Printer and binder: Data Reproductions